D1710912

MYTHS AND TALES OF THE JICARILLA APACHE INDIANS

Morris Edward Opler

DOVER PUBLICATIONS, INC.
New York

Published in Canada by General Publishing Company, Ltd., 30 Lesmill Road, Don Mills, Toronto, Ontario.

Published in the United Kingdom by Constable and Company, Ltd., 3 The Lanchesters, 162–164 Fulham Palace Road, London W6 9ER.

Bibliographical Note

This Dover edition, first published in 1994, is an unabridged and unaltered republication of the work first published in 1938 by The American Folk-Lore Society, New York, as Volume XXXI in the series, *Memoirs of the American Folk-Lore Society.*

Library of Congress Cataloging-in-Publication Data

Opler, Morris Edward, 1907–
Myths and tales of the Jicarilla Apache Indians / Morris Edward Opler.
p. cm.
Originally published: New York : American Folk-lore Society, 1938, in series: Memoirs of the American Folklore Society ; v. 31.
Includes bibliographical references and index.
ISBN 0-486-28324-0 (pbk.)
1. Jicarilla Indians—Folklore. 2. Jicarilla mythology. I. Title.
E99.J5066 1994b
398.2′089972—dc20 94-40592
CIP

Manufactured in the United States of America
Dover Publications, Inc., 31 East 2nd Street, Mineola, N.Y. 11501

PREFACE

So rich is Jicarilla Apache mythology that, despite the apparent fullness of this volume, it has required merciless slashing and steady pruning to reduce it to its present size. Therefore, before discussing what has been retained, it is perhaps advisable to make some comment concerning those stories which have been excluded from this collection.

In the first place all stories which have to do primarily with raid or war-path have been eliminated from this volume. Though these stories are always represented as a record of events which actually occurred, many of them are overlaid with tales of encounters with supernaturals, and the exploits of their heroes have grown to legendary proportions. Consequently it may be felt that they belong in the present collection. Yet they bear so completely upon the war and raiding complexes and follow so closely the warfare and raiding practices of the Jicarilla that they will serve as invaluable documents with which to illuminate an ethnological account. I have accordingly decided to reserve them for that purpose.

There is another group of tales which has grown up around behavior patterns between relatives and affinities. The strong joking relationship which obtains between Jicarilla cross-cousins of the same sex, for instance, is celebrated by stories which have become the common and traditional property of all Jicarilla. But again, these stories refer so particularly to an ethnological context that I feel justified in retaining them to implement a monograph on Jicarilla social organization.

Likewise excluded is a group of stories which have to do with visits of the sick and dying to the land of the dead. The necessity for dealing with this material in descriptions of the death rites is so patent that I have no hesitancy in saving it for such use.

The section dealing with bird and animal stories could have been much expanded. One of the longest story cycles which I recorded from the Jicarilla, that which recounts the adventures of Blue Jay (see p. 349) has been omitted entirely on the grounds that it contains too much repetition, too few themes not found elsewhere in this collection, and, considering its length, too little material of ethnological and comparative interest to justify its inclusion. The same can be said for a long story of the adventures of a group of animals. Some day, for the sake of completeness, these tales may deserve publication. For the present, however, those stories found in this volume should serve to give an adequate and representative picture of Jicarilla mythology.

A further economy of space has been effected by choosing the shorter of two versions of a story where the story itself is not of the greatest moment and the condensed version furnishes all the essentials. Such a selection was made in the story of Dirty Boy (p. 384). In the longer account, a series of raiding and war-path experiences which the boy undergoes and the details of the Jicarilla war and raiding complexes are described at length. Since most of this material will be treated in ethnological monographs, the version which has less to say concerning all this is utilized here.

From this explanation of what has been rejected we may turn to a consideration of the character and arrangement of those tales which remain. In an effort to bring together the stories most similar in spirit and theme, the contents have been divided into ten major sections. These sections fall naturally into two parts. Sections I—V comprise the stories which are predominately sacred and associated with ceremony. Sections VI—X consist in those stories which are generally secular or profane in character.

It must not be thought that this dichotomy is a neat and indisputable one. The tale of the misbehavior of the women of the emergence which I have recorded as a part of the coyote cycle (p. 266) and therefore have placed with the stories of a secular nature, is very often told as a part of the most important of the sacred myths, the origin story. Again, the exploits of Killer-of-Enemies, who rids the earth of obnoxious monsters, is part of the sacred origin myth. But a similar deed on the part of Coyote, who liberates the people by overcoming the monster bear (p. 336) has fallen with the secular stories, since most of Coyote's other adventures picture him as the trickster and buffoon.

Not only is the division between the secular and sacred stories somewhat blurred, but the distinctness of the several sections is also open to question. For example, in Section IV, the attempt is made to bring together all tales which deal with the origin of games and artifacts. Yet the reader will readily appreciate that the story of the first moccasin game (p. 231), which has been placed in this section, might well have been thrown with the animal trickster stories of Section VI. And no section, it is frankly admitted, redeems the promise of its title to the letter. Section III has been set aside to harbor myths devoted to ceremonies for rain or agriculture. Not only is the first of the tales of this section (p. 210) concerned as much with hunting rites as with those to aid agriculture, but there are almost as many references to rain and rain ceremonies in the origin myth and the myth of the Hactcin ceremony as can be found in this section.

Sometimes the contents of a section are less a function of the realities of Jicarilla mythology than they are a matter of such variables as the ceremonial prerogatives of the informant from whom the tales were recorded. The man who told the origin myth, for example, did not feel that he had the right to talk of the ceremony in which the most powerful of Jicarilla supernaturals, the Hactcin, appear. Therefore the account of the origin which I have utilized here, and which is otherwise very complete, omits reference to this important rite. An informant who felt qualified to discuss the ceremony of the Hactcin would doubtless have had something to say in regard to it in the course of his version of the origin myth. As it happened my prudent informant later made it possible for me to consult an older man whose knowledge of the ways of the Hactcin was most extensive, and an account so detailed and unified of the Hactcin ceremony resulted that it has been set aside as a separate section. (See Section II.)

Despite these obvious limitations the arrangement here attempted does furnish the reader with a ground plan for the exploration of Jicarilla mythology. The origin myth of Section I is the most important of Jicarilla legends and logically deserves its introductory position. It explains the Jicarilla conception of the creation of the earth, sky, and all living beings and their relations to each other. It introduces the principal groups of Jicarilla supernaturals and the rites with which they are associated. It contains more explanatory material than any other story. The dominant Jicarilla symbologies, sacred objects, ritual patterns, and conceptual biases are unmistakably adumbrated. One may read no farther than the end of the origin myth and still gain a surprising amount of information concerning most aspects of Jicarilla life.

The stories of Section I which follow the origin myth are so grouped as to supplement it. They deal with events introduced or referred to in the origin myth and are arranged in the order in which the occurrences to which they relate received mention in the myth. In the opinion of other informants various of these supplementary stories belong in the origin myth itself. It may be assumed that the entire contents of Sections I and II constitute a storehouse from which the Jicarilla raconteur may draw at will for material with which to embellish his version of the origin myth.

There is, theoretically, one correct manner in which to relate the origin story. Actually, no two individuals tell it exactly alike, with the same events included and arranged in the same order. Once, at an important ceremony, I listened to a discussion of the learned ceremonial men of the tribe. Their subject was the legendary events which govern the cosmology and ceremonial life of the Jicarilla, the events described in the origin myth. It was soon evident that no one of them agreed perfectly with any other. Upon all major points and essential meanings they were of one mind, of course, but on details such as the exact order of the deeds of the culture hero, the kind of weapon he used in each adventure, etc., there was a difference of opinion which threatened to interfere with the business at hand.

Despite such fluidity, there are essential cores withing the origin myth which show a surprising rigidity in regard to order of events. The creation, the loss of the sun and moon, and the emergence form a nucleus which stands as a logical narrative unit. The birth of the culture heroes, their journey to the sun, the adventure at Owl's home, and the slaying of the monsters are likewise major episodes which have a fixed order in the minds of most informants. It is the accounts of ceremonies and the adventures of the culture heroes after the slaying of the principal monsters which vary most in position and in the importance attached to them. Some of these are handled by one narrator as an integral part of the origin myth; another Jicarilla may treat one or more of these same episodes as separate stories.

The tales which have to do with the origin of games and artifacts (Section IV) have been brought together in that part of the volume which has to do with ceremonial matters because these games and artifacts are considered, in nearly every case, to be the gifts of supernaturals, and their use and care are often connected with ritual observances. The myths of Section V are thought of as sacred rather than secular because they involve supernatural encounters with animals and because of the hunting rites and ceremonies which flow from them. The titles of the other sections give an adequate hint of their contents.

There can be no better introduction to Jicarilla ethnology than the myths. One informant, whom I shall soon quote, likened the mythology of his tribe to a "Testament." The simile is apt; Jicarilla mythology is truly the codification of the beliefs and mores of the group. There are few matters of conduct which the Jicarilla do not refer back to this body of lore. It is thought of as the proper guide to action, positive and negative; consequently the telling of myths is not a casual and lightly regarded undertaking.

An informant's comments in regard to the subject will indicate the native attitude:

"The stories were mostly for instruction. When the children wouldn't behave or listen the older people would stop talking. They wouldn't allow anyone to make fun of them. When a man has a group of children listening to his stories, he gives them kernels of corn to eat. They eat these while he tells his stories and then they never forget them.[1]

"The winter was the time when stories were told most, for then the nights were long and the people got tired of lying around. The story of the emergence can be told any time, day or night, and during any season, but it was most often told during the long winter

[1] A man who knows a ceremony, when he is telling stories connected with his ceremony, puts down a kernel of corn for every one he finishes. At the end he passes them out to those who are interested. Then those people will remember the stories well. (Inf.)

nights. It is not dangerous to tell it at any other time, however. The story of the killing of the monsters by Killer-of-Enemies or stories about the bear, snake, any monster, or any of the evil ones can be told during the winter only, for then those dangerous ones go high in the mountains and are not where the people live. And these stories are always told at night.

"The stories are of different kinds. Some make you happy, some make you sad; some frighten you. They have a little feast when stories are being told, for the stories are just like a 'Testament' to the Indians. The one at whose camp the people have gathered furnishes the feast. About midnight they eat. It is a sort of 'sacrifice' for they are talking of holy things, of the time when the earth was new and all were holy.

"They tell the stories all night. When the morning glow comes they eat again. Then they paint their faces with red ochre, everyone there, even the children, and all go away. They leave the red paint on all day. The paint stands for the holiness of the story.

"To begin, one man would tell a story. He would tell it in the best way he could and explain its meaning thoroughly. When he got through he would get another man to tell a story. The women who were there told stories too. In the old times no one would interrupt a man who was telling stories. He had the floor as long as he wanted to talk. No one could take it away from him. But now everyone wants to talk at the same time. Very likely one person would not tell the whole origin myth. They pass the story on if it is very long.

"They told the children to pay attention, that these stories would show them what to believe and learn. If a child got very sleepy they would let him sleep, though; they did not have to keep him awake. But a child who did not pay attention and made a noise would be whipped. In the old days when they 'gave' these stories such as 'codi' (Coyote) and the 'traveling people' tales to the children they advised them not to be foolish like this. Stories of that kind make the children think. The old people were always giving advice to the children.

"After the night of story-telling they did not sleep during the next day. They waited till the next night, and no stories were told that night. All went to sleep early the next night.

"We have a way which we call 'he gives him something for the story.' If a person stays at your house all night to listen to your stories, you give him something in the morning. We still do this. It is done only when stories are told all night. But if the people at whose camp you are staying serve something to eat about the middle of the night, presents are not expected. This takes the place of giving out presents.[1]

[1] Another informant corroborated these statements as follows: "We used to give gifts to those who came to listen to a person tell stories and who

"Once over at my aunt's place, all of them were fighting. They called me over and I got them together. Just as soon as they were together they began to talk against one another. One said, 'It was her fault.' And another said, 'No, she said the first bad word.' Each was blaming the other. I made them all quiet down.

"I turned to my aunt. She was the oldest one there; she's an old lady. I said to her, 'You are very foolish. Here you are taking sides and helping the trouble along. Have you no good advice to give your grandchildren? Why don't you tell them stories of the old times?'

"So she began with all these stories. Pretty soon they started laughing and all were friendly and at peace before long."

From these remarks it is plain that the myth is of greatest functional importance to the Jicarilla in the guidance of his behavior, his beliefs, and his ceremonies. I do not doubt that many readers will be intensely interested in the complete manner in which world cosmology has been worked out in Jicarilla mythology. The generous amount of detail, the introduction of all classes of supernaturals, ceremonies, sacred objects, and sacred places in the Jicarilla myth will not go unnoticed. Likewise will attention be drawn to the introduction of all important animals in these tales and the consequent definition of attitude in respect to them. For the Jicarilla this is essential; he requires all this information to be in ready form. The mythology represents for him the summation of knowledge on the basis of which he must act. Jicarilla mythology, therefore, carries an enormous load. The mother or grandparent schools the child in accordance with its dictates. The ceremonial man conducts his rite in terms of directions found therein.

Many tales have a function in the ceremonial life which is not always discernible from their contents, and a wider understanding of the culture is essential for the evaluation of these. A myth which has become one of the most important in the Jicarilla repertory is the story of the contest between Killer-of-Enemies and One-Who-Wins (p. 128), for in it is to be found the basis of the purification rites held after a death has occurred in a family. The Jicarilla lay great emphasis upon the necessity for purification after contact with death or anything that has to do with death. Those involved in mourning or death rites are thought to have been swept over to

---

stayed all night. This happened to me the other night. Some men came to my place and I told stories till it was nearly daylight. In the old days I would have given them something, but now I am poor. In former times as much as a horse was given." The Mescalero Apache have a similar practice which they call "stealing the night away from him," the inference being that the story-teller, by keeping his listener so interested that he does not go home, has "stolen" the night from him and owes him amends. Behind this rationalization is the true motive that serves for both the Jicarilla and Mescalero, a rule of hospitality which decrees that a courteous guest should not go home hungry or empty-handed.

the "death side" and thereby contaminated. Until they have been brought back to the "life side" they are a menace to the health and good fortune of their fellows, and may not mingle with others. The ceremony which purifies or "brings them back" draws its inspiration from this myth. The singer symbolically takes the part of Killer-of-Enemies. His ceremony serves as the contest in which he wars against the forces of evil who have won life and health from the people. Those elements which seek to win the people to sickness and destruction are personified in the character of the gambler, One-Who-Wins. The songs and prayers of the ceremony recount the bitter contest and celebrate the ultimate triumph of Killer-of-Enemies and the liberation of the people from the tyranny of One-Who-Wins.

The relation between Jicarilla culture and mythology is manifestly a close one. No great disjunction between behavior patterns and the rules laid down in mythology may be permitted to disturb this nexus. The adjustments necessary to maintain the balance flow in two opposite directions. In the first place the greatest pressure is exerted upon the individual to force him to conform to the advice given in the myths. Today the Jicarilla faithfully oppose the cutting of their hair because hair was fashioned from the clouds by the Hactcin (p. 5), and to cut oneself off from the clouds of the Hactcin is to invite drought and want. In most cases, due to the force of this mythological sanction, Jicarilla youths who have their locks shorn when they are at school resume the long braid as soon as they return to camp life.

On the other hand Jicarilla mythology has been raised to a high measure of flexibility and receptivity by the need to accommodate itself to changes which could not be successfully opposed or avoided. Thus Jicarilla mythology has come to take for granted the presence of the Americans, the Mexicans, of adobe houses, chimneys, guns, and priests, and, in terms of the principle of explaining that which cannot be ignored, accounts satisfactorily for all of them.

This rule has its exceptions, of course. The Hactcin ceremony was the accredited Jicarilla method of warding off epidemics. When the smallpox scourge threatened to decimate the tribe the natives looked to the Hactcin ceremony to relieve their sufferings. White medical men thought otherwise and opposed vaccination to the native conception. This time the Jicarilla remained inflexible. They took up the challenge to their supernaturals and decreed that anyone who allowed himself to be vaccinated could not impersonate a Hactcin. But the pressure to have the young Jicarilla vaccinated continued and resulted in the disqualification from the masked dancer ceremony of nearly all Jicarilla youths. The Hactcin have not danced for many years, and it may be that they will never perform again.

To the high correlation of the details of Jicarilla mythology with the actual conduct of the bearers of the culture and the forces which maintain it, we shall return in a moment. Just now I wish to call attention to the tremendous validity of Jicarilla mythology for the affairs of everyday life. So complete and conclusive does the Jicarilla believe the dicta laid down in mythology to be that behavior which violates admonitions stemming from the legends is most often considered a proof of deplorable ignorance. It is accepted that one who knows of the injunctions embodied in the mythology will not ignore them. Those who "give" the stories to the children stand usually in a grandparental relationship to them and so it has become customary to chide abberant conduct by inquiring scathingly of the transgressor, "Did you have no grandparent to tell you the stories?" And the reprehensible behavior of a tribesman is many times explained and condoned by the statement, "He doesn't know any better. The poor fellow never had a grandfather to give him the stories." As a means for the control of conduct there is no measure more used or more successful then the telling of a myth. If a child is unruly at night, the story of the monster owl and his basket is enough to force quiet and obedience. Should a boy be seen playing with an older sister or a female cross-cousin, a few pointed stories of mishaps likely to follow such thoughtlessness make him more discreet. Should a youth, angered that he has been called from play to tend horses, treat one of the animals roughly, there is a story which will cause him to think well before again allowing his bad temper to master him.

The absorption of the Jicarilla in his mythological lore is not without its disadvantages to the ethnologist at times. I well remember the occasion when I went to a very old Jicarilla man to discuss with him the Jicarilla agricultural complex. I suspected that the complex, or at least some phases of its development, were of recent origin, and that this man, if he would think over the matter in a practical and realistic fashion and in terms of his own life-span, could give me some valuable clews concerning its growth and the provenience of some of its elements. After long and fruitless conversation it was plain to me that this aged informant and I were talking at cross purposes. I was determined to have him think in terms of history and consecutive events; he was equally insistent that I listen to the myth (I had recorded it twice before) which accounts for the origin of agriculture. Two qualities of interest were here opposed. As so often happens on our planet, myth prevailed over history this time, and to the self-righteous satisfaction of my informant I meekly listened for a third time to the familiar legend.

Since Jicarilla mythology is so completely a rationalization of a mode of living, to function acceptably it must be held down to the requirements of the actual round of activity. The compensations for satisfactions denied in reality by the culture, the elaborate day dreams, the exultant departures from the true culture ethic which are characteristic of many mythologies, are seldom encountered in Jicarilla legends. The culture heroes perform deeds that may be expected of no mortal, of course, but when a rite or observance is attributed to a supernatural or an animal, one may be sure that the Jicarilla carry out the details of that procedure in much the same way. And when feelings, attitudes, judgments, likes and dislikes are described for the protagonists in the myths, one may be fairly certain that the same responses belong to the normal reaction pattern of the average Jicarilla. In other words, the myths provide a surprisingly accurate guide to Jicarilla culture. The reader may follow the narratives confident that through the eyes of supernaturals, animals, and the people of the emergence, he is being introduced to something more substantial then entertaining stories.

As he turns these pages the sensitive reader will be thoroughly cognizant of the signs that delineate the contours of Jicarilla culture. A few examples may illustrate the manner in which the gap between the mythology and the culture is frequently bridged. Early in the origin myth the roving propensities of the Jicarilla are rationalized. The creator, Black Hactcin, tells Ancestral Man and Ancestral Woman, "Stay anywhere you like to be. There is your place. There is your home." And the narrator went on to explain: "That is why the Jicarilla Apache went from place to place. They would come to a desirable place and say, 'This is pretty; let's stay here.' Then they would go to some other place later." (See p. 9.) This outline of the Jicarilla attitude toward a particular locality is remarkably sound and is borne out by accounts of the life experiences of living men.

Again, on page 14 of the origin myth, the power and characteristics of the shaman are considered. As I have indicated in a footnote at that point, the light in which the shaman is portrayed in the myth is singularly faithful to the role he plays in Jicarilla religious life today. Later in the same myth (p. 80) there is a clear expression of the dependence of the Jicarilla on both vegetable and animal food. On page 86 an origin for the two bands, the Ollero and Llanero, is offered. Very little space is devoted to the subject. It is merely stated that the two bands resulted from the choosing of sides for a ceremonial relay race. This lack of elaboration is a true index of the place of the band in Jicarilla culture. Band affiliation is accepted most casually and has few serious implications for the individual or for the culture. The only time the bands figure prominently, and this might be guessed from the origin myth, is in the ceremonial race of September fifteenth.

There is scarcely a story in this collection which does not reveal fidelity to the cultural round. In the story "When Tanager and Robin Were Chiefs" (p. 119) the relation between the bird chiefs and the people to whom they are giving advice and directions differs little in spirit from the responsibilities of Jicarilla chiefs as this office is described in less legendary accounts. It would prove too lengthy an undertaking to proceed methodically through the mythology and point to all the ethnologically accurate and significant statements. Some footnotes are provided to throw the most arresting items of this nature into relief. In the sphere of social life and organization alone there will be found mention in the myths of the relative freedom of the Jicarilla boy from the parental bonds; the contrasting dependence of the Jicarilla girl upon her parents and her duty of obedience to her parents in all things; the obligation of the body of relatives to see that a young couple is provided with the necessities at marriage; the practice of matrilocal residence; the giving of presents by a man to his future parents-in-law; the use of polite forms of speech to in-laws; the avoidance of the mother-in-law; the man's obligation to provide and care for his parents-in-law; polygyny; brother and sister reserve; the joking relationship between cross-cousins of the same sex; the nepotic-avuncular joking relationship; and the family feuds which sometimes took a heavy toll — to mention a few conspicuous examples. From time to time there appear passages outlining Jicarilla death customs, war and raiding practices, and descriptions of such activities as the training of the boys.

It was in spite of initial scepticism that I came to recognize the degree to which Jicarilla mythology mirrored Jicarilla culture. I recorded a number of Jicarilla myths before I had worked out the details of aboriginal Jicarilla economy. The numerous references to corn and an agricultural complex in the myths left me very much puzzled, for there was nothing in the meager literature concerning the Jicarilla to lead one to believe that this tribe had ever paid much attention to the raising of crops. Yet there was a consistent alternation when one passed from Mescalero — Chiricahua ceremonial and mythological data to comparable Jicarilla material which pointed to a greatly enhanced regard for corn on the part of the latter. Whereas the Mescalero singer, on the last night of the girl's puberty rite, placed pieces of wood taken from a useful wild plant around the fire for every song chanted, for instance, the Jicarilla singer placed a kernel of corn in a like position for the same reason. It was not long before I learned that corn and its derivatives were not only highly regarded in ceremonial contexts but were of considerable importance in the food economy of the Jicarilla as well.[1]

Again, as I recorded the myths, my attention was drawn to the fact that in them most of the major disasters which befall mankind and most instances of unworthy conduct are laid at the door of the women. A woman's faithlessness is made to account for the separation of the sexes in the underworld; the misconduct of the women

[1] For a sketch of the Jicarilla agricultural complex see "A Summary of Jicarilla Apache Culture," American Anthropologist, n. s., Vol. 38, No. 2, April-June, 1936, pp. 202—223.

results in the birth of the monsters; the thoughtless actions of two girls cause the emergence mountain to stop growing, and man's ascent is made difficult; deer, once tame, are frightened and scatter because of the act of a woman; and in the stories of perversion it is almost always a woman who engages in the shameful act. This feeling tone which pervades the myths is neatly followed out in actual practice. Jicarilla women are considered somewhat weaker mentally and morally than men. They are supposedly less stable; they are represented as more fickle, more likely to succumb to love magic, more prone to quarrel, and their presence at parts of certain ceremonies is held undesirable. Some of the major rites, such as the Hactcin ceremony, cannot be conducted by a woman.

There are, of course, occasional lapses from the accuracy which can be claimed for Jicarilla mythology as a picture of cultural realities. A few of the items retained in the myths are definitely dated and have no validity for the contemporary scene. A dislike for coffee is expressed in one or two of the myths. That dislike for the taste and smell of coffee was genuine at one time, before the Jicarilla became accustomed to the beverage. But it certainly does not hold for the present; the Jicarilla are inveterate coffee drinkers now. The white man is described in one story as dressed in buckskin clothing. The frontiersmen with whom the Jicarilla first became acquainted were probably so dressed, but it has been many years since the Jicarilla have seen a white man so attired. The myth, or this part of it, evidently crystallized at about the time of first white contact. There are other departures from Jicarilla usage which cannot easily be explained even on a basis of culture lag. In the story of the man who was carried down the river in a log (p. 213) a fire is located by means of a forked stick. There is no evidence that the Jicarilla themselves used this method of determining the position of distant objects. In the tale of the man who traveled with the buffaloes, there is mention of armor made of willow. I was not able to learn that wooden armor had been used within the memory of living Jicarilla. With these few exceptions, however, the correspondences between Jicarilla mythology and Jicarilla usage are impressive.

Jicarilla mythology is not only relatively accurate concerning details of the culture, but also quite realistic in describing them. The scene between Coyote and his wife following his misadventure with the crane (pp. 298—299) is as intimate and convincing a picture of family life as one could imagine. The first class overhauling which the talkative husband earns at the hands of his wife in the tale of the origin of clay pots and pipes (p. 243) has a special appeal for anyone who has seen an Apache man hurry down the road under the spur of his wife's tongue. There is a genuine note in the all too human impatience of the people whose curiosity leads them to gather long before the appointed time to listen to the words of their leaders (p. 120).

In order to retain this ring of authenticity Jicarilla mythology has had to develop a rare degree of vitality and flexibility. The movement toward this end has been in two directions. In the first place the mythology admits of continuous change to accommodate or explain phases of the white man's culture as it impinges upon the Jicarilla. Secondly, tales of European origin are refashioned to suit the Jicarilla pattern.

Let us take an example of the latter process. The Jicarilla story "The Flood before the Emergence" (p. 111) is undoubtedly inspired by the Biblical flood story. But by the time it is recorded from a Jicarilla informant one is conscious of a decided transformation. The ark disappears; people are saved by means of four sacred mountains which they ascend; the water-covered earth is spanned by eight individuals who travel by means of sight, a favorite mode of travel for Jicarilla supernaturals. Finally there are twenty-four survivors (a multiple of the sacred number four is used) and they are at length disposed of by having them go into sacred mountains, a typical abode for Jicarilla supernaturals.

There are probably more instances of the opposite process, of the recognition in Jicarilla mythology of adjustments made necessary by contact with the white man. The explanations are given with as little damage to Jicarilla pride and patterns as possible. The white men desire a square chimney so that each corner will point to a cardinal direction (p. 97). The white man has hit upon using turkey as the chief dish of the Thanksgiving feast because of the important link between turkey and the crop according to Jicarilla precepts (pp. 3—4). Guns were once given to the Jicarilla culture heroes by Thunder but were later taken back (p. 55). The Mexicans learned how to make plows from the Jicarilla (p. 249). Jicarilla mythology now provides answers to numerous questions involving the ubiquitous whites. Among other things we learn why the white man cannot be harmed by sorcery; why the white man goes to heaven; why carvings of animals grace the buildings of the government in Washington; why the Indians are afraid of the white men; why priests live in adobe houses; why priests address others as "my son" and study interminably.

Objects associated with contemporary American culture are drawn within the circle of Jicarilla myth materials. There are references to the telegraph and to the automobile. For imagery with which to embellish the tales, phrases and similes which have no relation to aboriginal Jicarilla culture now appear as a matter of course. Thus the boy who was raised among the bears returned with his body "black like a Negro's" (p. 116), the singing of the songs of the Hactcin ceremony is "just like turning pages to the end" (p. 195), and the boy who runs a long distance in one night is compared to an automobile (p. 386). Mexicans, rations, and even dynamite find mention in Jicarilla tales.

There is a manifest relation between the educative function of the Jicarilla tale and the ready introduction into it of allusions and materials which the narrator deems *a propos*. The narrator, who is more bent upon driving home a point and moral than in strictly following a verbal pattern, often pauses to dilate upon a theme suggested by the story. Consequently there is an attractive air of freedom and spontaneity about the narration of the Jicarilla myth. The speaker is dealing with traditional materials it is true, but in reaching the audience they are filtered through his own personality and mode of expression. The charm of such asides as the one addressed to me while I was recording the origin story, "It was because the animals were so eager to see what Black Hactcin was making that people are so curious today, just as you were eager to know this story," is patent. They are evidence of the vitality of Jicarilla folk-lore, of the common bonds of interest, participation, and belief which hold together the narrator and his hearers.

That the narrator is allowed a liberal amount of artistic latitude is indicated not only by the individual touches he lends to his rendition of a tale, but also by the fact, previously mentioned, that one person will include as part of a tale material which another will reject. The freedom permitted in the handling of episodes is suggested, moreover, by the variants of the same myth or episode which have grown up side by side. I have included a number of these variants (such as the second version of the creation of man) for illustrative purposes, but there are many others which have not been set down in this volume. The ease with which an episode or motif may be transferred from one mythological context to another is an added indication of the plasticity of the mythological material in the hands of the native artist. Thus we find that the incident in which the deer are driven away from the camps of man is found attached to two separate tales, "How the Animals Were Recovered from Raven" (pp. 259—260) and "The Man Who Floated down the River in a Log" (p. 215). Bat carries a man down from a high rock in the origin myth (pp. 63—64) and in the coyote cycle (p. 287). A person is blown to pieces and resurrected when his blood is boiled in a pot in both the origin story (p. 95) and the story of the spotted enemy (p. 376). The latter story, to be sure, is a queer compilation of episodes and themes drawn from a number of other tales.

Yet in spite of the generous concessions to individual taste, artistry, and imagination permitted in the treatment of Jicarilla mythology, the close correspondence between the myth and the reality acts ever as a brake to hold each tale to a consistent and intelligible part of the mythological whole. The unifying threads which run through all the myths are themal associations, fundamental to Jicarilla thought and culture. Turkey and corn; grasshopper and wheat; the bear and evil; wind as messenger; Coyote as trouble maker and buffoon; the woodpecker as worker in wood; the swallow as the worker in mud; baldness and untruthfulness; sunlight and pollen; moonlight and specular iron ore; clockwise circuit and the handling of sacred objects: these are a few of the stable elements, found with little variation of detail and spirit throughout the mythology, which impart to it a common flavor and unmistakable character.

I shall not pretend that the contents of this volume do justice to Jicarilla folk-lore. The Jicarilla, and this is true of many other preliterate peoples, of course, have developed a vivid oral art in which gestures, pantomime, and onomatopoeia, impossible to reproduce here, carry much of the dramatic burden.

It was a temptation to attempt a comparison of the Jicarilla myths, the myths of the other Southern Athabaskan-speaking tribes and the myths of the Pueblos. But I have decided that such a comparative treatment, to be comprehensive and of maximum use, should wait upon the publication of rather complete collections of Mescalero, Chiricahua, and Lipan mythology which I am now arranging and editing. A careful comparison of the myths of the Southern Athabaskan-speaking peoples is of decided importance for the establishment of the picture of inter-tribal relations. Lipan mythology, for instance, shows more correspondences to Navaho and Jicarilla folk-lore than it does to the tales of the Mescalero and Chiricahua, though these latter peoples were nearer geographically. Therefore it is well to have the significant materials in available form before attempting generalizations. Meanwhile it is scarcely necessary to call attention to the marked similarity between Jicarilla, Navaho, and Pueblo mythology, especially in those elements which have to do with the masked dancer cult.

An attempt has been made to render the tales as readable as possible, and to that end all native terms for which an English equivalent could be supplied have been eliminated. It is enough to ask the reader to grapple with native conceptions (such as the one which describes the four aspects of one priest, each associated with a color and direction) without making it necessary that he master an Apache vocabulary. The abbreviation "Inf." following a footnote signifies that the informant volunteered the statement or explanation at that point. Other footnotes not so marked are my own comments.

There are three publications on Jicarilla mythology to which reference is made in this volume: P. E. Goddard, "Jicarilla Apache Texts," *Anthropological Papers of the American Museum of Natural History*, Vol. VIII, 1911; James Mooney, "Jicarilla Genesis," *American Anthropologist*, Vol. II, 1898, pp. 197—209; and Frank Russell, "Myths of the Jicarilla Apaches," *Journal of American Folk-Lore*, Vol. II, 1898, pp. 253—271.

The myths of this collection were told by four men, Cevero

Caramillo, John Chopari, Alasco Tisnado, and Juan Julian, between the spring of 1934 and the spring of 1935. To the first of these men I am exceedingly indebted for his continued assistance, interest, and patience. Mythological material and variants were recorded from other Jicarilla, notably Juan Elote and his grandson, Balis Elote, but space does not permit their inclusion.

My thanks are due to the universities and organizations whose financial support made the collection of these tales possible: Columbia University, the National Research Council, the Social Science Research Committee and the Department of Anthropology of the University of Chicago, and the Southwest Society.

I am greatly indebted to Dr. Ruth Benedict and Dr. Elsie Clews Parsons who read much of this material before its final arrangement and gave me excellent suggestions for its treatment; to Dr. Harry Hoijer of the University of Chicago who aided in the translation of native terms; and to Professor E. F. Castetter of the University of New Mexico and Professor A. L. Hershey of New Mexico State College who identified the various plants mentioned in these tales.

TABLE OF CONTENTS

I. ORIGIN MYTH; EXPLOITS OF THE CULTURE HEROES; TALES CONCERNING EVENTS REFERRED TO IN THE ORIGIN MYTH

A. THE ORIGIN OF THE JICARILLA APACHE AND THEIR CUSTOMS

1. THE CREATION OF EARTH, SKY, ANIMALS, AND MAN

In the beginning nothing was here where the world now stands; there was no ground, no earth, — nothing but Darkness, Water, and Cyclone. There were no people living. Only the Hactcin existed. It was a lonely place. There were no fishes, no living things.

All the Hactcin were here from the beginning. They had the material out of which everything was created. They made the world first, the earth, the underworld, and then they made the sky. They made Earth in the form of a living woman and called her Mother. They made Sky in the form of a man and called him Father. He faces downward, and the woman faces up. He is our father and the woman is our mother.[1]

In the beginning there were all kinds of Hactcin living in the underworld, in the place from which the emergence started.[2] The mountains had a Hactcin, the different kinds of fruit each had one, everything had a Hactcin.

It was then that the Jicarilla Apache dwelt under the earth. Where they were there was no light, nothing but darkness. Everything was perfectly spiritual and holy, just like a Hactcin.

Everything there was as in a dream. The people were not real; they were not flesh and blood. They were like the shadows of things at first.

The most powerful Hactcin down there was Black Hactcin. The Hactcin were all there already but in the darkness Black Hactcin was the leader. It was there, before anything else was made, that Black Hactcin made all the animals.

We dwelt for many years there. It was not a few minutes or a few days. But we do not know how long it was.

---

[1] This is one of the moot points of Jicarilla cosmology. In another version (p. 141) the Hactcin are said to be the children of Black Sky and Earth.

[2] The Hactcin are supernaturals, personifications of the power of objects and natural forces.

This is how animals and men first came to be made. Black Hactcin first tried to make an animal. He made it with four legs of clay and put a tail on it. He looked at it. He said, "It looks rather peculiar." Then he spoke to the mud image. "Let me see how you are going to walk with those four feet." That is why little children always like to play with clay images. Then it began to walk.

"That's pretty good," said Black Hactcin. "I think I can use you in a beneficial way."

He spoke to the image. "You have no help; you are all alone. I think I will make it so that you will have others from your body."

Then all sorts of animals came out from that same body. Black Hactcin had the power; he could do anything.

Now there were all kinds of animals. Black Hactcin stood and looked. He laughed to see all those different kinds of animals; he just couldn't help it when he saw those animals with all their different habits. That is why people laugh today at the habits of animals. They see a hog and laugh at it, saying, "See that dirty animal lying in the mud." All animals were there, some with horns, like the deer and elk, some with big horns like the mountain sheep. All were present. But at that time all those animals could speak, and they spoke the Jicarilla Apache language.

And those animals spoke to Black Hactcin. Each one came to speak to him. They asked him many questions. Each asked him what he should eat and where he should go to live, and questions of that order.

The Hactcin spoke to them. He divided all foods among them. To the horse, sheep, and cow he gave grass. "That is what you shall eat," he said. To some he gave brush, to some pine needles. Some he told to eat certain kinds of leaves but no grass.

"Now you can spread over the country," he told them. "Go to your appointed places and then come back and tell me where you want to stay all your lives."

He sent some to the mountains, some to the desert, and some to the plains. That is why you find the animals in different places now. The animals went out and chose their places then. So you find the bear in the mountains and other animals in different kinds of country.

Hactcin said, "It is well. It looks well to see you in the places you have chosen."

So all the animals were set apart.

Then Black Hactcin held out his hand and asked for water to come to his hand. A drop of rain fell into his palm. He mixed it with earth and it became mud. Then he fashioned a bird from the mud. He made the head, body, wings, and two legs.

He spoke in the same way to the image he had made. "Let me see how you are going to use those wings to fly," he said. He didn't know whether he would like it. Then the mud turned to a bird. It flew around. Black Hactcin liked it. "Oh, that is fine!" he said. He enjoyed seeing the difference between this one and the ones with four legs.

"I think you need companions and someone to help you. By yourself alone you will never be satisfied. From your body there will come others with wings."

When Hactcin said this the bird became lonesome. He flew to the east, south, west, and north and came back saying, "I can find no one to help me."

The Hactcin took the bird and whirled it around rapidly in a clockwise direction. The bird grew dizzy, and, as one does when he is dizzy, this bird saw many images around. He saw all kinds of birds there: eagles, hawks, and small birds too. He could hardly believe his sight, but when he was himself again, there were really all kinds of birds there. And because Black Hactcin turned the bird around and made him dizzy, birds now circle when they rise in the air.

All different birds were there now. Birds like the air, dwell high, and seldom light on the ground because that drop of water which became the mud from which the first bird was made fell from the sky.

Then the birds came to Black Hactcin. "What shall we eat? Where shall we dwell? Where shall we rest?" they asked.

He sent them all in different directions. "Find the place you like best and tell me about it," he said.

The birds flew in all directions. All came back. Each one told of the place it liked.

"That is all right," Black Hactcin told each of them. "You may have that place for your home."

Then they asked about food. Black Hactcin held his hand up to the east, south, west, and north in turn, and because he had so much power, all kinds of seeds fell into his hand. He scattered the seeds before them. The birds were going to pick them up.

"All right, now pick them up," he said.

The birds went to do it, but the seeds turned to worms, grasshoppers, and all insects. The Hactcin was trying to tease them. They couldn't catch them at first.

Then Black Hactcin said, "Oh, it's hard work to catch those flies and grasshoppers. You can do it though."

Then they all chased the grasshoppers and other insects around. That is why many birds today use the insects for food and chase the grasshoppers around.

At the time when Black Hactcin threw the seeds down he said to Turkey, "You must be the one who takes charge of all these seeds." That is why Turkey has control of the crops now.[1] That

[1] The origin of agriculture is credited to Turkey (p. 212). The association of the turkey and corn is a common motif of Jicarilla folk-lore.

is why some of these Indians and the white people too use the turkey at Thanksgiving. The white people put the turkey in the middle of the table and have the fruits and vegetables all around it. The Indians use the turkey feathers too. When they plant a crop they put one turkey feather in each corner of the field. The turkey is striped just like corn. The head is like the corn tassel. Every part of the turkey's body stands for some part of the corn plant.

There was a river nearby. "You must drink from that river," Black Hactcin told them. The birds thought that was a beautiful place.

"Now I'm going to make something to scare you," Black Hactcin said. He was always teasing them.

He picked up some moss and began to roll it between his hands. Then he threw it into the water. And it became frogs, fish, and all that live in the water. That is why, often, when the birds come to drink at the water, something sticks its nose out of the water and frightens them and they jump back. Sometimes even humans are frightened in this way.

While the birds were flying around some of their feathers fell out and into the water, and these turned to water birds such as the duck, heron, sandhill crane, and others.

Now the birds and animals had everything, food and a place to stay and rest.

Black Hactcin started to make more images of animals and birds. The ones who were already made called a council and came together. The birds and animals were together at this council, for they all spoke the same language in those days.

"Now what are we going to do?" they asked Black Hactcin. "We need a companion, we need man."

"What do you mean?" asked Black Hactcin. "Why do you need another companion?"

The birds and animals said, "You are not going to be with us all the time; you will go elsewhere some of the time."

"I guess that's true. Perhaps some day I'll go away to a place where no one will see me."

So all the birds and animals gathered all different objects: pollen, specular iron ore, water scum, all kinds of pollen, from corn, tule, and the trees.[1] They put these all together. They added red ochre, white clay, white stone, jet, turqouise, red stone, Mexican opal, abalone, and assorted valuable stones. They put all these before Black Hactcin.

He told them, "You must stay a little distance from me. I don't want you to see what I make."

---

[1] This list is a fair inventory of the chief sacred substances used in ceremonial contexts by the Jicarilla.

He stood to the east, then to the south, then to the west, then to the north. He traced an outline of a figure on the ground, making it just like his own body, for the Hactcin was shaped just as we are today. He traced the outline with pollen. The other objects and the precious stones he placed around on the inside, and they became the flesh and bones. The veins were of turquoise, the blood of red ochre, the skin of coral, the bones of white rock, the fingernails were of Mexican opal, the pupil of the eye of jet, the whites of the eyes of abalone, the marrow in the bones of white clay, and the teeth, too, were of Mexican opal. He took a dark cloud and out of it fashioned the hair. It becomes a white cloud when you are old.

This was a man which Black Hactcin was making. And now the man came to life.[1] He was lying down, face downward, with his arms outstretched. The birds tried to look but could not make out what it was.

"Do not look," said Black Hactcin.

Then the man braced himself up, leaning on his arms which were outstretched.

"Don't look," said Hactcin to the birds, who were very much excited now.

It was because the animals were so eager to see what Black Hactcin was making that people are so curious today, just as you were eager to know this story.

"Sit up," commanded Black Hactcin to the man, and he was sitting up now. This was the third time Black Hactcin had spoken to him.

Then Black Hactcin went over to him and facing him, picked him up. Now Hactcin tried to teach him to speak.

"Speak to me, speak, speak, speak." Black Hactcin said it four times. Then the man spoke.

Then Black Hactcin said to him four times, "Laugh, laugh, laugh, laugh," and the man laughed.

"Shout, shout, shout, shout," and the man did so.

Now Black Hactcin was teaching him to walk. "Step forward," he said and made him step with his right foot first, then with his left, then right, and then left again.[2] Now the man could walk.

Then Black Hactcin said, "Run," and made him run four times in a clockwise arc. That is why they have to run at the girl's puberty rite just like that.

---

[1] Later the informant supplied a detail he had omitted at this point. Black Hactcin sent Wind into the body of man to render him animate. The whorls at the ends of the fingers indicate the path of the wind at the time of the creation of man. This detail is important for an understanding of Jicarilla conceptual life, for at death "breath" or Wind is said to leave the body from the soles of the feet, the whorls at the bottoms of the feet representing the path of the wind in its exit.

[2] In ceremonial contexts the right foot, hand, or side takes precedence over the left.

When the birds saw what Black Hactcin had made they sang and chirped as though it were early morning. That is why, when the girl who has come of age runs at the time of her puberty ceremony, an old woman stands there and makes that noise in her ear.[1]

Now the man could talk and he understood what the birds were singing and what Black Hactcin was saying, for all had one language then. The man was the only human being living; he was by himself.

The birds and the animals thought it was not good that he should be by himself and they all came together and spoke to Black Hactcin.

Black Hactcin asked the birds and animals for some lice. "Who has lice? You must bring some to me."

They brought some. Black Hactcin put some on the man's head. He scratched and scratched. Then his eyes became heavy and he went to sleep.[2] He was dreaming and dreaming. He dreamt that someone, a girl, was sitting beside him.

He woke up. The dream had come true. A woman was there. He spoke to his wife and she answered. He laughed and she laughed too.

He said, "Let us both get up."

They both arose.

"Let's walk," he told her. "Right, left, right, left." He led her for four steps.

"Run!" he said, and they both ran.

Now another person was there. The birds sang and chirped. They wanted to make pleasant music for them so they wouldn't become lonesome.

The names of these first two were Ancestral Man and Ancestral Woman.

THE CREATION OF MAN (SECOND VERSION)

In the beginning the dog was just like a Hactcin in appearance. This was because the Hactcin made everything. He was listless, however, and didn't do anything.

And Hactcin noticed this and spoke to him. He said, "Why don't you do something? Why don't you work?"

"I don't care to work. I'm too lazy. I'd better turn to the form of a dog I guess. Let my hands be round."

At first his hands were like ours, but he didn't use them and just stayed home so they became round.

When Hactcin made the dog in his present shape he took some

[1] The reference is to a high-pitched call, indicative of applause, which the pubescent girl's attendant utters in her ear. (See p. 90).

[2] That lice cause sleepiness is several times mentioned in the tales (p. 26 and p. 282).

of the yellow from the afterglow of the sunset and put it above each eye. And he took some of the white of the morning glow and put it on each paw. This was a sign that the dog would protect people.

And so today in the girl's ceremony, the girl has yellow ochre on her face and the boy who dances with her has white paint over his face.

Hactcin spoke to the dog and asked, "Where are you going to stay now?"

"Oh, you can make some people so I will have companions."

Hactcin asked, "What is the idea you have in mind? I never thought you would say a thing like that."

So the Hactcin lay down at a smooth place. He said to the dog, "Now draw a line around my feet and body. Trace my outline with your paw." So the Hactcin lay with his face down and his arms outstretched, and the dog drew his outline.

Then both got up. Hactcin said to the dog, "Go a little further on and do not look back yet."

The dog went on for a short distance.

"Now you can turn and look."

Dog looked back. "Someone is lying where you were, Grandfather," he said.

Hactcin said, "Face the other way and walk off again."

Dog did so.

"Now turn around."

The dog did so.

Someone was arising from the ground, bracing himself with his hands and knees.

"Grandfather," said Dog, "someone is on his hands and knees at the place where you were lying."

Hactcin said, "Turn and walk away again."

Dog did so. Then he was told to look once more. When he looked he saw a man sitting up.

"Grandfather, someone is sitting up!" he cried. There were surprise and happiness in his voice.

But Hactcin only said, "Turn once more and walk away."

He did so again.

"Turn around now and look," he was told.

He did so and cried out in astonishment and delight, "My grandfather, he is sitting up and moving around!"

Then Hactcin said, "Now come. We will go and see him."

They came to the man. He was sitting facing the east. Hactcin first faced him from the east. Then he went to the south, the west, and the north of him and then faced him again from the east. Then Hactcin went around to this man's back, and after motioning four times lifted him to his feet. Then he went around his body clockwise and returned in front of him at the east again.

Then Hactcin addressed the man. "You must watch me. I am

going to take four steps, moving my right foot first. As I do it you must do it too."

Hactcin did walk this way and the man followed.

"Now," said Hactcin, "let's run," and with Hactcin leading, the two ran. They ran to the east and back again in a clockwise manner. That is why they run like that in the girl's puberty rite.[1] They came back to the starting place.

Then Hactcin shouted into the ear of the man four times, twice from the right side and twice from the left and asked, "Did you hear that?" Because of this the old woman shouts into the ear of the girl in the puberty rite four times from the right side, so that the girl will have good hearing always.

But the man could not yet speak. Hactcin stood before him. Four times he said to the man, "Talk, talk, talk, talk," and then the man spoke. "Laugh, laugh, laugh, laugh," he said, and the fourth time the man laughed. "Now shout, shout, shout, shout," Hactcin told him, and the fourth time it was said the man shouted.

"Now you are ready to live around here."

The dog was very happy. He jumped at the man and ran back and forth just as dogs do now when they are glad to see you.

The dog was very happy, but the man, with no one but the dog to talk to, soon grew lonesome.

He told Hactcin the cause of his sadness and Hactcin thought about it. Finally Hactcin resolved to make a woman for him. So he told the man to lie down on the ground, face downward with arms and legs extended. The man did so. Then Hactcin traced his outline on the ground and bade him rise. Then Hactcin had the man do exactly what he had had the dog do when he had been making the man. He had the man face the other way and walk to the east four times while the figure he had drawn successively rose to its knees, sat up, and moved. Then Hactcin lifted this figure in the same manner and taught it to speak, hear, laugh, shout, and walk and run. Then Hactcin was satisfied and sent Ancestral Man and Ancestral Woman off together.

These two people who had been created also came to Black Hactcin and asked, "What are we to eat? Where shall we live?"

He showed them all the roots and leaves and plants. "These are your foods," he told them.

They went to taste all that he pointed out. They tasted them all and found them good.

Then he took them out and showed them the animals. "Those who are cloven-footed will be your meat."

In those days the animals were very gentle, very mild. They all stayed around there.[2]

---

[1] For an account of the girl's puberty rite cf. p. 87.

[2] In the Jicarilla myths the animals are represented as being extraordinarily tame in the beginning. For an account of how animals became wild see p. 215 and pp. 259—260.

He told them, "When you kill the animal you must save the hide and use it for clothes."

After that they did so.

"Where shall we put our heads?"

"Right on the earth. Stay anywhere you like to be. There is your place. There is your home."

That is why the Jicarilla Apache went from place to place. They would come to a desirable place and say, "This is pretty; let's stay here." Then they would go on to some other place later.

In those days the two people had no hair on their bodies or on their faces. The man had no moustache.

Hactcin told them the first day, "You must not let water touch your lips until I give you permission." He gave them tubes of reed and told them to use these. For three days they drank from the reeds as they were told.

The fourth day they grew impatient. It took too long to drink water that way, they thought. The man put his reed aside and lay down and drank from the stream. The front of his face touched the water and after that hair grew on his face. The woman had just stood there, however. Black Hactcin had told them what would happen if they disobeyed. The woman thought, "It would not look well for a woman to have hair on her face," so she did not do as her husband did.

Immediately the hair grew out on the man's face. The girl started to get angry because her husband looked so strange. In her rage she dashed some water under her armpits and around her pubic region. Hair grew at once in those places.

When the man saw this he thought, "I'd better do the same," and he splashed water on himself at those places too and hair grew there.

Hactcin came then and spoke to them. "Don't do that." He told the man, "Go up in the woods and find two branches which have been rubbed against each other by the wind and have become smooth. Rub your face with that."

To the woman he said, "Rub your face with abalone."

Now at the time of the girl's puberty rite when the girl acts as White-Shell Woman and the boy as Child-of-the-Water, they do this to themselves and then they do not get much body hair. It is not part of the ceremony. The young people do it by themselves.

A few generations passed. The animals, birds, and people increased, but they all lived in darkness. They had no sun as yet. The people were used to it, and because they were used to it they could see things. Still, one could not see objects clearly. But they did not have any hard times. All the animals were friendly. They had no enemies. If they wanted something to eat, it was present.

But Black Hactcin didn't think it was right. He sent for White Hactcin. They came together and talked of what they were going to do. They sent for a male eagle's white tail feather and a female eagle's spotted tail feather. And they sent for one tail feather of the blue jay too and for the yellow tail feather of the western tanager.

One mountain stretched upward. All around it lived the people. The Hactcin worked together. At the east side of the mountain, resting against it, they put the feather of the white male eagle. On the south side they put the blue feather, on the west the yellow feather, and on the north side the feather of the spotted female eagle.[1]

The white feather sent a long beam of white light to the east. Because of the blue feather, everything looked blue to the south. To the west all looked yellow because of the yellow light of the feather. And on the north side the feather of the female eagle gave a flickering light, sometimes light and sometimes shadow.

The people kept gathering to the east and living there because of the greater light in that direction. On the blue side the light was not so clear. Just a few people liked that place and stayed over there. And for the same reason very few were living on the west and north sides.

Down in the underworld there were many brooks and streams. The people had all kinds of water.

2. THE CREATION AND LOSS OF THE SUN AND MOON

Holy Boy was not satisfied. He thought there should be more light. By himself he started to make a sun. He tried hard in many ways. The first time he tried by himself. He used all kinds of specular iron ore and pollen. The result was not very satisfactory though. He used abalone too, but that didn't work any better. He tried turquoise and red beads and white beads, but without success. But he kept on. He tried over and over.

One time when he was at work the little whirlwind came. The little wind asked him, "What are you doing here all by yourself? You never go outside. I have not seen you for a long time."

Holy Boy said, "I have not been doing anything. I've stayed right here."

Wind said, "There must be some reason that you stay home."

Holy Boy said, "Yes, there is. I am making a sun. But it is not very bright."

Wind said to him, "There is a man who has a sun. Why don't you go to him?"

---

[1] The usual color-directional association, used whenever the materials or objects to which reference is made will permit is: east, black; south, blue; west, yellow; and north, glittering. Spotted or white is sometimes substituted for glittering and is associated with the north. The circuit is clockwise, beginning with the east. The association of east with white, as occurs in this passage, is unusual.

"Who is he?"

"Oh, it is White Hactcin. You go and ask him. But don't tell him who told you."[1]

So Holy Boy went to White Hactcin. He went into the home of White Hactcin.

"What do you want?" asked White Hactcin. "There must be some reason for your coming here. You never come to visit with us. What do you want, my grandson?"

Holy Boy said, "I came here to ask you for the sun."

White Hactcin said, "How do you know I have it? Who told you? No one could have seen that I have that sun."

White Hactcin sat there. He tried to think who could have seen it and reported it. Then he remembered that there was one who came often to his house. It was the wind.

"I believe it was Wind who told you I have the sun."

Holy Boy didn't mention Wind's name. He just continued to ask for the sun.

White Hactcin said then, "Yes, I have it." He picked up his bag and looked into it. He found it and he took it out. It was a very small sun and hard to see. It was just like the present sun, but it was no bigger than a pin head. He gave it to Holy Boy.

"This is for daylight," White Hactcin said.

Wind had told Holy Boy when he had talked to him, "There is a moon too, but another person has it. Black Hactcin has it.[2] You can get the moon from him."

So now Holy Boy went over to Black Hactcin.

"What do you want, my grandson?"[3] asked Black Hactcin. "You never came to see me before. There must be some reason."

"Yes, I have come for the night light. I have come for the moon."

"How do you know I have it? Who told you I have it?"

Black Hactcin thought a while. "I believe that little wind told you," he said. "He's the only one who comes to see me often." So he looked in his bag and found it. He gave it to Holy Boy. It was a tiny one too.

Then he said, "You must go back and put it on a deerskin which has no holes.[4] First make a circle to represent the sun and one for the moon too. Paint them with pollen and other coloring matter.

[1] The use of the whirlwind as a messenger or spy for the supernaturals is an ever recurring theme in Jicarilla folk-lore and will be encountered many times in these pages.

[2] The association of Black Hactcin with darkness and the things of the night is here continued by representing him the possessor of the "night light" or moon, thus contrasting him with White Hactcin, who owns the sun material.

[3] The term grandson is honorific in this context, referring to relative age and not to kinship.

[4] Unblemished buckskin was much prized by the Jicarilla for ceremonial purposes. It was required, for instance, in the rite conducted four days after the birth of a child. (p. 44.)

Then put the sun that you have been given right in the center of the sun that you make with pollen. Make a painting of the moon in the same way with specular iron ore on the deerskin and put this moon that I have given you exactly in the center of it.[1] When you get ready perhaps White Hactcin and I will come over, and Red Boy will come too.[2] There will be four of us.[3]

"Make rays for each of your designs too. Let there be four black rays to the east, four blue rays to the south, four yellow rays to the west, and four glittering rays to the north. On each, within the first outer circle of pollen or specular iron ore, make a circle of red paint. Make this near the edge. This red one stands for the rainbow. Then bring downy eagle feathers and white tail feathers of the eagle and spotted feathers of the eagle so that we can sing over this sun and moon."

Then Holy Boy went back to his own home. He worked on the sun and moon as the Black Hactcin had told him. He sent for Red Boy, and Red Boy came over and assisted him. They painted what the Hactcin had told them on the buckskin. They were nearly finished when the two Hactcin came in.

They walked in and looked at the designs. They said, "Oh, it's pretty good!" They put pollen in their own mouths and the two boys did likewise. Then the Hactcin put some pollen on top of their own heads and the boys did it too. Then each threw some to the east, south, west, and north, then straight up in the air, and then on the sun and the moon both. Each one of the four did that. They sprinkled pollen on the sun and the moon four times after throwing it upward in the air.[4]

Then White Hactcin took the white feathers and the Black Hactcin took the spotted feathers. The downy feathers they gave to Holy Boy and Red Boy. One bead of a certain color was placed in each direction on the outer circle of each design: a red stone bead on the east side, turquoise on the south side, a white bead on the west side, and abalone on the north side.

The two drawings lay before them. Everything was ready. They asked each other who was going to start to sing and pray.

Then White Hactcin spoke to Holy Boy. "You are the one who started to make the sun. You had better start the singing too. You must know how."

---

[1] Pollen is often used to represent the light of the sun; specular iron ore the light of the moon.

[2] Red Boy and Holy Boy do not appear in other Jicarilla stories. Holy Boy is mentioned in the Navaho origin legend also. See Matthews: *Navaho Legends*.

[3] The Black Hactcin and White Hactcin were leaders of all the Hactcin. All the rest were just helpers. I think that Holy Boy and Red Boy were the children of Hactcin, but I am not sure. (Inf.)

[4] This is one of the few references in Jicarilla mythology to offerings of pollen to upward and downward directions as well as to the cardinal points.

"Yes, I started it. I can't deny that."

So Holy Boy sang songs. He sang a song to the pollen. Then he sang a specular iron ore song.

Now Red Boy sang, and he sang to the beads. And he sang a song to the red ochre too.

That is why they rub paint on the face of the girl and the boy the last morning of the puberty rite. They put the red paint on then. If the boy and girl would go out without having their faces painted with red paint it would be like going out without being under the care of these holy things. Then if you prayed the Hactcin would not hear you or help you, nor would anything else.

And the pollen is just like a summer offering. After they used the pollen and sang of it, all kinds of fruit of the summer were mentioned. That song gives long life too. They sang it for both the sun and the moon, that they would have long life.

Then White Hactcin sang in the same way. He sang the same songs. He sang to make the sun and the moon come to life.

As he sang the pictures began to move a little. They began to come to life.

Then Black Hactcin sang too. He sang to make them move.

Red Boy helped each of them sing; he joined in. He didn't sing alone himself though.

Now everything was ready. The sun and moon were ready to go. Then all went out, the four of them. White Hactcin had the sun in his hand. Black Hactcin had the moon in his hand. They stood in a single file facing the east. Holy Boy stood first, then White Hactcin, then Black Hactcin, and behind him Red Boy.

Holy Boy and Red Boy had pollen in their hands. Each threw some towards the north and then up and to the south. They were making a path, just the way the sun and moon were to go.

Then White Hactcin and Black Hactcin released the sun and moon, and the sun and moon went up that path. In the sky they came up from the north and moved toward the south.[1] It was a long time before they reached the sky. Then they could be seen faintly, just as at dawn. The light began to get stronger and stronger. The light began to show on the mountains.

The other people of the underworld didn't know what it was.

Then the sun came out and in the bright sunshine everything could be seen clearly. It was just as it is now in daytime.

There were all kinds of shamans around there among the people. These were men and women who claimed they had power from all sorts of things. They saw the sun going from the north to the south across the sky.

These shamans began to talk. One said, "I made the sun."

Another contradicted him and said, "No, I did it."

---

[1] At first the sun and moon moved from north to south. For an account of the change to the present direction of movement see p. 22.

They got to quarrelling about it.

Hactcin told them not to talk like that for four days. "After four days say what you want to." That's what White Hactcin told them.

But the shamans didn't listen. They kept making claims like this and fighting. They talked all the more. One would say, "I think I'll make the sun stop overhead so that there will be no night. But no, I guess I'll let it go, because we need some time to rest too." And another would say, "I might get rid of the moon. We don't need any light at night."

But the sun arose the second day and was overhead at noon. The birds and animals were happy. The third day it was the same way; the sun rose as before.

And the fourth day came. The sun rose early. But the shamans, in spite of what the Hactcin had told them, continued to talk and kept it up till noon of the fourth day.

Then, at noon, there was an eclipse of the sun. It grew black. The sun went straight overhead, through a hole, and on to this earth. The moon followed and came to this earth too. That is why we have eclipses today.[1]

The rays of the sun came straight down through the little hole that connected the underworld with the earth above. The people could see the light faintly.

3. THE EMERGENCE[2]

The Hactcin said to the boastful shamans, "All right, you people say you have power. Now bring back the sun."

And so they lined up. On one side were all the shamans and on the other side were all the birds and animals. The shamans started to sing songs and make ceremonies. They showed all they knew. Some would sit singing and then disappear into the earth, leaving only their eyes sticking out. Then they would come back as before, but it couldn't bring back the sun. It was only to show that they had power. Some swallowed arrows, and the arrows would come out of their flesh at their stomachs. Some swallowed feathers. Some swallowed whole spruce trees and then spat them up. But they couldn't do anything about regaining the sun and moon.[3]

---

[1] Another account (p. 160) attributes eclipses of the sun and moon to jealousy of their spouses.

[2] For abbreviated accounts of the emergence see Goddard, p. 193; Mooney, p. 197; Russell, p. 254.

[3] The attribution of the loss of the sun and moon to the boasts of shamans (those who obtain supernatural power through a personal encounter with some animal or natural force) and the ridicule heaped on the ceremonies and legerdemain in which the shamans subsequently engaged in order to retrieve the loss, are indicative of the subordinate place shamanism plays in Jicarilla religion. Shamanistic ceremonies are used for emergencies and minor crises. For important occasions and for times when planning and preparation are possible, "long life ceremonies," traditional rites, which have their genesis and rationalization in the myths and not in any personal experience of an individual, are invoked instead.

Then White Hactcin said, "All you people are doing pretty well, but I don't think you are bringing the sun back. Your time is up."

Then he turned to the insects and the birds and animals and said, "All right, now it is your turn."

The birds and animals spoke to each other politely, just as though they were brothers-in-law.[1]

Hactcin told them, "You must do something more than speak to each other in that polite way. Why don't you get up and do something with your own power and make the sun come back?"

The grasshopper was the first one to try. "That's not a difficult thing to do," he said. He put up his hand to the east, to the south, to the west, and to the north in turn and then put down bread which had been baked in ashes.

White Hactcin asked, "What is this?"

Grasshopper said, "That is bread."

"How do you make the bread?"

"Oh, with grain," he said.

"What is in it?"

"Wheat. It grows. It has roots and leaves and pollen and a stalk."[2]

"All right, I can use that," White Hactcin said.

Then the deer's turn came. He said, "Hactcin hasn't asked such a difficult thing." He put out his hand in the four directions. Then he put down some yucca fruit.

White Hactcin asked, "What is it?"

"That is fruit. It is what I live on. It is a growing thing too. It has roots, stalk, leaves, blossoms, and pollen."

"I can use that too. It is wonderful," said Hactcin.

Then the bear stepped forth. He too put his hands out in the four directions. Then he put down a handful of choke-cherries. "This is what I live on," he said.

"What is it?" asked White Hactcin.

"It is a fruit too. It grows. It has root, stalk, leaves, blossom, and pollen."

"I can use it. It is good."

Then came Ground Hog. He too put out his right hand to the four directions. In his hand was a berry.

"What is it?"

"It is a fruit. It is what I live on. It has a root, stalk, flowers, and pollen."

---

1 A number of Jicarilla affinities must be addressed by a special third person form, called "polite form" because of the restraint and circumspection which are supposed to accompany it. By taking pains to be more formal and dignified, the birds and animals hoped to avoid the excesses of the thoughtless shamans.

2 The grasshopper is considered the guardian of wheat. See pp. 177—178 for further development of this theme.

"I can use it."

Then Chipmunk came out. He too put out his hand in the four directions. He put down a strawberry.

"What is it?"

"It is a fruit. It has roots, stem, blossom, and pollen. It is what I live on."

In the same way all the animals came forward in turn. Each put his hand to the four directions and each gave something which was his food to Hactcin. The birds and insects came too. The birds brought all kinds of seeds.

The last one to come was Turkey. He went to the east, strutting. Black corn lay there as if spilled. He did the same to the south, and blue corn lay there. He strutted to the west, and yellow corn lay there. And then he went to the north, and all kinds of vegetables and fruit lay there.

Hactcin asked him, "What is all this?"

"This is what I live on. They have roots, stems, pollen, and the corn has tassels on top. It has dew on it too."

"That is very good. I think I am going to use you. You can help us make it grow," he said to the turkey.

Then White Hactcin sent for Thunder of four colors from the directions. And these thunders brought clouds of four colors. The rain fell from these clouds. Then Hactcin sent for Rainbow to make it beautiful while they planted these things on the mountain.

Then those four, White Hactcin, Black Hactcin, Holy Boy, and Red Boy, brought sand. It was sand of four colors. They brought pollen from all kinds of trees and from the fruits. They leveled off a place so they could work with the sand. They smoothed down the place with eagle feathers.[1]

They had earth of four colors there too: black, blue, yellow, and glittering.

First they laid the sand down evenly. Then they made four little mounds of earth with the dirt. In each one they put some seeds and fruits which the animals had given. And on top they put the needles and leaves of the trees that were to grow on the mountains. On the top of each one of the piles of earth they put a reed. On top of the reed was attached the downy feather of an eagle and the downy feather of a turkey. The mounds of earth were in a row extending from east to west. The first one was the one of black earth, next the one of blue earth, then the one of yellow earth, and last the one of glittering earth.

Before the mountain started to grow, the Holy Ones took a black clay bowl and filled it with water. They did this because water was needed to make the mountain grow. How could it grow that tall without water? When they did this there was still no single tall

[1] Sand on which ground drawings are to be traced is leveled off with eagle feathers today.

mountain there. But they put the clay bowl of water there and then added all the things that the animals gave, and the mountain began to grow. That is why the black clay bowl, full of medicine, is used in the bear dance.[1] And when the old people wanted holy water after that, they always got it from the mountain tops.

All the birds of the mountain and the mountain animals were there helping to make these mounds of earth grow. They all prayed. Then the two Hactcin and Holy Boy and Red Boy started to sing. They sang and sang and after a while all the fruit began to grow in these piles of earth.

The turkey was gobbling and strutting. When the mountain expanded he always did this. But they did not know how many times the mountain grew, for they had no sun and could not count.[2] Now we watch the sun and see the days pass, and in this way learn to count.

Every time the mountain grew there was a noise as though something was squeezed, a squeaking noise. All the four mounds of earth, as they grew, merged and became one mountain.

When the dirt had all grown together into one mountain, the two Hactcin and Holy Boy and Red Boy picked out twelve shamans who had performed many things when the people were showing off their power before. These were the ones who had been able to cut themselves and to swallow arrows. These people had ceremonies from different sources, from animals, from fire, from Turkey, from frogs and others things. They each had a shamanistic ceremony and they were shamans. They could not be left out. They had power and they had to help too. All with power were helping to make the mountain grow. Each animal and bird was contributing his power.

The four Holy Ones painted these twelve men and made them appear like the Tsanati of today.[3] They dressed them up with spruce branches and yucca leaves, using the narrow-leafed yucca and the broad-leafed yucca too. They wove the yucca and made a short skirt of it for the men to wear. They stuck spruce branches in around their waists. They tied yucca at the wrist and lower part of the arm and spruce at the upper arm. Six represented the summer and six the winter season. Therefore six were painted blue all over and six white all over. Yucca was tied to their ankles and to a place

---

1 For a description of the bear dance see pp. 27—44.

2 Another version: Some say that the mountain grew twelve times; that it grew eight times and then the foolish girls stopped it. Then the Hactcin fixed it, and it grew four more times. (Inf.)

3 The marked tendency of the Jicarilla to discourage shamanism in favor of the "long life ceremonies" finds unmistakable expression here. To become effective in this rite of the growing emergence mountain, shamans have to be transformed into a dance group which functions in the traditional or "long life" ceremonies today. The word Tsanati refers to ritual gesticulation. Since a literal translation would be awkward, the native term will be retained in these pages.

above the knee, and spruce branches were stuck in these circles of yucca. The faces, hands, and feet were painted. A line of black ran outward and down from each eye. They wore buckskin moccasins. One white eagle feather was tied in the hair of each, on top. In their hands were branches of spruce and blades of yucca. They held four kernels of blue corn in each hand.

Then the four Holy Ones made six clowns.[1] They were painted white all over except for four black stripes, one across the face, one across the chest, one across the upper leg, and one across the lower leg. The stripes went around the whole body. Each arm also had four black stripes. On their wrists they wore a band of narrow yucca and one around the neck. They wore loin cloths of deerskin, and they wore moccasins. Yucca bands were put around their ankles. Rattles of deer hoof were tied to the yucca at the ankle, two to each foot. The hair was gathered up and brought to a point on each side. These "horns" were painted white with four black stripes. They stuck out like horns. And at the top of each one was one eagle feather.

In the right hand they carried the broad blades of yucca. This was called their whip. It had a downy eagle feather at the very end. With this the clown protects the holy places against any woman whose menstrual period has come. If a woman is in that condition the feather points to her and the clown chases her away with it. This whip is used against sickness too.

In the left hand they carried a branch of spruce. These people are powerful. If you have touched the bone or marrow of a man or dog, though you did not realize it, and then later put your hand to your mouth, it makes you sick. You can't digest food. You vomit all the time. Then these clowns are the people who can cure you.

All those who were present helped. They all worked to make the mountain grow. It was getting large. The people wanted to travel on it. The mountain had much fruit on it now. There were cottonwood and aspen trees on it and streams of water flowed from it too. It was very rich in everything. Yucca fruit and all other fruits were growing on it by this time, all kinds of berries and cherries.

The turkey, more than anything else, was the one who made the mountain grow. When he gobbled and strutted it would begin to rise.

It was very dark and they couldn't see well. They had the feathers by which they obtained some light, but they could not see all over.

Two girls went up on the mountain when no one was watching them. A little later the mountain stopped growing and would rise no more.

[1] The literal translation of the term for the Jicarilla clown is "striped excrement." Their ability to cure stomach ailments is connected with scatological practices which will be presently described (p. 184). The clowns of the emergence were decorated with four black stripes. Clowns which function in war-path ceremonies are designed with six black stripes.

Then the Holy Ones[1] said, "Something must have happened up there."

They sent the whirlwind to find out about it. The wind went up there. He saw tracks.

They all continued with their songs and prayers, but the mountain would no longer move.

Whirlwind sent a message to the two Hactcin telling them to go up and fix the damage. Turkey was responsible for all growing things and so he first went up and saw what the two girls had done. He came back and told the two Hactcin. The Hactcin requested that the people remain where they were.

The two Hactcin went up with Holy Boy and Red Boy. They saw all that the girls had done. They saw how the reeds and many other plants were damaged. The girls had been chasing each other and wrestling and trampling on the holy plants. They had even used the holy mountain as a toilet. So the Holy Ones cleaned up everything and fixed it up. The girls were no longer there. They had gone down the mountain again.

The Holy Ones came down to the people again after performing a ceremony there. They asked the people who had been on top of the mountain, and they found out which girls had done it.

"Why did you go up there?" they asked these girls.

They blamed each other. One said, "She wanted me to go up." The other said, "No, she told me to go." They said they had intended to go only a little way but that they had seen berries and fruit ahead, and so had gone from one plant or tree to another until they had climbed to the top.

Now all the people came together once more and sang, and the mountain began to grow again. It grew just a little higher. It grew four times and then it wouldn't rise any more.

The four Holy Ones went up the mountain again. They saw that the top of the mountain was still a little way from the sky and from the hole through which they could see to the other earth. So they all held a council to decide what they would do next.

They sent up Fly and Spider. The spider put his web all around, and the fly and the spider went up on it. That is why, in February or March, when the first warm weather starts and the first flies appear, they come on the sunbeams, which stand for the spider's web.[2] You will see the sun's ray come through the window and the fly will come in on it, right into the house.

---

[1] The Holy Ones are White Hactcin, Black Hactcin, Red Boy, and Holy Boy. Actually the informant mentioned these four names each time, but to avoid repetition this convention of referring to them collectively will be followed.

[2] The Jicarilla will not kill spiders for this reason. The nexus in Jicarilla ideology between the spider's web and the sunbeam is made explicit in the birth rite, where a cord of unblemished buckskin, called in the rite "spider's rope," is stretched from the umbilicus of the child towards the sun.

Those two went up where the sun was. They took four rays of the sun, each of a different color, and pulled on them as if they were ropes. They pulled them down to the mountain top. The ropes came down, black, blue, yellow, and glittering, one on each corner of the opening. From these rays of the sun the four Holy Ones made a ladder. Out of the same material they made twelve steps and placed them across.

When Spider first came up on this earth, there was only one mountain, and that was to the east. Flint Mountain was its name. It is still there, west of Abiquiu.

The first animals to be sent up after Spider came down and announced that water was plentiful there, were two wild ducks.[1] These are the ones they hunt now in October. They were sent up because it was thought that they could get along well in the water. But as soon as they came up they flew over to this mountain and stayed there until the water was sent away. When everyone was up on the earth, they came back and joined the others.

Now the fly and the spider went upward again on that ladder. They saw a great deal of water up there. They could see no ground at all. The spider made a cylinder of web which protected them and they went up to the top through this. Spider then wove four webs on top of the earth of four different colors and stretching in four directions so that the four Holy Ones could ascend.

The four came up. Black Hactcin stood on the black web to the east, and the others took their places too. They talked of what to do, for the sun was past the middle of the sky already.

Then they said, "Let us make four hoops of the different colors, one black, one blue, one yellow, and one glittering."[2]

They did so and threw the black one to the east, the blue one to the south, the yellow one to the west, and the glittering one to the north. Every time they threw one, the water rolled back and grew less where they were standing. By the time they threw the fourth one, there was land where they stood. The water had receded from the land and had made the oceans as they are now.

But everything was still muddy. So they sent for the four Big Winds of the different colors and for the little winds too. The winds blew and made it all dry. But the winds couldn't dry off certain places where the springs and rivers were.

When the wind was hurling the water back and exposing the land, it lifted the water high in the sky and held it there. Over by the oceans the water is still held there by the wind.

White Hactcin said to the wind, "Hold the water there and when it is needed we will let you know and you must blow and bring the rain."

---

[1] For the origin of the water found on the earth at the time of the emergence see p. 267.

[2] The device of rolling back waters by the tossing of colored hoops occurs in more than one place in Jicarilla mythology. See p. 106.

Hactcin talked to the thunder, "You must lead," he said, "so people will hear and know the rain is coming and get ready. They will prepare buckets to fill and be ready to receive the rain."

Then he spoke to the sun saying, "You must shine on the lakes and rivers so that the steam will arise and turn to water and give rain. But Wind, you will always carry the water in the air; you are responsible for it. If the heat does not pick up the water but leaves it around on the earth in the same way all the time, the water will become dirty and unfit for use. But by changing it in this manner it will be made pure and good for the people."

High in the air there are four winds: the black wind from the east makes the water warm, the blue wind from the south makes it cool and fresh, the yellow wind from the west freezes the water and turns it to snow, and the glittering wind from the north turns it to ice and hail.[1] These four people are always there handing around the moisture of the air. When it is handed to the wind of the north, it turns to ice. Then, when it is handed back to Black Wind of the east, he warms it and it turns to water again. That is why we have the moisture of the air in all these forms.

And some people who also control water live in the mountains. These are the people who were directed by the Hactcin to stay in the mountains and take care of them and of all within them.[2]

When the people first came up on earth there were no mountains. But when the monsters began to grow, the mountains too began to rise, for Hactcin made them to be barriers so that the monsters could not get to the people easily.

And Hactcin stationed people in those mountains then, saying, "This mountain will be your home."

These people allow the water of the mountains to flow out, and thus there are springs.

We say that the fly is the messenger of the sun. It carries the news of the coming of the sun. And the spider has long ropes, we say. In ceremonies he helps people, and when he helps it is just as if a rope were lowered to one who has fallen in a deep place.

The four Holy Ones said to Fly and Spider, "We need your help still. Make a web and extend it to the sky," they said to Spider, "and then you two bring the sun down."

The Hactcin sang and sang so the sun and moon could be gotten down, for the sun and moon had not asked permission when they went up as they did. It was the fault of the sun and moon that the people had such a hard time and had to come up on this earth.

---

[1] Like other natural forces, Wind is often personified. The Jicarilla's conception is of an animate universe which understands and responds to his needs.

[2] The belief that people or supernaturals have been stationed within mountains for one purpose or another is a common theme. See also p. 112.

Spider did as he was told, and he and Fly brought the sun and moon down. Then all held council and they decided that they would change Sun to a person, a living person, because he had disobeyed. They were afraid that if they didn't do this the sun would go up again to some other place, and they had had a difficult time regaining the sun. They decided to do the same to Moon too. Before this Sun and Moon were alive, but they were not people.

So the four Holy Ones talked it over and said, "Of the sun we will make another people." And they made the sun into a Taos Indian boy. And out of the moon they made a Jicarilla Apache girl.[1]

"Let them marry," said the four Holy Ones, "and then the Jicarilla Apache and the Taos Indians will be good friends and will not fight over little things."

And so these two helped each other after this. They helped each other shine and give light.

Now they sent the sun and the moon back to the north again after they had become living persons. So they went back to the north. Then the sun started to go to the south. The moon followed. They went like this for one full day.

But then they thought about it.

"I don't believe it's right," Sun said, "for one side of the earth has light when we go this way and one has not."[2]

The Holy Ones thought about it. Then they changed it and had the sun and moon go from east to west. And the Milky Way that you see stretching from north to south across the sky is the first path of the sun and moon.

At first the sun and moon went together, at the same time.

"That's not right," they thought. "We will hold back the moon. Let the sun go first and then the moon can go at night."

The moon was flat and round. It followed the sun, coming later. When the sun set in the west, it could be seen. The moon is a girl and was having her menstrual period just at that time. She was tipped up so that only the rim could be seen. That is what we call the new moon when it occurs now. So it is that our women have a period after a new moon, and that is why the girl's puberty ceremony is always held at the new moon. And the new moon is used now for keeping track of the seasons.

The sun just kept going all the time.

---

[1] Apache cosmology is not consistent concerning the sex of the moon. When the moon is thought of in connection with the woman's menstrual cycle it is given female attributes. But Moon is also associated with Water, and Water becomes the father of one of the Culture Heroes. In an important ceremonial race Moon is represented as a male (p. 81) as is the case in the origin myth of the Hactcin ceremony (p. 141).

[2] The earth is said to have the form of a woman whose feet point toward the east and whose head lies to the west.

When everything was ready in this upper world the Holy Ones went down below to the place where the people were waiting.

The people had a great deal of food on that mountain. They had much to eat while they were traveling. But they had not yet started upward. They were still below, in the underworld.

Then the four Holy Ones sent up the crows, the four crows of the different colors. "You must go up there and see how everything is getting along."

The crows came up. Some of the fish and water animals had died when the water was thrown back by the Holy Ones. The crows began to eat these dead bodies.

The other people were expecting them back. They wondered why the crows did not return. So finally they sent up White Weasel.

White Weasel went up and saw what the crows were doing. He returned and told the people, "No wonder they don't come back. They are busy eating."

So they sent Badger up then. Badger stepped into some place that was still muddy. He thought it must be muddy like that all over, so he went back and told them, "Oh, it's still very muddy." Because he stepped in the mud he has black on his paws now.

Then they sent up Beaver. When he got up there he tried to dam up the water. He stayed up there working and making dams.

Then Black Weasel was sent. Black Weasel came to Beaver and said, "What are you doing? The people are waiting for you."

"Oh, I'd better dam up this water so that the water will be ready when the people come up."

The rivers that are left us here today are the ones he dammed up.

Beaver knew that the people were on the journey to this earth and would be very tired. So be built a sweat house there where the people could come and get rested.

When Weasel came up he saw it. He asked, "What are you doing here? The people are waiting for you."

"I'm making a dam for the poeple, so they will have water. When the people come they will already have water for drinking and to bathe in."

"And what are you building?"

"That is my house. I call it *keltca*."[1]

"Is this for the people?"

"No, it is my home. But whenever the bodies of the people are doubled up they will use it. When they are tired they will use it too. After a long sickness when they are run down they will use it. When they come up I will explain to them how to use it. I'll

---

[1] This word means "beaver pelt" and is quite similar to the word for sweat-house, *kiltca*. The informant is employing a bit of folk etymology to hint that the word for sweat-house originally came from "beaver pelt." Since there is a difference of tone as well as outline between these two words, this is extremely unlikely.

explain to them what they should do. They should build a fire outside and put rocks in it. When these rocks are well heated they must throw them into the sweat house. The doorway must be closed by my own skin, by beaver skin, for when I go into my house I never wear my skin but take it off and hang it at the door. So let the people do likewise when they take a sweat bath. The door must always face to the east. The people must roll the hot rocks in with sticks and pile them all on the north side. Then they must throw water on the rocks and steam will arise. When it begins to cool down, more water must be thrown on the rocks. And the songs that are sung should be about Little Night. They must sing these, for they go into that small dark place which gives them the sweat bath and the cleansing.

"Two or four may go in and all can sing in there. And they should sing for long life too and sing of the sun and moon. Women may go in but not with the men.

"The sweat house shall be made of bent pieces of wood with brush and dirt over these. And it must be made by the water's edge so that all can go into the water and wash after the sweat bath.

"The men must not use the same sweat house that the women use. If they do so they will become blind, and the women will become blind too if they go into the one the men have used.

"The sweat house, after use, is to be left standing, and it may be used again."

Then from below the Holy Ones sent the birds up first, because they have wings to fly. They came up in a flock.

Hactcin told the animals and people. "Now get ready. We must go up in the sky."

At this time the girls were big with children.[1] This was the result of the things they had used on themselves in the absence of the men, when the women and the men had separated. They were already in late pregnancy when they started.

Now they all began traveling on the mountain going toward the top. The Hactcin made sure that everything was right and holy before they let the people start. There was no sun and so one cannot say that the people took four days to reach the vault of the underworld. But they traveled four times until they were tired and then stopped each time. The top of the mountain where they stopped last was twelve ladder steps from the earth hole. That was the distance between the mountain top and the earth hole. They had four ladders. The black ladder to the east was the one the men climbed up on. The blue ladder to the south was for the girls and women. The yellow ladder to the west was used

[1] For the explanation of these pregnancies see p. 266. The account of the misbehavior of the girls in the underworld is as often told as a part of the origin legend also.

by the young boys. The north ladder of a glittering color was used by all the little children.

First they prayed before the ladders. Holy Boy was the real leader of the ascent. It was due to him that the people were coming on this earth. So he prayed for the ladders and for the Hactcin, the clowns, and Tsanati.

Then the clowns came up first, for they had the whips of yucca with which to chase sickness away. At that time it was not known whether there was sickness on earth. They thought that perhaps the water animals which had died had some sickness. So the clowns came up and made everything wholesome for the people. They made the path that the people could follow.

White Hactcin was the next to come up. Holy Boy first dressed him up. He put a downy eagle feather on top of his head. He dressed him up with spruce. White Hactcin held a big whip made of yucca. A downy feather was at its end. In his left hand he held spruce branches.

The clowns uttered a certain laugh when they came up, so that all the sickness would be frightened, and the Hactcin made a different noise for the same reason. Black Hactcin ascended immediately after White Hactcin did. He had black specular iron ore and pollen all over his face. White Hactcin had pollen all over his face, and on the right side the seven stars of the Big Dipper were painted with specular iron ore. A sun of specular iron ore was designed on the middle of the forehead. On the left cheek was the moon, designed with specular iron ore. The bodies of both Hactcin were covered with white clay. They wore skirts of woven yucca like those of the Tsanati. At the arm and leg joints they wore yucca bands tied, and spruce branches were fastened on these.

Next Red Boy ascended. He, like the Hactcin, went up the ladder of the east. Then the twelve Tsanati came up. Then Holy Boy came up. After him came Turkey. All these came up the ladder to the east.

Now all these were up on this earth, and they prepared everything so that no harm should befall the people.

Now it was the turn of the people. Ancestral Man was the first of the people to ascend. Ancestral Woman followed and was the first woman to emerge. Both walked up with age sticks in their hands.[1] They were dressed as White-Shell Woman and Child-of-the-Water dress for the girl's puberty ceremony now. The other people followed. The men were to the east, the women to the west, and the children to the north and south.[2]

[1] The age stick, or the staff which an old person uses for support, is here mentioned as a symbol of the long life that man shall have on earth. It is constantly named in Jicarilla ritual songs.

[2] At the time of the emergence, the man who came out last had his hair parted, not in the middle, but on the side. The line of the parting was painted red. If you know this emergence story well, you can wear your hair that way. Both men and women did this. (Inf.)

After the people the animals came.

The people emerged from a hole in a mountain. At that time this was the only mountain on the earth, besides Flint Mountain to the east. The other mountains grew up later, at the time of the monsters. Some say that the emergence mountain lies north of Durango, Colorado. Others say it is near Alamosa, Colorado. It was called Big Mountain.[1]

Sky is our father, Earth is our mother.. They are husband and wife and they watch over us and take care of us. The earth gives us our food; all the fruits and plants come from the earth. Sky gives us the rain, and when we need water we pray to him. The earth is our mother.[2] We came from her. When we came up on this earth, it was just like a child being born from its mother. The place of emergence is the womb of the earth.[3]

The animals came up, the elk, the deer, and all the others. But they were not wild animals. They were gentle and tame then. The animals came up any ladder which was nearest. After a while the ladders were all worn through, so many had passed over them.

There were two old people, an old man and a very old woman who were far behind the animals. These two couldn't see well; their sight was dim. Those two silly girls who had interfered with the growth of the mountain before were far behind too. They had been chasing each other and playing, and the people didn't know it.

When the two old people came to the ladders, the ladders were worn out and they couldn't get up. They stood there and called, "Come and get us. Take us too." But there was no ladder nor any way to get them up. The old people tried to get the others to help them.

Finally they became angry. "All right," they said, "we shall stay here. But you must come back some day." They meant that the people must return to the underworld when they die.

Night came. The people on top tried to sleep. But they couldn't sleep the first night. They couldn't sleep the second nor the third. They wondered why. They wondered whether it was because something had been left behind.

Then they discovered that they had no lice in their hair. There were three kinds, black ones, grey ones, and the small ones, the nits. So they sent down to the old people for these. The two old people threw some up. The people divided the lice among themselves. The fourth night they all slept soundly.

---

[1] For identification of the emergence mountain as the San Juan of Colorado see pp. 163—164.

[2] Taos is at the heart of the earth. Our own country used to be the Cimarron region. (Inf.)

[3] That the emergence tale is a myth of gestation is patent enough. It is seldom, however, that the native draws the parallel so conclusively.

The people looked down through the hole, for they couldn't find those two silly girls among those on top. The light of the sun went through the hole and hit the tip of the mountain, illuminating it. There, in the light, sat those two foolish girls sewing shallow tray baskets.

They called to these two girls, but they wouldn't come up. They wouldn't obey.

Then Holy Boy made two butterflies out of the flowers. He made the kind that always go in pairs, the yellow ones.

The sun had power now. Holy Boy sent word to Sun. "You must help us and send a beam for the butterflies." The sun did so and the butterflies went right in on that beam.[1]

The two silly girls caught sight of the butterflies.

"Let's catch them and make designs. We have always made mountain designs on our baskets. Now we'd better make a butterfly design," they said. "That is more beautiful."[2]

So they started to chase the butterflies. The ray of the sun came down and provided a ladder. The butterflies kept just out of reach above them. So they began to ascend the ladder, trying to get those butterflies. Before they knew it they were on top.

4. THE ORIGIN OF THE BEAR DANCE[3]

On top was the bear lying in wait, and next to him sat the snake. Both were evil. As soon as the girls reached the top, the bear stole one and the snake the other. There were four hazes, one black, one blue, one yellow, and one glittering. Bear and Snake used these to hide what they were doing,[4] and the people couldn't see what was happening.

The relatives of the girls gave downy feathers and four different kinds of stones to various shamans so that they would make a

[1] Butterflies and the rays of the sun are connected with love charms in Jicarilla theory and are therefore well designed to lure the girls to the upper earth. One way to gain the favor of a member of the opposite sex is to flash a beam of light in his direction by means of a shiny object. The butterfly, symbol of the fluttering and inconstancy of women, is encised or painted on flutes which young men play to attract sweethearts.

[2] A woven basket, one of the ceremonial gifts of the bear dance, is decorated with designs of mountains and butterflies to commemorate this.

[3] As will appear from the description which follows, the "bear dance" is designed to cure sickness from either Bear or Snake, and serves a number of subsidiary functions besides. "Bear dance" is the name given to the rite by the white men, largely because a blackened and spruce-covered figure, symbolic of the bear, makes an entrance at one point in the ceremony. The natives have two names for the rite; in neither of these names is the bear or snake mentioned. Because the rite has become known in the literature as the bear dance, however, that name will be retained for it here.

[4] Haze or fine dust in the air are often thought to be sent by sorcerers to cover up their designs or actions.

ceremony for them and find out the whereabouts of the girls. That is what we do today. They gave this to the leader of the shamans, and the shamans began to invite each other to make a ceremony and find the girls. They all got busy and started to do what they could. They cut themselves and disappeared and did all the different things they had tried below when they were seeking to bring back the sun. They did their best, but they could accomplish nothing. They couldn't find out who had taken the girls or where they were.[1]

Then the relatives came to Holy Boy. Then they came to Red Boy and to the two Hactcin also. Holy Boy asked for the baskets the girls had been making. It was the ceremonial present he wanted.[2] They brought them to him. The girls had made them with the withes going around clockwise.[3] But Holy Boy stepped in them and reversed them, and now the ceremonial basket for the bear dance is like that, the coils run counter-clockwise. And the designs on the basket were mountains and butterflies. Now the basket for the bear dance is made with two mountains and two butterflies. Then Holy Boy asked for a pipe, a clay pipe. He told the relatives to make the design of a moon on it. He showed them how to do it. He had them incise the sun on it, too, and the big dipper with seven stars in it. And he had them put on it also the seven stars of the Pleiades, the north star, and the morning star. He told them to get mountain tobacco[4] and put it in the pipe and to put jet on top of the tobacco in the pipe. He also asked for pollen, specular iron ore, and corn-meal. Then he asked for six white eagle tail feathers and six spotted ones and for two tail feathers of the yellow-tailed hawk and two tail feathers of the magpie. He needed, besides these things, a branch of spruce, six white downy eagle feathers and six downy feathers from the turkey.

The relatives gathered together all these things and gave them to the four Holy Ones. The Holy Ones divided them. "I'm going to use this," one would say. "I shall use this," another would say. Thus they divided the ceremonial gifts among themselves.[5]

Then they began to inquire about the girls. They asked the wind, "Did you see anything of those girls?"

The wind answered, "I know nothing of it."

---

[1] The inadequacy of the shamans is again made the rationalization for the origin and performance of a major rite.

[2] The ceremonial presents are gifts which must be offered to those in charge of a rite before they may begin their work. They are presents of sacred substances and objects associated with the rite and used in the course of it, and are considered payment to the supernaturals or power and not to those officiating.

[3] This is the usual direction in which the coils run in the Jicarilla basket.

[4] Mountain tobacco has been identified as the bearberry.

[5] This follows out the native theory that ceremonial gifts are payment to the supernaturals who assist with their power.

They asked all the different animals. First they asked the mountain animals. Then they asked the animals of the plains. None of them knew. So they called the birds. All the different birds came together. The birds all said that they hadn't seen the girls. Then the Holy Ones called upon all the ducks and water birds. But they had not seen the girls either. Then they asked the frogs and the creatures of the water. Neither had they seen anything of the girls.

Now they asked the season, Spring. He didn't know. They came to Summer Season and asked him. His answer was the same. They went to Autumn but without any better result. Finally they went to Winter, but he could tell them nothing.

They called the clouds and asked the same question, but Cloud didn't know either. Then they asked Thunder. Thunder knew nothing about it. They asked Mist, but he couldn't tell them anything more than the others. Then they approached Heat Waves but learned nothing more.

They called on the sun next. The sun didn't know. He said he had been traveling to the west and had not seen the girls. There was a cloud beneath him, he told them, and therefore he had not been able to see what happened.

"When it is clear I see everything," he told them. "I saw shadows," he said, "but I didn't know what was going on in those shadows. And I cannot tell what goes on in caves or holes or dark places. I did not see through the darkness. And I cannot see at night."

The sun sent them to the moon. Those people inquired of Moon. Moon said, "I can see everything at new moon, for then I am high and can see all over. But even then I cannot see into shadows or dark places. And I cannot see under a cloud, and the clouds were thick. Nor can I see anything in the daytime. No, I cannot help you."

So they sent for Dipper. He had seen nothing of the girls either. They told North Star to come to them, and he told them the same.

They had called everything on the earth and up in the sky and under the water and had even inquired of the seasons. But none knew the whereabouts of the girls. All four of the Holy Ones had been doing this together till now. Every time they had called upon someone they had given him something.

Now the two Hactcin started alone. They were going to use all their power. The Hactcin pushed the earth all together and made it small. That is why they make a corral when they have a bear dance. That corral represents the earth as it was made by the Hactcin. They use all sorts of brush to make the corral because when the earth was pushed together like this, all the different plants and trees were pushed closely together. At the door of the corral they put a spruce tree on the right side and a piñon tree on the left. Those two trees stand as a guard. When people enter the corral they cannot go out without permission. That is what those two trees mean. The corral stands for the sun, too, for the Hactcin pushed the earth together and made it the size of the sun.

All the people were on this earth that had been made small. The animals and birds were there too. All living things were there. The plants were there too.

Now all the animals, birds, and insects came to the Hactcin. They did just as they had done under the earth when they sought to make the mountain grow. They put their hands to the directions and each got something. They gave these things to the Hactcin saying, "This is what I live on." The squirrel brought nuts. Each brought something.

The Hactcin told the women to go over on the south side. And the men they sent to the north side. At the west they told the people they would have a holy place.[1] They made a fire from the north star and they kindled four fires on the south side and four on the north side going around in clockwise fashion from the door.

All the people were there. Hactcin told Small Wind to find the girls now. Wind went after Bear and Snake. Bear and Snake had been taking the girls directly through some mountains. There were forty-eight mountains scattered around. Each day they would take the girls into another one of these. But Wind found them and told them that the Holy Ones wanted them to come back to the holy place, return the two girls, and free them.

But the bear and snake said, "No, no one is going to tell us what to do."

The wind came back with this answer.

The wind was sent three times with a message and each time they gave him the same answer.

Hactcin then said, "If they do not obey, if they do not bring the girls back, I shall mete them out a severe punishment."

The first time the wind was told to order Bear and Snake to bring the girls back, he was not told to give them any other message. But the second time he was told to tell them, "If you don't come back with the girls, you will be severely punished. There will be no food for you two."

The bear was a little frightened and wished to give in at first. But the snake was hard, he was unafraid.

The third time the wind brought this message to them, "If you don't come back to the Hactcin with those girls you will have a hard time hereafter. You will have no friends. Everyone will be against you. Everyone will hate you."

Then the fourth time the wind was told to give them this message. "Tell those two," said the Hactcin, "that if they do not obey us·

[1] The "holy place" is the tipi erected at the back or west end of the corral In it the ground drawings are traced and the sick are treated.

we are going to make an arrow of the snake and shoot it into a cliff, into the rocks. When the skin dries we'll be happy. And tell the bear that if he does not obey at once he will burst."

When this word was brought to them by the wind they were much frightened. "All right," they said.

First night

It was night now. The people were all present at the holy place.[1]

The Hactcin turned over the basket[2] on the ground so that it lay with the face down. As they did it they said, "The bear, the snake, and the two girls are coming at this very time."

The bear and the snake were on their way back with the girls now.

The Hactcin began to sing. They sang their sacred songs.

Then the bear came in with the girl he had stolen. The girl was very fat. Then the snake came in with the other girl. This girl was pitifully thin. She was nothing but skin and bones.[3]

The Hactcin looked at the girls. Then they turned to the bear, "Now you have to make a ceremony for the girl you stole and make her well again. She is too fat now. You have done this."

So the bear began to sing in his own way. He performed a ceremony over the girl.[4] The bear was sitting facing the girl. He put his right foot against her right foot and then his left foot against her left foot. He repeated this once more.

When Bear had done this, all the little animals of the cliffs and mountains, — the jack-rabbit, the cottontail rabbit, the squirrel, the chipmunk, the magpie, — all the birds and animals came around and helped sing. These were what they called mountain songs, for this was just like a mountain ceremony, like the ceremony which had made the mountain grow in the underworld. When that was over the Hactcin talked to the bear and told him it was his turn again. While they were singing they had used the basket, hitting it with the moccasins of the girls who had been stolen. As they did so they sang, "This is your home. Right here is where you belong." They used these moccasins to accompany the singing because it was with these moccasins on that the girls had been stolen away and had been made to walk all over.

Hactcin then gave the feathers and the spruce branch to the bear and told him to hold these.[5] He gave them to the bear to hold in

---

1 For a brief note concerning the bear dance see Goddard, p. 263.

2 The basket drum is one of the important ritual objects used in the ceremony. It is placed over a hole in the ground which is dug deeper four times during the ceremony. A buffalo hide is placed over the basket.

3 These are the symptoms diagnostic of bear and snake sickness respectively.

4 Now the bear dance can take place only in winter when the bear is hibernating and the snake is away. (Inf.)

5 In another version of the origin of this dance, it is said that Bear taught it to a human who lived among the bears for some time. (pp. 116—117.)

both his hands. The bear took the feathers and objects he had been given and stood in front of the holy place facing the east. He danced forward four steps, starting with his right foot, and then danced backward. He did this four times. The music changed while he was dancing. Now they were using notched sticks made out of choke-cherry wood without any knots. There were twelve notches in the stick. They had two sticks like this, one resting on each side of the basket. They called one the summer and one the winter. The scrapers were made of deer bone; they were made of the shin bone of the deer. While the bear was dancing he motioned to and fro with the feathers, driving away the sickness. When he finished he sang one song and then he gave those feathers to the girls.

Now the women on the south side got up and chose men with whom to dance. The partners danced through about twelve songs. The songs were all about sickness, asking it to go away. The men and women danced to make the sick girls feel better; to make them more comfortable. And the dancing brought the people back to a better state of mind too. For they had been frightened by the stealing of the girls.

That was the first night. After dancing they went to sleep.

Second day

The next morning it was the snake's turn. They brought the girl Snake had made sick back to the holy place. This was the thin one. She was very thin and sickly.

Hactcin said to Snake, "You must perform a ceremony over this girl."

So he began. While he was making his ceremony the girl just shook.[1] He did as the bear had done. He touched his right foot to the right foot of the girl, then touched the girl's left foot with his, and so on for four times. He rubbed his body against the girl from all sides, moving around her clockwise. After he finished this he touched his head to hers.

Then he brought some medicine in a clay bowl[2] and she drank it. Some was left, and he rubbed this all over her. Then he rolled a cigarette. He puffed at it four times and handed it to the girl, and she puffed at it four times and handed it back to him.

Hactcin said, "You must sing a song for the kind of medicine you have."

And so Snake sang a song to the medicine he had given her and which he had rubbed on her.

---

[1] The trembling of the girl constituted proof that the right disease was being treated. Today, when the snake songs are being sung, those ill from snake shake in this manner. Those suffering from bear sickness do so when the songs of the bear are sung.

[2] This is the clay bowl referred to in the story of the emergence, p. 16.

When he got through he sat down. Holy Boy, Red Boy, and the Hactcin began to sing. They sang of the girl's improving health and of the sickness which was going away entirely. They sang a pollen song too. They had put the feathers all around the holy place. Holy Boy picked them up now. They had had them around like a fence.

When Holy Boy picked up the feathers the other Holy Ones began to sing songs. They sang about how Holy Boy should pick the girls up. So Holy Boy went behind the girls and motioned as if to lift them three times; the fourth time he lifted them. Then another song was sung to make them walk. And the girls went out.

Second night

They waited now until night came. The Holy Ones were there now, but not the snake nor the bear. They put the basket down the same way. They made a little noise under the basket with their mouths so that it would give more sound. The girls had not come in yet. They hit the basket with the moccasins once, pounded several times steadily, and then stopped. That was done once. Then they did the same thing four times, and the girls got ready to come in. They made a place for the girls. They gave them each some feathers to hold. They sang the songs of the mountain, just as they had done the first night. Then Holy Boy took the feathers from the girls and went with them and danced as Bear had done the first day. He motioned as Bear had done. Then he returned and gave the feathers back to the girls. When he motioned all the people did likewise and motioned all the sickness away with their hands.

Now the women were going to choose men for the dancing. Holy Boy sang while the people danced. In the songs he told the sickness to go away. At first the dancing went on to the accompaniment of the basket drum. Later the notched sticks were used too. After the dance all slept for the night.

Third day

The next day the Hactcin asked for white sand. They wanted to use it for a ground drawing.[1] And they asked for "sand that rises." They wanted it for the ground drawing too. This kind has life. And they spread out the sand and on it put some of the birds and animals and also the fruits used by the different birds and animals which the Hactcin had been given.

The two girls were to sit in the middle. A place was left for them there. On the outside, around this place, the animals and birds and foods were placed. They heaped up the sand and made a mountain out of sand in the back, directly behind the place where the girls

[1] In the ceremony held today four ground drawings are made during the course of the rite.

were to sit. And right on top of the mountain was put the black clay bowl with holy water in it, water obtained from a holy place, a place near Albuquerque. In it they put four small pieces of wood from an evergreen tree[1] which grows high on top of the big mountains. The sticks were each about an inch long. In the bear ceremony today those who do a great deal of hunting take the sticks at the ceremony's end. Then they tie the stick to some part of their clothing and when they go hunting in dangerous places the bear won't bother them.

All the animals and birds were sitting there now, and then the four Holy Ones began to sing and pray. They sang for each of the animals that sat there. They sang, "After this all you people must help, must help the sick ones." And they sang, "When the people are sick from Bear or Snake after this you should be there and help."

Then the Hactcin were ready to sing the song that had been sung to call the snake and the bear when they had stolen the girls away. But it was being used now to call in the girls. When the song began the girls came in. They took their shoes off outside the corral. They came in and stood up in front of the holy place. There in front was a bowl of corn-meal.

The Hactcin said, "You must take this corn-meal and throw some on the birds and animals here. And while you are doing it you must pray."

The four Holy Ones went out there and they did the same, throwing the corn-meal on the birds and animals. Then the Holy Ones sat down and told the girls to sit in the middle.

White Hactcin had a rattle of young buffalo bull tail in his right hand. He shook it to the directions, beginning east and going clockwise. He touched the rattle gently against the bodies of both girls.

Then the Hactcin started to sing the bear songs to make the girls shake. The girl which the bear had made fat began to shake. The next song was the snake song. When this was sung the other girl was much frightened and nearly died.

Then White Hactcin gave the rattle to Holy Boy. White Hactcin took off his shoes. He did just as the bear had done. He touched his foot to the bottom of the right foot of one of the girls. And then he did it to her left foot with his left foot. He repeated it four times and then did the same to the other girl. Then he clasped the right hand of the first girl with his right hand and pulled each of her fingers in turn. This was to pull the sickness from her.[2] And he did

[1] Limber pine is the tree mentioned.

[2] Sickness is extracted from the body or chased away by a number of different methods. Chief among these are pulling, sucking, blowing, brushing, and frightening by gesticulating. The impartation of health and strength is often accomplished by supernaturals or ceremonial men by rubbing their own bodies against those of the patients.

likewise with the left hand. Then he went to the other girl and did the same. The Hactcin was still facing the girl. He touched his right arm to hers. Then he went behind her and touched his back against hers. He touched his left arm to hers next. He came around and touched her head with his four times. Then he motioned, sending the sickness to the north. Sickness is always sent to the north.

Then Hactcin rolled a cigarette. He drew smoke. He puffed on the right foot of the girl, on the left, on the right hand and the left, on the right shoulder and the left, and on the head. He did this to both girls. Then he gave the cigarette to them to smoke and each drew four puffs of smoke. They gave it back to him. He finished the rest of the cigarette himself.

Then he went back and sat down. The bowl was there, full of medicine. He stirred it with his forefinger. As the others sang and Holy Boy shook the rattle, he dipped his finger into the medicine and sprinkled some on the sick girls and the animals. They sang twelve songs. Hactcin now got up. He picked up the bowl of medicine. He moved it four times towards the girl, and the fourth time she took it and swallowed some of the medicine.[1] He did likewise to the second girl. Then he rubbed some on her legs to the knee and on the upper part of her body and arms and face. Then he gave the girl some in her hands and she applied it to her privates herself. This was done for both girls. Then he put away the bowl.

He started to sing again. He was going to send the bear and the snake away to the other side of the earth. That was the first song. The second song was about sending them beyond the sky. And the third song was to send them beyond the water.[2] In the fourth song he sang to send them to the other side of the seasons.

Then White Hactcin sent all the animals off the sand. "You are all through," he told them. They all went out. He picked up the feathers which had been put around like a fence.[3] When he had gathered them all up he gave them to Black Hactcin. Black Hactcin smoothed them and fixed them nicely together and returned them to White Hactcin. And while the girls were still sitting there White Hactcin brushed off the girls with the feathers to brush off all the sickness that might still be on them.

The four Holy Ones now began the song which told how to pick up the girls. White Hactcin went behind the girls during this song.

---

[1] The ritual feint of three preliminary gestures before the actual performance of an act, runs throughout Apache ceremonial life. Thus impersonators of masked supernaturals raise the headdress three times before putting it in place on the fourth, and so on.

[2] Reference to earth, sky, water, and seasons is a formula much invoked in Jicarilla prayers and songs. It is the figurative manner of encompassing the entire universe.

[3] The fence is one erected against the forces of sickness and evil. It consists in the feathers and ritual objects asked for as ceremonial gifts in the beginning of the rite.

He motioned as if to lift the girl three times, and the fourth time he really did pick her up. Then he did the same with the other girl. He motioned as though to push the girl and make her walk. He did this three times. The fourth time the girl did walk. The girls went out now. The others were waiting for something to eat. Now the girls' relatives came in with the food and gave it to the Holy Ones.

There were two kinds of food prepared by the relatives. One was what they brought to the Holy Ones. This was an offering. No one else could eat it. It was prepared in different pots too. The other kind was for themselves. This division is still made in the bear dance today. The Holy Ones ate the food that was brought. Now nothing more was done until night came.

Third night

At nightfall the basket drum was beaten four times again to notify the girls to come in. They entered. The Holy Ones sang the song of the basket first. Then they sang the songs of all the fruit and all the animals. These songs were accompanied by the music of the moccasins and basket drum. Then the notched sticks were scraped four times. The fourth time the men doing it motioned to the north, sending all the sickness there.

At the last basket song the Tsanati came and danced, just for that one song. They were not yet painted. It was just the men who were going to dance Tsanati later who did this.

After the notched stick had been scraped four times Holy Boy got up. He took the feathers which the two girls had in their hands. He stood up. He did as the bear had done. He danced back and forth four times during the singing of one song.

Then the women chose the men with whom they wanted to dance and they danced until about two o'clock. Hactcin told the people that when they danced they should not talk of anything foolish or bad. He told them that they must talk only in a good way.[1]

"Someone will get sick from Bear or Snake if anything evil is done or said here," he told them.

And he told the men that they must not give any presents to the girls, no rings or earrings. So they obeyed and danced and sang as directed. When the dancing was over they all went to sleep.

And around that holy place, the people, even husbands and wives, were told that they could not have intercourse. They would have to go far away for this, so far that they could not even hear the music.

Fourth day

They all stayed there until the next morning. After breakfast the people assembled around the holy place again.

[1] Much emphasis is laid on the fact that the dancing is not for entertainment or for the purpose of attracting the other sex, but should be regarded as a prayer for the sick.

They swept out the sand which had been used, they just brushed it aside. They brought fresh sand of the same kinds. When the sand was put down they smoothed it out with the feathers. In the middle of the sand four mounds of sand were pushed together and "mountains" were made in this way. The first was called Black Mountain and it was painted black with specular iron ore. The second was Blue Mountain and it was painted blue with a paint made of a mixture of white clay, yellow ochre, and black earth. When this was stirred together it gave blue. The next one was Yellow Mountain and it was painted with yellow ochre. And the last one was Striped Mountain. It was made with alternating black and white stripes. On top of each one they put four white downy feathers of the eagle.

White Hactcin and Black Hactcin talked to the birds and animals. "You must each give what you live on and we will put it in these mountains."

This was before the mountains were made. Each came and brought his food. They gave it to the Hactcin and the Hactcin put these things in the four mountains.

To the birds, animals, and insects the Hactcin then said, "You must trace your figures in the sand here, and before your images put the fruit that you live on." So these animals and birds busied themselves doing this. And they were told to put pollen on top of the fruits. It was done all around in that sand.

Then around the edge of the sand the Holy Boy traced a *kabaskin*.[1] Now it was the turn of the Hactcin. Near the center, but leaving room for the two girls, they put their own images, the black one on one side and the white one on the other. The girls were to sit between. And the pictures of the sun and the moon were drawn too. They were all drawn in color.

Then they put the feathers all around the outside. In front they put two spruce trees, one on each side, and downy feathers were tied to the top of these.

Then the four Holy Ones got up. They picked up the bowl. There was corn-meal in it, and each sprinkled a little of it on the drawings. The animals and all who had drawn their images on the sand were now called and the Hactcin told them, "You must throw this four times on the sand."

Holy Boy had the rattle in his hand. He shook it in the four directions. Then they began to sing about all the different animals represented and all the different birds. And they sang for the long life of the girls and all the birds and animals too. Then they sang for the pollen and for all the fruit that the animals had put on the drawings. And they sang for the holy mountains too, and for the downy feathers on top of them. Then they sang for the feathers

---

[1] The *kabaskin* is an elongated border figure such as is often seen in Navaho sand-paintings. It is symbolic of the waters surrounding the earth in the Jicarillla ground drawing.

which had been placed around as a fence. Then they shook the rattle four times and called the girls in this way. Holy Boy was singing while he did this.

The girls heard and came. They took their moccasins off before they came in. They stood in front of the ground drawing. They, too, picked up the cornmeal and sprinkled it over the sand four times. Then they sat down on the sand.

Now the Holy Ones sang of long life. They sang the bear song first. The first girl did not shake much this time because she was getting better now. Then the snake song was sung. The girl who had been stolen by the snake was not so much affected either. The girl who was so fat the first time she was brought in was not so very fat now. Her weight had decreased a great deal. The other girl had been terribly thin, but now she was beginning to gain weight.

White Hactcin got up. He began to sing. He began to send all that sickness away. He took his shoes off. He picked up the spruces and picked up the feathers placed towards the front around the right side of the *kabaskin* and those in front on the left too. While he was singing he rubbed out some of the drawings with his feet. Then, during the second song, he picked up the feathers on the right and left, but a little further back. During the third song he picked up the ones quite far back on each side, beginning with the right side. And during the fourth song he picked up the rest of them in the back. All through these songs he was rubbing out the paintings.

White Hactcin did this. Then he gave the feathers to Black Hactcin. Black Hactcin put them in order. Black Hactcin gave them back to White Hactcin who used them to brush off the girls. The girls were still seated. When this was done White Hactcin came back to his place and sat down again. He took the bowl of medicine once more. He put the medicine in front of the girls and he sprinkled it on them. Then the song of how to drink that medicine was sung. The medicine was motioned toward the girls three times and the fourth time it was given to them. They swallowed some of it four times. Then White Hactcin rubbed the medicine on the girls to the knee and on the upper part of the body too. The girls were given some with which to rub the middle part of their bodies.

Then more songs were sung. They were all songs about the medicine. The songs told how the medicine cures in one day. Fifteen songs of this kind were sung. Then they sang the songs of the forty-eight mountains. The songs rehearsed what had happened: how the Hactcin had asked all the shamans where the girls were, and none had known; how he had asked all the animals and elements too. The songs told how the bear and snake had power to make the hills grow into mountains and how they had done this and had gone through these mountains with the girls, zigzagging until they had brought the girls back to the holy place. That is where the mountains ended. Then the Hactcin sang their own songs, for they were the ones who had more power than all the rest and had forced the bear and snake to bring back the two girls.

In the same way as he had done the other day, White Hactcin now put his feet, body, and head against the girls and pulled their fingers. He pulled them to their feet in the same way too and then pressed their bodies four times. They made a noise when pressed like this, for they were squeezed very tightly. This is always done at the bear dance. The Hactcin did it from behind.

Then White Hactcin made them walk out.

After all had gone out, White Hactcin rubbed out the four mountains with his hand. He had rubbed out the other designs with his feet but he had left the mountains until now. Now he rubbed out these and he called all the animals who had no fruits to come and pick out the foods they wanted. He told them to take the seeds of what they wanted and to carry them home and plant them where they lived so that they could have that kind of food thereafter.

It was about noon now. They gave the Holy Ones food to eat in the same way as they had done before.

After eating, the Hactcin called twelve different men to them who were shamans. These were to be Tsanati. And they chose six more to be clowns.

Now they picked out the two sets of dancers, one of twelve men and one of six men. They were all placed in one circle but the six stood together and the twelve were together. Holy Boy began to sing. The men began to dance in place to the singing. They sang four songs.

Then the Hactcin said to these men, "You must bring narrow yucca blades." They all went then. Hactcin told them, "Bring spruce branches too." He told this to the group of twelve.

Then he turned to the six men. "You bring the broad yucca," he told them. "And bring the root of the slender yucca too."

They went. Later all these men returned to the holy place.

When the twelve men came back they were put to work to weave skirts of the yucca.

When they had finished the skirts, the work was put away. Then they were all sent to take baths in the river. Then nothing more took place till night.

Fourth night

Night came. Two tipis were set up outside the circle of trees. The one on the right side was for the Tsanati and the one on the left for the clowns. Then they were dressed up. The Tsanati had the feather across the hair. Holy Boy and Red Boy painted the clowns and the two Hactcin painted the Tsanati. Paint belongs to Wind, and when you use it you must pray; then Wind will give it to you when you ask for it. But if you don't you may get sick. So these Holy Ones prayed and sang as they put on the paint. The yucca also belongs to someone, an animal of the mountains. Yucca is just like the home of this animal. So the Holy Ones prayed and sang before they used the yucca. It is the same with spruce; it belongs to the Hactcin and it may not be used without asking them. When the painting was finished two songs were sung by the Holy Ones, and the Tsanati and clowns danced while the singing went on. This was done in the two tipis. In the corral the events of the preceding nights were being repeated.

Holy Boy went back to the corral as soon as the painting was finished to take care of the work there. Holy Boy sang six songs in there. He sat near the basket with others and sang for the basket. After the six songs were over the painted dancers were to come in. The sick girls were already in the holy place and Holy Boy was taking care of them. The other three Holy Ones were taking care of the Tsanati and the clowns.

The painted dancers came slowly and quietly towards the door of the corral. The clowns led. Their leader entered the corral without the others first. He went over to the south side where the women were. The downy eagle feather sought out those among the women who were having their menstrual period, and he sent them out. Then all was ready. He went back to the door and the dancers began to file in, led by the clowns. They moved in an undulating line, going the way the snake goes. They came towards the holy place. Then they came to the middle and formed two lines, both facing south. The clowns were in the first line and the Tsanati came behind.

When they first came in all the people had to throw corn-meal in their direction so that none might be frightened or get sick, for if anyone is foolish or does a wicked thing while the corral is being put up or while the ceremony is taking place, that individual may become ill.

Then the twelve Tsanati showed their power.[1] Each one of them did something before the people. One would cause a squirrel to rise before him by a sweep of the hand. Another would make fruit appear before him. When they had finished they sang and the other people picked up all that they had caused to appear. Each used his own power. They were all men who had great power; that is why the Hactcin had chosen them.[2]

Now they all formed in a single line again with the clowns leading, and went up to the girls. Each made a motion as if to drive the disease away, and then all went out.

---

[1] Now they do not have to pick out men who have power when they choose for the bear dance. (Inf.)

[2] This is the heritage the Tsanati carry as a result of their descent from wonder-working shamans. They are the magicians of the bear dance.

Now the other people started the basket dance. After about six songs the painted dancers were ready to come in again.

Two songs were sung and then they re-entered. The twelve Tsanati were in front this time. That is the way it is now at the bear dance too. The people inside were all quiet as they entered. They came in with their line undulating like a snake. They shuffled their feet and advanced in this way. They came towards the holy place and passed the girls, going the way the sun goes. Each motioned the disease away with his arms. Then they came to the middle and formed two lines as before, but this time they faced the men. The people just bowed their heads. They did not dare to look at them.

Each one of the Tsanati performed some wonderful thing again. Then they danced for two songs. The six clowns took care of the Tsanati. When the Tsanati dropped anything, like a feather or a piece of yucca, the clowns would pick it up and give it back. When they finished they formed in line and went back to the holy place and around and out again, moving in an undulating line as before.

Now the notched stick was scraped four times and the singing began. Holy Boy took the feathers and danced forth and back as the bear had done the first day. This is called the path dance. Holy Boy was making a path for the people, after which the women could choose partners and dance. Then they knew how to dance correctly.

The women chose their partners then and danced while six songs were sung.

Now the painted dancers were ready to come in and the clowns were leading this time. They came in as a snake moves, went to the women along the south side, chased the disease away, and came around to the center where they formed two lines, this time facing the women.

At this time the clowns began their clowning. They wrestled. They rolled on the ground. They pretended they were having intercourse. They said funny things, laughed and shouted. They did everything that the people should not do while the ceremony is going on. They have the right to do it, for they are holy. They showed their power in this way and they showed the people what must not be done. The Tsanati are not like this. They do not talk or laugh. They just sang the holy songs, but not loudly. It was more like a hum. This is the way they do now at the ceremony too. But the clowns are always funny. Every time they come in they are talking and laughing and making fun. They imitate the Tsanati too. They danced like this for a while and then went out as before.[1]

The people began to dance to the music of the notched stick once

[1] For comparative material which will summarize the close similarities between Pueblo and Jicarilla clowns see "The Sacred Clowns of the Pueblo and Mayo-Yaqui Indians" by Dr. Elsie Clews Parsons and Dr. Ralph L. Beals, *American Anthropologist*, n. s., Vol. 36, No. 4, Oct.-Dec., 1934, pp. 491—514.

more. They danced for six more songs. Back in the tipis the painted dancers were eating. When they had finished the meal they arose and danced for two songs.

Now they were ready to come into the corral again. The Tsanati led. They came in as before, went to the holy place, and drove the sickness away once more. Then they came to the center. They formed two lines facing the women. They danced as before, and the clowns did many comical things. Then they went out and put on their own clothes. Inside the dancing of the people had started again.

When the painted dancers were in their own clothes, they formed a line. They started to come in. When the people saw them coming they all sat down. The dancers came to the holy place and then separated into two lines before the holy place. They faced each other. A song was begun for them and they danced to it. The singing was accompanied by the music of the notched stick. Then they formed a single line facing the east. The women came to them and chose partners from among them. Then the singing began again and the women danced with these men. As the men danced they motioned as though driving sickness away from the girls. This was done for one song. Then they separated and the women went on their side and sat down. The men who had been the painted dancers went and sat with the other men. By this time it was about four o'clock in the morning.

Each time the clowns came in, they gave a little bread to some men and women. The people were told to keep it, that it would be good if one became ill from having unintentionally touched any kind of excrement and carried it to the mouth. Or a dog may defecate or urinate on something later touched or used for food, and the bread s good for the resulting illness.

Fifth day

They danced again until the sun came up. Then the four Holy Ones got up and picked up all the feathers. The two spruces with the downy feathers on were picked up too.

White Hactcin then chose a good girl who had not yet come to womanhood. The basket that had been used for the drum was filled with corn-meal. The girl walked ahead with this. The four Holy Ones came next. They carried the notched sticks and all the objects which had been used in the ceremony. Next came the two sick girls. The rest of the people came in a line. The procession went to the east. They walked for about one hundred or two hundred paces, until they found a young tree. Then the girl went to the left of the tree and the Holy Ones stopped behind the tree. They put down the two spruce trees, one on each side to the north of this tree, and then they sprinkled corn-meal on the tree. The sick girls were behind the Holy Ones. Then all the people, men, women, and children, came and sprinkled the tree as the Holy Ones had done. Then the women formed one line and the men another. Both lines faced the corral. The Holy Ones were in line too. They spoke to the men and women. Then the men and women turned to the east and shook their blankets four times. Then they turned around and all ran to the corral as fast as they could. They ran to the holy place and went around it clockwise. Then they waited inside the circle of trees.

The Hactcin were outside the corral with the two sick girls and those who couldn't run. The Holy Ones were all there. They took the notched sticks and, while these infirm people sat with their legs straight before them, the Holy Ones crossed the notched sticks over their legs, their abdomens, the upper part of their bodies, and the top of their heads.

When they were through with this outside the corral, the Holy Ones came back. They entered the corral. The men there were sitting in one straight line and the women in another. The same thing was done to them with the notched sticks. All this takes place in the bear dance today.

When this was finished all the people went out. There were men and women and animals too. All were called "the people" in those days.

Now the Holy Ones took the cover from over the holy place, for it had been covered with buffalo skin like any tipi. All the tipi poles, twelve of them altogether, were taken down. They went to the other two tipis outside and took them down too.

The girls who had been cured were told not to go back to their own home at once, but to go to some other place first. Their relatives were told to move camp and go to some other place. That is why camp is moved after a ceremony now. The one who sings for you always tells you to go to another place.

During the ceremony the tree squirrel, the chipmunk, the porcupine, and some birds were using the scrapers near the basket drum. The fire was right behind them and their backs were scorched. It shows on their bodies still.

Now that the ceremony was over, the people went back to their homes.

Because the earth had been pushed together the sun had come nearer. Now the Hactcin made the sun go back to its place. And he made the earth large again; he changed it to its former size.

And the Hactcin said, "Perhaps some day you people will forget how to make this ceremony." So he made three mountains with white sand all around them and told them, "These mountains are sick people sitting in a row on the sand. If you forget how the ceremony goes, you must come back and see what was done the first time."

There is a place near Taos where the fire of this first ceremony stood. There the ground is soft still and feels like a mattress when you walk on it. That place is the heart of the earth, they say. Once a fire came out of the earth at that place and the Taos Indians were much frightened.[1] They could not stop it, for they had no power. So they called on an old Apache woman and she came and stopped it for them.

5. THE BIRTH CEREMONY IS GIVEN; DEATH AND THE MONSTERS COME; THE PEOPLE SCATTER

The people had emerged on the shores of a large lake called Big-Water-Lying-on-Top. They knew nothing about the rest of the world. They knew only the region immediately around this place. Four rivers ran west from this lake.[2] One is called Big Water. This is the Rio Grande. And the rivers are thought of as two married couples.

White Hactcin told them, "When you have a baby, use this water. Go to these rivers and get some of this water. Sprinkle it on the child four days after birth."[3]

And the people were told to use the water for bathing and drinking.

"When you use the water of these rivers in the right way, you will have long life," Hactcin said.

When the people were first on this earth, the children used to grow up to adulthood in four days. Both boys and girls grew up in four days. They married immediately after reaching maturity, and so there were many people.

The people talked it over. "It isn't right," they said. "It is too fast."

First they thought they would retard the growth of a baby so that he would not grow to manhood before twelve days. The people were still holy. They were living as in a dream in those days, and White Hactcin who had more power than anyone was there to help them, so they accomplished it.

But it was still too short a period they found, for the people were still increasing at a rapid rate. So they made it that one who was born at the new moon would be grown at the full moon and would be old and die at the last quarter, so that a life was only about thirty days long.

But the people didn't like that. They thought, "We have only thirty days to live; it is too short a time. What can one accomplish in so short a time?"

---

[1] The final destruction of the present earth by fire is a common Jicarilla theme. See p. 112.

[2] The four sacred rivers to which reference is made are the Rio Grande, the Arkansas, the Canadian, and the Pecos. Water from two of these, one a male, the other a female, must be obtained for the ceremony held four days after the birth of a child. The Rio Grande and the Arkansas are considered to be male rivers; the other two are female.

[3] For a reference to this rite see Goddard, p. 269.

Then White Hactcin spoke and said, "Well, how about measuring your life against mine? I never die. Shall we make it so that you will be like me and never die?"

Coyote, Raven, and Buzzard were all there. They were all talking about this.[1]

Coyote had a leaning stick made for taking hair off hides. He said, "Let us throw this into the river. If it sinks in the water, people will die. If it comes out of the water again, people will return four days after death."

They tried it. The leaning stick came back out of the water. So for a while people came back to life four days after death.

The people liked this arrangement very much, for death was not final and they could return to life. That is why we know now what is going on in the place of the dead; these people used to come back and they told many stories which are remembered by us now.[2]

"You don't have to be afraid to die," they said. "It is a good place down there. The people have a good time there. They hunt; they play the hoop and pole game."

By this time the people had learned sorcery and some were sorcerers. In that place of the dead the sorcerers and the good people were separated. One group lived on one side of this place and one on the other. There was a great wall of rock between. The sorcerers had a difficult time. They had no games. They had almost no food. The only thing they had to eat was lizards which they hunted in the rocks.[3] They heard the sound of singing and laughing on the other side of the wall cliff that rose right to the floor of the upper earth and separated them from the good people. They tried to cut their way through to the others with stone axes. They would work all night and for fear of being found out they would stop just at daybreak and sleep. By that time they would have a tiny hole hacked out through which they could look. But when they awoke the wall would be as before. The hole would be filled up and they would have to start over again the next night. This went on night after night.[4]

But the people were coming back from the land of the dead continually and new people were being born all the time. Again there were too many people. So now it was Buzzard's turn.

He took a small round stone used for pounding meat. He used this because this rock helps the people. It "chews" the meat for

---

1 For references to this incident see Goddard, p. 194; Russell, p. 258.

2 A number of these stories have been recorded, but, since they seem more in place in ethnological context to explain death rites, none has been included in this collection.

3 The imputation is that sorcerers practice incest. Sorcery, incest, and lizards are connected in Jicarilla ideology.

4 No other Apache group with which the writer is familiar has a similar belief in punishment of the wicked after death. Despite the typical Apache setting it is more than likely that this conception is a result of Christian influence. The Tantalus motif is unusual for Apache mythology.

them and it "chews" the roots to be used for medicine.[1] Even today it is used. But today people die nevertheless, because the stone will not help people any more.

Buzzard threw the rock into the water, saying, "If this sinks people will die. If not, it will be as it is now."

But the water washed the rock on the shore, so death did not come this time either. That is why the rivers carry rocks along today and anyone who looks at the river will find such stones in it.

A few days later Raven said he would try something, for things were not yet satisfactory.

He took a flat metate. He said, "I'll throw this into the water. If this comes back again, the people will also come back to life after death," and he threw it in the water.

It didn't come back.

So then he took the mano and threw it in the water also. He used these two because they are just like a mother to the Indians. The mother chews the food for her child when it is helpless and without teeth. In the same way do these two stones help so the Apache will have food to eat and sustain them. And that is why today, when a person dies, all his material possessions are destroyed. For these things which he needed and used were thrown ahead to prepare the way for him. It is not because they are afraid of that stone that the Jicarilla dispose of it at its owner's death, but because they are sending it away so the dead person can use it wherever he is.

This is why the Indians hate the raven and call him a sorcerer. When Raven threw in that mano, that too stayed there. So after that people died. The raven knows when anything is dead, therefore. Even if a horse dies, or a snake, though Raven is on the other side of the mountain, he knows it. Then he is happy. And the same is true of Buzzard. He too flies around, and when he sees that something is dead he is happy.

The people are still afraid of those two and even of the shadows they cast when they are flying. If the shadow of either of them passes over you, it means that you, too, are going to die.

They say that Buzzard always has that rock that he used in his nest. Some people use that rock in games. A man gets such a rock from the nest of the buzzard and ties it somewhere on himself. Then he goes and plays a game, perhaps the moccasin game, perhaps the hoop and pole game. His opponent gets tired. His arms ache. He doesn't feel like playing. He pays little attention to the game and loses all he has.[2]

---

[1] This is a good example of Jicarilla Apache feeling for an animate universe consisting of objects and beings which respond to human needs.

[2] Because the buzzard's "nest" (usually nothing more than a place in a rocky crevice for concealing eggs) is so hard to find, anyone who obtains a stone from the buzzard's nest will be able to conceal objects without difficulty and will become a proficient thief, the Jicarilla believe. In stories Buzzard is represented as being able to hide others easily. See p. 348.

And because he was interested in shortening man's life, people are afraid of Coyote and his tracks and do not dare to touch him. And the feathers of the buzzard and the raven cannot be touched.[1]

About this time the girls who had abused themselves with feathers, stones, and different objects were going to have children.[2] They felt ashamed of themselves and they went and hid and gave birth to their children. They brought forth the eagle, the running rocks, and all the monsters which were afterward to kill and eat man. They were scattered all over with their children. And these children grew rapidly and were soon of abnormal size. At the same time that they grew, the mountains grew too, and that is why some of the mountains are so very tall and hard to climb. The mountains grew because they knew now that the Indians would have a hard time and would be pursued by the monsters, and that the mountains would be the only place where they would be safe. The mountains grew as barriers to the monsters.

The people thought, "We are free now. We can do as we please." And they started to move to the east.

They all started out together. But soon some began to play games. The others did not want to wait and went on. They went around the earth clockwise. At different places various groups wanted to remain, and these broke away from the main group. But the main group kept on and continued in a spiral which grew smaller and smaller. On the way many disobeyed and wanted to stop. Finally some reached the center of the earth. These are the Jicarilla Apaches. The others were changed into all other tribes because they disobeyed.

When a small group broke off from the main body the children would begin playing games. The children of one group would say, "Let's play we are Pueblo people." The grownups paid no attention at first, but the children kept on using this strange language and carrying on in these strange ways. Soon everyone began to know this manner of talking and these ways, and before long this was the way everybody talked and acted. The people gradually forgot their own language and used only this new speech. This is how the different groups originated and the different languages and customs came to be.

6. THE BIRTH OF KILLER-OF-ENEMIES AND CHILD-OF-THE-WATER

About fifteen miles east of Taos is the place where the Jicarilla Apache stopped. This is the heart of the world. The earth is thought of as a woman, as the mother of all people. The sky is the

---

1 Grackles, red-winged blackbirds, yellow-headed blackbirds are all right. Only the big black one, the raven, is dangerous. (Inf.)

2 For the full account of the impregnation of the future mothers of the monsters see p. 266.

father of all people. The sun is our grandfather; the moon is our grandmother. We call the sun and the moon our grandparents, but they, too, are the children of the earth. They were born under the earth and came up, as I have told you. But the earth and the sky are our father and mother. They help each other to provide for us. If they did not take care of us we would die.

Other Indians stopped at different places during the journey and live at the arms or the legs of the earth or in some other part of her body; but the Jicarilla went straight to the heart of the earth and stopped there.

When the people were scattering all over the earth the Jicarilla stayed in Arizona somewhere for a while. But Red Boy and Holy Boy, who were still with them, told them to travel on and to take care of the heart of the earth. So they journeyed on. Some went across to the north.[1] They came back and told that there was nothing but snow and ice there and that the sun never shines there. They traveled many years before they reached the heart of the earth. Every time they stopped they saw a better place ahead and went onward. The reason the Mescalero and the Navaho have different stories from ours is that they stopped off before the end of the journey and, of course, they do not know what happened after that.

At first the Mexicans were all Indians. But their children, too, began to play that they were a different people. There were a rooster and a chicken there. The children listened to the fowls. "Perhaps they are talking," the children said and began to imitate the rooster and hen. After a while they turned into Mexicans. That is why, when the Mexicans talk rapidly, they sound just like chickens.

All the animals and plants were still talking at this time.[2]

Two girls went out somewhere and were lost during their travels. The people were all looking for these two, but they couldn't be found. The two girls had gone up a mountain. They lived there on fruit of all kinds. Those girls stayed there a long time. By that time they weren't afraid of anything.

One day one of them was sleeping. Sun came and slept with her. She woke up. There was a man lying beside her. She arose. It was a young man who was there. He spoke to her and she spoke to him. The sun brought food to her, for she had had nothing but fruit to eat for a long time.

That same night Water came to the other girl. In the morning she saw him lying by her side.

---

[1] The story of the travelers to the north is told in Section I, D, p. 117.

[2] My grandfather, my father's father, traveled all over. He didn't go by horse or with a woman, but just on foot. He found a place where everything still talked. When you went past a stick it went, "Hist!" And the stones and trees and all other things talked too. It is somewhere around here. (Inf.)

The sun spoke to the girl in the morning. "I must go to the east," he said. "It is time for me to do my work." Before he went he said, "When you need anything, ask me for it." He left and went back to the east.

Water was about to leave too. He said to the other girl, "Call me if you need anything." Then he left.

Soon the girls learned that they were with child.

After the sun had spent a night with the girl, her period started.

"This is my fault," the sun said. "I'll fix it."

She had been a perfect person. Now, because she had spent a night with the sun, she became like other women and menstruated.

She was White-Painted Woman. The sun dressed her up as the pubescent girl is dressed now, with white paint on her dress and yellow ochre on her face. He told her to stay inside for four days and work.[1] And the sun told the other girl to do likewise. This girl was White-Shell Woman. And because Water gave White-Shell Woman the child, the pubescent girl cannot look up in the sky when she has her ceremony. To do so might bring rain.

The girls were in the mountains. They made a brush shelter and in this they stayed and worked. The sun gave them just a little bread to eat, a little bread made of corn-meal. The girls thought it would not be enough, but they learned that it was too much.[2] If they ate just a little of this bread they became satisfied. This ceremony was held before they had their children. This was the beginning of the girl's puberty ceremony.

For three days the girls carried their children, and on the fourth day the children were born. The two children were boys and they began to grow rapidly. Both were very poor. They had nothing, no good clothes, nothing at all.

Holy Boy knew what was going on at the mountain. "Those girls have become White-Painted Woman and White-Shell Woman," he told the people.

Whirlwind always finds out what is happening and brings the message to Holy Boy. That is how he knew. Holy Boy was with the Jicarilla Apache at this time and didn't do anything about it, for he was protecting the Jicarilla on their journey.

So the two little boys were born and began to play around. They had no playthings. They asked their mothers for something with which to play.

Their mothers told them, "You must go to your fathers; they will give you something with which to play."

---

[1] That is the way they used to do in the girl's puberty rite. In the old days the girls didn't dance at this time. Now they do, but it was only after they went to Mescalero and saw them there that they started this. (Inf.)

[2] This motif, of a small amount of food or drink, given by an animal or a supernatural, becoming more than enough, recurs continually in Jicarilla tales.

"Where are our fathers?"

The children already knew, but they asked anyway. The point on the inner margin of their ears had spoken to them and told them, "Your father is living towards the east."

Each woman said to her son, "Go to your father and ask him for something with which to play."

7. THE JOURNEY TO THE SUN.

The two boys began to travel. There were all sorts of obstacles that the boys had to pass before they could reach the sun.

The first thing that happened to them was that they became very hungry and thirsty.

That point on their ears told them, "Your stomach is like a living person. Tell him why you came."

So the boys said, "We are going to visit the sun."

The antitragus said, "Give him a present."

So the boys gave him pollen and passed on without danger. Their hunger and thirst grew less. After a while their legs began to ache.

The antitragus said, "Talk to your legs. Tell them why you have come so far."

So the boys said, "Legs, we came so that we might visit the sun and ask for playthings."

So the legs grew strong and carried them on.

Then their throats began to ache.

The antitragus said, "Tell your throat why you have come."

So the boys talked to their throats too and offered their throats pollen, and then their throats grew well.

Then they became hot and sweaty. Because of this they also spoke and offered pollen.

The antitragus told them, "Put pollen on top of your head and tell this heat to go away."

They did so and were relieved.

Then they were seized with weariness. They both said, "Oh, this journey is difficult!"

But to this, too, they offered pollen and went on refreshed.

Then they met Night. He was so dark they could not pass. Their eyes turned against them and would not pierce the darkness. Their eyes became heavy, sleepy.

The ear told them, "You must sleep for a little while."

They slept a little while and then they started again. But the darkness made them imagine all sorts of things and frightened them. Sticks looked like snakes and all sorts of things seemed ready to harm them.

Then the light came and dawn brought dew and cold. They suffered from the cold. The dew made them wet. Again the point on the ear told them to speak and tell Dew of their errand. They did so and were relieved.

Then they met Big Rain-Storm. They were soaked by the rain. Thunder came and frightened them too. The antitragus told them not to fear, that they would not be harmed. So they went on.

Before them a tree was struck and split by Lightning. They were frightened once more. In every danger that was connected with the water in any way, Child-of-the-Water heard from his ear. So he learned about Thunder-Storm and Lightning. Before this Killer-of-Enemies heard from his ear about the dangers and how to evade them. Ear now told Child-of-the-Water to go on.

Now the rainbow was in front of them. They backed up before it, for they did not know what it was. But the ear of Killer-of-Enemies told him that there was no danger in it, and they went on.

Then they were engulfed by Mist. Later they had to go through Mud. Then they were confronted by Heat Waves. Killer-of-Enemies knew about the heat waves.

"That's all right. I'm going to take care of it," he said. He could say this, for he was the child of the sun, and the heat waves come only when the sun is out.

Then Cyclone blew at them. Killer-of-Enemies was told what to do about that. He offered pollen and told Cyclone of their errand.

Then Strong Wind breathed fiercely at them. Killer-of-Enemies was warned of that too and offered pollen and prayer.

Now Whirlwind came and Child-of-the-Water was afraid. But Killer-of-Enemies knew what to do, and the boys went ahead safely.

Then they met Winter. They had to pass through cold, frost, and snow. The snow was blown against them.

Child-of-the-Water spoke now. "I'll take care of this; this is nothing but frozen water."

"What makes it freeze?" asked Killer-of-Enemies.

"The wind," answered Child-of-the-Water.

"Oh."

Child-of-the-Water offered pollen to Winter, and then it was not so cold. But they were shivering and chilled while they were with Winter.

Now they arrived at Ice. It was so slippery that they could hardly stand. Child-of-the-Water's ear spoke and told them what to do.

Then they met Big Hail. The hail stones were very large and they were hit in the head and hurt. But Child-of-the-Water brought them safely through this. Nearby they met Sleet and all things of that nature.

After they had passed the obstacles of Winter, they came upon the bear. The bear had just come up from his hole because winter was over. He was about to swallow them up, but Killer-of-Enemies threw pollen in his direction and he let them pass. It was spring where they were now.

A little further on they met Snake. They were walking in the path when Snake crossed it.

"Where are you going?" Snake asked.

"To see my father, the sun," Killer-of-Enemies answered and offered Snake pollen. This was what his ear told him to do.

Then they met the singing birds. They, too, asked, "Where are you going?"

"To the east to see my father, the sun," and they offered pollen to the birds too.

The boys, when they met one of these creatures, always asked each other, "What is it?" And the one who knew would tell the other.

Now they came to all the animals of the mountains, such as the mountain-lion and wildcat. All these animals stopped them and asked them where they were going. To each they answered and offered pollen.

They passed on. Before them rose a great mountain. They were afraid of it. It was very steep and it had thick brush on it. It grew taller as they approached and would not let them pass. But Killer-of-Enemies, at the advice of his ear, explained their errand and offered pollen. The mountain grew no more and they passed easily. This mountain was called Long Mountain.

When they got over the mountain they found that they had a desert to cross. In this desert were large lizards whose bite was fatal. But they appeased the lizards too and passed on.

At the end of the desert they came to a big river. They didn't know how to get over it.

But, after his ear spoke to him, Child-of-the-Water said, "Do not be afraid. Walk right on top of the water."

They walked over it in this way.

Beyond the river they saw all kinds of fruit growing. They were hungry and wanted to eat, but the fruit told them not to eat until they explained where they were going. So they told of their journey to the east and how they hoped to get playthings from the sun.

Then they met the Pollen People. These Pollen People asked, "Where are you going?"

There were all kinds of Pollen People there representing all the sources of pollen.

The ear spoke to Killer-of-Enemies and said, "Put pollen in your mouth and sprinkle these people with some. Tell them what you are doing here."

So they did this and passed safely.

Then they came to the people who represented all ripe fruits and vegetables. These people barred their path too. But pollen was offered to them and the two boys went on.

Then they met the seasons. They met Spring first, then Summer, then Autumn, and then Winter. All these were people and stopped them to ask where they were going.

After this they met Day. Day also inquired about their journey and let them pass when he heard what they were doing.

Then they came to Fright. They met him there because they began to be afraid of seeing their fathers. Their journey was nearly over now. But they gave Fright pollen in his mouth and passed. Soon they were at the door of the sun's house.

They began to rejoice. They were there before morning, before the sun was up. They stood near the door.

The wife of the sun came to the door. She saw two boys standing there. "For whom are you looking?" she asked.

"We came to see our father, the sun," the boys said.

The woman was jealous at once. She began to be angry. This is the first time there ever was jealousy. After that people became jealous.

She went inside to the sun. She said, "I thought you said you go to the west for a good purpose and never visit other women. You have lied to me. Here are two boys who say you are their father."[1]

Then the sun came out and met his children.

"I'll test them before I'll admit they are my children. If they come safely through this test they are my children. I'll try them with four things." He said this to his wife before he came out to meet his children.

Then he came out and asked them, "What do you want?"

"We came to see you."

"Who told you that I am your father?"

"Our mothers told us to come to see you."

The sun had four rooms. One was filled with ice. He put them in that one, saying, "If you are my children this won't hurt or freeze you."

Child-of-the-Water said, "Oh, this is all right. I can take care of this."

Sun left them in there a long time. But when he opened the room the boys were still living. Child of-the-Water was from Water and could stand it for that reason, and Killer-of-Enemies was the real child of the sun and could stand it because of that and because he had heat within him.

[1] There is some ambiguity here concerning the parentage of the boys. In some passages the impression is given that both are the children of the sun. Possibly the confusion exists because Moon and Water are associated in Jicarilla thought and there is difference of opinion as to whether the moon should be thought of as masculine or feminine. In some stories (p. 141) the moon is introduced as the father of Child-of-the-Water.

Then Sun threw them in a room full of fire. Their feet and hands were tied before they were put in. When Sun opened the room the boys were still living.

There was a room of boiling water. Into this the boys were next thrown. But Child-of-the-Water could stand any kind of water and so both came out unharmed.

In the last room was the heat of the sun. They were thrown into this, but when the room was opened they were still living. Now the tests were over.

"All right, come to my house," Sun said. "You are really my children."[1] Then he asked, "What do you want?"

"Our mothers told us, 'Go and see your father,' and they told us you would give us something with which to play."

Then the sun gave them the hoop and pole game.[2] He gave them two poles and the hoop. He took the ring from around himself and this was the hoop. He already had the poles to give them.

"What else do you want?" asked Sun. Then he thought for a while and said, "I believe you came to save your people. There are monsters around your home now."

Again he asked them what else they wanted.

"We just came to get playthings."

"I think you came for another reason too. I can give you bows and arrows too."

So he gave each of them a bow made of the rainbow and arrows made of lightning. He gave each a quiver and bow carrier of mountain-lion skin. They put them on their backs.

Down below Holy Boy knew what had happened, for Whirlwind had again told him.

Sun told the boys, "You must play this game of hoop and pole in the day. And you can play it all around the world the way the sun goes, east to west, but do not roll the hoop to the north." And Sun told them, "You must wager when you play this game, but if anyone dies before the wager is paid or on the same day as the game was played, you must not take what you have won. Return the winnings under such conditions, for you do not want

---

1 The same informant who told this origin story later said, "When they sing hoop and pole game songs they sing to the sun and the moon, for both helped to make the hoop. Both gave their rings." This would indicate that the moon, a symbol of water, is often considered the father of Child-of-the-Water, and that in the story Sun stands for both of the heavenly bodies, in order to eliminate the male—female confusion which attaches to the moon.

2 For this game a pole with incised bands at the butt end and a hoop upon which bands have been carved are used. The hoop is first rolled along the ground and when it is about to fall the two players slide their poles after it in an attempt to cause the incised bands of the hoop to fall upon the bands at the butt end of the pole. A count is made according to the relative positions of these bands. Women are not allowed to approach the playing grounds or to see the game played.

anyone to 'die on your game.'" And he told them, "After a death if you wish to play hoop and pole again, you will have to paint the red part of the hoop with red ochre again and sprinkle a little red ochre on each pole. And paint your face with red ochre again before you play. This will wipe out the blood." And he said, "You must not play when there is blood from slain animals on your hands or on your clothes. You must clean your hands and change clothes or clean it off first."

And the sun gave songs and prayers for the hoop and pole game to the boys too. Then Whirlwind made the hoop roll to the east, south, and west. But Sun said, "You must not roll it to the north."

So they took leave of Sun and started home. They liked that game and had good times playing it on the way.

On their way home the boys came to the house of their grandfather, Thunder. Thunder gave them guns at first. But they were just children and didn't know how to handle them. They began to shoot at everything in sight and soon were destroying many valuable possessions, such as horses.

So Thunder saw that they were too young to have the gun. He called them back and said, "I think you had better give me those." He gave them arrows instead.

When the boys got home they were very proud of the game. They showed this game to their mothers.

And their mothers said, "How did you get along on the road? What did you meet?"

They told of all they had endured and suffered on the way. Then they began to play hoop and pole. They had a good time.

By and by they became tired of playing in the other directions and thought of playing to the north.

Killer-of-Enemies said, "Let's throw it to the north and see what happens."

But Child-of-the-Water said, "No, we had better obey."[1]

8. THE ADVENTURE AT OWL'S HOME.[2]

But while the boys were talking, the hoop began to roll to the north by itself. They walked after it and tried to stop it, but it just kept going in that direction.

It went right to the owl's home. It rolled directly into his home and lay in the corner. Owl was there.

He looked around and saw them and said to his wife, "Two handsome boys have come to see us. Let's boil them and make a soup of them."

The mothers of the boys had a fire drill which told them whether

[1] Killer-of-Enemies is often described as daring and impetuous, in contrast to the more cautious and obedient Child-of-the-Water.

[2] Goddard, pp. 196—197.

their sons were in danger. When they were in danger the wood flared up by itself and began to burn, and when they were safe again it would become restored. This time the fire drill burst into flame and the two women were very much frightened.

When the owl spoke like that Killer-of-Enemies was afraid, for the owl had his cooking kettles right there.

But Child-of-the-Water said, "It's all right. Let him try to make soup of us."

Owl put the boys in the kettle and tried to boil them. The boys were playing at the bottom of the water. Child-of-the-Water made it so they couldn't be hurt. They were splashing the water at each other and having a good time. Above them the water boiled, but it didn't hurt them.

The owls waited for a while. Then they said, "They must be cooked by this time." They had a big forked stick. They thought they would take the boys out with this. But instead, when they opened the kettle, the boys jumped out unharmed. They jumped out, one after the other. The owls looked at each other in surprise.

They said, "Well, we'll put them in the fire place then." So they pushed away enough ashes to make a place large enough for them.

This time Child-of-the-Water was afraid. "I guess we're going to die," he said.

"No," replied Killer-of-Enemies. "I can stop that."

Owl threw the boys in that hole and covered them with ashes. But the boys played and had a good time under there. They were not scorched at all.

The owls said again, "They must be done." They started to uncover them and the boys leaped out. They were not hurt at all.

Then the owls said, "Let's cut them up. Let's chop them in pieces."

They carried the boys to the place where they were going to do this. Killer-of-Enemies was not afraid, but Child-of-the-Water was much frightened now.

They put the boys on a block. They were ready to chop. But just as Owl raised the ax, it shattered in his hand.

Then Owl was frightened. "I think these are the children of the sun," he said. "We had better untie them, give them back their hoop and pole, and let them go before we get into trouble."[1]

So they loosened the bonds and let the boys go. The boys had learned their lesson and knew what disobedience meant.

Now, back home, the fire drill went out again and the women knew their children were safe.

---

[1] Only three attempts to kill the boys are mentioned in this version. Four may be the correct number, since this is the sacred figure and such events usually transpire in fours. Sometimes an informant will omit a detail which he does not consider important, to spare himself censure or supernatural punishment.

Whenever you play the hoop and pole game, or a group of people gets together for playing games, or there are horse races going on, there are some sorcerers present who try to harm you. They try to injure you in every way. But Killer-of-Enemies protects you from them. For when he was given the hoop and pole game and was told by his father to roll the hoop towards all directions except the north, he allowed it to roll to the north and went to the home of the owl to regain it. After he escaped from Owl without being harmed, he determined to help all those who, when they try to play games, are menaced by sorcerers or evil ones.

When you are rich, when you have many sheep and horses, the sorcerers are jealous and try to kill you. But if you use Killer-of-Enemies he can protect you and the sorcerers can't do anything to you.

9. THE SLAYING OF THE MONSTERS

The children returned to their mothers' home. On the way they agreed not to tell what had happened to them. That is what Killer-of-Enemies advised. But Child-of-the-Water wished to tell his mother. When they got home Killer-of-Enemies wouldn't tell anything about it. He wanted to cover up the fact of his disobedience. But Child-of-the-Water told all about it.

Holy Boy and Red Boy, too, knew all about what was going on and about what was happening to their grandchildren. Holy Boy came to visit them and see what they were doing.

Holy Boy spoke to the two women. "You must come back to your own people," he told them. "That is where you should be."

Before the women left with Holy Boy, Killer-of-Enemies heard of some monsters living to the east. He came to his mother and asked permission to go and kill these monsters. He had heard of a monster elk living to the east.

She said, "No, it is too dangerous."

But the boy wanted very much to go. "I have arrows," he said. "Why do you keep me from this?"

He made up his mind to go. So he started to the east in spite of his mother's objections.

And the two women and Child-of-the-Water went back with Holy Boy.

The heart of the earth is near the place of emergence.[1] These Apache had stopped in Arizona, but Holy Boy brought them back to the place of emergence.

---

[1] There is general agreement among the Jicarilla that the heart of the earth is somewhere near their old territories, in the vicinity of Taos. Concerning the place of emergence there is less agreement. Some locate it in Colorado, near the San Juan Mountains (pp. 163—164). Others claim that it is not far from the heart of the earth.

Now the people were dissatisfied with life on this earth. They wanted to go back to the place below.

But Holy Boy had told them, "No, wait here. I will go and find those two women and learn what we should do."

Thus it was that he came to the two women and urged them to come back to the people with him.

The women came back with him to the place where the Jicarilla Apache were. Holy Boy told White-Painted Woman and White-Shell Woman what the people said; how they wished to go below.

The women told the people, "You had better not go back until our grandson returns, for he is going to have a difficult time for your sake."

White-Painted Woman went about and talked to the people. "You must wait until Killer-of-Enemies, my grandson, comes back. He is going to bring you good news."

Killer-of-Enemies was on the way to fight the monsters. All this was the plan of Sun and Water. It was their means of helping the people of the emergence.

The two girls, White-Shell Woman and White-Painted Woman,[1] had become angry because they had been ordered to stay near camp. They had run away from the people on purpose and had stayed on top of the mountain. While the girls were on the mountain the monsters began to prey upon mankind. Sun and Water saw this and determined to help mankind. So they came to the girls. After they had spent the night with the girls, Sun told White-Painted Woman to call her child Killer-of-Enemies, and Water told White-Shell Woman to call her son Child-of-the-Water.

The people now wanted to go back into the place from which they had emerged because the monsters were beginning to come around. They said, "This is a dangerous place. We had better go back."[2]

But White-Painted Woman and White-Shell Woman told them to wait and see what befell Killer-of-Enemies.

Elk was one of the monsters.[3] He was lying down with his face to the east. The giant elk was just like other elks in appearance but was much larger and had half human blood. That is why he turned to an enemy. His mother was Apache and his father was an elk horn which a woman had used underground for the purpose of abusing herself.[4] The monster elk was able to transfix the people

---

[1] These were the names of those two girls to begin with; they were not given these names after they had the children. They don't say whether the two girls were sisters. The children grew up in four days. In those days people grew fast and no one died. (Inf.)

[2] The despair and fright in the face of the dangers and realities of living, and the longing for a return to the quiet and security of the womb of the earth are clearly indicated. For a further development of this theme see p. 109.

[3] See Goddard, p. 197; Mooney, p. 204; Russell, p. 256.

[4] For an account of the circumstances of this perverse conduct see p. 266.

with his eyes and they couldn't run away when he looked at them. So they would stand immovable, and he would come up and kill them.

Killer-of-Enemies' ear spoke to him. It told him, "You must put on clothes of heat wave. Then run around and come from the east side."

Killer-of-Enemies had four suits of these clothes, one for each direction and color. Each time the monster looked he changed to another.

The monster glanced in his direction. He thought he saw something moving. Then afterward he couldn't see anyone. He could see through the heat wave but he couldn't see Killer-of-Enemies. He looked carefully, but in vain. So finally he lay down again.

Killer-of-Enemies took one more step. The monster again saw something move. He looked straight at Killer-of-Enemies but could see nothing. Killer-of-Enemies stood still, clothed in the clothes of heat waves, and couldn't be seen.

The third time it was the same way. Killer-of-Enemies moved and the monster saw the movement and jumped up. But he could see nothing further.

Killer-of-Enemies moved a fourth time and again the elk was alarmed. But Killer-of-Enemies stood still and nothing more of him could be seen.

Then Killer-of-Enemies saw the whiskers of a gopher sticking up from a hole. He heard a voice coming from the middle of the whiskers, "Grandson, what are you doing around here in front of this monster?" The voice went on, "This monster kills the people. That is why I live under the earth all the time. I have not dared to come up since the monsters came on earth."

Killer-of-Enemies said, "I have come here to kill this elk."

"How are you going to do it, grandson?"

"With this arrow of mine," Killer-of-Enemies said. "Will you help me in some way?"

"Yes, I will."

Killer-of-Enemies told him, "You must dig out a hole underground to the place where the monster lies. Make one tunnel towards him from the east, one from the south, one from the west, and one from the north."

Then the ear spoke to him again and said, "You must ask the spiders to help you too."

So he called the spiders. The four spiders of different colors came. Each one stationed himself at the end of one of the four tunnels, at the end furthest from the monster. They waited there. And a piece of flint was put beside each of the spiders. The piece of flint at the east tunnel was black, the one at the south was blue, the one at the west was yellow, and the one at the north was glittering. And a piece of sacred black stone was placed at the east, a piece of sacred blue stone to the south, a yellow one to the west, and a glittering one to the north.

Killer-of-Enemies talked to Gopher. "Now make a hole to the place where the monster is lying, right to his heart."

The monster felt the drilling beneath him. He woke up.

Gopher said, "My grandfather, I want to use your hair; my little children are freezing. I want to make a nest of your hair."

The monster said, "You may use all you want."

Then Gopher filled up his cheek pouches with hair from both sides of the elk under the front legs. That is why Elk and Deer have no hair there.

Killer-of-Enemies asked Thunder for power, for Lightning was his arrow. He asked the rainbow for power. They all came near to him. His bow was of rainbow; that is why he asked Rainbow for power. Then he made four fire drills of four colors. One was black, one blue, one yellow, and one glittering. He started to go directly to the east.

"This hole is too small for me," he said.

"No," answered Gopher, "this hole will stretch to fit your body."

He went in. It was true. He could walk and run in there.

Gopher said, "Look at your arrow."

He did. The point was swinging and ready to fall off, it was so loose.

"Let me fix it for you," Gopher said, and Gopher fixed it for him.

Then Killer-of-Enemies said to Gopher, "You must pray for me, for I may be in danger." He told this to the spiders too.

He went below the monster. The ear spoke to him again. "Motion three times with your bow as though to shoot and let the arrow fly the fourth time."

He did this and shot the monster under the heart. The monster leaped to his feet. Killer-of-Enemies then shot the black fire stick to the east with his bow. Where it fell a cloud of black smoke arose. The monster ran to the east to learn the cause of the smoke.[1] He could find nothing. When he came back Killer-of-Enemies shot the blue one to the south. Killer-of-Enemies was under the earth. He heard the noise of the monster's hooves. The monster was still running.

When the monster got back, Killer-of-Enemies shot the yellow one to the west. He listened. On his return the monster was walking heavily, hardly running. He was tiring. So Killer-of-Enemies shot the glittering one to the north immediately. And when the monster got back from the north he was so tired and weak that he almost fell down.

The monster came back to the place where he had lain. He put his horn down and plowed through the hole which Gopher had made

[1] Smoke is a sign of human habitation to the monster. Since he preys upon mankind he always investigates the least sign of smoke.

to the east. At the end of the tunnel to the east Black Spider put up a black web and the black flint. The monster struck the web and flint, and these stopped him.

The ear of Killer-of-Enemies had told him, "Run to the end of the tunnel to the north," and Killer-of-Enemies was there waiting.

Now the monster put down his horn and raked up the tunnel to the south. At the end he was stopped by the blue spider's web and blue flint. He tried the west now, digging up the earth in that direction. He was finally halted by the yellow spider web and flint.

Then he started to dig up the tunnel to the north with his horn. He crashed into the flint and shattered it to pieces. But when he struck the spider web he fell down and died. Killer-of-Enemies was sitting on the other side of the spider web and was saved.

Gopher was very happy.

White-Painted Woman, too, was happy. She was watching all the time with her fire drill to see whether her son was in danger. The fire drill had flared up and now it subsided. She knew what was happening and told it to the people. She always told the people, "My grandson is doing this," or "My grandson is doing that." Many of them didn't believe her.

They said, "That White-Painted Woman must be crazy to talk that way."

But Whirlwind brought the message to her. That is how she knew.

Killer-of-Enemies was ready to butcher the monster. He had a flint knife. He opened up the monster and took all the skin off. He put some of the blood from the heart into the stomach. The monster elk had two small horns in the middle of his head as well as the big ones on the sides. Killer-of-Enemies took the smaller horn, the right one, with him and it was with this that he later killed the monster eagles. His ear talked to him and told him to cut off the right horn.

While the skin was still fresh he made clothes of it for himself and sewed them all up tightly. Right inside, at his chest, he put the stomach filled with blood.

After Killer-of-Enemies had killed the monster elk he went over to the elks and the deer. These were the animals which were not monsters but had come from the underworld with the people.

He spoke to them. He said, "You must help the people. You must help them in the 'life way.' When they ask for clothes, give them clothes; when they want meat, give it to them."

In those days the deer and elks were just like the horses. They were tame.

And Killer-of-Enemies said to the elks and deer, "Do not grow large. Remain at your present size."

He started now for the home of the monster eagle. He went to the big rock near the Navaho Reservation.[1]

[1] This has been identified as Shiprock.

The ear told him, "Face to the east."

The eagle looked down and saw someone walking below. The eagle swooped down and tried to pick him up. But he couldn't hold him, for the skin had begun to dry and was hard. The eagle rose again.

Killer-of-Enemies faced to the south. The eagle swooped down again. It struck at his feet and scratched all the way up trying to retain a hold, but it was unable to pick up Killer-of-Enemies. So the eagle went up and circled overhead once more.

Killer-of-Enemies now faced to the west. The eagle tried again but without success.

The fourth time Killer-of-Enemies faced the north. He opened up the hide and bunched up his cloak to give the eagle a chance to seize him. This time the eagle hung on and carried him high in the air and to his nest. The eagle threw him down on the point of a rock. Killer-of-Enemies opened up the stomach full of blood and spilled it to make it appear that he was killed.[1]

The eagle, after dropping him, sat on a point of rock at the north side. He said to his children, "Help yourselves. Eat it."

When a child tried to reach out toward him with its claw, Killer-of-Enemies said, "Cit, cit!" just as though he were chasing away a dog.

The children were frightened away twice and then they said to their father, "Father, every time we get near this dead person he says, 'Cit!' to us."

The father said, "It's all right. The dead always sound like that. Air comes out of the wound and causes that noise." Then he flew away.

Then Killer-of-Enemies stood up and spoke to the children. "When does your mother return?" he asked.

"When the fine rain comes."

In about an hour she came. She had a Pueblo Indian in her talons. He was crying for help. She threw him on the rock and killed him. Then she sat on the west side.

Then his ear spoke to Killer-of-Enemies. "You must motion towards her three times and hit her the fourth time with the elk horn."

Killer-of-Enemies did as he was directed, and she fell from the cliff. When she struck the ground it made a noise like thunder, she was so big.

Then Killer-of-Enemies asked the children, "When will your father return?"

"When it hails," they told him.

"Where does he sit?"

"He sits to the east."

[1] Goddard (p. 198), Mooney (p. 205), and Russell (p. 257) all mention this encounter with the monster eagle.

The ear spoke to Killer-of-Enemies. "Lie down at the end of the rock," it told him.

In a little while the father eagle came carrying a human being in his talons. He dropped his burden and sat and stretched his wings.

Just then Killer-of-Enemies came up to him and knocked him down as he had the mother bird. The father, too, fell with a loud crash.

Killer-of-Enemies turned to the children. He pressed their wings and bodies together and made them small. He sent one up to the other side of the sky, saying, "The people are going to use you sometimes for feathers." Later Killer-of-Enemies visited these eagles and saved them from their enemies, the bees.[1] These eagles are smaller than the eagles of earth.

This eagle turned and said, "Whenever the people touch our feathers they will get sick. They will become doubled up and stiff."[2]

Killer-of-Enemies answered, "Don't talk like that; go where I send you."

"Well, there will be medicine to cure these people even if we make them sick." Then he went up and his descendants became the eagles of the sky.

Killer-of-Enemies made the other one small too. He reduced it to about the size of the present eagle. He sent it down on this earth.

This one said as he went, "People will become ill because of me. They will be doubled up and stiff from touching my feathers."

"Don't say that," Killer-of-Enemies told him.

"Well, there will be a cure for it even when they become sick from us." Then this one flew away.

Now Killer-of-Enemies was up on the rock and didn't know how to get down. Far in the distance he saw a woman approach the rock. She was carrying something on her back.

His ear said to him, "You must call to her."

She was going towards the woods.

He called, "Grandmother, help me. Take me down."

But the old woman paid no attention and just went on. She made believe she was deaf.

He called a second time and a third, but she would not look.

The fourth time he called, but she would not come. She knew someone was calling all the time, but she wouldn't pay attention. She went into the woods instead. She came out of the woods and put her hands above her eyes then and peered around. She looked and looked. Finally she found him high on top of the cliff.

She began to come to him. She came under the rock and began to climb. She sang as she climbed. "Stick to it, stick to it," she sang to her feet. Finally she was at the top. She was Old Woman Bat.

---

[1] For the account of this adventure see p. 103.

[2] The plucking of eagle feathers is considered so dangerous that it is a minor ceremony in itself among the Jicarilla.

"What are you doing up here? How did you get up here?"

"That monster eagle brought me up. I want you to take me down."

Killer-of-Enemies looked at the burden basket she carried on her back. He noticed that the rope was of spider thread. He thought, "That can never hold me. It will break and I shall fall."

The old woman knew what he was thinking. She said, "Don't think that! Get in."

But Killer-of-Enemies was afraid to get in.

"Why, I've carried a big-horned sheep in that basket."

But Killer-of-Enemies didn't believe it. He was afraid. So he filled up the basket with big rocks to test the strength of the rope, and she jumped up and down with the load.

"Do you believe it now?"

"Yes," he said. He took the rocks out and got in.

The old lady said to him, "You must close your eyes when we are going down."

She began to sing again and descended. Killer-of-Enemies tried to open his eyes.

Bat Woman called, "My grandson, don't open your eyes or we'll fall."

So he closed his eyes again. They got down. She was dancing around and singing, "We're on the earth again." But he wouldn't open his eyes for a long time. He knew they were down but he was just playing and teasing her.[1]

He got out of the basket finally and the woman started to go away.

"Don't go away," he told her. "I'm going to give you something."

He took the basket to the place where the dead eagles were. He filled up the basket with the downy feathers of the male eagle. Then he told her, "Do not go to the fields with this, or these feathers will get caught in the plants and all the feathers will stick to these plants.[2] Take these feathers home with you and make a nest for your little children of them."

But Bat Woman forgot, and when the basket was filled she went past the plants and all the feathers were lost.

She came back and said, "Give me some more feathers. I forgot and went near the bushes, and the bushes took all of them away from me."

He filled it up this time with downy feathers and wing feathers of the female eagle. He warned her, "You must not go to a place where there is brush with these. All the little birds might take them away from you."

---

[1] This was because she had teased him in the beginning by pretending not to see him on the top of the rock.

[2] The plant named is a member of the composite family (*Coleosanthus brachyphyllus*).

Again she forgot and went to the wrong place. The little birds came and took them. That is why some of these little birds have downy feathers just like the downy feathers of the eagles.

She came back to Killer-of-Enemies again. This time Killer-of-Enemies gave her a piece of old hide. It was scorched from the fire and all soiled. She drew it up around her as the women put a blanket over themselves. She was very happy and went away. That is why the bat has a black skin today.

Then Killer-of-Enemies started to go home to his mother. His mother knew what had happened. She always told the people, but they did not believe it at all.

She said to the people, "My grandson is coming."

They looked to the east. After a while a figure was seen.

She was very happy. "See, my grandson comes," she said. When he came near she said, "See, it is my grandson."

When he came close she said to him, "The people don't believe me though I have told them what you were doing and how you were killing the monsters."

She called four different birds, the robin, the western tanager, the bluebird, and the road-runner. They all came to the place where Killer-of-Enemies was with White-Painted Woman. Then Killer-of-Enemies told all about his experiences. White-Painted Woman told the birds to go everywhere and tell the people all over the world.

"Act as chiefs and tell them," she said, "for the chief stands up before all and talks."

Each bird went in a different direction to tell what Killer-of-Enemies had accomplished. The birds told the people of all the deeds of Killer-of-Enemies, and so after that the people knew what had been done and had songs about it. And later, when a man became chief, he sang of these four birds, for they were the ones who had made the announcement to the people.[1] And if a chief sang of these four birds he would never get bald.[2]

The birds told the people, "Now we'll all be at peace. People can sleep with confidence because of what Killer-of-Enemies has done, and food shall be plentiful."

After that, because the birds spoke well to the people, the chiefs, who also speak to the people, who tell them what has happened and who advise them, always sang of these birds.

The people all gathered to listen. Then they departed for their homes.

There was a kicking monster too. He was a real person called

---

1 For a story of the bird chiefs which takes its inspiration from this incident see p. 119.

2 He would never become bald because, following the precept of these birds, he would tell no untruth. Baldness is attributed to chronic lying by the Jicarilla.

He-Kicks-them-in-the-Water.[1] He lived where there were some hot springs. The water was boiling and seething all around that place. He lay on top of a ledge beside a mountain road that wound along above the hot springs. As people passed by he kicked them into the water. Below, under the water, he had a home, and there his four daughters lived. And all those whom he kicked in the water, these girls ate.

He lay there across the road. Always when people were passing he would draw his feet back as though to allow the people to pass by. He would say, "Now you can pass," but when the traveler tried to pass, he would throw his foot forward again and knock his victim into the water.

Killer-of-Enemies missed some people. He noticed that people who went on a journey in that direction never came back. So he followed that trail and came to that road. He found the monster lying across the road.

"Brother," said Killer-of-Enemies, "why are you lying down like this?"

The kicking monster said, "It's all right. There isn't much room, but I'll withdraw my feet and you can pass." He pulled his feet back.

Killer-of-Enemies seemed to be just about to pass. He acted as though he did not suspect, but he knew all the while what the monster was going to do. He really watched the kicking monster very closely. When the kicking monster was just about to give him a violent push, Killer-of-Enemies stopped and the monster missed him entirely.

Then Killer-of-Enemies asked, "Why do you try to kick me?"

Then Kicking Monster answered, "Oh, my leg was cramped. That is why I had to kick. I really did not mean to kick you."

But Killer-of-Enemies knew that he was doing it on purpose and just to harm people.

Three times this same thing happened. Killer-of-Enemies would start and the kicking monster would try to kick him, and each time he missed.

The fourth time the kicking monster pulled his feet back. By this time Killer-of-Enemies was very angry and decided to end it. As the monster flung his feet forward, Killer-of-Enemies caught him and threw him into the hot water below. The kicking monster was cooked in the hot water. Soon the four girls were eating their own father.

Killer-of-Enemies came down to find out what had happened to all the people who were kicked into the water. He went into the monster's home. He found the four girls there. The four girls were very eager to get Killer-of-Enemies.

---

[1] Goddard (p. 202) makes mention of this kicking monster, but the true identity of the monster and his children is not apparent from his account.

Killer-of-Enemies said to them, "You must not touch me. Stay away from me. I'll give you some medicine, and then you may do whatever you wish."

These four daughters of the kicking monster were the only women who possessed vaginas. They were vagina girls. They had the form of women, but they were in reality vaginas. Other vaginas were hanging around on the walls, but these four were in the form of girls with legs and all body parts and were walking around. It was because of them that so many men had gone along the road. But the father of the girls, the kicking monster, had not let these men have his daughters. Instead he had kicked them into the boiling water.

When Killer-of-Enemies went down there, all four girls approached him and wanted to have intercourse.

One of them said, "Oh, you have come to see us, to have intercourse with us."

But Killer-of-Enemies said, "No, not I. Perhaps someone else."

The girl was angry. "Then after this our blood will make people sick."

"Don't talk like that. Close your mouth," Killer-of-Enemies commanded her.

"Well, there will be medicine that will cure it, blood medicine," she said.

Killer-of-Enemies asked them, "Where have all the men gone who were kicked into this place?"

"We ate them up because we like to," the girls answered.

Then they all tried to embrace him. But he drove them away, saying, "Keep away! That is no way to use the vagina. First I must give you medicine that you have never tasted before, medicine made of sour berries, and then I'll do what you ask."[1]

But he promised this only because he knew that he would change these girls and that after that the vagina, which had been used for evil alone, would be used for good. He gave them sour berries of four kinds to eat, sumac berries, currants, red raspberries, and gooseberries.

The first time he gave the medicine to them he said, "The vagina is always sweet when you do like this."[2]

Then they all chewed the medicine and swallowed it.

He said the same thing the second time. This time they didn't chew it much. The third time they chewed it still less, for it puckered their mouths. The fourth time they couldn't chew it at all. They

[1] The oral fixation runs throughout this entire episode. For these girls, eating is the equivalent of intercourse.

[2] The reference to the vagina and sexual intercourse in terms of sweet and sour is a continuation of the oral erotic motif. In many Jicarilla contexts intercourse is referred to as something "sour." The theme is followed out in a number of aspects of Jicarilla culture, e. g., there may be no intercourse at the time of a salt gathering expedition.

just swallowed it. They liked it very much though. It felt just as if Killer-of-Enemies was having intercourse with them. They were almost unconscious with ecstacy. Really Killer-of-Enemies was doing nothing at all to them. It was the medicine that made them feel that way.

When Killer-of-Enemies had come to them they had had strong teeth with which they had eaten their victims.[1] But this medicine destroyed their teeth entirely.

Then Killer-of-Enemies chose the largest vagina and the smallest there, for the vaginas were not on the girls but were hanging on the walls. Many of them were hanging there. The girls had been guarding them.

Then he left the girls and went back to his mother. He had the two vaginas along with him. He gave them to his mother, and his mother chose two girls and gave these vaginas to them.

The people did not know what they were. They had never seen anything like these before. The people were all crowding around, for they were eager to see what would happen. They had a big council about it.

First someone said to the girls, "Put them on top of your heads."

But others said, "Oh, that wouldn't look well! Put them on your chests."

When that was tried many didn't like it either. Then the back was suggested. The hand was tried too, but that didn't look well either. Someone thought of the knee, but when it was tried most of them were not satisfied. The feet were next tried, but after viewing it they said, "No, that is not the right place."

Finally the vaginas were put between the legs where the vagina is now, and the people said, "Yes, that is much better."

Killer-of-Enemies then spoke and said that women would have it there always.

He then went to the hoop and pole grounds. Those four vagina girls from the hot springs had come up and were looking for him. They found him there.[2]

They said to him, "You are the one who lay with us once. Now you have run away from us. We have been lonely for you since then."

This was the beginning of loneliness. That is why when people separate for a time they long for each other. The girls came up because no one was feeding them any more.

Killer-of-Enemies said, "I am not the one who was with you. I think you must mean someone else."

---

[1] This is the familiar toothed vagina theme with the proper displacement to accommodate the oral element.

[2] The girls not only came on an evil errand, but also disregarded all proprieties by seeking Killer-of-Enemies at the hoop and pole grounds, a place from which women are banned.

But the girls just kept saying, "You are the one. You never come to us any more. You ran away from us." Three times they spoke to him this way.

Each time he said, "No, it must have been someone else. People all look the same.[1] I have never been with girls."

Then the girls said, "All right! If you claim that you are not the one, it is all right. Even though you spoiled our teeth by making us chew those sour berries, we have still another power. Because of us people will get venereal disease. And when anyone touches menstrual blood he will become ill. The only thing that will cure the illness is the long roots in the ground which have 'blood' (red tendrils) at the end when they are pulled up. Blood medicine is its name. 'Medicine for venereal disease' will cure this disease after which it is named."

When White Hactcin planted all the roots and flowers which were to be used for medicine, he knew that these diseases were coming, and so these plants which the girls named were already growing.

So now, when a woman is going to have a baby, the one who acts as midwife puts some of the "blood medicine" on her hands and in her mouth, and after the baby is delivered the mother blows four times on the hands of the midwife. The mother does this because it is her own blood and she doesn't want the sickness to spread because of her. After this the midwife is safe; she could not get venereal disease even if she were with a man who had it, and she would not get the blood disease that gives you rheumatism either.[2]

Killer-of-Enemies spoke to those four vagina girls. "If you use your vaginas and your power in the wrong way and cause harm to people, you too must suffer when you have a baby."

That is why a woman who is kind and good does not suffer when she has a baby, but one who is mean and wicked and always harming others is the one who will have a hard time at childbirth.[3]

When White-Painted Woman gave the two girls the vaginas, the big one and the small one, she spoke to the boys and girls. She told them that if a girl used it too early, before she was grown up, she would not grow any more. And she said that the boy who went to girls and women too young, when he was fifteen or under, and before he had attained full size, would remain short the rest of his life.

"You have this vagina that you may have six kinds of relatives," she said. "There will be grandmothers, mothers, aunts, daughters, sisters, and nieces. If you use it in the right way you will have those six relatives and live in the proper way."

---

[1] The people were not yet differentiated as to appearance. Cf. p. 109 for an account of this differentiation.

[2] A woman cannot become ill from her own blood, but she can be made ill by the blood of other women. (Inf.)

[3] This is what the Jicarilla Apache believe today. (Inf.)

The four girls said, "Even though we hurt the people with disease there will be a medicine for it."

Now these girls became like others and turned to a good way of living. They stayed among the people.

This all happened because the women under the earth had been evil and wished for the men at the time of the separation. Their evil actions led to the birth of the monsters. The women of the emergence had had vaginas in the underworld, but not real ones as the women do today.

Now Killer-of-Enemies went to his grandmother. He always talked to her before he started out to kill another monster. Each time he told her what he intended to do, she was somewhat frightened and exclaimed, "Yi!" She would tremble for him and advise him not to go. But Killer-of-Enemies would answer, "I must kill them. That's the reason I'm here."

Killer-of-Enemies had heard about two running rocks which were killing people. One was black and the other white. They had been racing around the earth. They were preparing to kill the people, and they were practicing running for that purpose. Two-Rocks-Racing-Together they were called. They were both round, smooth rocks such as are found in the rivers. One was black and made of the kind of stone that is found in the Archeuleta Mountains. The other was white and was made of a rock called Holy Rock.

Killer-of-Enemies first asked the rainbow to help him, because he knew how fast those two rocks could run. He said, "Watch me when I race with them. When they get too close come under my feet and lift me up so they cannot harm me."

The ear of Killer-of-Enemies spoke to him. "Those two rocks are good runners; despite Rainbow's aid they will still be able to catch you. You had better ask someone else for help too."

So Killer-of-Enemies asked help from the sun. When something shiny is held up it throws a gleam of light and that light travels as fast as eye can see.

"Let that be my legs," Killer-of-Enemies asked.

And Sun said, "All right."

Then he came to four birds who were good runners, Sandhill Crane, two hawks, and Humming-Bird. He said to these four birds, "You must stand close to the north."

Then he let the rocks see him. The rocks saw someone on the race track. At that time his ear spoke to Killer-of-Enemies and told him he must start running for his life. At first Killer-of-Enemies used his eyes. He fixed his gaze on a distant mountain and as soon as he saw it, he was there. Then he looked to another, and as his glance fell on it he was already there. He continued to do this until his eyes got tired.

Then Ear spoke to him and told him to use his power of thought. He would think of some distant place which lay ahead, and as soon as he thought of it he would be there. But his mind tired of that after a while.

At the advice of the ear he began to use the speed of light which the sun had promised him. The sun would throw a beam of light ahead and he would travel with it to that place. The rocks were coming fast behind him all the time. But Killer-of-Enemies was tiring of this now.

So now he was told by the ear to use his word. So he said, "Let me be there," mentioning a place, and he would be there. Behind him the rocks were approaching all the time. Every few minutes he would hear them.

After a while his ear said, "Now use Sandhill Crane."

So he said to Sandhill Crane, "Now it is your turn."

This was the first of the birds, all of whom were in a line, each a long way from the other. So he used the speed of Sandhill Crane, though he didn't have to change bodies or ride on him. He came to the second bird before the rocks reached the place. A hawk was the second bird to help him. With the power and speed of this hawk he came quickly to the place where the second hawk was waiting. Then he came to the fourth bird, the humming-bird.

But the rocks were coming nearer and nearer. So Killer-of-Enemies ran to Old Man Spider. "Grandfather, save me!" he said.

The old spider asked, "Where are those many leaders? I thought there were many leaders around. Just go in my house."

Killer-of-Enemies entered, and the spider made a black web before the door. The rocks came running after Killer-of-Enemies and ran right into the web. Meanwhile Killer-of-Enemies was going into the house.

There he met Old Woman Spider and he called to her, "Grandmother, now it's your turn to help me."

She too said, "I thought many other leaders were helping you." But she made a blue web between the rocks and Killer-of-Enemies.

The rocks had run into the first web and were all enmeshed in it. It clung to them and retarded their progress, but they came onward with the strands of the web streaming behind. Then the rocks ran straight into the blue web and through it.

Meanwhile Killer-of-Enemies had met Young Man Spider in the home of the spiders and said to him, "You must help me."

The youth replied, "I thought you had many leaders to help you. Why could they not save you?" But he made a yellow web and stretched it between Killer-of-Enemies and the running rocks.

The rocks were still coming nearer all the time, though they were entangled in the webs.

So Killer-of-Enemies ran to the spider children. "Children," he said, "you must help me."

The children answered in the same way. "We thought there were many people to help you," they said. Nevertheless they made another web, a glittering one.

The rocks were still coming onward. They had gone through the third web and were approaching the fourth. Now the spider people all gathered there.

"Why do we let those rocks run through our webs?" they asked angrily. "Let us hold them back this time. Let us all take hold of the web and pull the ends taut."

They all began to pull it. As they took hold of it, the rocks ran into the web. So these people pulled four times, each time harder, and broke the rocks all to pieces.

Because the spiders spoke to Killer-of-Enemies as they did, people now when you ask help of them always say, "I thought you had some other strong men to help you. Why don't you go to them?"[1]

The reason the rocks could run so fast was that they encased other monsters, monster mountain-sheep. These sheep in the rocks were like the engines in automobiles. When Killer-of-Enemies killed the rocks they broke in many pieces. The female mountain-sheep came out of one, the male mountain-sheep out of the other. Both looked around.

Killer-of-Enemies said to them, "Hereafter you will not be monsters. You will live in the high cliffs and the people will use you."

Those rocks were completely shattered. Some of the pieces of the white rock were small and some large. And the pieces of black stone were of all sizes, and some of the pieces had sharp edges. After that some of the people used the kind with sharp edges for axes. And the round pieces of the white stone were used for pounding meat or medicines.

From all around the people came to see these rocks. Some were going to pick up fragments of them but Killer-of-Enemies said, "No, do not touch those pieces."

He picked up four, two black ones and two white ones. "Now you may help yourselves," he said.

So all the people picked up the pieces of rock. Spider picked up some. That is why some spiders live in the rocks.

Killer-of-Enemies took his four pieces of rock and went back to his grandmother. She took a piece of the round white rock and put it in the back of the house, in the corner. She buried it there. That is why the Apache man puts such a rock in the back of his home. It is done so that his wife will never run away from him but will stay there always.[2] In the old days the man used to dig up this rock when moving camp and put it in the back of the house at the new site. A man's wife may see him put it there or she may not. She knows what it is for. The women never do this.

The black stone is used in another way besides as a pounder.

---

[1] The Jicarilla shaman delights in emphasizing the obligation of his patient to him for his services.

[2] Only the man does it now. (Inf.)

If you have a bad cold in the chest or a pain there caused by pneumonia, you put this rock in the fire, heat it, and put it on the spot. This is for both men and women. Then the pain stops. You put a rag around the stone so it does not burn the flesh. This is done because White-Painted Woman, when Killer-of-Enemies came back with the rock, said, "This rock was used in an evil way. Now it shall be used in the 'life way.'" And she used it for this purpose.

Now everything was at peace for a while. But then the people saw a galloping rock coming. It had not yet started to eat the people. It was only one canyon removed from the people by the time it was discovered. It was at the Rio Grande River coming toward Taos. All the people gathered, frightened, to see it come. It was near Taos, at Picuris.

Early in the morning all the people armed themselves and waited. This was before the light had come. They were going to start shooting as it passed them. As the rock approached the people started to shoot at him with their arrows. But they could not kill that rock. The arrows struck it but could not go through or hurt him in any way. So the rock passed by all the people.

Killer-of-Enemies was there too. He had three others to help him this time.[1] Now it was his turn. He was ready to shoot. He motioned with his bow and arrow three times and the fourth time he let the arrow go. The arrow struck the monster under the arm and the monster tried to bite at it. As soon as he started to bite he fell over dead. That rock is still there, where it was killed, in the form of a rock dyke.[2]

After this, when an Apache passed this place, he would shoot two arrows through a hole there in the rock dyke. If he had no arrows he would pick up stones and throw them through instead. Then he could pass. This same rock was used to determine whether a man had been with a girl or not. If a man was accused and could not shoot through that hole, it showed he had been with the woman. But one who had not had intercourse could throw a rock or shoot an arrow through the hole easily.

And a person who passed the rock would chip off a little material from the hole which was made when Killer-of-Enemies shot his arrow and killed the monster. They carried this in the buckskin bag on the string over the shoulder. This kept the wearer from being hit when someone was shooting at him.

When someone was shot they always used this rock from the monster's wound too. A little of it was pulverized and put in the medicine which the wounded one drank, and then he would not die but was sure to get well.

And fragments of this rock are used as medicine when someone

[1] The three helpers of Killer-of-Enemies were supernaturals who told him what to do. The informant did not know any names for them.

[2] For another account of the conquest of this rock see Goddard, p. 204.

falls from a rock or on a rock and hurts himself badly, for Killer-of-Enemies killed this rock and made it good for man to use.

There was now an owl who was living in the woods. He was called Big Owl. He had great power. At that time he could make a noise which frightened the people. Whenever the people or the birds or the animals heard the owl's voice they all trembled and were afraid. His voice was just like thunder. It made everything shake.

Every time when he came out of the woods he would hunt for people. "I need them for my meal," he would say.

No one who met the owl could escape from him. This owl had great round eyes, just like the moon. He could use them to hunt the people too. When he saw someone, that person could not move away even if he knew the danger. He was held there just as though the owl had reached out with a long stick and pressed him to the ground.

Then the owl would come up to him and put him in a basket, throw the basket over his back and carry him home. There he would chop his victim up and cook him and eat him. Sometimes he would bury his victim in the hot ashes and eat him when he was roasted.

Once Big Owl went out to hunt for people. He took with him his bow and arrows. On the way he met Coyote. He frightened Coyote, and Coyote fell down in a faint. He picked Coyote up and put him in his basket and started for home. While he was on the way the coyote recovered consciousness. He thought all was over with him, but he was sorry for his children and tried to think of some way to get away.

It was daytime and very hot. Big Owl stopped and sat by some rocks for a rest. Coyote crept out, put several rocks in the basket, and then reentered it. Then Owl picked up his basket and started off again. The basket seemed very heavy and he soon tired, but he thought it was because of the heat and the weight of the coyote. Several times they stopped and each time Coyote put in rocks when the owl wasn't looking. Soon the basket was very full and Coyote made his escape. Before he went he defecated on top of the rocks.

The owl carried his basket of rocks home. When he got there he said to his children, "Help yourself. I just killed this meat for you."

The children peeked into that basket and saw nothing but rocks.

Owl was furious when he saw the trick that had been played on him. He went back to the place where he had caught Coyote, but he could find no trace of Coyote now.[1]

Then Owl went down another canyon and there he found a turkey. He transfixed the turkey with his glance and the turkey fell down. Owl picked him up and put him in his basket. Again he grew very

---

[1] The Western Apache of the San Carlos and Fort Apache reservations have similar stories of Big Owl. The Chiricahua and Mescalero Apache tell the same tales of a giant.

warm while on the way, so he stopped under a tree in the shade. The turkey regained his senses at this time and found himself in the basket. He knew he would lose his life unless he acted quickly. Turkey made up his mind that when Owl passed under some low-hanging branches of the trees he would reach up, hold on to a limb, and pull himself out of that basket.

The owl got up and started for home again. Turkey pulled himself up and, as he clasped the branch, he defecated in the basket.

The owl took the basket home. There was nothing in it but excrement. He was very angry again. He ran out to look for Turkey.

He didn't find Turkey, but he did come upon Killer-of-Enemies. He looked at Killer-of-Enemies, and Killer-of-Enemies, although Owl couldn't hurt him, fell down, making believe that he was dead. He wanted to see how strong Owl was and he wanted to be taken to his home and to see what had happened to the other people Owl had captured.

Owl picked him up and put him in the basket. At his home Owl had a block for chopping up people. On this he put Killer-of-Enemies. He tried to chop him to pieces. But his big knife could do nothing. Every time he raised the knife over his head, it fell down behind him. This happened four times, and the fourth time the knife fell from his hands it broke into pieces.

Then he tried to frighten Killer-of-Enemies with his voice, but Killer-of-Enemies was not frightened. Finally he tried to frighten him with his eyes, but Killer-of-Enemies was not afraid. The eyes were large, just like a moon.

Killer-of-Enemies said, "You are not using those eyes in the right manner. I thought they belonged to the moon. Did Moon let you have them?"

Owl answered, "When I was still unborn my mother looked at the moon, and now I am like this."

Apache women who are pregnant must not look at the moon for this reason. They must not look at the sun either or at anything like the bear, snake, or any harmful animals. And they must not look at someone who is all doubled up and paralyzed, for then the child may be like that too.

Killer-of-Enemies said to Owl, "You had better not use your eyes for evil. And you had better not use your voice for evil either or to harm the people."

Owl said, "Even though I hurt the people, there will be some songs and prayers which can cure them."

Owl had a fire poker. Killer-of-Enemies picked it up. With it he hit the owl four times. And as he did it, four different kinds of owls came out of this monster. They flew in different directions. Then Killer-of-Enemies came back to the two children. He pushed their bodies together and made them smaller. And he told them to fly away, saying, "After this do not hurt the people. Fly around only at night." Before this they say that Big Owl had been around even in the day, bothering the people.[1]

Again Killer-of-Enemies went back to his grandmother and told her what he had done. But before long he heard of another monster, a giant fish in the water.[2] That fish could swallow people, even if they were on land and a long distance away. And it swallowed many birds and animals too.

Killer-of-Enemies had a long black flint knife. He made ready to go after the fish. His grandmother begged him not to go, but Killer-of-Enemies resolved to attempt it, for he was eager to see and conquer the monster.

He tried to get near enough to that fish to see it well. The fish saw him and swallowed him.

Child-of-the-Water was on land. He missed his brother.

Killer-of-Enemies sat in the fish. He didn't know how he could get out. Rainbow shone over the fish and one end pointed directly to the place where Killer-of-Enemies was. The inside of the fish was like a big room. In this space something large was hanging down. It was the fish's heart. So, with his knife, Killer-of-Enemies started to cut at the heart. The fish floundered around in the water as Killer-of-Enemies cut at its heart. Killer-of-Enemies had almost cut through it now. The fish tossed till it was on the shore by the side of the water and there it died. But Killer-of-Enemies didn't know how to get out of the fish's body.

Child-of-the-Water knew what was going on during this time. At home he prayed, for he had power over the water. He knew that he had not lost his brother.

Now Killer-of-Enemies made up his mind to cut his way out. He took his knife and cut at the neck region, and where he cut the fish have slits in the neck now (the gills). Then he came out of the body of the fish holding the heart in his hand. He spoke to the fish then and said, "You had better become small now, and you shall have no heart."

He took the heart home with him. When they saw it Child-of-the-Water and White-Painted Woman were very glad. He gave the heart to his grandmother.

They all talked of what to do with the heart. They wanted to put it where no monster could get it, for the fish was the leader of all the monsters. So they gave the heart to the moon[3] and that's where it is now. They say that some day the moon is going to give the heart

---

[1] There is another version in which Killer-of-Enemies explodes something in the Owl's eyes and thus bests him. (Inf.)

[2] Goddard, p. 201; Mooney, p. 209.

[3] The fact that the heart of the giant fish was put in the custody of the moon is another affirmation of the nexus between water and moon in Jicarilla thinking.

back to the fish and then all the monsters will come to life again. At every full moon and every new moon Killer-of-Enemies, Child-of-the-Water, White-Shell Woman, and White-Painted Woman pray for long life and good luck for the people and ask the moon not to give the heart back to the fish.

Killer-of-Enemies stood with the blood of all the monsters whom he had killed on his hands, beginning with the eagle and including all the others. He went up to the top of a big mountain, White Mountain near Mescalero. With him he took the club of elk horn with which he had killed the eagles, and he had some reed with him, a flint knife, and a clay bowl with some water in it that White-Painted Woman had given him for washing his hands when he got to the top of the mountain.

He took the reed and threw it to the east. "This will be white people, Americans," he said.

He then rubbed his hands which still had on them the blood of the monsters and then he made a motion as though throwing something to the east. "Those white people will be strong in a life way. They will be like White Hactcin. They will help all peoples."

And this has come true, for the white people know everything and are ahead. They teach the other peoples and give them clothes and the way to live.

And he threw the stone knife to the south, and that is why those people, the Mescalero and those to the south, had knives like this, many of them. And that is why those people have more ceremonies than we have[1] and many different kinds of cactus.

Then Killer-of-Enemies washed his hands in the water which his grandmother had provided for him. It was holy water. He raised his wet hands and shook them. As the drops fell he said, "These will be sheep and cattle of all kinds."[2]

That is why lamb and mutton taste a little peculiar. And that is why, when people eat freshly slaughtered meat, still warm, it makes them sick and gives them a fever. This is especially true in the case of anyone who is not feeling just right. If anyone is a little weak, it is very unwise for him to eat freshly killed meat.[3] The meat of the sheep tastes as it does and the fever comes from warm meat because of the blood of the monsters which was mixed with the water from the hands of Killer-of-Enemies.

---

1 The informant said, "We, the Jicarilla Apache, have more power than other tribes but not so many ceremonies." For a few years following 1884 the Jicarilla Apache were stationed on a reservation with the Mescalero Apache and became acquainted with Mescalero ceremonialism. The greater importance of shamanism among the Mescalero results in a larger number of minor rites than the Jicarilla have, and the latter evidently have been impressed by this.

2 Also see Goddard, p. 205. Many Jicarilla still do not care for mutton.

3 We will not eat meat of any kind that is still warm. We believe that all kinds of meat will give you fever if they are eaten while they are still warm. (Inf.)

10. EVENTS IMMEDIATEIY FOLLOWING THE SLAYING OF THE MONSTERS.

After Killer-of-Enemies had killed all the monsters he came before the people. He was telling them how to protect themselves thereafter. He brought a basket of ashes before them.[1] He dipped a small piñon bush into it and then drove all sickness and evil to the north. That is why people place a dot of ashes on the forehead to keep away evil things.

Coyote came up to this earth with the people. All the animals came up and Coyote did too. He had power in those days but he was not so bad as he is now. It is only since the people drove him away that he has become so harmful. It was when Killer-of-Enemies had destroyed the monsters and was telling the people how to take care of themselves and how to cure themselves that Coyote became as he is now.

Coyote began to mock the ceremonies and make fun of all that the people did. He came in to the place where they were making ceremonies. At first he listened and was interested. But he grew tired of it and started to pay less attention. He was making all sorts of remarks and acting funny. He would say, "That's no good. It's best to do it in our old way. Let's just have a good time and pay no attention to this."

Finally Killer-of-Enemies grew angry. "After this you will not be able to talk with man. Your language will be different. And you will not be allowed to stay with mankind, for you do nothing but laugh at others and act foolishly. It will be all right for the dog to stay with man and be his companion, but you will have to go by yourself."

Before he lost his voice Coyote said, "Well then, if man touches me he will become sick."[2]

"Don't talk like that."

"Even though I make him sick, there will be a song to cure him," said Coyote and sang the song. Then Coyote went away.

At this time Cyclone and Lightning were quarreling. Each wanted to be the leader.

Cyclone said, "Let me see your power."

So Thunder showed what he could do. He broke to pieces trees, rocks, and everything he touched.

Cyclone asked, "Is that all you can do?"

"That is all."

---

[1] Ash is a specific used against sorcerers and ghosts by the Jicarilla. Evil is customarily driven away to the north. See p. 143.

[2] To touch the fur of coyote or even to step in its tracks may bring sickness. This is the second rationalization of the fear in which Coyote is held that we have had. (The first was that Coyote strove to bring death into the world, p. 45.) More important than either of these is the belief that the ghosts of sorcerers turn into coyotes.

Then Cyclone started to show what he could do. He picked up trees by the roots and great rocks and lifted all of them up in the sky. He showed that he had more power than Thunder. And so he became the leader. When they came back they agreed that Cyclone would be the leader.

Cyclone said, "I will always help you. How can you get along by yourself? I carry all the clouds above the sky. Without me you could not travel."

Now, after slaying all the monsters, Killer-of-Enemies stood in the center of the world. He sang a song of how he had moccasins, leggings, shirt, and hat of black flint, blue flint, yellow flint, and glittering flint. He sang of how they protected him.

The sorcerers heard him, the sorcerers from among the people. They were proud of their wicked power. They wanted to see whether they could do what the monsters had failed to do. They all tried to harm Killer-of-Enemies.[1]

That evening he went to the home of his mother, White-Painted Woman. Her home was of flint of the four colors. She was living right among the people then. The sorcerers could not do anything against him.

Then Horned Toad let Killer-of-Enemies have his clothes. Killer-of-Enemies put them on and the sorcerers were still more powerless to harm him. They couldn't do anything at all against him.

Every time he went out, the sorcerers tried to "shoot" him, but their "arrows" merely fell down. And the "arrows" all came back to the sorcerers and they themselves died.[2] That is what Killer-of-Enemies was here for, to protect the people.

Turtle watched while the sorcerers tried to harm Killer-of-Enemies. He saw them all fail. So he made up his mind to see how strong his power was. He walked out.

Lightning saw him and thought, "All right, we shall see whether you can stand it."

So Black Lightning from the east came down and struck Turtle. He gouged out some of the marks that are on the turtle's shell now but he could not harm the turtle. Then Blue Lightning from the south struck at Turtle, but with the same result. Yellow Lightning from the west hit him too, but he was still unharmed. Last of all Glittering Lightning from the north struck at him, but he, too, failed to injure Turtle.

Then Turtle held up his hand and said to the people, "You see. I am strong and after this I shall be a leader. When the lightning comes, have my shell near.[3] If you are eating when the lightning

---

[1] Goddard records this exploit, p. 205.

[2] They say that if a man tries to harm another with evil power and fails to do so, he dies himself. His own sorcery kills him. Some little incident is the apparent cause. He may choke or fall down, but it is really his own sorcery that kills him. (Inf.)

[3] A turtle shell is often kept around the dwelling to ward off lightning.

comes, scrape some of my shell into the food and then you can continue to eat. Otherwise do not eat until Lightning has passed.[1]

Now Killer-of-Enemies and Child-of-the-Water were having a hard time. Because they had gone after the monsters and had touched them, they grew thin and gaunt. Nothing was left of them but skin and bones. The two women, White-Painted Woman and White-Shell Woman tried everything. They sent for Thunder to make a long life ceremony over them. It came about this way.

White-Painted Woman said to Killer-of-Enemies, "Go with Child-of-the-Water to see your grandfathers, White Hactcin and Black Hactcin."

These two performed a ceremony over these boys and used Thunder to cure them. The ceremony lasted four years.

Then they used the ceremony of the whirlwind on the boys. Now the boys started to get fat. At first they thought they were getting well. But, though they were now very fat, the fever remained and they felt no better. They would feel better in one place and worse in another. The sickness kept right on. The Hactcin kept busy making ceremonies of all kinds for them.

Then the boys began to be doubled up with their sickness. It took a long time to get the boys over this. The Hactcin made all sorts of medicines from plants and rubbed them on the afflicted parts.

Now at last they were getting stronger. They went back to their grandmothers.

11. THE FIRST CEREMONIAL RACE

Today we have a race and feast that are just like Thanksgiving. We hold this ceremony in the fall, September fifteenth, and the people all help each other then, for the birds and animals helped each other when the race first began.

The reason for the first ceremonial race was that there was too much food of both kinds, meat and plants, at the same time. The food was all mixed up and people didn't know how to use it. The food did not come in season then as it does now. Sun and Moon decided that it must be divided up and that there should be seasons for the different kinds of food.[2]

Moon said, "I'll bet all my fruits against you."

Sun said, "I'll bet all my animals."

The fruits and plants were on the side of the moon, all those that are used for food.

---

[1] Tuberculosis is thought to result from eating at the time of lightning.

[2] The ceremony is a testimony to the dual food supply (plant and animal) of the Jicarilla, and is an attempt to insure the continuance of all sources of sustenance. Interestingly enough, the moon, acting as a symbol of water, is considered the guardian of the plant life for the purposes of the rite.

The birds all helped each other get ready for the race, the birds of the water such as the duck, and those of the sky such as the eagle, and all others. They all assisted and worked together. But not the owl; he was the only one that didn't help. Many of the birds went on the moon's side.

On the other side were all the animals, those of the water, the mountains, and all those under the sky. They all separated into these two groups.

The sun and the moon took sides. They were all getting ready And all kinds of fruit came together too.

The sun went on the east side, and the moon went to the west. They all began to separate, going in these two directions. The sun chose all the animals. All birds that flew fast were there. Sun and Moon took turns choosing these birds. The race was going to start the next day. This day they were just choosing sides.

The sun took all his young fellows to the east where no one could see what he was doing. Moon did the same, taking those on his side to the west.[1] Moon placed them on a line at one end of the race track and he stood at the other end of it. He kept them in line and started them off at a signal. Then he watched to see who would reach him first, who was the best runner. The sun did the same. He lined his men up and made them race toward him.[2]

That night those on each side got together by themselves. The young men sat around and sang songs against the opposing side.

Meanwhile, during the day, the others had been making corrals, two of them. One was to the east and one to the west. The doors were toward the north. The corrals were made of aspens and cottonwoods. They were about twelve paces across, circular, and with a fire pit in the middle. They were called kivas.[3] Inside each corral they had a fire. This fire stood for North Star, the star that never moves. The Jicarilla fire place stands for this star because you always make the fire there in that same place. Someone may take the brands away, but you always make a fire in that same place when you have a regular fire place.

These first corrals had doorways of cottonwood trees, and on top of each side post was a downy eagle feather. This was to protect those inside and to prevent the women from coming in.[4] If a woman comes in the corral, the race will not be successful at all. And if any woman who is menstruating comes around, and a young fellow comes in contact with her blood, he will have rheumatism. That

[1] Note that Moon is definitely considered male here.

[2] Preliminary races in which the best two runners of each side are chosen to start the ceremonial race are held today.

[3] The word translated as "kivas" here is a general term for a holy place, either Jicarilla or belonging to some other group. It is the word used for the Pueblo kiva.

[4] When you see a man with feathers on his hat you think, "That's protecting him; I'd better not touch him." (Inf.)

is why they keep the women off the track too. The women stay in camp and cook and get the food ready for the feast.[1]

The ones who were going to run and the ones who were going to paint them went in the corrals that night and the singing took place. In each corral they made a ground drawing of many colors, a drawing of the sun, the moon, and two birds.[2] They sang and sang. Each side sang against the other, and they sang for the benefit of the young men too. They sang to make them strong in the race and to give them long life.

The next day came. Between the two corrals lay the world. To begin the race they started at the east and ran around the world clockwise. They lined up. Right to the east the runners came.

The stone on the outer side of the race track at the east was black, and on the inner side the stone was blue. The sun stood up behind the black stone and all his runners formed in line behind him. In front of the black stone stood Killer-of-Enemies. He had made himself into an old man and looked like a ceremonial man. On the inner track, behind the blue stone, stood the moon, and Moon's runners were lined up behind him. Before the blue stone stood Child-of-the-Water.[3] The runners were to encircle the earth and come back to two stones which marked the end of the course. Of these the one on the inner side was yellow and the one on the outside was glittering. Underneath the four stones lay all kinds of bird feathers. At the yellow stone which marked the end of the race course on the moon's side stood White Hactcin. On the sun's side by the glittering stone stood Ancestral Man.

Killer-of-Enemies and Child-of-the-Water started to run forward slowly. They were not really racing. Killer-of-Enemies held in his right hand two tail feathers of the male eagle. In his left hand were two long wing feathers. Child-of-the-Water had the same kind of feathers, but they were from a female eagle. They went around the world and ran to the end of the race track. They came to the two at the end of the track. These two had the same kind of eagle feathers in their hands. These two went counter-clockwise around the world. They approached the stones at the starting place. Ancestral Man ran clockwise around the black stone of Sun, and White Hactcin ran counter-clockwise around the blue stone of Moon. They did not complete the circle, but as they passed the stones the race was on.

Sun and Moon started off, running at top speed. First one was ahead and then the other. That is why the sun is ahead sometimes in the sky, and sometimes the moon.

[1] This is an example of the slight handicap under which the Jicarilla woman labors. At a number of crises in Apache culture, it is thought that contact with women will disqualify a man for certain functions.

[2] In the ceremony that takes place at present, the ground drawing is made on the morning of the race, immediately before the running.

[3] It will be noted that Moon and Child-of-the-Water are here paired, and that Sun and Killer-of-Enemies are likewise associated.

In this first race Killer-of-Enemies, Child-of-the-Water, White Hactcin, and Ancestral Man ran only to make the path. Killer-of-Enemies and Ancestral Man made the path of the sun's side just like pollen, and Child-of-the-Water and White Hactcin made the track of the moon's side like specular iron ore, so great was their power.

When Sun and Moon ran, the race started in earnest. By the time they reached the end of the course the sun was ahead just as it is now (July twelfth). The sun is far ahead now. But pretty soon the moon will be ahead in the sky again. In January they are even again. The sun and the moon come out then at the same time on the same day.

As soon as Sun passed his rock at the finish line Sandhill Crane started running for that side. When Moon came in, Cliff Swallow started off for Moon's side. But Cliff Swallow couldn't catch up.

The last of the fast birds to run for Sun was Humming-Bird. Hawk ran last for Moon. He couldn't catch up with Humming-Bird though, and Humming-Bird came in far ahead. All the little birds were divided between the two sides, and now all had a chance to run. The sun's side kept ahead and won the race.

So the sun won, and his side was able to hunt all kinds of animals and had a great deal of meat to eat that year. The crops were a failure though. Many plants dried up. Because the moon's side had lost, they had to forfeit the fruits and plants that they had bet to the sun's side. That is why the crops were so meager that year. That is why the losing side throws up fruit and provisions for the winners after the race now.

All the animals were there, even the grasshopper and the bear. They had the feast as we have it now. Each animal brought his own food and fruit. That is the way it is now. Different people come, Navahos, Mexicans, and all bring their food and articles to sell at the feast. This is just like Thanksgiving to us.

The sun and the moon agreed that they were going to run like this every year for four years. The second year the moon's side won. The third year the sun's side won. And the fourth year the moon won again. The sun and the moon took turns winning because people can't eat meat all the time, and they can't eat vegetables all the time. It was to insure both kinds of food for mankind.

After the fourth race the ceremony was handed to these Apaches. They were watching it during these four years, so Sun, Moon, White Hactcin, Ancestral Man, Killer-of-Enemies, and Child-of-the-Water decided to give it to them.

"This is your ceremony now," they told the Apache. "If you stop holding this ceremony you will starve."

That is why the Jicarilla are afraid to stop holding this ceremony.

The corrals were made of cottonwood and aspen because these woods are light in weight. Other kinds of wood are too heavy. You have to be light-footed to run. The corral of the sun was made of cottonwood, the corral of the moon of aspen. They had these corrals the first time the race was held, for they had to have a holy place in which to rest.

After that the people were supposed to run in this race each year. But they did not. They forgot about it.

Four large birds wanted to start it up again. So they arranged the second race. This was to be a race for two pretty girls.

These four birds, Sandhill Crane, Goose, White-Headed Bird, and Hawk came to the Hactcin. They told them, "Things should be different. Now we have everything at once. The fruit and the meat come at the same time. We can't take care of it all. We don't want everything at once. All kinds of food should not be plentiful at one time. Let it be divided."

"What put these thoughts in your heads?" exclaimed the Hactcin. Nevertheless they listened and talked about it.

The four big birds asked the Hactcin, Holy Boy, and Red Boy for a ceremony. They said, "Let us race for food, for the fruit or the meat."

And they took two pretty Indian girls and put them at the end of the race course. "Whoever wins the race, the first two to win, will have these girls," they said.

The girls were placed there that the Jicarilla people, too, should multiply and be numerous.

The Hactcin talked it over among themselves and discussed what kind of a ceremony it would be. They decided to make it a racing ceremony as the birds had suggested. They stood at the edge of the world as they talked.

The earth is flat and has the shape of a woman. Her head faces the west and her feet the east. The sun travels from her feet across her body to her head.[1]

The two pretty girls were chosen and they stood at the eastern extremity of the earth. From this place there was going to be a race all around the world and back again to the place where the girls stood. The first two who came in were each to get one of the girls, so the people would increase. The four birds were not going to try to win the girls. They had suggested the race for the others. They were going to run, but only to see how the race came out.

As soon as the race was announced, the others told Gopher, "You'd better start now. You're so slow that the people will beat you if you don't."

So Gopher, even before all the others had gathered, started off. After he started, Mouse, Frog, and many other animals and birds also started.

Two of the best runners were Coyote and Water Beetle. They stood to one side and let the others run first. By the time they started, the others were far off and Gopher was nearly half way

[1] At first, before it was changed, Sun took a short cut and went from north to south. (Inf.)

around.[1] Before these two started, Goose and Sandhill Crane prayed over them and brushed them off with their long wings so that they would run fast.[2]

"Don't be discouraged. Don't stop," the birds told them.

Then Coyote and Water Beetle started off towards the west. Both were running fast. Soon they began to catch up with the slower runners who had started ahead of them.

Behind, where they had stood, to the southeast, the four large birds were lined up, and in the same line to the northeast were all those who considered themselves fast runners — Humming-bird, Cliff Swallow and many others. This whole line started at once. Behind them sat the two girls.

But the four big ones who had suggested the race soon drew away from the others. They were the swiftest and the ones with much power. They would look at a distant point and draw in their wings and they would already be there.

By this time Coyote and Water Beetle had passed all the animals and also the gopher. Now the four big birds came along. They were all in line. One couldn't get ahead of the others.

They came to the place where Gopher was running. They all stopped. The white-headed bird picked up Gopher and put him on his back, for they felt very sorry for him.

He told Gopher, "Hold tightly. If you fall off it will be your own fault."

Then those four birds started on again. They passed Coyote and Beetle. About four miles from the finish line these four birds began to race in earnest. Each tried his best, but not one could get the advantage. They finished at the same time. But they were all far ahead of the other racers. They went directly past the two girls, paying no attention to them.

But the white-headed bird said to Gopher, "Get off my back now."

So Gopher got off and took one of the girls. Gopher took the girl who stood for the fruit, for the fruit comes from the ground.

Meanwhile Coyote and Water Beetle had been racing. Coyote was one step ahead and he crossed the finish line just a little ahead of Water Beetle. He took the other girl.

Beetle expected to get a girl too, but when he went to claim her, he saw that Gopher was already there.[3]

"I thought we passed Gopher a long time ago," he complained. "So how did he get here first?"

---

1 Now the four best runners wear two eagle feathers to represent Coyote's ears and the horns of the water beetle. (Inf.)

2 In the old days they used goose and sandhill crane feathers with which to brush off the boys before the race. Now they use eagle feathers and anything they have. But they shouldn't do this. (Inf.)

3 In another version of the story of the first race it is told that Gopher hid himself and then, when he saw the others coming, ran across the finish line and in that way won the race. But that is not right. (Inf.)

But the four large birds said to him, "No, you must be mistaken. He was here ahead of us."

No one paid attention to Water Beetle.

The four holy people, when the birds came to them with the request for this ceremony, selected the two girls and said, "One will stand for the fruits and the other for the animals."[1]

The ceremony was held so that the winners would marry the girls and raise children. Thus the people would increase. And the children, because the older people couldn't live forever, were taught this ceremony, so that people might continue to increase on the earth. And the children raced against one another so that the fruits and the animals too would increase and be plentiful. And each year this must be done or the fruits and animals will disappear and the people will starve.

A long time ago the people had forgotten about the ceremony and were not holding the race any more. Then some thought it was best to have it again; many wished to restore it. So all the Indians were called together. They began choosing sides. To one they said, "You will be Llanero," to the next, "You will be Ollero." This went on till all the men were on one side or the other. In this way the Llanero and Ollero were formed, and they have raced against each other ever since.[2]

After that the two groups lived separately. The Ollero stayed on one side of the Cimarron and the Llanero stayed on the other side. But the Jicarilla are all one people; there is no difference in customs, in language, or in anything else. Now we are all mixed up, the Llanero and Ollero.

People now can't run around the world. So they just run between the two points which served as the starting place and the finish of the race around the world. The Ollero take the sun's side. The Llanero take the moon's side. The sun's side still has the white flag, the others the red. The sun's side is on the east and has its corral there; the moon's side has its corral on the west side.

The sun is connected with the animals and the moon with the fruit because the sun is a man and the moon a woman. The moon takes care of the seasons. Therefore, as a woman brings forth children, the moon brings forth the fruit.[3]

---

[1] The story of the race for the two girls in which animals and birds participated is also told as part of the coyote cycle without ceremonial implications. (p. 268.) Then the story explains the origin of polygyny, for the winner was to marry both girls. In the writer's opinion this is the older form of the story. When the ceremonial race was taken over by the Jicarilla (possibly from the Eastern Pueblos) this story of a race around the world fitted in nicely. It was embellished with ceremonial detail and became the leading myth of the September 15th ceremony.

[2] The Llanero and Ollero are the two bands of the Jicarilla tribe.

[3] The equivocation of the Jicarilla in respect to the sex of the moon is again in evidence in this passage.

12. THE FIRST PUBERTY CEREMONY[1]

When Killer-of-Enemies came back he spoke to the people. He told of all his experiences and described how he had conquered all the monsters. And he told them that he had always had some prayer or song by which he had accomplished all this.

He said, "You must remember these prayers. And what I have done for you, you must remember also. And when the girls become women you must use these songs and prayers and sing songs about what I did."

This talk took place at the point of emergence. Holy Boy, Red Boy, Child-of-the-Water, and Killer-of-Enemies were there. White-Painted Woman and White-Shell Woman were there too and also the two Hactcin.

White-Painted Woman and White-Shell Woman sang a song of how they came up from the underworld and of what they did until the time when they were with the sun and water and had therefore become holy. White-Painted Woman sang of Sun's visit and of her memories in the morning of what had happened. Everything was ready then.

At this time there were some girls among the people who were becoming women, who were having their first menses. One was selected. A boy of her age was brought too.

Right there they made a tipi. Black Hactcin took pollen and put it around as a foundation where the tipi was to be set up. The tipi was built then with the door facing the east.

When the ceremony started twelve poles were brought. These were of aspen. Three were put together first and tied at the top. Then they were raised, and while they were being raised a song was sung by Black Hactcin. The three main poles were sprinkled with pollen before being put up and when they were tied together a plant with yellow flowers, often used for cleaning the spines from prickly-pears, was tied there too.[2] Then the other eight poles were brought around. The tipi cover was attached to the twelfth pole, and this was raised in place from the back, and the cover was spread around. The cover used in this first ceremony was of buffalo skin. Buffalo skin should always be used. Above the door four sticks of mountain mahogany were inserted. These were the pegs to hold the cover together. After this pegs like these were used for the regular dwelling also.

On either side of the tipi was put a downy turkey feather. This was done because the turkey was the leader of all the growing things. The feathers were put there so that the two young people would be fortunate in finding good plants for food. A handful of

[1] For a description of some of the elements of the girl's puberty rite see Goddard, p. 266.

[2] Snakeweed is the plant mentioned.

weeds was put into the fold of the tipi at the bottom where it was tied around the pegs driven into the ground. This was to hold it down.[1]

They called the tipi cover, the night, the yellow evening glow, the white morning light, and dawn. They called it these things in the songs. The tipi cover was unpainted.

After the tipi was built, North Star made the fire with his light. Then Black Hactcin took pollen and sprinkled it in toward the fire from the four directions, starting with the east and from the inner wall of the tipi. The girl was already inside.

The girl's relatives brought her four pieces of bread, one for each day, made from four different kinds of corn. This was to be her food during the rite.

The boy and girl were told that their behavior during the ceremony would decide their natures during life. They were told that they would be able to help the sick while they were dressed like White-Shell Woman and Child-of-the Water. By rubbing an arm or a leg that was crooked, they could restore it to health, they were told. And parents were advised to bring to this boy and girl any children who were too small for their ages. If either the boy or the girl lifted the child by its head or its neck, the child would grow rapidly thereafter.

The bread that the boy and girl used for food was baked in the ashes. They ate nothing else for the four days. They were not supposed to have a good time but were to work and be thoughtful.

The relatives brought yellow ochre, white clay, and the clothes the girl was to wear. Hactcin arranged these clothes in a line, just in the order that they were to be put on. Then he put the shoes on the girl, singing as he did it. Next he put the leggings on her, then the dress, then the buckskin shawl, and two magpie feathers in her hair. Then the girl's hair was unbraided and allowed to hang loose.[2] Beads were put on her ears as earrings, bracelets were put on her arms, and beads were hung around her neck. Then Black Hactcin painted her face yellow. It was still early in the morning when he did this. The girl was called after White-Shell Woman. The real White-Painted Woman helped Black Hactcin dress the girl.

At the same time a boy was brought forward, and he was called Child-of-the-Water. White Hactcin dressed the boy and White-Shell Woman helped him. Before they put any garment on him, they motioned with it four times. They put on the right moccasin first and the right legging first when they came to these garments. While the girl's face was being painted with yellow ochre, the boy's face was painted with white clay. While the girl's hair was being let down, the boy's hair was being bound with otter fur and decorated with two white eagle tail feathers.

[1] The cover of the regular tipi was pegged down in the same way. (Inf.)

[2] The girl's hair is let down to show what good thick hair she has and so that she will be holy. (Inf.)

Before the faces of the boy and girl were painted, Black Hactcin pulled out the girl's eyebrows and White Hactcin pulled out the boy's eyebrows. This was done because man had acquired the eyebrows when man and woman first disobeyed the Hactcin and had failed to use the reed for four days for drinking water as they had been instructed to do. Now we always try to get rid of the hair, but those who constantly disobey the Hactcin have it grow on their faces.

Then they rubbed a shell called Big Shell on the place from which the eyebrows had been removed, and over the girl's face, under her armpits, and over her pubic region. This was to be done once each day of the ceremony.[1] And they took a stick which was smooth from rubbing against another branch of the tree, and rubbed the boy's brow, face, armpits, and pubic region with this.

The boy and girl were given little sticks shaped like a horse's leg and hoof, and then they were told not to scratch themselves with their fingers but only with these sticks. They were told that if they used their finger nails, there would be a scar left where they scratched. And they were told not to look up at the sky during the whole four days, that if they did so it would rain. They were told not to let their lips touch water for the four days. If they did, it would rain. So the boy was given a length of reed through which to suck up water, and the girl was given a ladle of split buffalo horn out of which to drink.[2] They were also told not to eat anything sweet or anything sour. If they did, they were warned, their teeth would decay easily.

The boy was given a bow, four arrows feathered with the feathers of the golden eagle, and a quiver.

On the head of each pollen was placed. Then everyone came up to these two and put pollen in their mouths, and on their heads. That meant, "We are joining this ceremony with you."[3]

Up to this point the boy and girl had been seated. But now they stood up and the Hactcin and the two women pressed them so that their bodies would be straight and so that the woman would not be bent over until she was aged.

Now Black Hactcin went out. He sang a song to long life. He sprinkled pollen to the east. When he finished the song he called to the boy and girl. They stood one behind the other facing the east, the boy in front of the girl. Then they both ran to the east. The first time they ran a little way to the east and returned. It stood for exercise, so that both of them would be good runners after that. They ran four times, each time running farther to the east. The

1 This is still done. And some, because of this, never get hair in these places. That is why I believe this girl's puberty ceremony. (Inf.)

2 In the old days the girls used the buffalo horn for drinking. Now they don't; they just use a reed also. (Inf.)

3 Now the singer does it first, then the father, the mother, and the close relatives of the two young people, then anyone who wants to do it. (Inf.)

relatives were sitting in a line outside. Each time the two came back in place White-Shell Woman uttered a call into the ear of the girl.

The boy now went into the tipi and Black Hactcin followed him. The boy sat down in his place in the back on the northeast side. The girl's place was to the south of him.

All the female relatives of the girl were in line outside. They sat in a line facing the east, at the door of the tipi. The girl now went into the tipi. Behind her place was a parfleche filled with corn kernels, four different kinds mixed. The parfleche was placed near her bread. She had a little gourd dipper too. With the dipper she took out a little of the corn and walked out to the woman sitting farthest from the tipi in the line of relatives. She put this corn in the hands of this woman and went back to get another dipperful. She continued until she had given corn to all. This corn was to bring good luck to them. They were told that when they planted in the spring they should mix this corn with their seed and everything would grow well. The gourd that was used was plain and undecorated. After giving corn to the women, the girl went back and sat in her place.

Now the boy arose. He went out to the east. He picked up anything he could find there, a piece of horse manure, for instance, and ran into the tipi and gave it to the girl. She put it away in her corner, behind her. Then he ran out again, but to the south and returned as before. He brought grass and weeds and always he brought back horse manure with it. He ran to the west and to the north also. When he had been to all the directions and had come back for the last time, he sat down.

Black Hactcin said, "This is the end for now." Then he told the girl to work hard all day and grind corn on a metate with a mano. She stayed right in the ceremonial tipi and did so.[1]

Hactcin told the boy to look after the horses of the people and to bring them to the camp early in the morning. And he was told to run all the time at his work and never to walk.

In this first ceremony the boy and girl did not dance in the evening.[2]

The morning of the second day the two young people had their faces painted again and then they were told to work for the whole day.

The same thing happened the third day. At sunset they were finished and they rested. All the Holy Ones and the two young people slept in the ceremonial tipi.[3]

[1] In the old days the girl used to stay right in the tipi and work. Now the girls go to their mother's tipis and work. (Inf.)

[2] The dancing in the evening is something new and has only been done since my people were at Mescalero. (Inf.)

[3] They are supposed to sleep in the ceremonial tipi too, but now many do not do it. The people don't believe now and don't care. They disobey. (Inf.)

And the fourth day was like the others. Then came the sunrise of the fifth morning.

The two young people were called. The two holy women washed the girl's hair.[1] They took a black clay bowl and put the water from the four holy rivers in it. They had two of these bowls. Then they put crushed yucca root in and worked up a suds. One bowl of water was for the moon. That was the girl's bowl. And they sprinkled pollen on the water in the shape of a full moon with four rays. Then they put specular iron ore on in the same way. And a sun symbol with four rays extending outward was traced on the top of the water of the other bowl. In the moon's bowl the girl's hair was washed by White-Painted Woman. White-Shell Woman washed the boy's hair in the other bowl of water.[2]

Then Black Hactcin sang. He put red ochre and grease on his hands and rubbed it around. Then with pollen he traced the outline of the sun on his right hand and the outline of the moon on his left hand. He rubbed them together. He was seated, facing the two young people. He rubbed his hands on his own face first and made it red. Then he put pollen on his face, tracing the moon, sun, stars, and dipper on his face. He rubbed grease and red paint on his hands again. Again he painted the sun and moon on his hands. This time he rubbed these off on the face of the girl. Then, beginning with the right side of her forehead and working toward the left, he painted the sun, moon, north star, and Pleiades on her face. He sang as he did this.[3] He then put pollen in the mouth and on the head of the girl.

Now he painted the boy's face in the same way and put pollen in his mouth and on his head. And to all those who were in the tipi he did the same.[4]

Then the clothes were taken off the young people, beginning at the top and working towards the moccasins. The moccasins were taken off last. They put on their old clothes again. The ceremony was ended.

The fire was kept day and night for the four days. The relatives of the boy and girl kept it going; they didn't allow it to go out.

Later they had a second ceremony of this kind, and this time the animals came and helped. The buffalo came near the place where

---

[1] Bathing and hair-washing are important means of purification in Jicarilla ceremonials.

[2] Now the mother of each child does it, or the grandmother, or some close female relative.

[3] He did not use a rattle. When the girl and boy dance in the evening now, the helpers of the singers and the people sitting around clap in time. This takes the place of a rattle. (Inf.)

[4] They do this now too. It means that all in the past has been forgiven and is wiped clean. Perhaps your relative has died. When you go in there and this is done to you, you become all right again. You forget it. You don't grieve any more. (Inf.)

the people were. It was in the summer time. The Holy Ones, who were teaching the people, said to the buffalo, "We need you to give us your clothes and to give us food to eat for this feast."

The buffalo answered, "All right, we're willing to help."

This was the leader of the buffaloes who spoke.

The people all needed help, so they said to the buffalo, "We need you. We need your meat and we need your hide for clothing."

So the leader of the buffaloes went back to his own people. He told his people what he had heard. He said, "Let all of you who have prepared skins with hair removed and tanned, bring them here."

Each one brought twelve skins so prepared. These were all taken to the place where the Holy Ones were. They were given to the people. And the people all sang songs about this, they were so happy to receive them.

Then White-Painted Woman and White-Shell Woman began to sew the skins and out of them they made a tipi. They used twelve skins for this tipi. While they were sewing they measured the skins off on the twelve poles they had used for the first ceremony. When it was finished they put the pollen around just as had been done the first time and put the plant on the first three poles. They did everything ceremonially as before. But this time the cover of the tipi was of buffalo hides which the buffaloes themselves provided.

Then the girl came forward.[1] Black Hactcin was going to conduct the ceremony again. Just as before, he sang. He told the others to assist him and told them what to do. He gave directions and they dressed the boy and girl as had been done before, putting on the moccasins first.

But this time the buffalo and the road-runner were going to help. Mountain-Lion and Goose were there also to help. Western Tanager, Robin, and Bluebird were present. These were the birds who had announced the exploits of Killer-of-Enemies to the people after he came back from killing the monsters. Turkey was there too and offered his services, and Badger came. All these people were in the tipi after it was erected.

The boy and the girl were dressed now and Black Hactcin was singing. The girl had yellow ochre on her face. That stood for the yellow evening glow. The boy was called Child-of-the-Water and had white clay on his face. That stood for the morning glow. The girl stood to the west, the boy stood to the east, for yellow stands for the west and white for the east.[2] They prayed for the people.

Black Hactcin was singing his songs. He sprinkled the pollen. He made trails with it, four of them, each farther to the east than the other. He made all of them before the running started.[3]

---

[1] The informant could not say whether it was the same girl who had been in the first ceremony.

[2] The association of white with the east is much rarer than the association of black with that direction.

[3] Now they don't make the trail, but just motion with the pollen. (Inf.)

As in the first ceremony, at the end of the running the girl gave corn to the people. The boy went to the four directions and gathered grass and manure for the girl just as before. Now everything was finished for the morning.

Then Black Hactcin said, "Now you are free to work all afternoon."

When evening came all returned to the ceremonial tipi. As soon as the evening glow was gone, they started the ceremony again.

Black Hactcin started singing. He sang of the first man and first woman, of how they walked in the beginning, of how they walked to the emergence ladder, and of how they climbed and came to this world. Then he sang of how the people moved, of how they moved camp four times before coming to this world from below. Then he sang a song of the badger, of how Badger was one of the first to come up on the earth and of how he got mud on his feet. And he sang, too, of Turkey, of how Turkey took care of the emergence mountain and helped it to grow.

Then the leader of the buffaloes began to dance in the tipi. And he said to the boy and girl, "You two stand up and dance with me."[1]

Goose arose now and danced with the others.

Then the voice of Sun was heard. Sun was singing, and the boy and girl danced to the sound of his voice. He sang to them of long life.

After that the road-runner danced for one song.

Now four life songs had been sung, and after the singing and dancing they stopped for that night.

The next night there were singing and dancing again. But this night there were more songs and they danced for a longer time, for all the birds and those who danced brought their own songs. Robin and Western Tanager did not dance, but they, too, contributed songs.

And the third night the singing was continued for an even longer period. More birds and animals were coming in each night, bringing their own songs and prayers. Even Thunder joined and sang, as did the wind and others. And the pollen, iron ore, and red paint all had songs, and even the dew had a song.

The last night the singing and dancing continued till dawn.

They always sang four songs for life before each two dancing songs. The songs for life told about the emergence and everything that Killer-of-Enemies had done and about how the people came to be. The first night only two dancing songs were sung. The second night four dancing songs were sung. The third night six dancing songs were sung. And the fourth night twelve dancing songs were sung.

---

[1] If, as the informant has already twice stated, the dancing within the tipi in the evening of the puberty rite dates since the Jicarilla were stationed on the Mescalero Reservation, this part of the story must be of recent development.

Yet there were many songs which were not sung, which were saved for another time, for no one would sing all of his songs at once.[1]

Road-runner was dancing with his tail up, facing the east, when the dawn came. The red of the dawn struck his head and turned it red. And his tail, which was sticking up, was struck by the morning light, and therefore is white at the end.

Now the hair of the boy and the girl was washed and all was conducted as in the first ceremony.

Then Black Hactcin spoke to the people who were assembled there. "After this you must use this ceremony. Do it generation after generation till the end of the world."[2]

The last night Black Hactcin laid down a kernel of corn for every song that he sang. He put them around the fire place starting from the east and going clockwise. The life songs were grouped in four's and the kernels of corn which stood for them were put close together. Then a little space was left and the kernels which represented the dancing songs were put together.[3]

In the morning, when the ceremony was over, Black Hactcin picked up the corn kernels and distributed them. He gave a kernel to everyone present and the people ate them to retain good health and a long life.[4]

The first three nights, after the finish of the dancing, food was served in the tipi. The fourth night they ate at about midnight, for they were going to stay in there till dawn. The two young people did not eat what the others did, though the others ate with them. The two for whom the ceremony was given ate the bread which had been provided for them.[5]

After this White-Painted Woman and White-Shell Woman went away to their homes in the east and west. They are there now, up in the sky. The Hactcin also left later as we shall see. Killer-of-Enemies was still on earth. It was after this that he left for Picuris and Taos. But Child-of-the-Water went back to his mother, for everything was at peace now. Holy Boy and Red Boy were not at this ceremony.

---

[1] In any ceremony the one who officiates is careful not to sing all the songs or recite all the prayers he knows for the one occasion. The Jicarilla feeling is that something should be held in reserve always; that no one should allow himself to be stripped entirely of his sacred protection.

[2] I believe there are about seven men who sing these songs. (Inf.)

[3] Now they always have four life songs together, but the number of dance songs might vary. Sometimes two, sometimes three, are sung together. If the dancers are not lazy the corn may reach all around the fire pit. I've seen this happen. (Inf.)

[4] This is done now too. If many people are present, each gets only one kernel. If few people are present, each one may get more kernels. (Inf.)

[5] Four pieces of bread are baked. Each day the boy eats half of a piece and the girl eats half. (Inf.)

The people had been called together by the four bird messengers. Now they started to move out and occupy the whole land.

White-Shell Woman went up in the sky to the east then, and White-Painted Woman went up in the sky to the west. And they are still there. They live in homes of the sun made of abalone. Both have fire sticks still and they watch the fate of their people, the Jicarilla, by means of these fire sticks. When the people are few in number, the fire sticks diminish; when the people increase, the fire sticks enlarge again. And when we pray and talk of them, Killer-of-Enemies, Child-of-the-Water, White-Shell Woman, and White-Painted Woman are always glad. They hear it all. Wind acts as a messenger and carries the report.

Now all was at peace. The Jicarilla had animals to kill, and there were birds, fruit, and plants of all kinds. Holy Boy and Red Boy left the people. They went back into the opening from which the people had emerged, for their work was now finished. There they wait and will stay until they are called. Some day when the monsters come back, Killer-of-Enemies and the Holy Ones will come back too.

13. THE CREATION OF THE WHITE MAN

One time Coyote was teasing Cyclone. Every day he went over there and teased him. Coyote could run fast and get away before Cyclone could catch him.

Then one time Coyote went to see Child-of-the-Water. He said, "My partner, let us go and visit our friend, Cyclone."

He lied about his friendship. Coyote was that way. He always tried to test the power of another, to see whether others were really powerful or were just ordinary people.

So they went to see Cyclone at his home.

When they got near, Coyote ran to Cyclone and began to mock him again. "You can't do anything! You can't catch me!" he said.

So Cyclone started to run after Coyote. Coyote ran away and left Child-of-the-Water behind, for Child-of-the-Water could not run very fast.

Cyclone was breaking things to pieces, and Child-of-the-Water, who was in his path, was lifted up and broken into many pieces and scattered all over.

There were some people living at a spring. The woman went to get some water. She saw some blood spilled on the leaves, little drops of it. She looked at it. "Oh, that will make good soup!" she thought. She broke off the leaves and carried them home with water. She was going to make soup with this.

When she got home she put the leaves in the pot. She started to boil the soup. After a while she heard somebody crying. She looked around all over. The only place she didn't look was in the pot.

At last she came near the pot and listened. The noise seemed to come from there. It sounded like a baby crying in that pot.

She took the pot off the fire. There was a baby in there, and she picked it up. It was a little boy. She took care of that baby until it was a big boy. The woman did not know it, but this was Child-of-the-Water.

He grew up. He was nearly twenty years old now. But he was always rather weak and puny and shy.

Evil, sickness, and sorcerers couldn't bother him; they couldn't make him ill.

Once, at this time, Child-of-the-Water was walking to the east. He came to the ocean. He walked on the water. He found a fish there with blue eyes. He picked up a female fish of this kind and a male fish. He took them along with him to the other side of the ocean. He put the fishes on the ground.

Then Child-of-the-Water sent for White Hactcin. White Hactcin came.

Child-of-the-Water said, "Help me make people of these fish."

White Hactcin said to him, "You lie down."

Child-of-the-Water lay face downward and White Hactcin traced his outline on the earth.

"Get up now and stand to one side."

Then Hactcin took both fish and put them within the outline of the figure of Child-of-the-Water.

Hactcin said to Child-of-the-Water, "Now turn around and face the east." He had him walk to the east, then turn to the south without looking at the fish and walk there. He had him walk to the west and the north in the same manner. Next Hactcin told him to walk once more to the east. Then Hactcin said, "Now turn around and look."

When Child-of-the-Water turned he saw that someone was lying there where the outline of his body had been traced.

Then Hactcin said, "Now face to the south," and Child-of-the-Water did so.

"Now turn around again."

He looked and saw that it was a man stretching out his arms to his knees and attempting to rise.

Then Hactcin said, "Turn to the west," and Child-of-the-Water did so.

"Now look."

He saw that the man was sitting up.

He went through the same procedure to the north and when he turned and looked this time, the man was sitting with his legs crossed under him.

Both White Hactcin and Child-of-the-Water came to the man and picked him up.

Hactcin said to Child-of-the-Water, "Make him get up," and Child-of-the-Water did so.

They motioned four times to make him walk. Child-of-the-Water led him for four steps, and then they turned around.

Hactcin said, "Talk, talk, talk, talk." The fourth time he said it, the man spoke.

"Laugh, laugh, laugh, laugh," Hactcin said. After the fourth time he was told to do it, the man laughed.

"Shout, shout, shout, shout," the man was told, and after the fourth time he did so.

Now he was fully formed.

Hactcin told the man to lie down this time. Child-of-the-Water traced his figure on the ground. The man was told to rise.

Again the Hactcin set out to give life to the figure. The man and Child-of-the-Water did exactly what Child-of-the-Water had done the first time. The man led and Child-of-the-Water stood behind him. White Hactcin gave this figure life and made it sit up and walk and talk and laugh just as had been done to the man. But the one that was made this time was a woman.

Child-of-the-Water asked Hactcin, "Where are these people to live?"

Hactcin said, "What home do you think will be best for them?"

They both thought it over. Hactcin sent for the swallow, and this bird came.

The bird went to the river. He brought back mud from the bottom. He put down the mud. Then he went away and brought back the wind. The wind blew into the mud and made it large and round.

Hactcin asked the people, "Do you want a round house?"

"No," they answered, "we want a square house."

So the mud was reshaped and the kind of house they wanted was given to them. Then the bird made them a chimney for the house. The roof was first made round and the two people did not like it. The bird did not know how to change the roof to suit them. So they sent for the woodpecker.

Woodpecker was to be the carpenter for this dwelling. And they sent for Lightning too. Lightning came and split the spruce and piñon trees. It was at this time that these people, the first white people, received the gun from Lightning.

They all brought over the beams. Woodpecker started to construct the roof. To hold the beams he used spider's rope (spider web thread). Then the people wanted the chimney changed. Instead of having it round, they wanted it square with each corner pointing to one of the cardinal directions. Woodpecker fixed this also.

Now the house was finished and the couple was told to enter. They went in and looked around. But there were no windows.

So Hactcin said, "I think we should give this house windows just as the human body has windows to let in the light."[1]

[1] This refers to the eyes. (Inf.)

So Child-of-the-Water gave Hactcin rock crystal of four colors, black, blue, yellow, and glittering. The black one was pushed into the mud wall at the east side of the house, the blue one was placed in the south wall, the yellow one in the west wall, and the glittering one in the north wall.

Now all came into the house, and all thought it beautiful, for there was plenty of light in the house now.

The Hactcin turned to Woodpecker and said, "Now you must stay here and work for these people until all is finished.[1] Whatever they wish to have, you are to make for them."

So the woodpeckers stayed on and worked as carpenters.

Now Hactcin sent for the turkey. To him Hactcin said, "Now make a garden for these people near the edge of the water." Water was already flowing there.

They called all the other animals too, for Hactcin had great power. All the animals and birds came around to have a conference with these people.

"Deer skins will be your clothing," Hactcin said to these people.[2] And he told them, "You must take care of all these animals. These are all your animals and these are all your birds too. All this meat is your meat. And the garden will yield food for you. Here you are, and all this is given to you. Now I am going back."

So Hactcin and Child-of-the-Water and the birds and Lightning and the others all went back. Child-of-the-Water started, then, to return to his stepmother's home.

Thus Child-of-the-Water made the white people when he went to the east that time. Now he is up in the heavens, above the earth. He went up in a cloud after creating the white man. That is why the white men say they will go to Heaven when they die. Child-of-the-Water, who made them, is up there. He is living to the east with White-Shell Woman, his mother.

And the reason the white man cannot be hurt by sorcerers and can handle snakes and evil things like that without harm is that Child-of-the-Water created him after being blown to pieces by Cyclone. Child-of-the-Water was not killed even though he was blown to pieces by Cyclone. Where his blood fell there was life. He made the white man to be just like that, so that nothing could hurt him. That is why the white man says, "We do not die. We are going to Heaven." The white men are following in the path of Child-of-the-Water.

When Child-of-the-Water was returning to his stepmother's home, he made a path for the white people to take in coming to this country. That is why the white people were not afraid. They knew a path had been made for them across the ocean.

---

[1] In the stories Woodpecker is usually called when work in wood is wanted.

[2] I guess the white people wore deerskin clothes when they first came here. (Inf.)

Child-of-the-Water came back to his stepmother's home. He got inside a cloud. The cloud began to sail upward towards the heavens. This woman who had cared for him was the only one who saw this happen.

Before he started, Child-of-the-Water said to his stepmother, "I've made another creation of man. They will come here some day."

So he went up on the other side of the sky. That is where Child-of-the-Water is now. No one halted him. What he meant by the other creation of man was the creation of the white people.

His stepmother did not know what Child-of-the-Water meant when he spoke of another creation. Child-of-the-Water said to her, "You do not understand what I mean by a new creation of man, but some day you will see them. They will be different from you, but they will be good people. They will be shaped like your people."

Many years later she heard of people who came from the other side of the ocean. She remembered what Child-of-the-Water had told her. She was eager to see what these people looked like.

The chief of her group received a message that some people were coming from the other side of the ocean. They were called White-Eyed Travelers. The chief told the people, "They are coming. They will give us guns, they will give us cloth for clothes. They will give us different food too. These are the people that Child-of-the-Water is sending to us. Child-of-the-Water has not forgotten us, even though he didn't do much for us about killing the monsters. He is helping us in some other good way."[1]

The other people did not know what the chief was talking about. Some of them began to joke. They said to each other, "When those people give you a gun, I'm going to take it away from you." Some said, "I'm going to hunt with the gun I shall take from you, so we will not have hard times any more."[2]

Not very long after this they heard that these people had really come across the ocean.

These white people met these Indians and became friendly with them. They took out some money and showed that it had a head of the president on one side and an arrow on the other. "One face belongs to us and one to you," they said. "Take this money and we will give you all our property." They clasped hands and were at peace with each other.

The white man said, "I'm going to live on your territory, but I am going to divide my property with you always. If I fail to do this,

---

[1] The Apache seem to associate the lesser of the two culture heroes with the white man. Among the Mescalero and Chiricahua Apache, where Child-of-the-Water is the one who slays monsters and, by a curious twist, Killer-of-Enemies becomes the weaker companion, the latter is represented as the benefactor of the white man.

[2] This incident happened about four hundred years ago. (Inf.)

you can chase me from your territory." And the white man signed a promise and gave it to the Indian.

The white man went back and returned with much property, guns and food, and gave it to the Indians. He gave them flour, sugar, coffee, baking powder, and cloth for clothes.

The Indians did not understand. Some did not know how the flour was to be used and some just dumped it out. But they recognized the salt and kept it and used it. The sugar they tasted and it was sweet, so they kept it and used it. But the baking powder they did not recognize, so they threw it away. Some tried to eat the baking powder just as it was and ate too much and killed themselves. Some put their hands right into the flour and ate it and made themselves sick. The coffee they thought was some kind of beans, so they cooked the coffee all day, and then for two days and a night trying to soften it. But the coffee beans never got done; they were as tough as ever. Some then ground the coffee beans on the metate, but they didn't taste good when cooked. The Indians didn't know how to use it. So they gave up and threw it all away.

After a while they took some coffee to the Mexicans and asked to be shown how to use it. The Indians called it "black water," and they call it that still. The Mexicans told them how to use it and said to them, "Put sugar in it and it is good." But some do not like it that way. After that some kept coffee, and some did not but gave it to the Mexicans. Some did not like the smell when it was ground and so didn't wish to have it.[1]

14. KILLER-OF-ENEMIES AT PICURIS[2]

Killer-of-Enemies went up to the pueblo of Picuris. When he came they said, "He is worthless. He is no good." They decided to use him in evil ways.

They took him to a place where an eagle had a nest. The eagle had a nest on a ledge at the side of a cliff some distance down from the top. They took Killer-of-Enemies to the top and put ropes around him, and they told him, "We will lower you, and you must take those two little eagles from the nest."

"All right," replied Killer-of-Enemies.

They lowered him to the nest. When he got there he threw off the rope and stayed there.

The Pueblo men called to him, "Why do you take that rope off? Keep it on and bring those little eagles up with you."

But Killer-of-Enemies didn't listen to them. He paid no attention to what they said. They all cursed him and called him names.

The two little eagles spoke to each other, "Shall we ask him what he wants?" one asked the other.

[1] The Jicarilla are inveterate coffee drinkers now. Certainly this part of the story crystalized some years back.

[2] Cf. Goddard, p. 210.

"Yes, let's ask him."

So they did. One of them asked him.

"I've just come to see you. I have come to stay with you because you are children all by yourselves. Perhaps you might become frightened sometime if you are left alone. Where are your mother and father?"

"Our mother and father went up in the sky."

"When will they come back?"

"In about four days." Then the two little ones asked, "Are you hungry? If you are we will feed you."

So they brought a little piece of bread for him on a small plate.

Killer-of-Enemies thought, "That's not enough for me. I'll finish it at one swallow."

The two little eagles said, "That is enough for you."

He began to eat. He couldn't eat it all. When he was satisfied some was still left.

He asked for water now. The young eagles brought a little hailstone.

He thought, "That won't be enough for me."

But he started to drink the water from it and couldn't finish it all. Some was still left and he gave it back. The young eagles put it away.

Four days passed. On the fourth day he looked up in the sky. Something was coming. The father and mother eagle came to that nest.

The male eagle spoke to him and said, "Something-Hanging-Down,[1] what are you doing here?"

"Oh, I just came to visit with you because I would like to see how it is up in the heavens."

"It's a good thing you came here," the eagle said, "We are going to take you up in the heavens."

The cliff looked solid, but the big eagle went to it and opened a door in that rock wall. Then he called Killer-of-Enemies to it. Killer-of-Enemies went in. He looked around. It was one large room, and hanging from the roof were suits like those the eagles wear. There were many of them, of all sizes. They told him to pick out one that fitted him, and he did so and put it on.

Then the parents said to the eaglets, "You must teach him to fly. But go only a little way at first."

So the eaglets began to play with Killer-of-Enemies. They flew a short distance with him at first. Every time when they went out to play and fly, they went a little farther. After a while the parents told them to fly all day with Killer-of-Enemies, and to come back in the evening. They taught him how to do many things, how to fly high and swoop down.

---

[1] This is the name by which the eagle addresses Killer-of-Enemies throughout this episode.

For four days they took long trips, trips that took all day. They would get back in the evening. Then they took longer trips and were gone all day and would come back the next day. Now Killer-of-Enemies was getting strong.

The father continually asked the children whether Killer-of-Enemies was learning. "Is he strong?" he asked now.

And the children answered, "Yes, he can fly ahead of us."

So the big eagle said, "Then tomorrow we will start upward. You go," he told Killer-of-Enemies, "and change your suit. Hang up the one you have been using and take a new one."

The next day they started to travel. They left early in the morning, just after sunup. They stopped at sunset and found a place to sleep. The next day, early in the morning, they started out again. They found a place at nightfall and slept. The third day it was the same.

They asked Killer-of-Enemies, "Are you tired?"

"No, I'm not tired. I'm still all right."

So the next day they went on. Killer-of-Enemies had no trouble until the afternoon. In the middle of the afternoon they were getting near to the heavens but Killer-of-Enemies was getting tired.

Both the big eagles got under him and tried to hold him up until he was rested. But he grew so tired that he began to fall. He couldn't help it. Both the big eagles were becoming tired now too.

The male eagle sent a message up to the heavens. He went up himself and got help. More eagles came down. Though there were many of them, they could not lift Killer-of-Enemies. He was too heavy.

So they sent up for more aid. They brought back some sandhill cranes. They all helped lift Killer-of-Enemies. But they, too, tired after a while.

They sent word up once more. This time a flock of geese came to their aid. They got under and lifted Killer-of-Enemies. After a while they also became tired. So they sent up word once more.

This time the grebes came to help. They were very strong, these birds. They got under Killer-of-Enemies and, without the help of the eagles or the others, lifted him up. At the top there was a hole and they brought Killer-of-Enemies through it.[1] On top there was a place just like this world.

When he stood up there Killer-of-Enemies asked the eagles, "Where is your chief?"

"Over here," and they showed him where the chief lived.

"What is his name?"

"Possessor-of-Authority."

Killer-of-Enemies went to that man.

---

[1] In a different version it is told that Killer-of-Enemies, when he tried to reach the home of the eagles and was falling, had Mountain-Lion put down his tail. Killer-of-Enemies clung to it and was drawn up. (Inf.)

The chief asked, "What are you doing up here?"

"I just wanted to see this place."

"When did you come?"

"Just now."

"When are you going back?"

"In about eight days."

The chief had a plentiful supply of meat, for he killed deer every day. So Killer-of-Enemies stayed there eight days.

The eagles came around and began to talk. They said, "We have our enemies nearby. They kill us every time we fight them."

Killer-of-Enemies looked around. "Where is the encampment of your enemies? Where do they live?"

The chief replied, "Right over there where the bushes are thick. They are bees. Three kinds of bees are living there.[1] They always try to fight us."

Some of the eagles went over there and started to fight them. Killer-of-Enemies watched the battle. The bees were darting in among the feathers of the eagles and stinging them. The eagles could not protect themselves. Some were swelling up and dying.

Killer-of-Enemies went back to the chief. He said, "Give me a thick suit of buffalo hide."

The fighting was still going on. The chief gave Killer-of-Enemies presents of beads. Then Killer-of-Enemies broke some brush. He took the brush with him and went into the fight.

With the brush he hit at the bees and killed every one of them. Then he went to the brush and destroyed all the hives. Then the eagles were all happy.

But he left two of the bees alive, a male and a female. He gave them sweet things, flowers and fruit. He told them, "You must not kill any more."

But they said, "When people tease us we will give them a shock."

That is why bees sting today.

The meadow-lark had been sitting there during the battle. He had made fun while some of those poor eagles were dying.

One of the eagles came to Killer-of-Enemies and said, "He is a sorcerer."

Killer-of-Enemies turned to that meadow-lark and told him, "You must go down to earth. I'm taking your power away and you will have no power there. You will just make fun of the people as they pass by."

The meadow-lark did not want to go, but he had to go when Killer-of-Enemies told him to. He came down to this earth.

Then Killer-of-Enemies went back to the chief.

The chief said, "It is a good thing that you came up. You have brought us peace."

---

[1] The three kinds of bees are described as black, grey, and yellow ones.

The next day Killer-of-Enemies started to descend. The chief gave him a horse before he left.

"How can I take this down?" Killer-of-Enemies asked.

"Well, if you can't take it down, I'll choose something else."

So the chief picked out a bundle of white eagle feathers, the tail feathers of a male eagle. He also picked out spotted tail feathers of the female eagle. He handed them to Killer-of-Enemies as a present. And the chief gave him a war-bonnet of eagle feathers in addition.

So the next day Killer-of-Enemies started down. He was accompanied by the same two eagles who had ascended with him. In four days they were back. Killer-of-Enemies landed on top of the same cliff from which he had started. He removed his suit of eagle feathers and returned it to the eagles.

Then he started to walk to the pueblo of Picuris. When he arrived there, he gave the headdress and the feathers to these people. He distributed the feathers to the people of Picuris. That is why they use them now. And other peoples learned to use them from the people of Picuris.

Variant

When the battle between the eagles and the bees began, Killer-of-Enemies saw that the bees were using sharpened reeds as spears. These spears had poison from some weeds on the tip. Killer-of-Enemies put on hide armor and the spears broke against it. Then he killed them easily.

The eagle with whom Killer-of-Enemies went up was the golden eagle. This is the one whose feathers are used for the bear dance ceremony and for the war-bonnet.

Very few bald eagles are here. They are called "eagle up in the sky."

The eagles on the other side of the sky were colored just like golden eagles. They used to come down and visit the eagles of this earth, and the eagles of earth used to go up and visit them.

From here Killer-of-Enemies went to visit the people of Taos.

15. KILLER-OF-ENEMIES AT TAOS AND HIS DEPARTURE[1]

Killer-of-Enemies made himself appear to be poverty-stricken. His dress was ragged and he had no possessions. Matter was running from his nose, and he was dirty. In this condition he walked to Taos Pueblo. He entered the village.

They disliked him. They chased him out, saying, "You get out, you old Apache."

He was out on the edge of the village. He begged them for

[1] Cf. Goddard, p. 200.

something to eat. They gave him a few crumbs left from their meal. They treated him like a dog.

They were having a ceremony at Taos. They have a holy place where they hold their ceremonies. It is the kiva.

Killer-of-Enemies was not invited, but he went into the kiva. They couldn't see him. They didn't know he was there. They were all praying and expressing thanks for the fruit and for all things. It was their Thanksgiving, I suppose.

Then one of the Pueblo Indians discovered him. This man called the attention of the others to the stranger, and they all began to abuse him. They told him that he was dirty and that he must go.

Killer-of-Enemies turned to go. But as he was being driven out of the kiva, he made a motion with his right hand and all the corn of the people changed to flies. He did this with a motion as though he were covering the corn with a blanket.

Then Killer-of-Enemies hid. The people tried to find him and bring him back. They searched until they found him and begged him to return and restore their corn for them. So he agreed and returned. With a reverse wave of his hand he made all the corn as it was before.

At the time of another ceremony, he again entered the kiva. Again someone saw him.

This man asked, "Why have you come here? Your clothes are all ragged."

Killer-of-Enemies started to walk out. As he was leaving he raised his hand and waved it before them. "All right," he said, "I will go, but all will be changed. Your corn will turn to worms."

And in all the homes the corn turned to worms at that moment. They were all astonished when they learned of it.

Killer-of-Enemies went away. He tried to hide himself.

"Who did this?" one Pueblo Indian asked another. But no one knew. By and by someone suggested that it must have been the man who was driven from the kiva. They all decided he must have been the one, but they did not know it was Killer-of-Enemies. They thought it was some ordinary Apache.

They all hunted for the ragged stranger. They found him and brought him back.

"You must change this corn and make it as it was," they told him.

He did it; he waved his hand once more and the corn was as before.[1]

Killer-of-Enemies came into the kiva for the third time. This

[1] Killer-of-Enemies was driven out of the kiva and had his revenge on the people of Taos four times, though only three of the encounters are given here. After he had restored the corn from the worms he turned it into some black substance. Because of this a black ball is sometimes found on the cornstalk. "My people won't eat corn from a stalk which has this on," the informant said. "No one can touch it. You get a boil where it touches you."

time they again drove him out. He waved his hand over them and their heads were stuck together. They cried and begged him to make them as they were before. So Killer-of-Enemies did so.

Killer-of-Enemies stayed there a few days more.

They said to him, "If you have power you must help us." Then they told him, "If you are so powerful, we can use you. Nearby is a lake. There is something in there which swallows people. He-Holds-in-the-Water is its name. You must help us to get rid of it and get our people back."

Killer-of-Enemies replied, "If you believe in me I shall be glad to help you. Dress me in turquoise. Cover my cap, my shirt, my leggings, and my moccasins with turquoise."

The first time they put only one piece of turquoise on his moccasins and one on each piece of clothing.

"That is not enough. That is not the way I want it. I said to put it on all over my clothes."

So the next time they put a few more on. They put two on each moccasin and two pieces on the shirt and other articles of clothing.

"That is not the way I told you to do it. Put them on thicker."

So the third time they took the clothes and put the pieces of turquoise on a little thicker. They put three pieces of turquoise on each piece of clothing.

But Killer-of-Enemies said, "No, I want them close together. I want the whole thing covered. I want no spaces between the stones."

So the fourth time they put them on as he directed. Then they all walked toward the lake.

But Killer-of-Enemies told them, "Do not follow me. Stand near your pueblo and watch from there."

He came to the lake. He turned around and looked at the sun. He motioned four times in a clockwise circle with his hand, and he had stone hoops in his hand, four of them — one black, one blue, one yellow, and one glittering. Then he stood and faced each direction in turn, standing first facing the east, then the south, then the west, and then the north, and last he faced the east again.

He threw the black rock hoop into the water and the water receded toward the middle. He walked to the south side of the lake and threw the blue hoop into the water, and the water diminished even more this time. He walked to the west and from there he threw the yellow hoop. This time the water level was much lowered. He walked to the north and from there he threw the glittering hoop. Now the water was gone. The land was dry where the lake had been.

Killer-of-Enemies came back to the east now. He stooped and looked down. There he saw a ladder pointing upward. It was moss-covered and the moss and seaweed hung from it and made it look like a tipi. But Killer-of-Enemies knew it was a ladder.

There were frogs all around. These were the spies of the one who captured the people. But they could not see Killer-of-Enemies and therefore could not warn the old man of his approach. There were all sorts of water animals present to warn the old man, but none of them could see Killer-of-Enemies.

So Killer-of-Enemies went to the ladder. He lifted up the moss that lay over the top and it came off just like a blanket. He looked down. There, at the foot of the ladder, sat an old man. He was ridding himself of lice. He had his clothes off and had put them in the sun so that the lice would get too warm and would come off the clothes. The old man was looking down at the clothes. When a louse came up he picked it off.[1] This old man was He-Holds-in-the-Water.

The old woman, his wife, was there too. She said to him, "Why don't you look around and see whether anyone is watching you."

So he put his clothes back on.

Killer-of-Enemies started to descend the ladder. The two saw him now and called to him angrily, "What do you want? Why do you come here?"

"I have come here to take out those people you have imprisoned here. I want those people."

The old couple said, "No one comes to visit us. We have been by ourselves a long time. There are no people here."

Killer-of-Enemies had with him a fire drill. He took it out and began to work it. Black smoke arose from it so thickly that the old man began to choke.

He called to his wife, "I'm choking. You'd better give him that one old man we have here."

Then Killer-of-Enemies stopped. The smoke settled and it cleared. Then they brought out this old man from a hole.

Killer-of-Enemies asked him, "Are there other people there?"

"Yes, there are many others there. Four rooms are filled with people."

So Killer-of-Enemies used his drill again. Blue smoke arose and once more the old man nearly choked.

He spoke to his wife in the same way. "You'd better take out two people from each room, eight in all," he said.

These eight were brought out. Killer-of-Enemies asked them, "Are there more people down there?"

"Yes, a great many people are there still."

Then Killer-of-Enemies asked the old couple, "Are there others there?"

"No, that is all. We have no more here."

Then Killer-of-Enemies used his drill again. Yellow smoke poured out of the drill and the old man couldn't stand it. He spoke

[1] This method of ridding the clothes of lice was much used by the Indians. (Inf.)

to his wife again, and then both went and opened the doors and all the people came up.

Killer-of-Enemies watched. Of the last one who came out of each cave he asked, "Are there any more there?"

"No, I am the last." he was told.

Then he commanded those people whom he had saved. "Go up the ladder and wait for me there on top. Don't go to the village yet."

They all went away. Then he spoke to those two old people. "I want you two to get out of this place because you are so merciless."

They pleaded with him. They said, "Grandson, don't send us away. Let us stay here."

But Killer-of-Enemies said, "No, you must do what I say and leave this place."

But they did not want to depart and they refused to go. So Killer-of-Enemies began to use the last drill. The glittering smoke arose, they choked and were afraid, and they went up the ladder.

Now all were above at a dry place.

Killer-of-Enemies said to the old man, "You will have to go to Lake-with-Serrated-Flints[1] and stay there."

The old man said, "I want my wife to be with me. We must go together."

But Killer-of-Enemies told him, "No, you two are too fierce. You had better not go together."

So the old man had to go alone.

Now Killer-of-Enemies spoke to the woman. He said to her, "You must go to Big-Water-Lake."[2]

They both turned as they went and said, "If anyone drowns in the water it will be because of us." Then they both left.

So if anyone drowns today it is because of these two people.

Then Killer-of-Enemies turned to the people who had been freed and told them to come with him to the pueblo. He picked out six handsome young men and six pretty young girls.

He said, "I'm going to take these twelve into the kiva." So he took them in there. He stayed there with them for a few days. They lived together in there and married there.

Then Killer-of-Enemies spoke to the older people and the relatives of these twelve. He said, "I want to take these twelve and distribute them all over. They will be like a foundation so the earth will be strong."

He took them to the holy mountains and they lived on top of these thereafter. They were put on six mountains, a boy and a girl on each one. They are the guardians of the customs. If anyone cuts his hair or cuts a horse's mane, or does anything which he should not do, they send a voice to him and warn him, or even call him into the mountains to speak with him sometimes.

---

[1] A lake somewhere near Alamosa, Colorado. (Inf.)

[2] A lake near the first one. (Inf.)

Then Killer-of-Enemies went back to his grandmother, White-Painted Woman, in the west.

This is the last story of what Killer-of-Enemies did on earth. Now he is in the west with his grandmother.

Until Killer-of-Enemies was ready to leave man, man was not living as he does now. All was as though in a dream.[1] If the people had been as they are now they would have been frightened and would have run back into the hole of emergence. But when all the monsters were killed and all was at peace, Killer-of-Enemies gave people their own minds and habits, and they began to live as they do now.

Up to this time the animals had talked and acted just like man, but Killer-of-Enemies was afraid that if they were left that way, more monsters might be born. So he changed all the animals and made them different from men.

Then Killer-of-Enemies left. After he left evil and sorcery came into the lives of men. Some men, though they did not know it, had become contaminated from contact with the monsters. Some, though they were not aware of it, were carrying disease on their hands and gave it to other people.

16. THE DEPARTURE OF THE HACTCIN AND PROPHECIES CONCERNING THE END OF THE PRESENT WORLD

The Hactcin were still living here on earth. There was a place here on earth where the Hactcin lived. It was a big tipi. Later it changed to a big mountain, but that mountain still has the form of a tipi.[2] My father knows where it is. There are other Hactcin places. My father knows them all.

Although Killer-of-Enemies had given man human attributes and his own mind, all humans, up to this time, were just alike. All were of the same size and had the same appearance.

Then one day the Hactcin saw the sky burning. The whole sky was red; it looked as it does where there is a great forest fire. The Hactcin said they were going to go up and stop it.

They said, "Before we go we will make you all different. Some of you will be ugly after this, some will be good-looking, some will be intelligent and some stupid. Some of you will be fat, some thin; some tall, some short." They made the people all different. And they made them expert at various things. Some were made good hunters, some good basket makers.

Then the Hactcin went up in the air to put the fire out in the sky. They put out the fire but they never came back. It was the last time they were seen by men on earth.

---

[1] The informant compared their condition to that of a patient who has been given ether for an operation.

[2] A mountain south of Abiquiu called White Flint Mountain.

Rocks are alive, just as much alive as trees or plants or animals or pollen. They are the bones of the world. Without them there would be no firmness to the world. All would be sticky mud. Your bones are part of your life, part of your body. You must then consider rocks to be alive as much as you consider your bones to be alive. If you treat rocks well they won't injure you; but if you do not, some day you will fall on a rock and hurt yourself or be harmed by a rock in some way.

Everything has life, the rocks, trees, grass, and plants. In the beginning they could all speak like humans and all spoke one language, the language of the Jicarilla Apache. But the Hactcin did not like this condition. They did not think it right for all different things to use the same words. It was too monotonous to have everything speaking the same way. People get tired of it. We like to hear the birds sing sometimes and to hear the dogs bark and to see different things occurring. So, for the sake of variety, the Hactcin gave different voices and different ways to all things.

But all these objects have power, though they do not speak to us. The plants, rocks, fire, water, all are alive. They watch us and see our needs. They see when we have nothing to protect us, and it is then that they reveal themselves and speak to us. They take the form of man and say, "Why don't you use me to help your people?"

But they have two ways. Fire, for instance, if you treat it well, helps you; but if you abuse it, it will do you harm. And a horse is the same way. If you treat it badly, it does not forget. Some day you will have an accident, the horse will throw you. Or, if you buy a good horse it will die from some little accident, and you will be left without any.

The white man, when he sees pollen in the fields, thinks it is nothing. But the Indian knows that it is living. Sometimes it speaks to the Indian. Sometimes it says to him, "Why do you not pay attention to me? We are the path of life."

They say that some day when the earth is no longer good for sustaining life, the people will ascend to a third place above the present earth and sky, just as they came from the underworld. This ascent will be just like the emergence from the underworld to this world.

The sun and moon of this earth will go up as before. This place will be dark and then the people will follow the sun and moon. They say that some of the material out of which the earth was made is still left. They say that the Hactcin made this earth and that there is material left for two more earths and skies. This material is kept somewhere now, covered over by a mountain. White-Painted Woman is taking care of it. She watches over it. The old men know just which mountain it is and what it is called.

They say that the earth is to be destroyed twice, once by water,[1] and this has already happened. This happened after the people came up from below. That is why they know about it, I believe. There is a story about it, but I don't know much of it.

Sometime in the future the earth is to be destroyed for the second time, by fire. It will occur some day when Killer-of-Enemies comes back. He is going to take care of these Indians before it happens. He is going to send them up to a place above the present sky. The earth above to which we will go is not yet made. It will have to be made of the material which is being saved. When Killer-of-Enemies comes back, he will tell the people how it is to be done and how the trip is to be made.

B. THE FLOOD BEFORE THE EMERGENCE

Before the beginning of this world there were an old man and woman living. They were sitting on the earth. Dios came over and told them what was going to happen. He told them there was going to be rain for forty days and forty nights.[2]

"Only four mountains will stand above the water. You must get on top of one of these mountains," Dios said. "Do this if you want to be saved."

These two old people told the others, but they wouldn't believe it.

Tsisnatcin was one of the four mountains mentioned; Tsabidziłi was another, Becdiłgai another; the other is not known, but there were four. All the people were warned to get on top of these mountains.

They were told, "When you get up there, do not look at the flood. If you do you may turn to a fish, frog, or duck." The old people were warned of this and told the others.

"Don't look up at the sky. You may turn to a bird," they were told.

They told all this to the people, but the people laughed at these two and called them great liars.

The time came. It started to rain. It rained and rained. The people wanted it to stop, but it continued to rain. The people ran for the mountains. Most of them were drowned. A few got to the mountain tops. They shut their eyes and kept them that way.

They were told, "When you get hungry, think of what you want and Dios will feed you."

Some who didn't escape to the mountains but were in the water

---

[1] "I have heard my father and father-in-law speak of a time when the earth was covered with water. There was a big flood. The people got in a boat. That's all I have heard of the story. I didn't ask about it. They say the boat is somewhere in Old Mexico now." (Inf.)

[2] Cf. account of flood in Coyote cycle, p. 261.

and didn't want to drown, said, "I want to turn to a fish," and they did. Some said they wanted to turn to frogs and other water beings.

The people stayed there eighty days. Whoever opened his eyes was missed by the others later.

After eighty days the people were sitting in a circle with their heads down.

"Open your eyes," Dios said. "Get down to earth again."

Only a few were left. There were only twenty-four people left.

Dios said, "Now you are each going into a mountain. Go into twenty-four mountains. New people are coming and then you can come out again. I am going to make another people."

This happened before the Apache came up from the underworld. These people went into the mountains. They were told that these new people were coming on top of the world from below and were going to be here 2,000 years. Now only sixty-five years are left. They were told that when these people, the Jicarilla Apache, were getting small in numbers, the earth would be destroyed again.

Dios told the survivors, "After those Apache come, when they grow few in numbers, there will be hard times. There will be starvation. Other people will come and these others will increase. But the world will be destroyed just the same."

Now there are many Mexicans and Americans, but just let them grow. They can't stop it, for it is the business of Dios.

When the flood was on the earth there were eight people who traveled with their eyes; they looked at the place where they wanted to go, and at once they were there. They traveled back and forth like this. The twenty-four survivors went into the mountains.

Then the Jicarilla Apache came from the underworld. They didn't know what had happened before this. The people came up and traveled all around the world. Then the people began to separate.

Dios told these eight people who could travel with their eyes, "Now you had better go back in the mountains."

These eight were separate from the twenty-four in the other mountains. These eight were among the Apache for a while. They told the Apache of what had happened before. That is why the Apache know this story. Four of the eight went to Wide Grass, a mountain. It is near Antonito, south of Antonito. Red Mountain was the other mountain. It is near the Rio Grande, south of Wide Grass Mountain. Four went in there.

Dios told them, "You must come back when the earth is destroyed again."

At the end of the world these people who travel with their eyes are going to come back and go to all directions and see what is happening in the east, south, west, and north. For the telephone and telegraph are not going to be here any more. They are all going to burn. Next time the earth will be destroyed by fire. All are going to be destroyed. Maybe another world will be made; I don't know.

At Taos where there used to be a lake there is now some soft ground. There have been two fires there. When four fires have occurred there, the earth is going to be destroyed. The first time there was a fire at that place the Pueblos went and dug a ditch to it and tried to put it out with water, but the water burned like oil. Finally they called upon an old Apache man and woman. The man's name was Bánàn; the woman's name I do not know. They don't say how these two put out the fire, but they did put it out.

The second time it burned I was alive. I saw it from a distance. An old Apache who just died a while back stopped the fire. It will burn twice more. The fourth time no one will be able to stop it. The fire is going to start there and burn all over the world.

That is all they say about this.

C. BEAR DANCE STORIES

1. THE GIRL WHO TURNED TO BEAR

This story is about some children who were playing in an arroyo. You know that children have a good time when they play there. They played one game. After they got tired of that they played another.

One of these children was a little girl. She was digging in the bank of the arroyo. She dug a hole big enough for her to enter. The other children were waiting on the opposite side of the arroyo. They couldn't see her. After a while she finished digging the hole and called to the other children. They came around and she told them what to play next. She told them what the game was going to be.

She said, "We'll play Bear next." She went in the hole then.

The children knew the "bear" was in the hole. They came to the door and called to the "bear" to come out. When she heard someone at the door the little girl ran out and chased them all around. It was just in play as yet. She was still a girl. That was the first time she ran out.

When the children had all run away she went back to the hole. This first time she had caught no one. The children thought this game was great fun.

For the second time the children crowded around the hole and called to her, "We are here." She came running out again. This time her arms from the elbows to the fingers and her feet from the knees to the toes had changed. They were covered with bear fur. This time she nearly caught one of the children.

But the children did not notice that her feet and hands had become the paws of a bear. Once more she went back in the hole. The children gathered around and called to her to come out again.

This time when she ran out, her entire body, all but her head, was in the form of a bear. Her head was still that of a little girl. She reared up just as a bear does. She faced the east, the south, the west, and the north in turn. After she had faced the north she started to chase the children, but she felt pity for them and didn't want to hurt any, for her head and mind were still those of a little girl. So she didn't catch anyone that time either.

The children had not noticed that she was turning to a bear. They were having a good time. They thought it was still a game.

This girl who was turning to a bear had a younger sister who was one of that group of children. This all happened away from the camps and the older people didn't know what these children were doing.

Now the girl who was turning to a bear went back into the hole. The other children came back and stood around the entrance and called out to her as before.

For the fourth time she ran after them. This time she was a real bear, a female bear. She reared up as the bear does and stood first to the east and then faced south, west, and north in turn. But now she was of a different mind. She chased the children and killed all of them except her sister. Her sister ran ahead so she couldn't catch her.

The little sister ran to the camps and told the people, "My sister has become a bear and you must all run for your lives!"

Some believed it; others did not. Some began to run for their lives; some just didn't pay any attention to what the little girl said. But the bear came running up and those who had stayed behind were killed.

The little girl, the little sister, was hiding in her tipi. She found a big burden basket and covered herself with it.

The bear ran all over. It could see no one. But then the bear saw this basket move and turned it over. There was the little girl beneath.[1]

The little girl started to cry. "You must not kill me. You know I am your little sister. You must not kill me. You must feel compassion and spare my life. I will help you. You can take me to your home and I will help you."

So the bear spared the sister. She took her to that hole she had dug. She made it bigger and they stayed there. The little sister became her servant.

The bear went back and took the heads of those she had killed, cleaned the skulls out, and used them for water buckets. She made the little girl use them and fill all of them with water.

The little girl knew that her father and five other men had been out hunting when the killing took place and were still unaware of what had happened. She wanted to save these men and to warn her father.

The bear was in the hole and the little sister tried hard to keep the

[1] This furnishes another reason for the use of the basket drum in the bear dance.

bear from coming out and seeing these six hunters. She was bringing much food and water and serving the bear in every way, making it comfortable so that it wouldn't come out of the hole.

Four days passed like this. Then the little girl saw these hunters coming from a great distance. The little girl was very much frightened. She peeked into the hole. The bear was sleeping at this time.

She started to run then and went to meet those who were coming. She met them and told them not to approach that place. She told them all that had happened; she told them what had become of her sister and all the others.

They were all frightened. They didn't know what to do. They all stood together and had a council. Then the father spoke to the girl and told her, "You must go and bring a great deal of wood and pile it all around the hole. When you have a great quantity of it there, come back and tell us."

The little girl went and did as she was told. The hunters stayed where they were and ate some of the meat they had brought back from the hunt.

Meanwhile the bear was sleeping and was not aware of what was going on.

They all decided on a way to kill that bear. The hunters had brought back with them the peritoneum of a deer. They were all resolute now.

They told the little girl, "You must set fire to that wood you have placed around the cave."

They put the peritoneum in the fire. It flared up. Then they all shouted. The bear woke up and started to run out. As she ran out they threw the flaming fat over the bear's face. She could not see and didn't know which way to go. She backed up into the hole again. She tried to come out but she couldn't, for the fire was raging now.

They covered the mouth of the cave with burning brush. They left the fire there. They didn't know whether the bear was dead or not but they started to run to the east for their lives. They ran up to the top of a big mountain — Holy Mountain they call it. They got on top. They saw no one around. Others had run away from the bear and escaped, but these six men didn't know where they were.

They started to pray. They asked for help and a way to get up in the sky. Then the wind helped them. It brought a cloud. They all went into the cloud. There were the six hunters and the little girl, seven in all.[1]

The wind started to blow the cloud to the east, for the wind knows the shortest way to get up in the sky. So in this way they

---

[1] In the bear dance ceremony the households of the six men and the girl are depicted by seven tipis in a ground drawing.

reached the sky. They found a place there on top. They all became stars. They became the seven stars that rise in the east.

When they started from the east, Wind told them, "You have grandmothers in the west, White-Shell Woman and White-Painted Woman. Go there."

These seven stars are the Pleiades. They are overhead at dark in winter. The Indians say that when you can put your head up and this constellation points to your Adam's apple at dusk, it is winter. That constellation moves from east to west.

Some day, when only six of these stars will be visible, it will be a sign that the bear is going to be the enemy of man again.

From this story the Jicarilla give advice to children. They tell them, "You must not dig a hole and play Bear or you might turn to a bear yourself."

2. BEAR DANCE STORY

At the time when the bear was killing the people and the people were running away, someone lost a baby and the bear took that baby. The bear fathered the child and it grew up. It was a boy. When he had come to the age of manhood, this boy returned to his mother.

The woman did not know what had happened to her child. She had forgotten all about him. It was four years after the boy had been lost that he returned. Upon his return he tried to tell his mother about it.

The boy called to the woman and called her mother, but she said, "No, you are not my child."

Then the boy told his mother what had happened. He proved that he was her child. Then his mother was very happy and fondled her boy.

The boy said to his mother, "I know all who are relatives to me."

The boy's body was black like a Negro's.

This boy asked the people, "Do any of you know how to hold a dance, how to have a good time?"

The people said, "We don't know anything about a dance."

The boy told them, "Make a corral. I'll show you how to dance."

So all the men cut brush and made a corral the same size as the one used for the ceremony today. That is why the men come and dance for the ceremony.

At first the people did not know how to dance correctly. They executed the wrong steps and were all mixed up. Therefore this bear boy had to dance by himself and show them how to do it. That is why the chief singer dances by himself in the doorway.[1] He takes the part of the bear boy. So that is how the people first learned to do that dance.

---

[1] For another explanation of the dancing the chief singer does in the doorway of the ceremonial structure see p. 32.

While this boy was growing up with the bear, Bear had taught him how to do all this. Bear told him how to make the corral and arrange the dancers. He also told him that the tipi was to be divided into two parts, one the south side which is the snake's side, the other, the north side, which is the bear's side. If a patient has snake sickness, that is, if his feet are swollen, he should sit on the snake's side. If he is too fat and can't sleep well at night, he has bear sickness and he should sit on the bear's side. When the patients sit on the designs, whatever is the matter with them shows up and is known to the chief singer.

The bear gave the boy all the medicine which is used today in the ceremony to make the patient recover. And the bear gave the boy all the songs and all the directions for singing them.

D. THE PEOPLE WHO WENT TO THE NORTH[1]

To the north there is no light, nothing but darkness and ice. There were four tipis of people, four families who ran away from the others. They did so right after the emergence, when the people were going around the world. They went north and continued until they came to the place where there was very little light; it was just like morning light. They lived there for a long time, until all the older people had died and a new generation had taken their places.

The new generation knew nothing of the sun, nothing of the moon. The old people had not told the children stories of the light and the sun, for they thought that if they told the younger people of this, they would want to see it and would go back. So they told other stories but not these. They covered up knowledge of the sun and of light.

The children grew up to manhood and womanhood.

One time four of these young people began to travel. The reason why the sun had not come to the place where they were living was that this place was down in a hollow. In their travels these four climbed, and then to the south they saw some light. They walked for four days until they got to the place where the light shone.

They sat there and watched the sun. They stayed there until the next day. They wondered at it, for they had never seen it before.

As they came south they took off more and more of their heavy clothing, for it was getting too hot. They just left the clothes at the place where they took them off.

The first time they peeped over the rim and saw the sun they were afraid. They said, "That is a monster with a big eye." They took the sun for the eye of a monster. But after watching a while they realized it was just light. Then they went to the west until dark came. They stayed there over night.

[1] The events which form the burden of this story are mentioned in the origin myth, p. 48.

At dawn they saw the morning glow. They wondered what it meant. They looked and looked at it. They were very eager to see what was going on in this world. And after a while they saw the light of the sun on the top of the mountain. Again they were all afraid. They ran to each other and held each other in fear. Then the sun rose in the east. It was all strange to them. They all lay down so that the monster could not see them. All day they watched the sun. As before they saw it go across the sky and to the west.

Night came again. Now they were sure. They said, "Let's go back and tell the people that we made the sun."

So after these two days and nights they started back. They arrived home in four days.

When they got home they told the chiefs to bring all the people together.

When all were assembled they said, "We have made light."

The other people didn't know what light was or what they meant.

They told a story of how they made the sun. Before they had started for home they had talked the story over. One had said, "What shall we tell the people?"

"Let us tell them that we made a round light," another said.

So this one said, "I will tell the people, 'The first time you see the light we made you are going to be frightened.'"

And the other said, "Yes, that's good. Let's all tell it one way."

So when they got back they gathered all the people together and told the story they had agreed on. The chiefs, when they heard it, were very eager to see what they had made.

So twelve of the best known men decided to travel first and see it. They traveled four days. On the way they, too, had to take off some clothes every day.

They arrived there. It was about noon when they got there and the light was high in the sky.

"Where is the place you made the sun?" they asked after they had seen it.

"Over here." The four men took them to a smooth place where they had traced a round figure. They had traced a nose, eyes, and mouth on it and made it just like a head.

"How did you do it?"

"We made it here and then held it to the east and then placed it up in the sky. It will go right to the west."

So they waited and watched. And the four showed the others how the sun was setting in the west as they had said it would.

The end of the day drew near. Night came. They all stayed there. The four who claimed to have made the sun told the others, "You must sleep only to the middle of the night and then wake up."

So they all slept until the middle of the night. Then they arose and waited for the sunrise. At dawn the morning glow shone faintly at first.

The four who knew of it said, "Look on top of that mountain and you will see the first light."

The light hit the mountain and came down. It came down and shone all over. So they all stayed there till the sun went down again.

Again they acted in the same way. They slept for part of the night and then rose to see the sunrise.

They waited until the sun came out and then the twelve who had come to investigate the claims of those four said, "Yes, now we believe you."

So all of them went back. It took them four days. On the way they gathered up the clothes they had left. They told all the people. Half of them believed it and half did not. Those who believed it wanted to go to the place where the light was to be seen and started the journey. Those who did not believe it decided to stay where they were.

So those who started the journey traveled four days, and came to this part of the world again.

They stopped at the place where the others had stopped and saw the tracing on the ground. They watched the rising and setting of the sun from this place. Then they started to travel around. They didn't know the best place to go.

As they traveled around they came on groups of the Apache. With these groups they would stop, but when they were to move on, one family would stay behind. This continued until none were left to travel on any more. They were all divided up now. So the people were mixed again.

That is the way the people are now. Sometimes a Navaho comes here and likes it and stays, and sometimes a Jicarilla goes to the Navaho Reservation for a visit but finds a good place and stays there. That's how it started.

The place where the people lived in the north is not under ground; it is on top of the ground, but in a hollow.

E. WHEN TANAGER AND ROBIN WERE CHIEFS[1]

When the world was new Turkey and Buzzard were not allowed to speak to the people, to become chiefs. They lied all the time. That is why they became bald. And the Apache now believe that if a man lies all the time he will lose the hair from the crown of his head.

All the people on the earth came together for a big meeting. They were going to pick out the one who would be their chief. At that time the people had no leader; the people were under no control at all. But they didn't wish it to be this way. They wanted to select a chief.

---

[1] For a brief comment on the burden of this story see Goddard, p. 237.

When the people were together, Tanager and Robin began talking to the people, and the people liked what they said and listened to them. And so these two were selected to lead the people. All the people admired the way they talked and gave advice.[1]

Tanager stood up in the center of all the people. Tanager said, "You people are all on top of the world and all of you are gathered together. I am going to ask my power to give me permission to lead you."

Robin too stood up and spoke to the people. "Now I am going to speak to all you people who are meeting under the sky and on top of this world. All you people want me to be your leader, for I have never had trouble with others and all people like me. I am going to ask my power to give me permission to talk to you always and lead you. I will not talk much today. In four days from now let us all meet again. I am going to find out what my power has to say about it."

Tanager stood up again and spoke. He said, "I'm going to ask my power whether he gives consent, for he is the leader of the sky, of summer, and of the water. Now let us all go home. But we must meet again in four days. When we come together again we will find out what the power says, for you people have already asked us to be your chiefs."

When this was told to the people most of them understood. But some were busy talking and did not hear aright. Some were having arguments of their own and did not listen. So some of them gathered again the next day at that place instead of waiting the four days.

The robin told these people, "Go home. Come back in three days."

But some of them still did not understand and came in before the appointed time again.

"All of you go home again and come back in two days," Robin told them.

The third day some more people came, though it was a day early.

They said, "We want to find out what is going on and what business is being undertaken."

Robin told them, "Tomorrow is the day. Come tomorrow and we will have the meeting then."

Some of the people didn't trust the tanager and robin. They said, "Perhaps those two are lying to us."

When the sun arose on the fourth day, the people streamed to the place. The trails were crowded. They continued to come all morning.

Tanager and Robin said to the people, "After the noon meal we will speak to you all. We will tell you what we are going to do."

After all had eaten Tanager and Robin stood up. They said, "Now listen everyone. Our powers have given us consent to lead.

[1] This passage summarizes attributes which the Jicarilla chief is expected to show: willingness to counsel others and ability to give sound advice.

Our powers said that the people should not war or fight on this earth. Our powers want us two to be the chiefs for you. We are going to be the chiefs from this time on for you people who like us.

"Our powers say they are going to give each of us a way to live on this world. You will learn and must remember which is your food too.

"Power told us that he will give a way of life to all who fly in the air too. Power will give consent to the way each of us must live, all the birds and animals, all under the sky; and all who depend on the seasons and live in the waters. At harvest time, in summer, there will be many fruits."

Tanager said, "Power is going to give water for our lives, because we need it for drinking and it is necessary so the fruits and plants will grow. That is about all we have learned up to now. But in four days we shall have to meet again."

All the people were glad to hear what the two leaders had to say. "From this time we shall have a good time in this world," they said.

The people did not know how these leaders would rule. So they wanted to meet again at once. They wanted to learn more about how to live and what to eat. The very next day they gathered. But again they had to be sent away. The people were in a great hurry, and it seemed to them that the time was going very slowly.

On the fourth day there was a big gathering again. All morning the people came. There were so many that they covered a great expanse. Shortly after noon they were ready to start the meeting. All the people were quiet.

Tanager was first to speak. He said to the people, "Listen, everyone! Now I am your leader."

There were so many people that Tanager's words could not be heard by those furthest away, and so what he said was carried to the ones at a distance by word of mouth; one told another.

"I am the leader of those on this world. I am the leader of all you people. You must obey me. Those under the sky must listen to me also. I am the leader for the summer time, the time when all the fruits grow ripe. And I am the leader for those who live in the water too, for the water raises the plants in summer."

Now it was Robin's turn to speak. "All you people gathered here must listen to me. I am a leader of this world and all the people must obey me. All under the sky must obey me. I also am a leader for the summer when everything grows ripe. And I am the leader for those who live in the water. People use the water for life and the water is necessary that the plants may bloom and all become ripe."

Tanager stood up and raised his hand. "You have all heard our words. I ask you to consider what we have said and tell us what you think of it."

The people talked for about fifteen minutes among themselves.

Then all had agreed that they were in favor of what Tanager had said.

Robin arose now to speak again. "I want everyone to listen," he said. "Go back home now, but in four days we shall meet again."

All the people now knew that Tanager and Robin had been selected as the leaders. Before that time the people knew nothing about chiefs.

After four days the people met again. They all came to the place. After noon the meeting started again.

Tanager stood up and said, "Now listen to me. I am the leader of all the men, women, and children so that you will have long life. That is the way I am the leader for you people. The children will grow up without trouble and everything will go well in summer. To bring these things to pass I am the chief for you people. I am the leader in those things.

"You people must tell my words to one another. Spread my words to all so that all under the sky will recognize that I am the leader. And then the people under the sky will all have long life. I am a leader for the things of the summer season. I make everything ripen so that people will have food to eat as long as they live. I make everything productive in summer. Everyone will like the summer. The people will never be hungry as long as I lead them. In the same way I am the leader for the people in the water. In summer it rains and feeds the streams, lakes, and rivers where they live and it gives them long life too."

Now the robin stood up and spoke. He said, "I am the chief of you people now also. You must obey me and do whatever I say. Then the men, women, and children will be living in a good way, without fighting or war, and with plenty to eat and to use. I am the leader for all under the sky. I make it so all of them have a long life. I am the leader for the summer too. I make everything ripen so the people may live well. That is the way I am leader for you people. I am also leader for the people of the water, giving them long life. I bring rain, I wet the ground so everything will grow. That is about all. Now you people may go home. And in four days you must all meet here again. It will be the last time. This is the last word I have to tell you now. Remember that you must all meet here again in four days."

In four days the people came for the meeting once more. They all knew who their chiefs were. They were all there. They came in the morning. They started the meeting a little after noon as before.

Tanager spoke.[1] "The land around every mountain stream is going to be peopled by some of you. Those of you who like the mountain streams are to live there, for on those high mountains there will be wild game which is necessary for your living. The

[1] What follows is a rather accurate summary of the principal uses to which the Jicarilla put the animals and wild plants most familiar to them.

deer has to be used for life. You must kill the deer, skin it, and eat the meat. The cords and sinews from the legs are to be used for sewing and for making a bow-string too. The sinew of the back must be used for sewing and for the bow also. The fur of the deer skin must be taken off and the skin must be tanned soft by the women. And the women must make buckskin moccasins and dresses too.

"The elk must be killed and the hide removed. The women must remove the fur, tan the skin, and make a sack out of it. The stomach of the elk must be cleaned, saved, and dried. When a baby has stomach trouble, boil a little of it and give the child some of the water it has been boiled in. It is a good medicine for the child when he has diarrhea too. Men and women may use it also. The canine teeth will be prized by the people too. And the horns of the elk will serve the people as war clubs. The horn must be tied to the wrist and used for this purpose. They will cut off one prong for this.

"Anyone who kills a mountain sheep on the top of a cliff must always place it so the legs are up. The mountain sheep, used in this way, will be medicine for the Indian people. His toes must be cut off and kept. When the people have stiff necks this toe will be warmed and put on the back of the neck of the patient, and he will recover quickly.

"When you kill the mountain sheep you must take the skin off and use the meat. And sometimes the people will use the mountain sheep horns. They must be boiled and then stretched out to make bows. Good bows will come from these. If the people have no other rope, when they kill the mountain sheep they can make rope from his entrails.

"And the buffalo must be killed and the meat used for food. Its meat has a good taste. Do not waste the sinew because it must always be used for sewing and for bow and arrows. The long hair on the top of the head of the buffalo must always be saved and twisted to make a strong rope. And the tail must be used too. The woman must soften the hides and make blankets out of them. If the children have blankets of three good buffalo hides they will never get cold. At night use the robes with the fur side down. The soft fur is like a warm fire that keeps one comfortable.

"And the people will kill the mountain-lion. They will use the meat, for it has a good taste. The mountain-lion's skin will be valuable to use for making quivers. The claws of the mountain-lion must be taken off and a necklace made of them.

"The people will sometimes kill the wolf and take the skin off. The wolf skin must be tanned. Four of them tanned and sewed together will make a robe the size of a buffalo hide.

"The hide of the cottontail rabbit must be taken off and used. The man who kills one must always cut off the four paws. These will be thrown away. The meat from the head of the rabbit, if it is eaten, will draw smoke. Whenever anyone who has eaten rabbit head sits near a fire, the smoke will come towards him. The tail of the rabbit is to be used for a horse that is too wild. If the rabbit tail is tied to the horse's tail, the horse will not be so wild, but will become tame. The rabbit fur will be used for mittens in winter. The top will be made of buckskin and the fur will be put inside. The leg bone of the cottontail will be used to decorate buckskin, and beads will be put on it. The people can eat the rabbit's flesh. The leg bones may be broken and strung to make necklaces too. Sometimes it will take the bones of four rabbits to make such a necklace.

"You must kill the ground squirrel. The meat must be put in the fire place with many ashes and cooked. It will taste just like buffalo meat. The end of the tail must be cut off and tied to the left or right shoulder of a child so he will not get hurt.

"If the wildcat is killed, remove its hide. The women must tan that skin until it is very soft and use it to keep the baby warm." Tanager did not tell the people to use the wildcat meat. "The tail of the wildcat must be used as a medicine for piles. The tail of the wildcat must be burned under the anus and the smoke made to enter the anus. The claws of the wildcat must be taken off and a necklace made of them for the children.

"The jack-rabbit will also be useful. He must be killed and his skin taken off. The people will use the meat. The people will cut off the black tip of the jack-rabbit's ear. If someone has a pain over the heart, these tips must be burned and the person must inhale this smoke. In that way the pain will be cured. The fur of the jack-rabbit will be used as a mat for the children to sit on. And the people will use the paw; they will put it in buckskin and bead the buckskin. The paws will be tied together to make an attractive necklace. The tail will be used for wild horses, tied to their tails to make them tame. The tail can be used in the same way to cure a horse of bucking.

"Now all you people keep in mind what I have told you. Remember the way of life I have given you and the animals I have told you to use. Be sure to use them as I have directed."

After a while Robin stood. "It is my turn now," he said. "When autumn is near and the foods are ripening, the people must go to hunt food. When someone sees prickly pears, he must twist them off, rub them with grass to remove the thorns, and eat them. This fruit will be sweet and good to eat.

"When yucca fruit ripens the people must gather it. When this fruit is ripe, soft, and sweet, it may be eaten without being cooked. You must gather a great quantity of it and bring it home. All the seeds must be taken out. The fruit must be split and set out in the sun to dry. Then it must be kept for the winter. The pulp can be ground, boiled, heaped together, and kept as a winter food for the children.

When the people gather many choke-cherries, they must grind the fruit, spread it out on a hide, and let it dry. When these choke-cherries are dark and ripe they should be gathered. After the fruit is gathered it can be pressed together, fresh, into a cake and dried in the sun also. Then the people can use it in the winter. Let them put it in the water and soften it and then eat it.

"And the wild plum will be a food for the people too. Let them gather the plums when they are very ripe and spread them out in the sun. When the fruit is very dry, it may be put in sacks. When the cold weather comes and the people are having hard times, these plums can be boiled up and used.

"If service berries are found, the people should gather them in great quantities and dry them. They are good to eat fresh, but they can also be dried and used for the winter.

"About July the wild currants are ready. When they are ripe they may be eaten.

"There is another fruit called the gooseberry which is sweet and good to eat.

"In the mountains are red raspberries. Use them when they become dark and ripe.

"In summer the strawberries ripen and then the people must gather these.

"The fruit of the staff-tree will be used too. These berries are so small that they are hard to gather. But they are sweet and good to eat and are always found on the mountains. These, too, can be caked and saved for winter.

"The wild grapes must be picked. They are also sweet to eat.

"And bearberry leaves will be good for smoking. The berry, a red one, will be ground up with corn and boiled with it."

These were the foods that Robin told the people about. "Live upon these things," he told them. "Listen to what I say and you will eat well."

Tanager's turn came now. He stood up and said, "The one who is my power told me to give you all these things to use while you are upon this earth. Then you will have long life and will not be sick.

"About June the pine tree has bark ready for you. That is good food too. Take oak wood and make the end flat and thin like a knife. With this tool scrape off the inside of the bark and eat it raw. Mountain mahogany is also a good wood to use for making this instrument to scrape the sweet part from the bark.

"Cow-parsnip is a plant good to eat. Its leaf is to be boiled and eaten.

"Osha, a plant that grows on the high hills, should be gathered and its leaves boiled and eaten. The leaves are good to eat and the roots are good for medicine. Mix the root with tobacco for smoking if you have a headache. If you have a long way to go and your legs are very tired, use the leaf of osha for smoking. It makes you feel strong and fresh again. Drink water in which the root has been boiled to cure a cough and fever.

"There is a sunflower plant that grows out in the fields. Its leaf should be boiled. Hit this plant to make the seeds fall out; then grind these seeds and use them for bread.

"Thimbleberry plants with wide leaves grow on the mountains. The berries of this plant are also to be eaten."

Then Robin spoke again. "The bee plant is a good food too," he said. "And the wild onions will be good for you to eat. Roast them in the fire place, or boil them. Some wild onions are ready in April. The children will like them and will dig them out.

"Wild potatoes will be food for the Indians too. Some will be ready about May. They will ripen early.

"The buffalo berry will be found along the banks of every river where there are many cottonwood trees, and the people will eat these too.

"The aspen will also be good for food. Use the inside of the bark which has a sweet taste.

"There is another gooseberry, one with a wide leaf and red berries. The leaves will be used for smoking tobacco. There are two kinds of gooseberry, a smaller one as well.

"The cottonwood bark will be good to eat, just as aspen and pine bark are.

"The juniper berries will be good mixed with piñon nuts."

Robin spoke now and told the people, "Use grouse, too, for a food, all the different kinds. Use the turkey also." Those were the foods Robin told the people to use.

"Go home now and in four days all come together and we will have another meeting," he told them.

So the people returned home. They were very much pleased, for they had had plenty of food given to them. "We have good chiefs," they said. All the people now knew and trusted their chiefs.

They met again in four days. They wanted to know what the chiefs had to say next. Many were around on all sides. Shortly after noon they started again.

Tanager stood up. "It is my turn to speak to you people," he said. "Today we are having an important meeting. All you people must listen closely." Tanager took his time and spoke to the people. He wanted all to hear his words.

"Now here I am standing before you. Look at me, all of you. After this the ones who obey me and believe me will have a good way of life and a long life. My head is red. Look at me. That means good luck. In the fall when everything is getting red, when the leaves are getting red, remember the color of my head. The color of my head stands for the reddening of the leaves in the autumn. My body is yellow. In the fall some leaves turn yellow. In the evening you see red clouds in the sky. They are made of the red of my head. The yellow clouds are made of the yellow of my body.

"In the summer you see many red leaves. The red of my head is made from them. When the blossoms of the plants are yellow, I take that yellow to make my body as it is.

"On the edge of the rivers you see reddish clay. I use this for the red of my head. And there is yellow clay there which I also use. All you people know me by this.

"Sometimes the weather is good for a long time. Sometimes it rains steadily. When it rains like this you will know I am causing it so there will be plenty of growing things at harvest time.

"Now all you people must help with your minds. Help me to make rain, so that plants will grow, so pollen will be plentiful and food abundant. In the summer after a rain, the children must always be happy."[1] Tanager stopped at this point and Robin began to talk.

Robin stood up. "All you people must listen. It is my turn to speak now. All you people look at me. The mist that hangs over a canyon after the rain is the white under my eye. My breast is made from the red and yellow clouds that show in the east. And those from the west I have used in the same way. You all know me. I am Robin.

"When you hear me sing, then you will know that all on this world will have a good time and that the people will enjoy long life. That is all I have to say."

Tanager said to the people, "You people must separate into tribes and live to the north, south, east, and west. Each group must have its own leader.

"Always you people must remember what I have told you. And remember the way you are to live. Even after I grow old and die, remember how you are to live. The world belongs to all you people. You must separate and settle wherever you wish, wherever you think you have found a good place. All you people who continue to believe in me will have good luck, plenty of food, and a good time as long as you live."

It was Robin's turn now. "When you hear me sing," he said, "all is well. You will know then that there will be enough rain in the summer and that food will be plentiful.[2] Then you people will have long life. This world will belong to the Indians. Each tribe will have a different language. Some will be called Pueblo, some Navaho, some Mescalero Apache, and some Jicarilla Apache."[3]

---

[1] Good or evil thoughts are considered by the Jicarilla to have decided influence on external events. Those who attend ceremonies are often adjured to have none but kindly and holy thoughts, that the purpose of the rite may not be hindered.

[2] At another time the informant said, "If we see those two birds (the tanager and the robin) singing close to us we are happy, for we know that these birds are calling for rain. These birds have not been singing around here for the last four years. That is why this world is getting so dry."

[3] For another explanation of the origin of linguistic differentiation see the origin myth.

The people all spoke one language up to this time. Now they all have different languages as a result of their separation. Tanager told the people to separate. Robin said that if they separated they must speak different languages. That is why every tribe on this earth has its own leaders.

"That is about the end of what I have to tell you people. Now all look at me. I am kind to everyone. I never did harm to the people. I never lied to them. If I had lied, I would have a bald head."[1] That is all Tanager said.

Robin said, "What Tanager said is true. I am chief for you people. My head is not bald either. After you people separate, if your leaders lie to you they will become bald. That is all we have to say."

This took place at the time when the world was new. This happened before Blue Jay gave the people the way to live.[2]

F. THE CONTEST BETWEEN KILLER-OF-ENEMIES AND ONE-WHO-WINS

When everything on earth was settled One-Who-Wins played hoop and pole with the people. The rattlesnake was his pole. Every time he played a game he tied a strip of narrow yucca around his head for a head band. He took mud that adhered to the stones of the ant hills and rubbed it on his hands before he played.[3] His opponents would become feverish, and he always won.

This gambler went all over the world. He played with men who knew how to play the game well, but he was always ahead. He won everything from those who knew how to play the game. He wanted to be the leader of the earth, sky, waters, and seasons. He wanted to be just like White Hactcin.

Even those who had power could not avail against him, for his pole of rattlesnake and his ability to give the fever were stronger. Every day he won more. The people who lost everything stood aside and others came. He won even the moccasins and clothes of the people.

---

[1] This remark is directed at Turkey and Buzzard, who tried to usurp leadership and became bald in consequence. Turkey plays a dual role in Jicarilla myths. Birds were not esteemed as food by the Jicarilla anciently, and many Jicarilla will not now eat fowls, turkeys included. Moreover, Turkey is identified with the untruthful birds because of its bald head. The late association of Turkey with agriculture and the development of a Jicarilla corn complex of some importance altered this markedly, and it will be noted that in the stories of the major rites Turkey is treated with the greatest respect.

[2] This is a reference to a long story, not included in this collection, wherein Blue Jay is empowered to give the way of life to all the birds and animals. For a shorter tale which carries out the same pattern see p. 345.

[3] Ant hills can be places of danger for the Jicarilla. Ants retaliate by giving bladder stones to those who molest their homes and also by stinging.

So the people who had lost the game came together. They talked it over. They asked, "How is it that this man is always ahead?"

One said, "I know a ceremony for this game, but it seems to have no power against this man."

There were only a few people left who had not lost everything by playing against him. The people did not like it. Each day someone else tried to win things back, but One-Who-Wins always came out ahead.

There were four left who knew how to play this hoop and pole game and who had not yet opposed him.

Some said, "Let us hide the ant hills and the yucca from him. Those are the things he always uses."

These people had power and they caused these things to disappear, but he had some at his home and they could not get these away from him. So he kept his power. He worked with the yucca, for it has a sharp point and stings and poisons one where it hits. The ants, too, bite one, and it stings where they bite.

Now there were only two men left to play against him. The people felt sad.

Killer-of-Enemies knew about it. He said, "Let him beat those two. I'll come down and play with him."

Then Killer-of-Enemies made a hoop. As he made each notch he called its name. He made it of oak. Then Killer-of-Enemies made the pole. He called the names of the incised rings from the butt to the tip. Then he made the first of the notches. "They will not count in the score," he said. Then he made another and called it "straight bottom." Then he made four notches and said, "They will be called 'lying knotted'." He made another band and called it "straight head."[1]

He took another stick. He shaved thin the parts of the two sticks at the ends where they were to fasten together and then he fitted them and tied the place four times with sinew. He tied on another piece in like manner. This third piece was not very long, about two feet long. He looked at the three. They did not look right. So he put on another piece, fitting it in the same manner. That made four pieces of which the pole was made.[2]

Then Killer-of-Enemies made another pole the same way. When these two were done, he painted the two notched places of the first one red. The second pole he colored a little black at the notches. He stood them erect. The poles were just right. He turned them to the east and they were just right. He turned them to the west and they were just right.

He laid the poles against a tree. He hung the hoop on the branch of a tree.

---

[1] These are translations of names now given to the encised rings of the pole.

[2] The description is a summary of the proper way to make the pole for the Jicarilla hoop and pole game.

Meanwhile one more of the men had lost to the gambler. One more contestant was left. This one now began to play. By the time the sun set One-Who-Wins had beaten him too and had won from all the men. He had won all their possessions. While the last one played, Killer-of-Enemies was making ready his hoop and pole.

Then Killer-of-Enemies sent a messenger to the gambler, "Tell him one is still left and is coming to play with him."

The next morning Killer-of-Enemies measured the distance of the sun from the horizon. The sun was four fingers above the horizon,[1] and so Killer-of-Enemies put red paint on his face at the chin, forehead, and cheeks, and on his body at the shoulders, sides, and legs. He rubbed the poles and hoop with it too. On the poles he put just a little; he merely touched it to the poles.

Then he went over to the hoop and pole grounds.

The gambler said, "Did you come to play with me?"

"Yes, I am the last of those you have not beaten, so I have come to play with you."

The yucca was already tied around the gambler's head.

"You have beaten people all over the world. Now let us play with my own hoop and poles," Killer-of-Enemies said.

"No, let us play with mine," said One-Who-Wins.

Killer-of-Enemies answered, "No, you have won from everyone. Why are you afraid? Let us play with my set this time."

One-Who-Wins still insisted, "We must play with mine."

Killer-of-Enemies replied, "No, you have won from all the people with yours. This time it must be with mine." This was the third time they had thus argued.

One-Who-Wins still wanted to play with his set.

Killer-of-Enemies said, "You had better not talk so much about this game. You always win. Why do you argue? I'm the last one. Let us play."

So One-Who-Wins agreed. "All right." He motioned with his poles four times and threw them. They were snakes and they went into a hole and disappeared.

Then One-Who-Wins picked up the grey pole and scooped up some dirt; he spat on it four times and rubbed it four times on the pole from butt to tip.

While he was doing this, Killer-of-Enemies prayed in his mind. He said, "Let him score only four or six; let him score only small amounts or nothing at all."

Killer-of-Enemies said, "How many shall we set for the winning score?"

"Five hundred."

"No, that's too many. Let's make it fifty."

---

[1] Hoop and pole can be played only while the sun is at least four fingers above the horizon. For a more detailed description of the rules of the game see pp. 219—225.

The other looked around. That is still too large," he said. "Let's make it twenty-four."

The gambler said, "Let us make a rule first. Let the sinew and 'straight bottom' each count sixteen."[1]

Killer-of-Enemies said, "Let us make another rule. Let the band we call 'center' on the hoop count sixteen also." That is a red band on the hoop.

The gambler replied, "All right, you can take that. But the black band will be my winner. If I get that, I will win sixteen."

So they agreed.

Then Killer-of-Enemies said, "Let us make the earth know what we are going to do on top of this ground."

"All right," said the gambler.

Killer-of-Enemies held the hoop. They threw the poles to the east without rolling the hoop; then back again to the west; then to the east once more; then again to the west.[2]

Killer-of-Enemies got ready to roll the hoop. He let it go. But he made it turn so that it came back to the place where he was standing. The gambler couldn't do anything. His pole was across the center of the hoop. The pole of Killer-of-Enemies was along the edge and scored more.

One-Who-Wins said, "Oh, my opponent knows this game very well!"

Killer-of-Enemies had bet against the gambler everything on which the people subsist on earth. This was the first bet and Killer-of-Enemies won.

Then Killer-of-Enemies asked, "Shall we play the same way?"

"All right."

They continued. The gambler lost every time. Killer-of-Enemies put up a stick every time he won.[3]

Before the sun went down Killer-of-Enemies said, "Let us count the sticks and you will have to pay for each." He knew he was far ahead.

When they counted them they found that the gambler had lost twenty-four times.

Killer-of-Enemies pointed to the first stick. The gambler had to put down all the clothes and possessions for this.

The second stick had to be paid for. Killer-of-Enemies said, "For this you have to pay all the animals."

---

[1] To make a game more exciting, upon mutual agreement a higher value can be arbitrarily assigned to any encised band. This corresponds somewhat to "deuce is wild" in a card game.

[2] These preliminary throws always precede the actual play. The field must run east and west so that the hoop need never be rolled to the north, a reminder of the encounter between Killer-of-Enemies and the owl (pp. 55—57).

[3] This is the customary manner of keeping track of the number of gains and losses.

The third stood for all the plants and trees on which the people live.

The fourth was for the fruits and berries.

The fifth stood for the fields where the people plant.

The gambler paid out all this and he was angry, for there were many sticks still left.

He pulled up another stick, "I will give back the springs on which the people live for this one," he said.

He picked up another. "This is for the sky," he said. "I give it back."

He picked up another, saying, "I give back the seasons."

He picked up still another. "This is for the rivers."

He threw aside another. "This is for the cumulus clouds."

Of the next he said, "This is for the mist."

He said the next one stood for the rain.

Previously this gambler had won everything. The people had had no moon, no sunrise, no rain, no seasons, and no crops when he had finished with them. He had won control over all these before he played with Killer-of-Enemies.

He pulled out another stick. "This is to restore the darkness that comes out from the north that the people may sleep."

The next one he called haze and threw it aside.

The next stood for the morning star. The gambler had won it away from the people, for he had not wanted it to rise.

The next one stood for the north star.

The next stood for all the rest of the single stars.

The next stood for the seven stars, the Pleiades.

The next stood for the two fighting stars, Castor and Pollux.

The next stood for the backbone stars, the sword of Orion.

The next stood for the large vertebrae stars, the belt of Orion.

The next stood for the big dipper.

The next one stood for the evening glow.

The next stood for the morning glow.

Now One-Who-Wins had given everything back. He was empty-handed.

The gambler stood then with his arms akimbo. He looked around. He had nothing more to bet. He was very angry. He said, "Sometime when a flood comes or when the rain washes away the land, I shall be the one who caused it."

Killer-of-Enemies told him, "You must not say more."

"I'm going to speak once more. Sometime when a big snow comes that kills many animals and freezes the people, that will also be because of me."

Killer-of-Enemies told him, "That is all you have to say. Say no more."

"I wish I could have used my own pole," said the gambler. Then he went away.

Now the good things of the earth and sky were restored to the people.

Because the gambler spoke as he did sometimes a big rain comes or a heavy snow and people die. But Killer-of-Enemies won't let him do it all the time, so it happens infrequently.

Killer-of-Enemies called together all the people who had played against the gambler. They all gathered at one place.

Killer-of-Enemies asked them, "Who was the first to play with this gambler? And who was next?"

As he called them they came forward and stayed on the other side. He kept calling till there were many on that side. He started calling them in the early morning and was not finished till noon. At about five o'clock he alone was left. He was the last who had played against the gambler.

Then he said, "Tomorrow morning come around here again. I want to tell you something."

Some had not played in the games, but they came and stood near and listened.

Then Killer-of-Enemies said, "Did all who played come?"

"Yes, we are all here."

Then he got up and stood before them. "Everyone listen. I am going to say something to you.

"This earth is my body. The sky is my body. The seasons are my body. The water is my body too."

He picked up the hoop. "This is called 'rock hoop,'" he told them.

He picked up the pole. "This is called *macka*," he said.

"You are all my children. When you play this game, it will make you happy. These poles can be called 'those two which care for good.' That is another name for them.

"After this, when you play, at every full moon and every new moon, you must paint this set and paint yourselves. Remember that you lost everything on the earth, all under the sky, all the seasons, and the water. But I restored them all to you You all must believe it until the end of the world.

"All of you watch me. Don't look around. Listen to what I say. The world is just as big as my body. The world is as large as my word. And the world is as large as my prayers. The sky is only as large as my words and prayers. The seasons are only as great as my body, my words, and my prayer. It is the same with the waters; my body, my words, my prayer are greater than the waters.

"Whoever believes me, whoever listens to what I say, will have long life. One who doesn't listen, who thinks in some evil way, will have a short life.

"Don't think I am just in the east, south, west, or north. The earth is my body. I am there. I am all over. Don't think I stay only under the earth or up in the sky, or only in the seasons, or on the other side of the waters. These are all my body. It is the truth that the underworld, the sky, the seasons, the waters, are all my body. I am all over.

"I have already given you that with which you have to make an offering to me. You have two kinds of pipe and you have the mountain tobacco.[1] Over here, from the east are some people coming. Their skin is white, their eyes are light, their hair is reddish, and they will have reddish whiskers too. And from the south people are coming also. Their skin is not white and their hair is black. And half of their faces are all black (beard). These two peoples will come.[2] When they are friendly with you and help you I shall be glad. But if they are mean, if they think they have more power, you must tell them what I say. Then I'll turn their guns and equipment to water."

Killer-of-Enemies called one old man, "Come here," he said.

The old man came forward, and Killer-of-Enemies said, "Stand over here in front of me."

The hoop and pole had been put aside a little distance away. Killer-of-Enemies motioned and the hoop was already in his hand. He motioned four times with his hoop and gave it to the old man. Killer-of-Enemies again motioned with his hand and the poles, which had been placed at a distance, were already in his hand. He motioned with these four times to the old man and handed them to him.

Then he told the old man, "Hold the hoop before you. Have it over your right arm. Clasp it in both hands. After this you will be the leader for this game. Later I shall explain more of it to you. Now go back where you were standing."[3]

He called another old man. "Come over here," he said.

He motioned toward the place where the first hoop had been hanging and though there was none there a moment before, a second hoop was now in the hands of Killer-of-Enemies.

He motioned four times and handed it to this old man. He motioned again and two more poles were in his hands. He gave them to the second old man.

"You must put your arm through this hoop," he told the old man. He motioned four times and gave it to him. "You must believe in this. Every full moon paint it with red ochre, even though you are not playing with it. And at the new moon do so too."

He called to the first old man. "Stand together," he said to the old men. "This is what I give to you. It is a very good thing. Take good care of it and you can play it with your people. Some of you people have no sense. You must do just as I direct. You must not

---

[1] For an account of the origin and use of the two types of ceremonial pipe see pp. 241—242.

[2] Americans and Mexicans respectively are meant.

[3] Cf. p. 221 for a further account of the passing of the hoop and pole game to mortals.

make a hoop of any other wood. You must let everyone know about these restrictions. When you make a hoop and pole playing ground, don't let the girls come around. Don't let the small boys come around that place. After they are mature it is all right for the boys to be there.

"Everything on which you were living, you lost. You lost the rain, the night. But I brought them back to you. I am going to say just a few more words.

"In February when the thunder sounds, that means that everything is going to come to life again. In autumn everything has the semblance of death. In spring things shake and come to life again. In March when it thunders, it means that it will not be long before everything comes to life. These two moons are the ones which will give you the signs. Then the spring will come quickly. The first flowers will bloom.

"The first flower to come out will be the wild anemone."

Then this flower, in the form of a man, came forward. "I am the one. I will be the first to come out," it said.[1]

Then a second flower came forward in the form of a man and said, "I am the first white flower to bloom; I am the second flower to blossom."

Then another man stepped out. Killer-of-Enemies motioned to him to stand back.

"Next comes May and then the leaves grow large. There will be more flowers," Killer-of-Enemies said. "Everything will be in bloom then.

"After you pass this moon, the next will bring out all the leaves; and the plants will have pollen. 'Antelopes give birth to young' is the name of this moon. Gather the pollen then. That pollen must be kept. Whenever you pray to me you must sprinkle some for me.

"At this time take some plant and put it in your mouth. Then put strawberries in your mouth and start eating them, so that there will be plenty to eat till autumn.

"In autumn all will become yellow and red. The leaves will turn red and yellow. It will be dry. In late autumn the leaves will turn deep red. They will be like the red clouds at sunset and they will fall to the ground.

"When the plants are growing and it rains do not worry about it. Do not be sad about it. It will make the plants grow. Some people are afraid when it rains.[2] They hate to hear the thunder, but remember now that it also is good.

[1] This is an example of the Jicarilla tendency to personify natural objects.

[2] The non-agricultural Apache tribes, such as the Chiricahua and Mescalero, show the liveliest fear of thunder. Though this apprehension is present to some extent among the Jicarilla, the growth of the agricultural complex has greatly diminished it for them. For example, though some Jicarilla spit when it lightens (the Mescalero and Chiricahua practice), many others do not.

"I have given you advice. You must keep it and live on it. I never speak much, but I must say these things because you people have a great deal to learn. This is the end of my talk."

He clapped his hands and disappeared from the sight of the people. No one knew where he went.

One-Who-Wins, the gambler, has two signs, a big flood and a great snowfall. But he must ask permission when he wants to use them. This game between One-Who-Wins and Killer-of-Enemies was played at the center of the world.

G. THE FIRST PRIESTS

At one time the priests used to come right from heaven and go directly through this world to another world beneath. They paid no attention to the Apache. At that time the Apache did not have any good things.[1]

They got together and said, "What is the matter that they go right by us like that and never look at us?"

The priests went up in the same way too. There were four of them, one black, one blue, one yellow, and one glittering.

So Killer-of-Enemies made up his mind to try to stop them. He wondered why they never stopped to teach the people. So Killer-of-Enemies met them at Santa Fé and stopped them. They were Catholic priests, the first ones that stopped around here.

Then Killer-of-Enemies picked up some mud and threw it. He told the priests, "You have to go into that mud."

That mud became a house then and that is why the priests always live in adobe houses.

Then Killer-of-Enemies went away. He was glad, for he had made a neighbor for the Apaches of the priests and had kept them there.

Killer-of-Enemies told all the Indians around there, "You must go to the priests; they will give you a good present."

One Indian around there was very quarrelsome. He was always causing trouble and starting a fight. He was the first one to go to a priest.[2] He was going to ask for some presents.

When he arrived the priest turned and asked, "What do you want?"

On the top of the roof of the priest's house was a big sword called Old Man Knife, whirling around and around.[3] It could hack anyone to pieces who came near it. It was put there to frighten the

1 This is undoubtedly a reflection of the greater attention bestowed by the first priests upon the more sedentary Pueblo tribes.

2 It is an incisive thrust which has the most troublesome Apache be the first to seek out the priest.

3 Possibly a weather vane was so interpreted.

Indians. The priest had power to do this. That is why, when an Indian sees a white man, he is frightened and shivers all over.

When the Apache got into the priest's house he forgot that he came to ask for presents; he was so frightened that he didn't know what to say. The priest was angry at him and put him in jail.

Then another Apache came. The Apaches thought that the first one must have obtained some big present and that the reason he didn't come back was that he had such a heavy load. So the second man went to find and assist the first. He was a mean fellow too.

When he came to the priest's house the priest asked him the same question, "What do you want?"

The priest had four doors to his house.

The second man acted the same way. He couldn't say a word but just stood there.

The priest became angry. He said, "All right, if you can't answer my question you'd better go into that dark room until you can."

He put him in with the first man.

The next one to come was Child-of-the-Water. He went in and the priest asked the question. The priest turned around angrily as before and demanded, "What do you want?"

Child-of-the-Water said, "I want some abalone."

The priest gave him the present and then said, "You go in that jail too."

That was the third one he sent into that dark place.

Killer-of-Enemies was wondering why those three people did not come back. He thought, "I guess I'll go myself."

He made four stone hoops the shape of those used in the hoop and pole game. They were of the different colors. Then Killer-of-Enemies called the four slim whirlwinds of the different colors. They came and they rolled the hoops toward Santa Fé, toward the priest's house. Killer-of-Enemies got in the first, the black hoop. His feet were on one side and his head on the other, inside.

The hoops were rolled directly to the priest and hit him in the back. He was a little afraid, "What do you want, my son?" he asked.

Killer-of-Enemies said, "After this you must call me 'son' all the time and not be angry at me."

The priest asked, "What do you want, my son?"

That is why these priests always call people "son," even if they are not their sons.

Then Killer-of-Enemies said, "Where are those people who came here and what did you do with them? They came here to get some presents."

The priest said, "I don't know. I never saw anyone come to my house. I am by myself all the time. I am too busy studying to have visitors."

That is why priests are always studying whenever you go to visit them.

Now Killer-of-Enemies sent the wind. The wind started to blow all the priest's papers away. It was the black wind which came from the east.

Then the priest was frightened. He said, "I have one man only in jail. He wouldn't answer me when I addressed him, so I put him in jail until his mind comes back."

So he let that first man out.

Then Killer-of-Enemies said, "Where are the others? You have two more in there."

"No, I know nothing of any others."

So Killer-of-Enemies sent the blue wind from the south. Then everything began to blow. The priest could hardly stand up.

"Wait," he said, "I have another man in there."

The priest had two servants in there guarding the prisoners. They were the snake and the bear. That is why, at the Office of Indian Affairs in Washington they have images of animals like this near the door. I haven't been there, but I've seen pictures of it. That is why the white people, when you go to their houses, always have something there to scare the Indians. Perhaps it is a soldier right inside the door, or a fierce dog to guard them. It started right there with that priest.

Then the second fellow came out. Now the two Apaches were free, but Child-of-the-Water was still there.

Again Killer-of-Enemies asked the priest whether more were imprisoned.

The priest said, "No."

Killer-of-Enemies did not believe him. He sent the yellow wind from the west. The wind blew fiercely and the priest was frightened. So the priest sent his servants, the bear and the snake, and they brought Child-of-the-Water out.

Killer-of-Enemies was laughing. He said to Child-of-the-Water, "What have you stolen? What have you got in your hand?"

He was just making fun of Child-of-the-Water. That is why people talk that way. Even if you give me something and I take it out, people may say, "What have you stolen?" They joke this way. This is where it started.

Then Killer-of-Enemies turned and told the priest, "You must give to the people all they need. Do not keep it. Help them with everything and in every way."

So after that the priest did. He gave those two Indians many presents. They took a big load home.

Then the priest said to Killer-of-Enemies, "You think you have more power than I. If you have so much power I want you to help me obtain a good house, not one of adobe."

Killer-of-Enemies said, "All right."

Then Killer-of-Enemies asked, "Why did you put that sharp thing on top of your roof?" He knew why all the time. He just wanted to hear what excuse the priest would have. That is why people always offer excuses.

The priest replied, "Just to make my house beautiful."

Killer-of-Enemies went up and got the sword. Out of it he made a plow and he made a bell for the church.

"This will make your house better," he said, "Up to now you have been unkind, but now you will be kind and this bell will call your people to the church."

That is why the churches always have bells.

Then Killer-of-Enemies sent for the swallow. He said, "You must build a house for this man."

Four of them came and they started to build a house. The bottom part was finished now and they were ready to work on the roof. So they sent for Spider. The four spiders came and they made webs all over the top. That is why the capitol at Washington has that round dome. It is made round like the spider's web. They still use it. I've seen pictures of it.

Then Killer-of-Enemies sent for Thunder and thunders of the four colors came. The lightning hit the trees and made shingles and that is how shingles came to be used. The shingles are of different colors because the thunders were of different colors. That is why you see shingles of different colors now.

And Killer-of-Enemies called in the woodpeckers. They fastened the shingles together. Now the house was all completed.

Then Killer-of-Enemies made windows of rock crystal. Then he stuck in the house rocks of four colors, jet black, white rock, yellow rock, and variegated stone. That is why in big cities some people have houses which are so pretty that you think they are made of glass. The foundation was made of four stones too, turquoise, Mexican opal, abalone, and assorted gems.

The woodpeckers acted as carpenters. They made all the furniture for that priest too. They made desks and chairs.

The priest said it was wonderful when he saw what was done.

The priest was one person, but they speak of him as of the four colors.

II. THE ORIGIN OF THE HACTCIN CEREMONY

1. INTRODUCTION

At the beginning of our work the informant said, "Before I can talk about the Hactcin I shall have to pray, for I am not a foolish man. The Hactcin always know. The wind carries messages to them. The Hactcin are very important. I have the right to 'make' them. My grandfather knew a great deal about them and he taught me. But they have not been made for many years. It's a great thing to see them. We won't allow any Mexicans or white people to come near the Hactcin ceremony or to see it. If they tried to see it the clowns drove them away with their 'whips.' That is why the people don't want me to tell this."

This introduction will give some indication of the tremendous awe in which the Hactcin are held. It proved futile to attempt to induce most of the Jicarilla to talk about the Hactcin. One informant offered to tell any other type of story but pleaded with me thus not to urge him to discuss the Hactcin: "I know the stories about Hactcin, but I wouldn't dare to tell them. I can't do it. If I did my mouth would become twisted. I could tell the stories if I had danced Hactcin. But I never have. I've never seen them dance either. They are used now against sickness, through song and prayer, but none have been made since I remember. I couldn't dance as a Hactcin if they were made because I have short hair. Only those with long hair can dance as Hactcin and no one who has been vaccinated can dance. That's why it died out, I guess, for all the younger men who have been to school have been vaccinated.

"The Hactcin are more powerful than all the others, more powerful than the clowns or the Tsanati. The Hactcin are for only the Jicarilla to see. The clowns watch. They have hollow bones out of which they look, and they see anyone who tries to watch the Hactcin. One time some Pueblo Indians got on a very high point and watched from behind some bushes. But the clowns looked through their bones and saw them and ran and drove them away. In the old days the clowns might even kill someone whom they saw spying like that. It is very serious when they make the Hactcin. My grandfather once danced Hactcin. Later he thought he knew all about it, though no one had taught it to him. He shouted as the Hactcin do. Then his face became crooked. And his children were born deaf mutes."

2. THE ORIGIN OF THE HACTCIN CEREMONY[1]

There are two ways of the Hactcin. The way I am going to tell it is for long life. There is one kind of Hactcin that has wings,[2] but that one makes the people sick. This one is the one from which our life comes. These two ways both have power. One is in the good way. It is the stronger. It is the earth Hactcin, the cloud Hactcin.

The mother of White Hactcin was the earth; Black Sky was his father. He was the first one created in the world. He is the one the Jicarilla Indians regard as the Mexicans regard Dios. The next Hactcin was Sun Hactcin. The third one to be made was Moon Hactcin.[3]

After Sun Hactcin was created the earth and the sky talked to each other. They said, "How are we going to create the people and have them live the Hactcin way?" They asked this question of each other. Then the earth and the sky spoke again. They said, "Let us make another person." Then they made Moon Hactcin. Moon Hactcin, after he was created, was to stand for the fruit and the plants.[4] There is only one Moon Hactcin.

The earth and the sky spoke to each other again. They asked, "How are our children, the sun and the moon, going to travel to the east and to the west? How shall we make it for them?"

Earth and Sky called Sun their child. The child of the sun was Killer-of-Enemies. His mother was White-Painted Woman. The moon's son was Child-of-the-Water.[5] The mother of Child-of-the-Water was White-Shell Woman.

Moon and Sun called in all the people who had power. The people talked it over. They discussed how these children should grow. All the Hactcin were called in. Everything that was called Hactcin was consulted. There were Hactcin of stones, of mountains, of everything that existed.[6]

The people all gathered around. The two children started to grow. All the people watched. All the Hactcin looked at them.

The moon said, "This is my son. His name is Child-of-the-Water. He is the one who is going to stand for everything growing all over the world. The plants of the earth will be just like the moon. From little they will grow, just as the moon becomes full. And just as the

---

1 When you understand the Hactcin stories very well, there are no clouds, no wind, no bad weather when you tell them. When Coyote stories are told it is likely to be cloudy and bad weather. (Inf.)

2 Another Jicarilla who knows the stories and rites of the Hactcin associates the poor-will with the Hactcin in some way. Hence the derogatory reference to the "kind of Hactcin that has wings."

3 Attention has already been called in the origin myth to the other version of creation.

4 Moon Hactcin is here regarded as a male, the guardian of the crops.

5 The close identification of moon with water is here made explicit.

6 This line furnishes the key to the identity of the Hactcin. They are personifications of the power or essence of the objects of the natural world.

last quarter comes and the moon grows small, so the plants will wither and die too. After this all growing things will watch me closely. The new moon, the full moon, and the last quarter will set the path for the plants. Like me they will be small, will increase, and then will again become small."

Then all over the world the plants began to grow. The Hactcin watched this in great surprise. Everything began to grow and flourish all over the world.

But soon everything was getting too large. The animals were becoming monsters.

So White Hactcin said, "Let us use Sun's child for this purpose. Let us send Sun's child to kill these monsters."

White Hactcin came over and called Sun. He said, "You must stand up and look all over the world. See the plants. See the animals. They are all growing too large. The animals are becoming monsters and are starting to kill the people."

Sun stood up and looked. He said, "It is true."

White Hactcin spoke to Sun's child. He told him, "You must wait. There are four more Hactcin who will help you. The first is Truthful Hactcin, the second is Hactcinyoyi,[1] the third is Dancing Hactcin, and the fourth is Hactcin's Child."[2]

To each of these four White Hactcin gave a whip.

Sky spoke to all the Hactcin. He said of White Hactcin, "This is my son. I give you all this, my son. You are responsible. You people must listen to what he says. He is going to be your leader."

White Hactcin said, "I am going to speak four words before these four Hactcin go out to drive away all the sickness." Then he uttered these four words, "Long life, everything good, old age, no evil."[3]

Sun Hactcin spoke, "I will give you the clothes. Your leggings, shoes, cap, and shirt shall be made of my heat waves. These are the four articles of clothing you must wear. When you go out and meet the diseases, they will not see you as long as you wear my clothes. And you will kill all of them.

"The next clothes I shall make for you will be of sunlight. They will be the same four articles of clothing. Wear these and the sickness will not be able to see you.

"And of morning glow I will make shoes, leggings, shirt, and cap for you also. Wear these and the diseases will not be able to see you.

"And still other clothes I will make for you of ground mirage: shoes, leggings, shirt, and cap."

---

[1] The exact meaning of the name, Hactcinyoyi, is in doubt, therefore the native word is retained.

[2] These four Hactcin are associated with color and direction and are sometimes called Black Hactcin of the East, etc., instead of the names here employed.

[3] These words constitute a formula which is much used in Jicarilla ceremonialism and which is expected to counteract and drive away all evil and sickness in the vicinity.

Sun Hactcin came forward. He shouted four times at Truthful Hactcin, four times at Hactcinyoyi, four times at Dancing Hactcin, and four times at Hactcin's Child.

Now these four were free to call like that. But the diseases could hear their voices only; they could not see these four Hactcin because of the clothes.[1]

Sun Hactcin gave to each of the four who were going out, two long yucca leaves. At the tip of each a flint was tied and hung down.

He said, "Now go out with these. Stand to the east, south, west, and north with them."

Truthful Hactcin started to sway. Hactcinyoyi did also, and then the other two began to sway. They all started to shout and drive away the illness. They drove all the diseases to the north. They drove them over to the other side of the darkness that lies to the north. Then they came back to the east.

The Sun Hactcin made them stand in the morning glow. Upon this they were brought to the very center of the world.

When they arrived at the center of the world they found people there. These were the people who had been made unclean and ill by the diseases. The sick ones had had to separate from the ones who were well.

The Hactcin brought young spruce trees, each brought two. Then they lined up with the spruce trees in their hands and approached the sick people four times from each direction. They brushed them off with the spruce trees and sent the sicknesses to the north where the others had been driven. These sick people were thus cured and "brought back" among those who were well.

When all were brushed and all diseases were driven away, those who had been ill had to spit upon the tips of the branches that were held by the Hactcin. The Hactcin held these with the yucca leaves, and the people who had been cured spat four times upon the tip.

But before the people spat, the Hactcin approached them and said, "You must not look at us," so the people lowered their eyes and bowed their heads. Then the Hactcin traced crosses on the body of each person. The first cross was on the chest, the second was on the right arm, the third was on the back, the fourth was on the left arm, the fifth was on the head.[2] While this was being done the people faced the east. Then the Hactcin hit each patient lightly four times on the right foot with the Hactcin rattle, then four times on the left foot, then at the right knee four times, then at the left knee four times, then on the right hand four times, then on the left hand, then at the center of the chest, then at the center of the back, then at the

[1] In the Hactcin ceremony of the Jicarilla the singer blows into the mouths of the dancers before they go out. Then they cannot use any other voice (their own) except that of the Hactcin they represent.

[2] This is the ceremonial circuit followed when a sacred object is being applied to the body.

right shoulder, then at the left shoulder, and lastly on the top of the head.

Now this was all done and the people spat. They were told not to look as they did so.

Hactcin told the people, "You must say four words: long life, everything good, old age, no evil. We stand for these four things."

So the people repeated the four words.

"No one is allowed to look at us," the Hactcin said.

The four of them went to the north. "We shall call," they said, "but you must not look at us."

When they were a long way off they gave their call. Then, with the yucca leaves, they made a mark on the ground where they stood. They passed beyond that mark and shouted again. Then they made another line on the ground. They walked beyond that and farther on they drew another line, and called for the third time. Farther on, for the fourth time, they did the same thing.

Now they were at the end of the world, at the north, at the darkness. They faced the north. The first one, Truthful Hactcin, held black spruce, Hactcinyoyi held blue spruce in his hand, Dancing Hactcin held yellow spruce, and Hactcin's Child held glittering spruce. All of them spat four times at the end of the branches of spruce which they held.

Truthful Hactcin said to the other three, "Let us close our eyes and bow our heads, for we are going to throw this spruce with this sickness to the other side of the end of the earth."

They shut their eyes. They spat on the spruce which they still held. They spoke to the sickness, saying, "You must not come back among the men; you must not come back among the women; you must not come back to the young boys; you must not come back to the young girls after this."

They did this because they were carrying the sickness away on the spruce branches.

Then Truthful Hactcin said to the sickness, "You Sickness People, if you disobey and come back to our country, the next time I'm going to cut you to pieces with black flint and throw you to the other side of the darkness to the north."

Hactcinyoyi said to Sickness, "Whenever you come back I will cut you the long way of your body with blue flint and throw your body to the other side of the darkness to the north."

Dancing Hactcin said, "If you should come back to my country, I will cut your body with my serrated yellow flint. I will slash your head and body and feet, cut you in pieces, and throw you to the other side of the north."

Hactcin's Child then spoke and said, "If you come to our country again, I'm going to cut you up with my glittering flint. I will cut you all to pieces and throw you to the other side of the world, the other side of the sky, the other side of the water, and the other side of the seasons. If I do this it will be because of your disobedience. We don't want to see you around here."

Then they were ready to throw the branches.

At that moment Wolf,[1] Coyote, Burrowing Owl, and Great Horned Owl cried out. All the sicknesses turned to these animals, for these are their animals, and cried then. The Sickness People had been around with these four. That is why they turned to these four animals.

Now the Hactcin lifted up the spruce branches. They raised them up to the different directions in turn and then hurled them to the other side of the darkness, to the north.

Then these four continued around the way the sun goes. They shouted four times. They started back. They came to the four marks they had made. These lines are a protection, like a fence, against the return of the sicknesses.

They came back to the spot where the curing had taken place. They asked of the people who had been sick how they were feeling.

They all replied, "We are getting better, but we are rather hungry."

Then these four Hactcin shouted four times. At the east Grey Hactcin was standing. His house in the east was made of jet. They told him to come over, and he approached with his dog.

Then they said to him, "We are going to rejoice and dance."

Grey Hactcin[2] was the one who was to guard against all this sickness, for his color made him invisible to the Sickness People, and his dog was going to protect the people from sickness and evil during the night. These two stayed there and watched.

The people who had been sick were getting hungry. They said, "Let us go back among our own people."

But the Hactcin told them, "You must wait."

Truthful Hactcin said to Grey Hactcin, "After four days you must go and get the food from the holy place."

The four Hactcin who had done the curing said to all the people and to the other Hactcin too, "After four days you must come and see us. You must come to the holy place, for we are going to have a great ceremony."

Winter Hactcin, Spring Hactcin, Summer Hactcin, and Autumn Hactcin brought food.

Truthful Hactcin told the people, "You must gather around the holy place because all over on top of the world everything is good now; all under the sky is good now; everything on top of the water

---

[1] The inclusion of the wolf in this malodorous company is puzzling, since the Jicarilla wore robes of wolf skin on occasion and do not admit to the same fear of wolf that they have of coyote. Interestingly enough other Apache tribes, such as the Chiricahua and Mescalero, do have a real supernatural dread of the wolf. The Jicarilla consider the owl a bird of ill omen, and their attitude toward the coyote has previously been discussed in these pages.

[2] The informant later identified Grey Hactcin with Wind.

is good now; all the seasons are good too. You must hasten and all gather around. You must get ready, for from the east where it is dark, the Hactcin are coming. From the south, where the blue skies are, the Hactcin will come. From the west, where the yellow glow is, they are coming. From the north, where the dipper stands, the Hactcin are coming.

The Hactcin from the east brought a bowl made of black clay. The Hactcin from the south brought a similar bowl, but it was blue. From the west where the evening glow rises, the yellow Hactcin brought a yellow bowl. From the north White Hactcin brought a glittering bowl. White Hactcin from the north was the one who is the leader of all the Hactcin. He is the one I have told you of. They all came from the different directions with the bowls.

White Hactcin said to the people, "Now you make a corral, round like the sun. All the people are going to this corral."

Truthful Hactcin asked, "How shall we do it? Shall we have this corral made black?"

Hactcinyoyi said, "I'll make this corral blue."

Dancing Hactcin said, "When my turn comes, I'll make that corral yellow."

Hactcin's Child said, "When my turn comes, I'll make it glittering."

Truthful Hactcin sent for two young black spruce trees. These were to be erected in the doorway to stand for that which guides the men.

Hactcinyoyi said, "I'll make those trees blue and then they will guide the women."

Dancing Hactcin said, "Those trees will be yellow and they will represent the young men."

Hactcin's Child said, "I'll make those trees glittering and they will represent and guide the little children when they come in."

The corral was made. Each of the four Hactcin made a different side of it. Young piñon trees were put around first. Truthful Hactcin spoke and to the east a quarter circle of black piñon stood. Hactcinyoyi spoke, and at his word the blue piñon stood on his side. Dancing Hactcin spoke, and on his side the yellow piñons stood. Hactcin's child spoke, and at his side glittering piñons stood. At the door stood the two spruces. Piñon boughs were tied to the posts to make the corral. At the top of each of the two spruces which formed the doorway they tied a downy eagle feather.

The Hactcin of Summer and the Hactcin of Autumn took pollen and began to sprinkle it around the inside and outside, making it holy.

Summer Hactcin had brought pollen. Four Rock Hactcin were present, Black Rock Hactcin, Blue Rock Hactcin, Yellow Rock Hactcin, and Glittering Rock Hactcin. They had brought specular iron ore.

To the east, a little way from the large corral, they constructed a smaller corral as a home for the Hactcin. It was made of young black spruce and of blue, yellow, and glittering spruce. Before they built this home they traced a circle at the site with pollen and specular iron ore. This corral was to be the home of all the Hactcin. They were to call into that place all the Hactcin above the earth, all under the sky, all above the water, and all those of the seasons.

When all were together in there they asked the question of each other, "How are we going to dance for these people, my companions?"

Then to Black Wind Hactcin they said, "Black Wind Hactcin, you must go over to Black Lightning Hactcin and ask him for some lightning riven wood. Bring that and invite him to come too."

When Lightning was asked to come, he agreed to do so. He stepped into a black cloud. He was going to travel in that black cloud. He entered it from the top of a mountain and then sent his arrow, the black flint, and split a spruce tree. He broke it. It splintered and pieces blew in different directions. The one which fell to the east, he picked up and brought along.[1]

With the piece he had picked up he made something. He cut it with his black flint. He made it the shape of that black flint. He brought it to the corral.

Now Blue Wind Hactcin was sent to invite Black Rock Hactcin. "You must go over there and tell him to bring along Mountain-Sheep Hactcin, and he must tell Mountain-Sheep Hactcin to bring along a hide of mountain-sheep."

Black Rock Hactcin said, when Blue Wind came and told him this, "How am I going to catch up with Mountain-Sheep Hactcin? Tell Bear Hactcin. He can catch him for you." Blue Wind Hactcin did so.

So everything was obtained. Those people agreed to come. Black Lightning Hactcin was already there with his stick.

Yellow Wind Hactcin was sent up in the sky to invite Sun Hactcin to attend, and Yellow Wind Hactcin also was directed to invite Moon Hactcin and Big Dipper Hactcin and North Star Hactcin. "Tell North Star Hactcin to bring fire with him," Yellow Wind Hactcin was directed. And Yellow Wind Hactcin was also told to invite Two-Fighting-Stars Hactcin, Pleiades Hactcin, Three-Vertebrae-Stars[2] Hactcin, and Morning Star Hactcin.

"Tell Big Dipper Hactcin to bring the moccasins that every Hactcin shall wear," Yellow Wind was told.

Then Glittering Wind Hactcin was sent out. He was told to go to Black Water Hactcin, Blue Water Hactcin, Yellow Water Hactcin,

---

[1] Thus was made the bull-roarer. Its use in the ceremony will be described presently.

[2] The Two-Fighting-Stars are Castor and Pollux. The Three-Vertebrae-Stars are the Belt of Orion.

and Glittering Water Hactcin. "Tell each one to bring some of his own water and tell each to bring his water pollen."[1]

And Glittering Wind was told to invite Jet Hactcin, Mexican Opal Hactcin, Yellow Rock Hactcin, and Spotted Rock Hactcin. "Tell them to bring yucca leaves with them," he was directed.

And a message was sent to Black Mountain Hactcin, Blue Mountain Hactcin, Yellow Mountain Hactcin, and Glittering Mountain Hactcin. Black Mountain Hactcin was told to bring black earth, Blue Mountain Hactcin was told to bring blue earth, Yellow Mountain Hactcin was told to bring yellow earth, and Glittering Mountain Hactcin was told to bring white earth.

Rosy-Cheeked Hactcin was invited and told to bring red paint.

All who were invited came.

The large corral was for the people. On the south side the women were to stand. On the north side the men were to stand. They separated thus.[2]

All the people came into their corral and all the Hactcin into theirs.

White Hactcin came forward in the Hactcin corral. With the north star he made fire in the Hactcin corral and took a burning brand over to the place where the people were.[3] White Hactcin told all the others to dress up. They were all decorated with the yucca and the many things that had been brought.

The Hactcin formed a line. At the head stood two small Hactcin called Hactcin's Children. Then came two Black Hactcin, then two Blue Hactcin, then two Yellow Hactcin, then two White Hactcin. After the white-painted Hactcin came those dressed in spruce brush. They were in single row, one for each color, black, blue, yellow, and white. They are called Spruce Hactcin. The White Hactcin of the first eight wore whiskers made of buffalo tail hair which was painted white. Each of the Hactcin mentioned had a downy feather tied to the top of his head.

Then there were two of the Hactcin of the Fighting Stars. They stayed together because the two stars are always together. They stood to one side of the line.

Truthful Hactcin was painted red from elbow to finger-tip and from knees to toes, and he came in advance of the rest. He wore no mask but had horns of yucca.

Behind him came Dancing Hactcin wearing a mask. He was

---

[1] Water pollen is the scum which forms on top of the water. (Inf.) "Everything has pollen. All growing things have it. Man has it. He has it at the ends of the hair, the long hair of the head. It can be seen there. We came from the earth and all other living and growing things do too; that is why. And we eat things that grow. The sun and moon have pollen. They were made of growing things by the Hactcin in the beginning. So they have it too. And every animal has it in its fur." (Inf.)

[2] This separation of the sexes takes place in the bear dance as well, p. 30.

[3] For a parallel procedure of the bear dance see p. 30.

painted black all over and had a downy feather tied on top of his head. He and all the other Hactcin carried a yucca leaf in each hand.[1]

And one was Lightning Hactcin. He tied a string to the lightning riven stick and spun it, making a noise while these Hactcin came forward.

Before they came out of the small corral, White Hactcin shouted four times at each Hactcin near him. The one with the thunder stick went ahead. He stood by the large corral and made a noise with this stick while the Hactcin entered.

At the holy place Talking Hactcin stood in the doorway. He held a rattle. He said to the people, "All of you, when the Hactcin enter, lower your heads and your eyes and sprinkle pollen in the direction of the Hactcin." The rattle he held belonged to Buffalo Hactcin.[2]

Before, when all the Hactcin were dressing up, the people brought an offering of food to the Hactcin home.

The people who were sick were told to come to the space between the two corrals. There Grey Hactcin and his dog were going to take care of them. The others, who were not sick, were told, "You had better not look at those sick people. Later on you can see them again." The one with the rattle told them that.

While these sick people were sitting there, because they were hungry, White Hactcin sent over Big Turkey Hactcin. Turkey Hactcin brought them black corn, blue corn, yellow corn, and spotted corn.

"Give it to them," White Hactcin told him.

White Hactcin said to the wind, "Tell the Turkey Hactcin to notify these people that after the ceremony they should go back to their own relatives."

Now all the Hactcin went into the corral. They kept moving all the time. They all shouted at the same time. Black Hactcin carried one young spruce in his right hand.

The Hactcin of the Holy Place, who always commands the people in there, asked, "Did you all sprinkle pollen on these Hactcin?" He was Talking Hactcin.

He is the one who sings in there, so he started to sing. The Hactcin sang and danced. They danced for two songs. Then they went out.

When they came out they stopped at the place where the sick people were. With the spruces they brushed the uncleanliness from the sick people. Then they went into their own Hactcin home.

---

[1] From this description it is probable that the dancers who impersonate these two are known as Solitary Hactcin with horns and Solitary Hactcin with mask, respectively. Cf. the description of these two dancers on p. 186. Their identity was specifically denied by the informant however.

[2] The rattle used in the ceremony is made of the tail of a buffalo.

Those who had been sick recently were made to sit in that group too. Some of the sickness might still be with them, the Hactcin said.

When the Hactcin were back in their own corral the singer who had led them in the large corral came over and they danced in their own home. Then they all sat down.

The singer went back to the corral of the people and said, "Now your own people can come back to you." He went and told this to the sick ones too. They were all glad to hear it.

The old man with the rattle stood in the doorway and told the people, "Listen, all of you, young and old. Whenever these Hactcin go away they give us something. The White Hactcin is the one who sends the wind as messenger. He commands his own people," he told the Indians. "These Hactcin are going to be with us just four days. Then some will go up in the sky. Some will go to the east, some to the south, some to the west, and some to the north. Some will go back to the winter, the summer, the spring, and the fall. So listen closely. You can go out now. But come in the corral again tomorrow because the Hactcin are coming again to dance for you."

When they started this ceremony, they danced in the night first. Then they danced in the day, and then at night. Then the fourth time they danced in the day, and then it was over. That is the way it is done now too.

White Hactcin spoke to Grey Hactcin. "Take some narrow yucca leaves. Take two of them. Go to the east, to the path on that side. Lay them with the trail between and their points toward each other. Have flints on the end. Do this to the south, west, and north also. If Sickness or Death comes at night he will be killed right there."

The next day the people began to come back into the corral.

White Hactcin asked Grey Hactcin, "Did you do as I told you?"

"Yes."

"Did you take the dog with you?"

"Yes."

"Did he make any outcry?"

"No."

"Good."

He said this because he knew that the dog could see well at night and could locate Sickness if he were around. Sickness kills many at night.

All was quiet.

The old man told the people, "You must bring pollen. If you have no pollen, bring corn-meal."

At this time Turkey Hactcin spoke up. He said, "I brought some tobacco. Who wants to smoke?" He brought out tobacco leaves and corn husks.

The man with the rattle said, "How are the people to eat this?"

At that time they didn't know how tobacco was to be used.

"Where did you get this?" he asked Turkey Hactcin.

"I raised it myself."

"How did you plant it?"

"In the spring I put the seeds in the ground and they grew. The plant has roots, a stalk, and large leaves. It also has a tassel and it has pollen. It is just like corn. This is tobacco, yellow mountain tobacco. That is its name." And the Turkey Hactcin made a cigarette for the man with the rattle.

And the old man asked, "How am I going to light this cigarette?"

Then Sun Hactcin came up. "I'll light it for you. Look at me."

The old man held it to the directions in turn. Then he puffed at it. Smoke came from it. The Turkey Hactcin took it and handed it back to the old man.

Turkey Hactcin said, "Now this is for an offering. Whenever you pray you must use it."

The old man puffed at it four times, then he handed it around to the Hactcin, and each puffed at it four times. After each had puffed four times the old man began singing for the Hactcin.

Thunder Hactcin stood in the doorway and whirled the groaning stick. All the Hactcin came out of their home then.

Then Thunder Hactcin took the groaning stick and came with it to the door of the big corral. Now the Hactcin came to the big corral. The one Single Hactcin with mask came first this time instead of the one with horns, as had been done the first time.

The leader made four motions as though to halt and then went on before he entered the corral. He trotted in.

The singer said to the people, "You must all pray. Give pollen to them. Try to blow everything evil away from yourself. Perhaps you were frightened one time when you lost your relative.[1] Blow it all away. Try to get rid of it."

The Hactcin with mask came first. The Hactcin with horns came second. Third came the Two-Fighting-Stars Hactcin. The rest followed. They all called out at once.

The one with the groaning stick went to the east. He stayed on the outside of the corral and whirled the stick, making a noise with it. He did this then at the south, west, and north points of the corral.

The man with the rattle started to sing.He said to the Hactcin, "You must call four times and then dance."

They danced. They stood in an east-west line, facing the east. When they started to dance they turned their faces to the north. They danced for one song and then faced to the south. After another song they faced the west. This was the third song. Then they all faced to the east and this time the Spruce Hactcin went out of the corral. They were the first to go out. The thunder stick sounded while they went.

---

[1] Fright is an acknowledged source of sickness for the Jicarilla and is often associated with death.

Whenever the Hactcin passed the sick people they hit them gently with what they had in their hands. Then the sick people brought corn which they gave to the Hactcin.

That was the end of the second dance. The people left the corral and went to their camps. The sick people stayed outside the corral. The Hactcin stayed in their own corral. The old man stayed in the corral too and sang.

Every hour or so they sent Grey Hactcin with his dog to the east, to the place where he had put that yucca. He went to see whether he could detect anything. He came back and went into the Hactcin's home each time.

The Hactcin stayed there and sang and prayed until evening.

At that time it was the turn of the Evening Glow Hactcin to act. He prayed and sang. At sunset the people all arose and came from their camps. From every camp food was brought to the Hactcin's home.

The old man told the people, "After you eat you must come with your pollen and corn-meal into the corral again."

The camp people brought food to the sick, but Old Man Hactcin had to pray over it before it could be eaten. And he said to the sick ones, "You must go back to your own relatives tomorrow."

The meal was over now and the people began to come into the corral. The Hactcin got ready too.

Turkey Hactcin came forward. He brought tobacco as before.

The old man asked as before, "How am I going to light this?"

North Star Hactcin came forward. "I know how to light this too," he said. He held it up to the directions and puffed and it was ignited. "This is my fire," North Star Hactcin said of the fire inside. He puffed at it from a distance without touching his lips to it, but it burned nevertheless. He motioned with it toward the old man four times and gave it to him at the fourth motion. The old man puffed at it four times and then handed it to the Hactcin. This was done in the daytime.

After it had been passed to all, the old man, Talking Hactcin, started to sing, and the Hactcin started to dance in place within their own corral.

White Hactcin asked of Thunder Hactcin who stood at the door, "Are all the people in?"

"Yes."

"Make that music then."[1]

They were dancing right at the Hactcin's home. Thunder was watching the big corral. The Hactcin had not gone over there yet.

[1] That is, "sound the bull-roarer." The Thunder Hactcin or the one who impersonates him in the Jicarilla ceremony does not enter the corral, for the bull-roarer is not supposed to be twirled in the sight of the people. Thunder Hactcin stands at the outside of the large corral and sounds the bull-roarer at each one of the cardinal directions; at another one, moving clockwise, each time the Hactcin are about to dance.

Finally the Hactcin came out from their home. They went toward the large corral.

The Two-Fighting-Stars Hactcin were the leaders this time. Next came the Hactcin with horns. Next came the Solitary Hactcin wearing a mask. The others followed. When they stood at the door the groaning stick was sounded. The Two-Fighting-Stars Hactcin went in first, then the one with horns, and then the one with mask entered.

The leaders circled around past the women who stood to the south. The women threw pollen to them. These were the Star Hactcin, the horned Hactcin, and the masked Hactcin who circled around. The other Hactcin came behind and went in a straight line to the center. Thunder Hactcin went around to the directions on the outside of the corral, sounding the thunder stick. When he got back to the east they were all ready.

The Hactcin were all in line, facing the north. Old Man Hactcin sang and the Hactcin sang and uttered their call. At the second song they turned to the west.

When the dance was over the Star Hactcin led the way out. The Hactcin did not walk as men walk. They had their own way, trotting and swaying from side to side as they went.

There were Deer Hactcin there also, two of them. There was one Large-Deer's-Child Hactcin and one Small-Deer's-Child Hactcin. Ahead of them came one carrying a quiver of mountain-lion skin. This was Animal Leader Hactcin. He carried a bow and arrows in his hand and had two eagle feathers at the top of his head. His face was painted with specular iron ore. His clothes were all buckskin. He wore leggings of deer skin too.

And there were eight clowns and each carried four arrows and a bow. They wore caps of buffalo hide with horns, not real horns; their hair acted as horns. At the tips of the horns they had downy turkey feathers. They were painted with black and white stripes. They had four stripes of black and four of white alternately across the face; four of each across the body, including the arms; four of each across the legs. All were painted in sets of four stripes; no one showed six stripes of black or white on any part of the body.[1]

The Hactcin and the clowns help each other; that is why the clowns were there. These striped people have medicine. The people can't eat that medicine. They take the excrement of a child and of a dog and make a mush of it. They mix it up with white clay and some plant.[2] They taste this and say it is sweet. They mix it at the Hactcin home. The Hactcin only watch this. The clowns mix

---

[1] There is a six-striped clown who appears in connection with war rites. In the Hactcin ceremony the clowns have four stripes over the entire body. (Inf.) Drawings of clowns in the possession of the writer bear out this description of the clowns of the Hactcin ceremony.

[2] The plant is beggar-ticks. The root of it is used.

it there and put it in each other's mouths. Just before they put it in each other's mouths, they say, "Wa," four times. They imitate the sound people make when they are going to vomit.[1]

That medicine makes the clown's body powerful. Whenever anyone, man, woman, or child, swallows some excrement and vomits, the clown can chew some bread and put it in the patient's mouth and it stops the vomiting. After the clowns eat excrement in this manner their ears are very keen and their eyes are sharp. They can see like an owl in the dark. Even if someone three or four miles away sticks his head up, the clowns can see him.

On the top of the foot the clown wears a rattle of deer's hooves, four hooves together. This is just for a rattle.

They are funny people; they are always doing something. While the Hactcin dance, the clowns do amusing things and make fun of the Hactcin. The old man, the singer, has to make the people stop laughing, but some of the young boys won't stop.

Both ends of the bow the clowns carried were tied with downy feathers. The clowns had one leader. He carried a yucca whip in his hand as well as the arrows.

When the clowns went out they hit lightly each sick person with an arrow and said, "You are getting well now. Our country and all of us will be well."

They had no call. They just had a way of laughing of their own. They are not like the Hactcin.

The old man sang and sang just for the clowns, and they jumped in place, high in the air. That is their way of dancing. They just jump high.

The last time, the fourth time, the dance took place during the day. The Grey Hactcin went with his dog to look at the yucca which had been placed at the directions. The Hactcin came out of the big corral and went back to their own home. This was on the second night, after the third dance.

The Old Man Hactcin said to the sick people, "Tomorrow you will go back to your relatives."

They were all glad to hear it.

The old man told the people, "You must go home now and go to bed. Come back tomorrow morning."

The Hactcin and the clowns stayed in their own home. They prayed and then sang. They did not sleep during the whole ceremony. They stayed awake day and night. The people in the camp were allowed to sleep. The camp people could not approach except when they brought food. If they came around the Hactcin home at other times, the clowns whipped them. The Hactcin and clowns sang until morning.

---

[1] The clown's medicine is taken only one day, the first day of the Hactcin ceremony. (Inf.)

Morning Glow Hactcin commanded now. He called, "All you camp people get up. Now it is my turn. The morning light is here. This whole country and all you people must forget sorrow. Today these sick people will go back to their own homes."

All the people woke up. The morning light was now all over.

White Hactcin said to Grey Hactcin, "All that you put to the directions you must bring over here. When these people go home they will take them along. This is the last day."

Each camp provided food again for the Hactcin. And they gave food to the sick people too. The old man prayed and put pollen on the food. And he put pollen and specular iron ore on the heads of the sick men and women, saying, "Today you are going back well to your people."

And the red paint that was brought by Rosy-Cheeked Hactcin was distributed, just a little to each camp and each person.

Sun Hactcin brought pollen, and this, his own pollen, was distributed. Specular iron ore was also distributed, for the people were all to paint themselves.

Now everyone was happy. They all hurried back with their dishes to their camps.

"Stay right in the corral. Do not go anywhere else even when the dance is over," they were told.

After breakfast was over the Hactcin lined up again. They were about to dance. The camp people went into the corral. The sick people were very much excited at the prospect of going back cured to their own relatives.

The old man asked all the camp people, "Did you all paint your faces?"

They all answered, "Yes."

"Last night did you sleep well and dream nothing bad?" the old man asked the people.

They all answered and said, "We all slept well and had no bad dreams."

"Have you forgotten all about this accident, this sickness? When this dance is over, stay right in the corral. Don't go out till I say you may. This is the last day. The Hactcin are going to leave you. Before they go, each will say some word to you. Each one of them is going to tell you where he lives. They will tell you of their homes so that when we need them we will be able to ask their help. Did everyone hear?"

"We heard your words," they answered.

"Now this is the last dance. Let everyone go into the corral. Take with you the pollen and corn-meal to offer to the Hactcin. And give some corn-meal and pollen to these sick people, for they will offer it to the Hactcin too."

Everyone came into the large corral. No one stayed in camp or went out to any other place.

Thunder Hactcin started to swing the groaning stick.

This time the eight clowns came in the lead and the Hactcin came behind. These eight clowns were first. The next was the Single Hactcin with mask. Then followed the one with horns. The Two-Fighting-Stars Hactcin were next. The rest came in line behind. In the very last group was Animal Leader Hactcin. He led the two deer.

The eight clowns came to the big corral. Their leader motioned four times, and entered. Then they circled to the south. They had strings of corn bread tied around them as a bandolier is worn. They broke this and distributed it all around, giving little pieces to each person.[1] They motioned four times and gave pieces to the women and children. Then they came to the men's side and they gave it to the men with four motions also.

When the clowns first came in, one of the little boys and a big girl were frightened, for they had never seen them before. The girl got up and told the old man who was the singer that she was afraid.

He said, "You must wait. You must be patient. After this dance is over these eight people will take care of what they have done to you."

The Hactcin were all in line facing the west. Then they turned and faced the north.

Then the old man told all the men and women present, "Everyone has to stand up before I sing."

Then he started to sing and the Hactcin called and the clowns laughed in their own way. All danced. The deer danced too.

Two clowns, the leader and the one next to him, walked out of line. "We are going to hunt," they said.

The animal leader knew what they were doing. He didn't pay attention however. He let them tease the deer. The others kept on dancing. The two clowns crawled up on the deer. After a while the deer acted as though they knew something was after them. They tried to run away. The big deer was shot. Four times the leader motioned toward that deer. Then he "shot" it. The other clown had his turn next. He motioned four times too and then "shot" at the small deer. The big deer was the female, the small deer was a male, her child.[2]

Then these two clowns called to the other six. They all came over. They circled around the slain deer. They rubbed their hands on the deer and then on their bodies, saying, "Now wherever I go I will

---

[1] The bread of the clowns is kept by those who get it. It is given to the child who has eaten some dirty stuff and has an upset stomach as a result. No other medicine is given with it. The clown's bread is given out during the last dance of the ceremony, not during the others. When the ceremony is nearly over it is given out. (Inf.)

[2] First you make a male and a female deer dancer. The second year you make a female with faun. Keep alternating like that. (Inf.)

find deer."[1] Some said, "Oh, these are fat deer!" They all said amusing things.[2]

Then the strongest clown tried to carry a deer. Another tried too. The others helped put the deer on their backs. They carried them to the girl's side. They circled around among the girls.

"Who is a pretty girl? I'll give it to her for a present, for I want to marry her," the one with the deer said.

The other six followed. They picked out a good-looking woman and offered the deer to her.

The one carrying the first deer put it down close to the woman and said, "I give you this for a present. You can eat it in the company of all your relatives. I'm a good hunter. You must believe me and give me your girls."

The clown carrying the second deer chose another girl, put it down close to her, and said the same thing.

The Hactcin kept on dancing while this was going on, paying no attention to it.

The clowns, after they put the deer down, danced joyfully and vigorously. They called it a wedding dance. They called the girl "our sister-in-law." They said, "We are happy over this marriage." They all acted joyful because those two people were going to marry. The women all laughed at this.

The eight clowns said, "They laugh because they are too eager to be married."

The clowns danced and danced and then went back to the center, saying, "We are going to hunt again."

They danced on the other side of the Hactcin then. This time the animal leader missed his deer. He looked around for it. He saw it over there by the girl. Then he approached and stood near to the deer from the east, south, west, and north sides in turn. He stood again at the east side and motioned four times with his arrow before touching the deer with the point. He motioned, "Get up," with his hand then and the deer got up.

The animal leader did the same with the small deer.

The Hactcin had been dancing right along all this time. Finally they stopped and Old Man said, "This is the end of the dance."

Sun Hactcin and Moon Hactcin went ahead. They were going home they said.

Sun Hactcin told them before he went, "Whenever you need me, roll a cigarette and puff four times and blow the smoke toward me. Say, 'My grandfather, Sun Hactcin, you must help me for I am sick and in trouble.'"

---

[1] Dancing as clown really helps the men to be good hunters in the future. (Inf.)

[2] The clowns talk; the Hactcin do not, except in their own home, the small corral. In the large corral or on the way to it the Hactcin use their call only.

Then Moon Hactcin spoke. He said the same thing and told them to call on him in the same way. "I leave this word for you people," he said.

Then these two went back.

The old man said to the people, "Wait. Do not leave yet. There is still work to do. Do not forget the sick ones. They must be brought among the people before you go away."

Moon and Sun started to go out of the corral. To the people they said, "Bow your heads, lower your eyes. Do not look at us as we go out."

The only one to look at them was Talking Hactcin. He looked among the women and among the men to see that no one disobeyed. Thunder was waiting outside; as Sun and Moon left he swung his groaning stick. When he did this Sun and Moon Hactcin disappeared. No one knew where they went.

Old Man Hactcin said to the people, "Look and see whether you can find them."

All looked but saw no trace of those two Hactcin.

"They have gone up in the sky," Old Man said.

Now all the Hactcin started to file out of the corral. Thunder swung the groaning stick. The Hactcin with horns was the first to go. Then the one with mask went next. When they passed the sick people all the patients had to lower their heads and the Hactcin brushed away the sickness.

Thunder went ahead to the door of the Hactcin home. Then Animal Leader and the two Deer Hactcin followed. They were the last of the Hactcin to leave the big corral. But the clowns were still in the big corral.

Now it was the turn of the clowns. Two of those in the corral had been frightened, a boy and a girl. The old man led them out. They knelt with bowed heads facing the east. The clowns came out and stood in a line to the east, facing west, facing the patients. The clowns were in single file.

They started to run toward the patients. They shuffled toward them. Four times they approached and retreated, and the next time they jumped over them, lightly touching them with their arrows as they went. Then they ran in a clockwise circle around the patients and stopped at the south.

They repeated the running and jumping from the south; then from the west after running in a clockwise circle again. Then they ran in a clockwise circle again and stood facing the patients from the north.

When they shuffled towards the patients they talked to them. They said, "Companion, you are getting better, for I am shuffling toward you."

They did it from the north too and then they stood aside.

The old man came over with his rattle. Four times he struck the patient on the top of the head with the rattle, and then four times on the right foot, and then four times on the left foot. "Now get up," he said.

The clowns were standing there till this was over. Then they ran back into the big corral where the rest of the people were waiting.

"We are going to chase all these people," they said.

They ran among the people hitting them lightly with their arrows, chasing away all the sickness. The people ran out of the corral.

The old man walked to the spot where the sick people were. He prayed the while. With his rattle he struck them first on the right foot four times, then on the left foot, then on the right and left knees, then on the right and left hands, then on the shoulders, then on the breast, then on the back, then on the head four times. Then he motioned four times to the north, sending away the sickness.

Now the old man was finished. He stood aside. The clowns had chased all the people out of the corral. They came to the sick people. The sick people began to walk to their camps, but slowly.

The clowns came behind them with their whips. They shouted and told them, "You're better now. Why don't you go faster and make one people?"

They tried to unite them with the others who had started for their camps before. It was just like chasing sheep. They were causing them to be one people again. They struck them on the back and on the backs of their heads. Thus the clowns chased all the people to their own camps. The sick people went back to their own relatives.

The old man told them, "All of you go right into your own homes. Do not stand outside, for the clowns are not yet finished."

Old Man said to the clowns, "All of you get in line and face the camps. All of you strike the camps with your arrows."

The leader of the clowns went first. The rest followed in single file. They struck the tipis, all of them struck the same tipi, one after another. After they had done this to every tipi, they ran to the north.

No one watched them. It was just as though they were chasing something.

They stopped far away on the other side of the hills. The leader shot an arrow far to the north. He averted his head as he did it. He shot it away. "Now the people will not remember unpleasant things; they will banish evil far away," he thought.

Then the others did the same in the order of their place in line. The shooting of the arrows was the shooting away of all the sadness and trouble connected with the sickness. They made the sadness into an arrow and shot it far away.

After this the clowns circled clockwise and returned, after a wide circuit, to the big corral, the holy place.

The old man said now, "Who is the first one who came into this place?"

"Morning Star Hactcin," they answered.

"And next?"

"Two-Fighting-Stars Hactcin."

The others were: Pleiades, Three-Vertebrae-Stars Hactcin, Morning Star Hactcin (there are two Morning Star Hactcin and two Evening Star Hactcin, one of each for summer and for winter), Dipper Hactcin and North Star Hactcin.

They all listened to what each said when he went. Each spoke and told where he was going and said, "You must not forget this ceremony. When a man gets very old, he must pass it on to a young person."[1]

They all left their whips; these they left behind. They all spoke as Sun and Moon Hactcin had spoken.

They all said, "When we go up to the sky you must look up at us and see what we look like. It is all right to look at us then, when we are far away."

Sun and Moon Hactcin went back. In the morning the sun rose. The moon was behind. Around each there were circles. The circle nearest the sun was black, the second was blue, the third was yellow, and the fourth glittering. Right on top of each circle were four rays. They were all white. On the sides of the sun, red fire showed. This was his red cheeks. Only the sun had red cheeks, not the moon.

The circle nearest the moon was white, then came one that was blue, then a yellow one, then a red one.

When Morning Star Hactcin first came on earth he fought against sickness. Another Morning Star Hactcin (for there are two) stayed up there. He had a long white ray. That meant he was angry with the sickness.

The Sun and Moon Hactcin each took one of the bowls used in the ceremony back with them. They had used them to eat from. They had food in them. It was corn, but a corn different from the kind that is usually eaten; it was a sticky corn.

The old man who had the rattle went on top of a hill to the east accompanied by his wife. These two were teaching the people.

They left two bowls in the holy place; the same kind of sticky corn was there.

Sun said, "Sometimes I will become discouraged and be disappointed. When an eclipse occurs, that means that I am sad because my wife is jealous of me.[2] Then use these bowls that I have left

[1] The singer has to teach three or four other men. He notices that these men come around and pay attention. He teaches the whole thing to the one who seems most interested. He doesn't sell the ceremony. We live on it. We don't ask anything of one to whom we teach it. A woman may be taught the songs and ceremony, but she cannot put it up herself (i. e., officiate at the ceremony). She may pass it on to her grandson and he may do it. She would not even put on the small ceremony (one in which the songs and prayers are used but in which no impersonators of the supernaturals appear). (Inf.)

[2] For another explanation of the eclipse see p. 14.

here for you. Use them with a clockwise circular motion as though you are telling me to come out again. When I see you do that, it will make me happy again and I will come out. Sing and pray as you do it. Put pollen in the bowl as you do this. Then the skies will brighten and the eclipse will be over."

Moon said the same thing. He told them to do the same when he was in eclipse. "I go into eclipse for the same reason the sun does," he said. "You must do the same and I shall come out again. When I come out again everyone will be glad."

The Moon Hactcin stands for the fruits on this earth, and has authority over them. Sun Hactcin is responsible for everything under the sky. Moon and Sun help each other.

Sometimes in the season of planting, when Moon is angry because his wife is jealous of him, there are circles around the moon. Then the frost comes at night and kills all the plants.

But Sun Hactcin talks to him then and says, "Why do you do that? The people need those plants. And those plants beautify the earth." Then the sun puts forth all his power and shines with all his warmth on the plants, and they are restored.

So the people know all about the ways of Sun and Moon. When they see the rings around the moon, they pray to the moon. "Let it be warm," they pray. "Do not let all the plants freeze."

Now we shall talk of Big Dipper Hactcin. He brought the moccasins. He let all the Hactcin have these moccasins for dancing. He took them all with him when he went up in the sky. His wife, too, a female Hactcin, was with him, and she helped him carry them.

The North Star Hactcin took back his fire when he left also.

As they went back, Dipper said, "When you look up at night, count the stars of the dipper first. Whenever you see only six stars there, something is going to happen, something bad.[1] This dipper will stand as it is as long as the sky stands, as long as the earth stands. When you grow old you must teach this ceremony to the young people.

"The moon increases and decreases. It stands for the plants. But the dipper does not grow. It is the same all the time. But when you see six stars we will send you a message, a warning. And the sun and moon will also warn you if you miss one star of the seven."

When Sun was going back to his home he said, "If something happens to the earth and the sky I will send my son, Killer-of-Enemies, and he will let you know about it."

White Hactcin went up in the sky next. He said, "Whoever keeps these instructions, these prayers, and this ceremony we have taught you, whoever has a good heart, he is one who is going up here and see me again."

Sun said, "When I send my son down he will let you know what

---

[1] This same idea is entertained in respect to the Pleiades. See p. 116.

will happen. Perhaps fire, wind, drought, snow, one of these will come upon earth and destroy the people.[1]

Morning Glow Hactcin went up next. Night Hatcin went next, then Evening Glow Hactcin, then White Glow Hactcin. These all left the yucca whips in the holy place. Now the four Hactcin of the east, Black, Blue, Yellow, and White, left. Now the Hactcin of the south left. They live where the sky is blue.

The old man told these four Hactcin, "Take your whips along with you." There were four of these, Black, Blue, Yellow, and White. These Hactcin took along their whips.

"When you get near to your home you will see a mountain," the old man said. "You must throw the whips on the other side of that mountain. Throw these whips and flints there. The people who live on that side of the mountain will use them, will live on that which you throw. Those are the Mescalero people, an Apache people too.[2]

"The white and the blue pots, take them and put them on top of a mountain as you go on your way," Old Man said to the four Hactcin of the south. Nagodaje is the place, the mountain where one of the pots was put, the white one. The blue one was put at Dziłgegonłtcił. "Two of you Hactcin must stay there where you put these pots. Stay near them. And two of you must go forther. You must go where the mountain Dziłcidjei stands and stay there."

Because the Hactcin threw their yucca whips on the south side, even the bushes and all the plants there have thorns. The people there picked up those flints. When they have ceremonies, they paint the pictures of the flint on their bodies. The Mescalero Gahe[3] are thus painted. But these Jicarilla people know all about it.

---

[1] I tell this story just as my grandfather and grandmother taught it to me. It is the true way. There is another way and it is about the Hactcin too, but they are mean Hactcin. They are shaman Hactcin. They use the snake side and things like that. It is just like poison. That serpent has no arms or legs; it just crawls around. That is why, when it is used, many men, women, and children are doubled up, are crippled. That is shaman Hactcin. (Inf.) This is another attempt to discredit the informant's competitor in Hactcin lore. It is significant that he tries to do this by identifying the other man's knowledge with shamanism.

[2] There is another explanation for the existence of the abundant cacti of the south utilized by the Mescalero. See p. 77.

[3] The Gahe are the masked dancers of the Mescalero Apache. Their homes are in mountains, as are those of many of the Jicarilla Hactcin, and they are used as are the Hactcin to cure wide-spread epidemic and sickness. In respect to calls, behavior patterns, and methods of curing, there are marked similarities between the Hactcin and the Gahe. The Gahe differ from the Jicarilla Hactcin in that the right to "make" them is obtained through a personal supernatural experience. The personal, shamanistic principle is never obscured when the Mescalero masked dancers perform. Then it is that the one in charge of the rite expects some message or sign concerning further steps to take to hasten the cure. Such an intrusion of the personal and shamanistic into the Hactcin ceremony is unthinkable. My Jicarilla informant had this to say: "I would never get any message from the Hactcin or hear any words when I sing. And the dancers would

The two Hactcin stayed in those two mountains. They taught things to the Indians of that country. Those people, the Mescalero, believed it.

The Malpais and the White Sands are down that way. Two Hactcin of the south went over there. They went toward Dziłnayis, a mountain. "You must go over where Dziłcidjei stands," they were told. "When you get there you must live in the rocks. Use that place for your home and help the people living there." Both of them stay there. Of the four who went to the east, two also were to come to Dziłcidjei, and this made four Hactcin there. Two of the Hactcin of the east stayed at Dziłyadna, a tall mountain. They stay there.[1]

Now the Hactcin of the west were going to go from the holy place. Two went straight to the mountain, Dziłcidjei. The other two went to a mountain in the west. It is a mountain near Flagstaff, called San Francisco Mountain. These two put their yellow pot on top of that mountain.

The Hactcin of the north returned now. Two went to that southern mountain, Dziłcidjei. The other two went to a mountain in the north called Dziłdibentsei. It is the big mountain the other

---

never get any sign or message. I just perform my ceremony; I go right through with it and I know it will do the sick people good."

The masked dancers of the Mescalero are not individualized and given distinct names, mannerisms, and appearances as are the Jicarilla Hactcin. Moreover they do not each represent separate sources of supernatural power, but must be thought of as a group to which appeal must be made. The Mescalero personify supernatural power, and their masked dancers are collectively the personification of one source of it. The individual Hactcin, on the other hand, are personifications of different sources of power, and the concepts that surround them are much more formalized and stylized than anything found for the Mescalero. An added distinction is that the Jicarilla Hactcin have become involved in rain-making ceremonies in connection with the agricultural practices of the Jicarilla, whereas no such development has occurred, of course, for the Gahe among the non-agricultural Mescalero. This alternation is indicated at many points. For instance, the bull-roarer, symbol of thunder, has no place in the Mescalero masked dancer ceremony, but becomes an integral part of the Jicarilla rite.

[1] In the ceremony that was later performed by the Indians, not all the Hactcin are represented. There are Hactcin of everything; every tree, piñon, pine, spruce — the rocks, everything has its Hactcin. In the ceremony the Indians hold there are Spruce Hactcin and Bear Hactcin, but not all animals and plants are represented. About thirty-two men, including the eight clowns, are made up in the ceremony.

The Black, Blue, Yellow, and White Hactcin of the ceremony are not the same as Truthful Hactcin, Hactcinyoyi, Dancing Hactcin, and Hactcin's Child. The latter are associated with color and direction, but are separate ones.

In the songs and prayers it is different. In prayers Truthful Hactcin is always mentioned first. In the dance Hactcin's Child always leads, however. (Inf.)

The reference to Bear Hactcin has to do with the bear dance, in which a blackened and spruce-covered dancer, impersonating the bear, appears.

side of Durango.[1] That is the place of emergence, the place from which the people came out. In the beginning the people emerged from a place exactly on top of that mountain. And the Hactcin put the white pot on top of that mountain.

Now two clowns were sent up to the other side of the sky, where White Hactcin lives. They were going to help up there. And one clown was sent to the east where a mountain, Dziłdiłxiłyan stands. He was going to help there.

And one clown was sent to the blue mountain in the south, Dziłdatłidj, and told to stay there and help. And another was sent to the west, to San Francisco Mountain and told to help there. And another was sent to Dziłdibentsei and told to stay there and help.

The two who were left were told to stay at the holy place. "You stay here and help the people. Whenever they have another dance you help them."

Then the old man sent for Grey Hactcin. He said, "You must go to the eastern mountain. Go in that mountain with those two Hactcin who have already been sent. You, too, must stay there. But take along your whip." His dog went too; his dog always went with him.

When he got to the eastern mountain, those two Hactcin made a home of spruce on top of the mountain and right in the center of it he put the pot. That pot was left there.

Then Grey Hactcin went to the southern mountain, he went on top of that blue mountain. He was supposed to go around to the mountains. The Hactcin had already built a tipi of blue spruce on top of that mountain and in the center they had put the blue pot. Grey Hactcin saw that it was done.

Then Grey Hactcin went around westward. He stopped at the mountain Dziłcidjei which lies between the south and the west. There they had built a tipi of white rock. He saw that it was a pretty one. All around were greenleaved plants[2] growing and it looked very beautiful.

"What have you done?" asked Grey Hactcin.

"Oh, this is to make it look pretty," they said.

This mountain was of flint. Four mountains were standing close together in a cluster. All together are called Dziłcidjei. Naidleidził is the one standing to the east. Dziłcidjei is the one to the south. Dziłikidj is the western one. The northern one is Becdidził. These four stood near each other. There you can find many black flints and white flints. There is another mountain there called Dziłdiłxił. This is the fifth one. They are all in a cluster.

---

[1] This is probably a peak in the San Juan Mountains of Colorado.

[2] It was a plant called taltcidetso (Bearberry?) The stalk and the berries are red and the leaf is green. It gets to be about three and a half or four feet high. The berries are not eaten. It was used just for beauty around that place. (Inf.)

Everything was all right, so Grey Hactcin went on to the west, to San Francisco Mountain.

On the way he crossed a mountain named Sodził. He got up and looked out from it. Then he passed on to San Francisco Mountain. When he got there he saw that those two Hactcin had built a tipi of yellow spruce. He saw that they had put a yellow pot at the center. All was in order.

So he started to the north. When he got there he saw that a tipi had already been built of glittering spruce. In its center they had put a white pot. Everything was all right.

He started to the east. Halfway there he stood on top of a mountain called Striped Mountain. He got on top and looked to the north. He thought that perhaps he could see some sickness or evil coming from that direction. He looked over there but could see nothing. He said to the dog, "You must make a noise." The dog barked and cried. They both listened, but there was no answer. All seemed to be well. So they started to the east.

They approached the holy place to the east. Grey Hactcin called the name of the doorway, "Small Spruce Doorway," and then he came to it.

When he got back the old man asked him, "How is everything?"

Grey Hactcin answered, "Everything is all right. They have all built tipis."

Grey Hactcin had spent four days on his travels. When he came back they gave him food from a Hactcin bowl. There was just a little corn in it, but it proved to be more than enough. His dog ate of it too.

Now it was the turn of Thunder Hactcin.

Talking Hactcin said to Thunder, "You must leave your groaning stick here. Whenever the people have this ceremony they will use this stick." And Talking Hactcin told Thunder Hactcin, "You go back to Flint Mountain and stay there and help the people."

Thunder was standing there. Talking Hactcin spoke to Grey Hactcin, "You must get under Old Man Thunder."

He did and Thunder went up just as though pushed up into the air. He went up into a cloud and then he went away. As he was about to be carried away the lightning flashed four times from under the cloud. A clap of thunder was heard in the cloud. And with that he started his journey back.

The old man told Thunder as he went, "When you make your thunder, when the people hear you, they will all be happy. The noise will spread and everyone will be happy. They will say, 'Grandfather, we like to hear you every year.'"[1]

As he went on his way Thunder Hactcin sounded his thunder

[1] The different attitude of the Jicarilla towards thunder in comparison with other Apache tribes can be attributed to the growth of a corn complex among them.

again. Then all the people on earth who had little children pulled them upward by the hair and the heads and said, "Let my children grow fast."[1]

Then Thunder continued on his way. He was near his home now. Then he made the noise of thunder again. The people prayed and asked for a blessing, for long life. "Every year we like to hear you, but you must not come near to us," they said. "You must go around and above us, but you must not strike close to us."

When Thunder was almost home his voice sounded for the fourth time. He moved once more and he was at home. The people looked in that direction. They saw the lightning flash there. Now he was at home.

Thunder was going to wait till the spring, till the people had planted their seeds. Then he was going to come over and pour some water on their fields. "When the people need me, I'll come," he said. "If the people do not need me, I won't come."

Whenever the people have a Hactcin dance they notify the thunder. Then they are all sure to be rescued from the sickness.

Now Winter Hactcin prepared to leave. The old man said to him, "All around the cliffs you must build your tipi. You must stay there and help the people. In winter time you must help the people."

Winter Hactcin asked, "How will we make a whip with which to appear when the people use us? What shall we use?"

"Use the leaves of wide-leaved yucca," Talking Hactcin answered.

Then it was the turn of Spring Hactcin.

"You must build your home in the cliffs that jut out from the east, south, west, and north. When the people need you, come to help them," he was told.

"What shall I use to make a whip to protect the people?"

"Use young spruce tree to protect the people."

Before they started for home they asked, "Will the people puff cigarettes and offer us the smoke?"

"Yes, they will do it. They will not forget you."

"We are the ones who will chase all the animals to the people. That is how we will help."

Spring Hactcin then left.

In spring the animals are all happy. They venture out in the plains and run in the mountains where the people may hunt them. Spring Hactcin causes them to do this.

Now Summer Hactcin came forward.

"You build a tipi in the high mountains. Make it of Mexican opal," said Talking Hactcin. "You stay there and help the people. Help in two ways. Help the deer. Change their fur in the summer. Make it red. In winter it is grey. And help the people hunt and eat the deer too. That is how you will help. And your whip will be of the big yucca leaf."

[2] The people still do that today. (Inf.)

Summer Hactcin turned to go. And now it was the turn of Autumn Hactcin.

"Where am I to go?" he asked.

"On top of a big mountain. Make your home up there of spotted stone. When you get there you must help the people and all these animals. You must take care of them too."

Autumn Hactcin said, "All right. When we take care of the deer we will change their clothes so they will get their bluish clothes. And the leaves will all get yellow because of me. The pollen on the trees and plants will be my offering for these people, my gift to them."

And the other people asked, "Why do you have homes of all colors?"

He answered, "That is my home, but it is for everyone, for you too."

The whips of Autumn Hactcin are of slender yucca, wide-leafed yucca, small spruce, and large spruce. All four of them have flint at the tip.

And the home of the wife[1] of Autumn Hactcin is Pollen Mountain.

Now it was the turn of the deer. Talking Hactcin spoke to Animal Leader Hactcin. "You must lead these deer to the black mountain to the east and leave them there. Dziłnadjin is the name of the mountain. And when you take them over there you must watch these deer, stay and guard them. You must guide them. Don't let them go into the mountain. Don't let them go into the rock. Some evil people may try to harm them. Remember the people exist on those deer."

Talking Hactcin continued, "Some people who live in the mountains are robbers and are wicked, and if they steal your deer it will be hard to get them back again.[2] And some people who live in the rocks are wicked and might steal your deer. It will be hard then to take them out again. When you have raised many deer you must lead them. They will follow you all around the world. Take them to the mountain tops and leave them there. But watch them, go around and inspect them from time to time."

Then Animal Leader started to go. "How shall I call my deer?"

"Say, 'Ee,' and they will come. When you say that they will follow."

So this man left.

Talking Hactcin said, "I will send someone to see you from time to time; I will send Grey Hactcin."

Now it was the turn of Bear Hactcin. That bear is a bad one, for he stole the people. He acted just like the Sickness People. He was given good advice by Talking Hactcin.[3] Talking Hactcin took

---

[1] The Hactcin all have wives, but the Hactcin husbands and wives do not live together. (Inf.)

[2] Cf. pp. 256—260 for an account of how the animals were stolen and later restored.

[3] The reference is to events described in the story of the bear dance, pp. 30—31.

Bear's clothes off and gave him other clothes. Now the bear was changed.

Talking Hatcin said to him, "Did you hear what I said?"

The bear answered, "Yes."

When the people see the bear they are frightened. They get sick and fat.[1] In this way Bear kills people. Sometimes he makes the bottoms of their feet hard and it hurts when they walk. Sometimes he makes them double up, paralyzes them.

So Talking Hactcin scolded the Bear Hactcin. "After this you must not steal people. You have plenty of food for yourself on the mountain. Whenever you feel like eating meat you can have deer."

Then Talking Hactcin gave him moccasins and leggings and a shirt and hat of black flint. He told Bear to put them on.

Bear put them on.

"How do you like it?"

"I like it very well."

"Wherever you steal people or go against man, this flint will oppose you. This flint will watch you."

That is why the claws of the bear are of flint. And his teeth are flint too.

"I give you these clothes and you must help the people all over the world. Did you hear? Are you willing to help? If you disobey what I tell you, if you hurt the people and make them sick, I will punish you severely with the clothes which I have given you. I will make you die; I will cause you to waste away and become skin and bones. Now go back to your mountain. In summer-time you will have plenty of food to eat. There is no need to bother man. In the winter go into the mountain and stay in a cave for two moons. When the two moons have passed, when you hear the thunder, you must turn over on the other side. But stay there till the spring. You will become very fat in summer and so you will be able to do this. After two more months, when you hear the thunder again, go out once more. Now go!"

The bear has no whip; he just uses his body. He is too ferocious and so was given no whip. And that is why he was scolded and given advice and directions.

Talking Hactcin left the rattle in the holy place at the large corral.

Grey Hactcin went around once more. He inspected everything. He stood a little way from the holy place. He went around with his dog. He inspected all. The dog barked as he went, as he approached the holy place and the holy home of the Hactcin.

Grey Hactcin went to the east and the south. All was well there. He started with his dog toward the west. As they neared it he yelled. Then he continued to the north. Everything was all right so they went back to the east, to the holy place.

Upon their return they approached Talking Hactcin and his wife.

[1] Evidently dropsical conditions are attributed to "bear sickness."

Talking Hactcin said to his wife, "Your children have come back, give them something to eat."

They swallowed some of that corn four times and then they had had enough. The food is called *alole*. It is corn but it is called that. It is the food of the supernaturals. There is no meaning to the name besides that. The *alole* has great power. It makes the Grey Hactcin run fast.

After Grey Hactcin had eaten he started to go around again. This time he made a smaller clockwise circuit. All was well. He found all well at the east so he continued to the south, then to the west, then to the north, and finally back to the holy place. He found all well there too. Again he ate some of the corn and so did his dog. After they had eaten they stayed there and Talking Hactcin prayed a long time.

The old man asked him, "What did you say when you went around?"

"This is the way I shouted," Grey Hactcin showed him.

"And what did your dog do?"

"He barked."

The old man was glad to hear this.

After this Grey Hactcin went out with his dog. He started to go again in a clockwise circle. The circuit was still smaller this time. He saw that all was well at the holy places that had been made. The homes he visited were the homes of those who lived below the mountains. These homes were of spruce too. The colors of the homes were black, blue, yellow, and glittering. He carried his whip as he went. He completed his circuit. He returned to the holy place. They entered. He had seen that everything was all right.

The old man inquired, "Did you ask those people whether they saw sickness or anything wrong?"

"They say that everything is all right. Nothing evil lies on the earth, everything is good. Nothing is harmed."

Talking Hactcin sent Grey Hactcin among the people. "Tell them to come to this holy place in spring and I will show them another ceremony. For I have sent Hactcin to stand in the mountains and in the directions to guard the people till the end of the world."

So Grey Hactcin went and gave this message to the people of the earth.

He asked the people, "How do you like what was done for you? Do you still remember the ceremony?"

Some of them said, "Yes, we remember."

Grey Hactcin continued, "We sent Hactcin to all different places and they are to guide you and stand for you. We are going to make another ceremony. But those Hactcin will not attend. Talking Hactcin sent me to tell you. When spring comes you should gather again, he says, and we will have another dance. That is what I was sent to tell you."

And all the people agreed. So all knew what the old man wanted them to do, even though sickness was not around. There was to be another ceremony. Grey Hactcin went back to the holy place with his dog.

They came to the holy place and entered. The dog entered too.

Talking Hactcin told him, "You must stay here with your dog and help. You must stay here all your life. This is your home. Everything used by the Hactcin in the ceremony must be left here and you are to guard everything."

Now everything was completed on this earth. One thing was yet to be done. Grey Hactcin was sent up to the sun to ask him how he liked what had been done, the work done on earth.

"Go to the moon and the dipper and his wife too," Grey Hactcin was told.

Talking Hactcin sent a message by means of his power. He spoke to Sun. Sun let his rays down. Talking Hactcin gave clothes of heat wave to Grey Hactcin and his dog.

Talking Hactcin said to his wife, "You must not look while these two put the clothes on."

Then Talking Hactcin gave pollen and specular iron ore to Grey Hactcin. "Whenever you pass those people who live in the center of this sky, the Cloud People, offer this to them, but do not go into their home, even though they want you to go in. Sprinkle these and then pass on."

Grey Hactcin and his dog traveled on the sun's rays. They arrived at the home of Black Cloud. They saw those people. Cloud People invited them to come in. Their home was pretty. Rainbows and lightning were inside. But these two passed nevertheless. They paid no attention to all this. They said, "No, we must go," and they sprinkled specular iron ore and left.

Next on the way they came to Blue Cloud People. They offered pollen and specular iron ore and passed on. Next they came to Yellow Cloud People and again refused to come in, but sprinkled pollen and specular iron ore instead.

Next they came to the home of Glittering Cloud People. They sprinkled pollen and specular iron ore as before. The people tried to make them come in as had the others, but they were afraid to enter. "We must hurry," they said. "We must see Sun Hactcin and Moon Hactcin."

So they passed all the four homes. They went on toward the home of Sun. They traveled on Sun's rays. That is why they could not stay in any other home.

The home of the sun was in Black Sky. There were four doors to it. They stood at the east door. The Sun Hactcin was not there. He had gone to the west. But another Sun Hactcin (there are two, one that stays at home and one that travels) was there. The wife of the absent Sun Hactcin and his daughter were there.

They entered the house. The floor was of turquoise. The interior was filled with many beautiful possessions.

Each Sun Hactcin had a home. A short distance away there was another home for the other Sun Hactcin. This one had the east half constructed of jet and the opposite half of turquoise. This was the home of the Sun Hactcin who did not travel.

Near these homes of the Sun Hactcin was the home of the moon. One side was yellow stone and the other half was of all kinds of beads.

There were two Moon Hactcin too. But the one who did not move had more power; he was the leader of the other one. This was true of the Sun Hactcin also. The ones who move work on the earth side, the others work on the sky side and are more powerful.

Grey Hactcin came to the home of the traveling Sun Hactcin first. He was gone; no one was there but his wife and girl. So he went on to the other Sun Hactcin and said, "Talking Hactcin sent me to see whether you have looked down on all the work that has been done and are pleased."

Sun Hactcin asked Grey Hactcin, "Did you take care of all the Hactcin and send them all to different places?"

"Yes," replied Grey Hactcin.

Then Grey Hactcin went to the home of the stationary moon. He stood at the door. Moon Hactcin came out and smiled and told him to come in. He asked, "Did you do all your work on top of the earth?"

"Yes," said Grey Hactcin and then told Moon Hactcin, "This coming spring we are going to have another dance, one just like we had before. Is that good?"

Moon Hactcin replied, "Yes, that is good. Do it. But do not let the other Hactcin come there. Tell Talking Hactcin to send for Thunder Hactcin so that he may guide you while you dance."

Moon Hactcin had given his permission.

Then he asked, "Are you going directly back to the holy place now?"

"Yes."

"No, you had better go to see your grandfather, White Hactcin, now, for he expects you."

These Hactcin know each other. They know what the others are thinking; they know through their power.

Then Grey Hactcin asked, "How do people travel on the sky?" He was afraid, because some fierce people live up there. "Do you think that those fierce people will kill us if they see us?"

"No," and then Moon called to Grey Hactcin, "You must not be afraid up here. For no one dies up here."

Sun Pollen Boy was there.[1]

[1] When the sun comes out suddenly and hits a place, you see something like a rainbow, a short rainbow. We call this sun pollen. People don't see the body of Sun Pollen. (Inf.)

"Go with him; he will show you the way," Grey Hactcin was told.

He started off with Sun Pollen Boy. They moved rapidly, just as the light goes.

Sun Pollen Boy is the child of Sun. He is the boy of the sun who travels. Traveling Sun's daughter's name is Red-Cheeked Sun Girl. Sometimes the sun takes his daughter along because she cries for him. You see her when the sun goes down with a reddish glow.

When they had gone a distance they saw a white house standing up. It was just like a white cloud rising. As they came near they saw a mountain there. There were four roofs crossing over that place. It was the home of White Hactcin and those who were sent up to help him. When they arrived at the mountain they asked for White Hactcin.

The two clowns there said, "White Hactcin is at home."

Now they saw that the home of White Hactcin was made of white rock.

Sun Pollen Boy was shining on White Hactcin. As they neared the door the dog barked, and then a white dog came out of the house.[1] They paused at the door which faced the east.

White Hactcin was staying there with his father, Black Sky. Black Sky said to White Hactcin, his son, "You must go and see why our dog is barking."

The two travelers who had come up saw someone standing there. They tried to enter. White Hactcin made the entrance slope downward, so that when they tried to enter they slid down and again found themselves outside. They circled to the east and again approached the door. The same thing was done to them as before. As they entered they suddenly found themselves outside.

White Hactcin bantered with them. "What's the matter? Come in!"

But they fell through the house again when they tried to enter. They turned around again.

The house had four doors, one in each direction. The first time they stood to the east and found themselves out at the west door. Then they came around to the south door and found themselves out at the north door. Then they came around to the west door, and White Hactcin called to them to enter again. The third time they tried to enter, and it was just as if they slid to the east and they found themselves out at the east entrance again.

Now they came around clockwise and stood to the north. It was a white door. Grey Hactcin looked at his dog. It had turned white. White Hactcin had changed it. He looked at himself. He was white too. He said to himself, "What is the matter? My body is getting white." It astonished him.

---

[1] Grey Hactcin's dog was greyish like himself. The people never saw the dog, but they heard the bark. All the Hactcin have dogs which are the same colors as the Hactcin are. White Hactcin's dog was white like himself. (Inf.)

They entered this time. They stood inside the doorway. Grey Hactcin looked at his dog. It was all white. But White Hactcin knew all about it. He had done it. White Hactcin knew what Grey Hactcin was thinking.

White Hactcin said, "You are Grey Hactcin. I know why you came up to see me. I know who sent you. There is nothing wrong with anything up here. Everything is all right. All who live around here are not going to die. I am in command here. You come here for good news and this is the good news I tell you."

Black Sky spoke and said, "I know Talking Hactcin. He has done all his work. I represent all the people up here. They are not going to die."

Black Sky Hactcin said to White Hactcin then, "You must take these two people to the top of the high mountain."

White Hactcin took them there. White Hactcin's dog went too. White Hactcin created a high mountain there where none had stood before. They ascended it.

"You will be able to look all around and see everything," he said to them.

They were told to look to the east. There on top of the sky, for it was the other side of the sky where this was happening, it was beautiful. They saw before them a beautiful land and it was all like the earth in the summer season.

They turned to the south. There too it was just like summer. To the south there was no mountain, but just a fine plain. It was the same to the west. There was a beautiful place there too. To the north they saw the same thing.

White Hactcin asked, "How do you like it?"

They answered, "We like it very much."

Then they came down. They went in the house again.

Black Sky Hactcin said to Grey Hactcin, "When you go to Talking Hactcin tell him he is the one to look after the people. For on the earth people must die. When the people pray let them pray to the earth and call her their grandmother. Let them pray to me and call me their grandfather. I am going to say another word to you, my grandchildren."

Both listened very carefully.

"I stand for the sky and I stand for the earth too. This is my son, White Hactcin. He has the same authority. He stands for all above the sky and under the sky, on top of the earth and under the earth. Now come near to me. Turn to the east."

Over there they saw their own images, right in the doorway. Grey Hactcin saw himself and his dog standing there. He turned to the south door and there in the doorway he faced another image of himself and his dog. To the west he turned then and there, too, was a Grey Hactcin standing with his dog. He turned to the north then and saw another Grey Hactcin standing with his dog. These that he saw were the images of the one who had come up from the earth. He had been changed up there.

Then Black Sky Hactcin told him to face the east again. "Now shut your eyes. Have your dog shut his eyes too."

They obeyed.

"Now open your eyes."

When they opened their eyes they were standing outside looking in. Now they were back in their own bodies. Before being allowed to enter they had been made different.

White Hactcin stood inside with his dog.

Then Black Sky Hactcin said, "When you are down on the earth listen and you will hear me. Make the people pray to me and to my son, White Hactcin. My son is the one who stands far ahead of all others.

"Stand there and look at me. I am going to get up. I am Black Sky Old Man. Now close your eyes while I arise."

They closed and then opened their eyes. Black Sky Hactcin had been an old man before with grey hair. Now he was a young man. His hair was somewhat yellowish.

He asked, "Who is it you are seeing?"

Grey Hactcin could not say. He could not think of anyone he had seen who looked like this. Black Sky Hactcin held his age staff;[1] still they did not recognize him.

He spoke then. "I am the same one. I had grey hair before. Close your eyes again and then open them."

They saw that he had changed himself to a middle-aged man, though he had been a young man before. Behind him his wife stood this time.

"Close your eyes again," he commanded.

Then Black Sky Hactcin asked his wife, "Shall we show him ourselves again?"

"Yes, let him look at us again."

"Open your eyes then."

They opened their eyes and they saw two people who were not very old but who were past middle life and beginning to grow old.

"Shut your eyes again."

They did so.

"Open your eyes again."

Then they saw a very old man whose hair was grey. His wife was aged too.

"You must tell the people of the earth all about us. Those who live over on this side of the sky are given a choice; they may live as they choose. Sometimes they want to change themselves to old

[1] The age staff is, in simplest definition, the stick which a very old person uses to support himself when walking. Symbolic reference is often made to it in ceremonial context, however, where it is used as a prayer for long life.

men. Sometimes they want to live as young people. When anyone gets tired of being old he can turn to a young person again. From youth to age, from age to youth, these people change, but they will not die. When you go down on earth you must tell this to Talking Hactcin and instruct him to relate all this to the people. I can do these things; that is why I can make the light for the sun and moon."

Then they called Sun Pollen Boy. They told him, "You must go back with these people to your father's home and to the moon's home."

Before they went Black Sky Hactcin told them, "You must stop and visit the sun. He will tell you something." Black Sky Hactcin knew what Sun was going to say.

So they went back to the home of the sun. When they got there they found Morning Star, Two-Fighting-Stars, North Star, and Dipper waiting for them. Three-Vertebrae-Stars and Pleiades were there also. Sun had sent for all of these.

Moon said, "This man came from the north and said that everything was all right." He was referring to Dipper Star Hactcin.

Only one Dipper Star Hactcin had come. Of Two-Fighting-Stars Hactcin only one was present. Of each group only one was sent. There was one Morning Star Hactcin also. They all said that everything was all right where they were.

The stars said, "Wherever we are we will help you." Then all the stars said, "White Hactcin has told us to work well and we all obey him."

Then Sun said to Moon, "Now it is your turn. In some way take them down to earth."

Moon said to Morning Star, "You must take them on top of the morning glow."

So Morning Star led these two people toward Morning Glow. Morning Glow Hactcin, who always stands in the morning glow, stood there. They got in with him. They were going back in a different way from the manner in which they had come.

They sat on top of the morning glow. Morning Star journeyed to the west and Morning Glow followed. When Morning Star got directly over the holy place he threw himself down as a meteor. And when Morning Star flew down, the light flashed all over. At that moment Grey Hactcin and his dog came down with that star.

They entered the holy place. Talking Hactcin was there. There they were given food. After they had eaten he asked questions. Talking Hactcin already knew what had happened, where they had been, and what they had been doing; but he asked the questions anyway.

He first asked, "How is everything up there on the other side of the sky? Did you go over to White Hactcin's home?"

"Yes, we've been there. When we entered they teased us and they changed our bodies."

"What did White Hactcin's father say to you?"

"He showed how he could change his body from youth to old age. He told us, 'You must tell the truth about me. Tell how you have looked all over the country up here. You must tell the people below, "Up there it is different." You must say, "Up there the people do not die, the old can change to young people and the young can become aged."' We saw those two clowns at the home of White Hactcin. They like the country."

The two travelers both told the story. They said, "When we first came up there to him White Hactcin took us and showed us the countries all around. 'You come up for good news; that is why I tell you this,' he told us. When we got to Sun's home and the home of Moon all the Star people were waiting for us. They all said that everything was well all over the sky. Sun Pollen Boy acted as our guide. Sun told Moon to take us down, and Moon spoke to Morning Star. Morning Star put us on top of Morning Glow and we traveled on him. Morning Star stopped overhead and brought us down. Thus we came to the very doorway of the holy place.

"When we first left here to visit the sun, halfway we met the Cloud People. They wanted us to come into their homes but we refused. We continued to the other side of the sky. When we arrived we were asked about the earth, and we told all that we had done and that all was well."

Then they said, "When White Hactcin spoke to us he told us, 'Some day I am going to tell Sun to send his boy to the earth, for some day monsters will be upon the earth and Sun's child will take care of that. I am going to tell the moon to send down his son too. And these two boys will help each other and clear the earth of monsters.'"[1]

Talking Hactcin spoke to Turkey. "Before Spring comes you must give corn to all these people so they will know how to plant. You must stay around and show them how. When they plant their corn you must stay around there and go nowhere else, for you are responsible for this corn. Stay there until harvest time."

Turkey Hactcin stood for the corn, because the corn was his body. His foot is the corn plant root. His leg is the corn stalk. His wing is the leaf of the corn stalk. The red wattle is the corn. The red around his neck is coral. Turquoise is in the top of his necklace. His comb is the corn tassel.

Turkey Hactcin, when he heard the request of Talking Hactcin, said, "Yes, that is my duty. I shall stay around there."

When the time came to give the corn to the people, Turkey Hactcin said, "You must make a smooth place."

He stood to the east and strutted, and as he went a large mound of black corn fell. He stood on the south side, strutting, and blue

[1] This is one thing I forgot to tell you. (Inf.)

corn fell. He stood on the west side and strutted, and yellow corn fell there. On the north side he strutted and corn of all colors fell.[1]

"Here is the corn," Turkey Hactcin told them. "All of you pick it up and use it. You must live on it. You must plant it. Use it in the right way, and no man, woman, or child will starve. I want this corn to make the surface of the earth beautiful. I want all under the sky to be beautiful with it. Let all on top of the water, all on top of the seasons be made beautiful with it."

Turkey said then, "Why don't you ask for some wheat too? That is good food to live on also. But another people have it now."

The people all picked up the corn. Then they questioned, "Whom shall we ask for the wheat?"

"Go to Talking Hactcin. He will tell you who has it. I know who has it, but I have no right to ask for it. But I will try. I will go back and ask Talking Hactcin."

Then Turkey went back to Talking Hactcin and said to him, "I gave them corn, but I don't think it is enough. There is another gift they need if they are to increase. That is wheat. I believe you know who has it."

Talking Hactcin called in Grey Hactcin and said, "You must go over to Grasshopper and tell him to bring along the food on which he lives."[2]

Grey Hactcin asked, "Where do these Grasshopper People live?"

"Over here, down below to the south. They live in the hot country. They like the hot country."

Then Grey Hactcin went. He was going to take his dog.

Turkey Hactcin said, "No, don't take that dog. You might frighten those people with your dog."

When Grey Hactcin neared that place the grasshoppers were jumping all over. They were hard to approach. When you went to one, he always jumped in another direction. There were many of them, and they were of different colors. All had horns.

Grey Hactcin stood among them. He said, "I bring a message to you."

"Where do you come from?"

"I come from the holy place."

"Who told you to come over this way?"

"Talking Hactcin sent me over here. I have come here for the wheat, because the people have not enough to keep them from starvation."

Then they all said, "Yes, we have it. But in spring when we planted we ate all the leaves. So the wheat didn't grow; the stalks were all dry. We have more to plant but it hasn't grown yet. If we give you our seed what are we going to eat afterward? We must

[1] Cf. the story of the origin of corn (pp. 210—215).
[2] Cf. p. 15 for another association of grasshopper and wheat.

exist on this wheat, so why should we give it away? If we do, then some day we will have starvation among ourselves."

They only said that; they just wanted an excuse.

They went on, "What if we should give you this wheat? Those people don't plant this grain. We are willing to give it away, but those people hate us, and that is why it is hard to give it away to them."

But finally the grasshopers said, "We will send four men along with you to carry the seeds. We will give you some."

Then Old Woman Grasshopper went into the ground. She opened up a cache and there was some wheat stored there.[1] The homes of the grasshoppers were of sand.

Then they called in a grasshopper with red wings, one with blue wings, one with yellow wings, and one with black wings. They told them, "You four must go along for you run fastest. You must stay there and show them how to plant the wheat."

Then these four grasshoppers took their caps off, filled them with wheat, and carried it along that way. They started off. Every time they jumped they spilled some.

So the leader said, "You must not jump."

So they started to fly, carrying the seed on their backs. This time it was carried all right.

They all flew to the holy place. When they arrived, those who were there said, "It is a good thing you have come."

After the grasshoppers had brought their burden to the holy place, Talking Hactcin said to them, "I am going to use this in some way. That is why I had you bring it. You must go over to the place where the turkey is, go to the other side of the field he has planted and show the people how to plant this wheat. Stay around and guard it. You must not eat the leaves when it grows."

One carried the seeds. Then they divided them. Each took a handful. They formed in a parallel line, and they threw seeds down and scratched up the ground as they advanced, for the grasshopper has claws.

They arrived at one end of the field. They had used up one bag going across. They turned around and did the same thing coming back, using the contents of the second bag.

The grasshoppers asked, "What are we going to eat while we are working over here?"

Turkey had planted all kinds of plants next to the fields, sunflowers and all the other plants. "You must eat these while you are working. You must not disturb my corn and you must not use my wheat." That is what Turkey said.

The grasshoppers were afraid of Turkey when they heard this and they obeyed.

[1] The Jicarilla stored surplus food in cave caches, but did not use ground caches.

The wheat began to grow. The field became covered with growing grain. Soon the grain was becoming ripe.

Then Talking Hactcin called upon a female cloud. "You must send some water and moisten this field. But do not send hail," he told her.

She said, "All right."

After a while a black cloud came. There was lightning and a storm. It rained steadily but not hard. It was just a shower. The grasshoppers were frightened because it was raining. They were afraid of getting wet.

The turkey said, "Come under my wings and you won't get wet."

It rained a long time. The earth was well soaked. Then the rain passed. The turkey gobbled. He was happy about it, for his corn was well watered. The sun was shining again. The grasshoppers leaped from under the turkey's wings. They were happy. They flew about and made noises, for they were joyful that the wheat was wet.

Talking Hactcin then said, "In springtime we are going to have a dance." Then he thought about it. "No, let us change it. Let us wait till fall when the people have plenty of food and plenty of pollen."

Before the coming of Morning Light, Turkey gobbled and Grasshoppers flew and made a great sound of joy. The turkey was watching the grasshoppers closely so that they would not eat the corn or the wheat.[1]

The corn became tall. In one month it was three feet high. The next month it was four feet high. The wheat was already high and had kernels. The next month the corn had tassels and the corn and the wheat were getting ripe.

The following month the corn had pollen on the tassels and the people were told, "You must gather all the pollen from the corn plant and save it."

The people were eager to pick and eat the fresh corn. They asked the turkey how they were to go about it.

Turkey went to Talking Hactcin and asked him, "How are we going to teach the people? What will be a good way for them to eat the corn?"

Talking Hactcin said, "Tell them to roast it fresh. That is a good way to eat it."

Turkey said, "I never roast it myself."

Turkey told the people, "Now it is harvest time. The corn is ready. All of you go out and collect the corn into one pile. Break off the husk. Look for good grinding rocks. Grind the corn kernels and eat the corn that way too."

---

[1] It will be noted that wheat and its guardian, the grasshopper, which represent an alien source of food, are subordinated throughout this account to corn and the turkey.

Some of the people roasted the corn fresh. They were all happy about it.

Now it was the turn of the grasshoppers, for the wheat was ripe. The grasshoppers would have liked to take some, but they were afraid that Turkey would eat them if they did so. They were afraid to touch it or handle it. So they called to the people and said, "Come over and take care of your wheat."

"How shall we put away this grain?"

"We just break off the stalks and put them away," the grasshoppers said, "but you people have fingers. You can break off the stalks, put them on a smooth place, and thresh the grain."

The turkey showed them how he ate the corn in his own way. He just swallowed the kernels whole without chewing them. The people thought it was a peculiar way, but they did the same. Then they defecated. The kernels were excreted in the same way, whole.

Turkey laughed and said, "You must grind it on a metate. Don't do just what I do. I have a grinding stone in my stomach."

Grasshopper said to the people while they were threshing, "You must not eat it all. Save some for next year for seed. That is all we have to show you. Now we are going home. Your place is too cold for us."

Turkey said, "This is the end of my work. I'd better go back to the mountains. In the spring I will come back again and we will then plant some more corn and wheat. And we will cultivate more land too."

And Turkey Hactcin said some more words about the dance. "I will give my downy feathers to Talking Hactcin, for he said he is going to have another dance next fall." He gobbled, "I do more work than other people." He jumped four times and then started to fly to his own country.

Truthful Hactcin[1] went back to White Flint Mountain. He lives in that mountain; it is between south and west where Dziłcidjei is. Hactcinyoyi went back to Sodziłi. He lives there. That is toward the west. Dancing Hactcin went back to Tcocgaidziłi, to the west. Hactcin's Child went back to Gockandziłi. It is between west and north. These were the four who sent all the sickness to the north.

[1] Truthful Hactcin wore no clothes. His body was colored black, including his face and hands. One downy feather was tied on top of his head, an eagle feather. He wore no loin cloth but was naked. This was the real one, the first one. After that, when he was represented, he had a loin cloth of narrow yucca leaves woven and left the natural color of the plant. He wore no mask. He had long curly black hair, hanging down loosely. He had no shoes. They borrowed the shoes from Dipper and returned them after the dance. At the ankle yucca leaf was tied. The first time he wore no spruce boughs. Now he wears them around the waist. The first one wore no yucca at the ankle either.

The original Hactcin had power of their own. They came to help the people, not to dress up. The first ones had nothing borrowed from man or the earth. (Inf.)

They said they were going to these mountains and were going to help the people from there. All these Hactcin who inhabit these mountains live inside of the mountains. They come out and go on top sometimes.

When the time came, in autumn, Talking Hactcin sent for Dancing Hactcin. He called him directly to the holy place. The people of the earth all gathered around. Talking Hactcin told the people of the new message they had received from the skies.

Talking Hactcin asked, "Do you all believe this new message?"

And the people answered, "Yes."

"I sent Grey Hactcin up there. He has returned to tell us this. Grey Hactcin has come back and brought us this message from White Hactcin and Black Sky Hactcin. They wanted me to tell you this. That is why I have called you here. White Hactcin said that you people must have faith. Many of your people are dying around you. Grey Hactcin brought good news from up there. Those who live up there are not going to die. They all pray for us. Sun Hactcin and Moon Hactcin are praying for us and watching over us. They want us to pray to them too. The stars gathered around and told Grey Hactcin that everything was all right in their country too. Sun spoke to the moon, and the moon to the morning star, and thus Grey Hactcin and his dog were brought down. They came to a place above this holy place, and they were brought down by a meteor."

Talking Hactcin said, "You people must all believe what White Hactcin says. All above you and from all the directions around you those people, the Hactcin, are guarding you. Those of them who are living in the mountains are going to stay there and watch over you and pray for you from there, but they are not going to come back and dance for you. You people must all have faith. If you like it we will have another dance.

"When the time comes I am going to choose a good man, one who has faith, and I shall make him just like me.[1] I am going to choose some man and teach him about this ceremony. Grey Hactcin and I will help you. We will teach you to dance. We will help you for two days and two nights and then we will leave you. We will have to go back. The man whom I choose will have to stay here from now until the time for the ceremony, for I shall have to teach him all.

"The rest of you people must go out and look for something to eat, and by the time the ceremony is ready to start you all will have enough. Then move your camps around this holy place.

"In autumn, four days after the new moon, all of you people must come here again. Then I will choose the young people and I will make them just like the Hactcin."

All the people went home.

The time came. They all gathered around the holy place. All the young men were called together.

---

[1] In the Hactcin ceremony of the Jicarilla, the singer takes the place of Talking Hactcin of the first ceremony. (Inf.)

Two young boys were chosen. One was painted black and one blue. They were about ten years old.[1]

Then two young men were chosen and they were to be painted black. They were told to stand aside. Then two were chosen who were to be blue. Then two were chosen who were to be yellow. Then two were chosen to be painted white, and they stepped aside also.[2]

Then two were chosen who were going to be dressed up with spruce branches. Their bodies were to be painted black. They stepped aside. Then two who were to be decorated with spruce branches but whose bodies were to be painted blue were chosen and they stepped aside.[3]

Then one was chosen and of him Talking Hactcin said, "I am going to make horns on him."[4]

And another was chosen who was going to wear a mask. His body was to be black.[5]

Then two other young men were chosen to represent the fighting stars.[6]

These chosen so far were to represent Hactcin.

Now some were to be chosen to represent the striped people, the clowns. Altogether eight were selected for this. The eight were so chosen that the leader was the tallest and they were graduated in size to a small one for the eighth.[7]

Then one big man and one small one were chosen. They were to be the deer. Then two more were chosen to represent the animal leaders, one was to come before and one behind.

They all stood there. Then they were dismissed for the time.

Talking Hactcin turned to the people, "Now all of you be here."

The people who were going to make a corral stood there. Talking Hactcin went around and sprinkled pollen on the ground in a circle. This was where the corral was to stand.

The men who were going to dance went around to gather yucca leaves, small and large, large ones for the whip. They looked for spruce boughs with soft needles. They sought white clay, yellow ochre, specular iron ore, and black clay. And they looked for abalone and downy feathers. They were not going to dance that day. The preparations were to take four days.

Some began to work on the corral for the ceremony.[8] Others were

---

[1] They are to impersonate Hactcin's Children.

[2] These are to impersonate the eight Hactcin of the colors.

[3] These are to impersonate the four Spruce Hactcin.

[4] This one is to impersonate the Solitary or Single Hactcin with horns.

[5] This one is to impersonate the masked Solitary or Single Hactcin.

[6] The two fighting stars are Castor and Pollux.

[7] Note that eight clowns dance in the Hactcin ceremony, whereas but six take part in the bear dance.

[8] The large corral is about forty yards in diameter. The Hactcin home, the smaller corral, is about thirty feet in diameter. They make the sides thick with brush so the dancers cannot be seen from the outside. The big corral stands for the sun; the little one for the moon. When the sun and

constructing a corral for the dancers, to take the place of the Hactcin home of the first ceremony.

The clowns were looking for deer hooves for rattles, for sunflowers, for white clay, and for buffalo hide out of which to make their caps.

The men who were to be Hactcin were looking for mountain sheep hide for masks.[1]

Some were looking for a piñon tree which had been struck by lightning, so that they could find a piece of lightning riven wood lying to the east.[2]

Some went to get the two young spruce trees for the doorway which would guard the people. And those who were going to be Black Hactcin went to find young spruce trees which they would carry.

Talking Hactcin was there still and Grey Hactcin and his dog, and the wife of Talking Hactcin was there also. They were the only ones present. Those three were the only real supernaturals who remained. They watched the young people. If anything was needed, they sent them for it.

The people who were constructing the corrals had to have pollen on top of their heads. They worked for three days.

Then Talking Hactcin said, "Tomorrow get busy and work all day. Go out early and take a bath in the river before you start on the fourth day.[3] Cleanse yourself first."

The third night Talking Hactcin and Grey Hactcin took two men in the holy place with them. One was to represent the clowns and one the Hactcin. They sang all night with these men, teaching them the songs and prayers. This continued till morning glow.

---

moon see these corrals they know what is being done. The doors face the east.

The sick people sit in between the two corrals in the open, for it is as if they were abandoned until they are "brought back" by the ceremony. They have no covering over them at all.

Inside each of the two corrals is a central fire pit. There is no fire in the corral in the daytime. There is a big one at night, though, and in the large corral there are four fires on the south side (the women's side) and four fires on the north (the men's side). (Inf.)

[1] Later the man who sang for the ceremony made and kept the masks. If the ceremony is handed down, the masks are given along with it. A man prays when he makes these masks, for it is not in fun. The masks can be of the hide of male or female mountain-sheep. It is hard enough to get either. The masked dancers sprinkle corn-meal on the masks first and then motion four times before putting them on. They pray while they motion toward their heads with the masks. (Inf.)

[2] In the first ceremony the supernaturals are said to have used a fragment of spruce for the bull-roarer.

[3] The dancers have to bathe in the river before the Hactcin ceremony. The camp people have to bathe and cleanse themselves before the ceremony too. The man who sings gives good advice to the people. He tells them, if there is much sickness around, that sickness will get them if they are not clean. (Inf.)

Then Grey Hactcin went to the camps and said, "Come in, hurry, you people who have been chosen to dance."

To the women he said, "Get the food ready, for at noon we must all eat."

Now all the young people came. To them they said, "If you have partners with whom you are going to dance, you have to stay with them."

The young people started to weave the yucca, making aprons. Some made wristlets and anklets.

Those who represented clowns made caps. The first two caps were painted black. Specular iron ore was used. The next two were colored blue with blue paint. The next two were painted yellow with yellow ochre and the last two were painted white with white clay.

For arm bands they wore woven yucca. The leaves at the base which come out white when you pull them were used for this. A band of the same material was worn at the wrist. The same kind was worn at the ankles and below the knee. These were put on all the Hactcin. The loin cloth was made of the whole leaf of the yucca.

One person was busy making a groaning stick.

They worked at these tasks until noon. The women brought the food at noon. They brought corn bread and wheat bread, because they were rich and were raising corn and wheat now. The food was handed all around. Before these people ate, the food was sprinkled, clockwise, with pollen.

Then the clowns brought the excrement of the dog and child. They merely put it there; they did not touch it, for it was not to be touched till that night when all were dressed up and the ceremony was ready to begin.

When all had eaten the dishes were put in a straight line to the east outside the corral, and the women came and got them.

Then one who was taking the part of Thunder Hactcin asked for a string for his groaning stick. It had to be of mountain-sheep hide.[1] The man who made it patterned it after the first one which had been made.

In the holy place two real clowns had been left. After these two they patterned the clowns they were to make.

The clowns had corn bread made for them in the shape of the new moon and full moon. Each one was given two pieces of each shape. This they put on a string around themselves.

The clowns were first painted white all over. Then four stripes of black were painted on the legs, body and face. The cap they wore had four black stripes on too. These black stripes were made of the ashes of the burned sunflower plants. The whole plant was burned to obtain these ashes.

---

[1] If they don't have mountain-sheep hide, they use deer. But they call it mountain-sheep string even though it is from deer, because this is a holy place. (Inf.)

The cap of the clowns was made to come down as far as the brow. It covered the top of the head only. On each side the hair of the hide was bunched up and tied. These bunches were called horns. At the ends of the horns there were downy feathers and the cap was tied under the chin by means of a cord. It came down in back to the nape of the neck. The hair, except for the "horns," had been scraped off the hide and the hide had been worked to make it pliant. This cap was painted white all over first. Then the black stripes were put on. Hide from any part of the animal and from either a male or a female animal could be used. In their hands the clowns carried bows and arrows. There were downy feathers at the ends of the bows. Both bow and arrow were made of willow; any kind of willow could be used. The arrows were not feathered. There were no stone tips on the arrows; they were just painted wood. Both the bows and arrows were painted white with white clay.

The clowns wore low cut moccasins of buffalo hide, sewed with buffalo sinew, and on top of the foot they tied the rattle of deer hooves.

The Hactcin Children were painted, one black and one blue all over from head to feet.[1] Each had a downy feather tied on top of his head. In each hand they held a spruce branch and a whip of wide-leafed yucca. Their whips had no feathers or flints on the end. They wore moccasins of natural grey color. Hactcin's Child was the only name they were called.

They next dressed the two called Black Hactcin. Both of them had masks which covered only the face and were tied under the hair in back. Each wore an apron of woven yucca tied about his middle. They wore yucca arm bands, wrist bands, and bands below the knees and at the ankles on both sides. They held a spruce branch about three feet long in the left hand and long-leaved yucca with the spruce brush in the right hand. These two were painted black with specular iron ore. They wore low uncolored moccasins. The mask was black also and had a small hole for the mouth. In the yucca bands spruce branches were stuck. Both of them were dressed exactly the same.

The two Blue Hactcin came behind. They were dressed and painted the same as the Black Hactcin except that their bodies and masks were blue. Otherwise they looked the same as the Black Hactcin. The Blue Hactcin held yucca in both hands and spruce branches in both hands also. The Black Hactcin had yucca in only one hand.

The two Yellow Hactcin came behind them. They were dressed in the same way except that their color was yellow. In their hands they held both yucca and spruce. On top of their heads all these eight Hactcin had downy feathers.

[1] To paint the one blue they used copper sulphate, and to paint the other black they used black ochre.

The White Hactcin, two of them, came next. The only difference in their costume was that they had whiskers of buffalo bull hair tied to the mask and painted white. Except for this and their color they were just like the others.

Then came two Spruce Hactcin. Their bodies were painted black. Around them they slipped circles of soft spruce[1] and these covered their bodies from knee to head. Buckskin string was used to tie the branches together in circles. These circles were slipped over the head and tied behind.

The next two were also Spruce Hactcin. And their spruce was the hard-leafed one.[2] Their bodies were painted blue. In each hand they held whips of yucca. All four of the Spruce Hactcin had these whips. They wore yucca bands with spruce thrust in at the knees and ankles. The moccasins they wore were not colored.

Now a single Hactcin came. This one was decorated with horns but wore no mask. His face was blackened with specular iron ore. On top of his head they tied a downy feather. From the elbows to the finger tips, his arms were painted red, and his legs were red from the knee to the foot. The rest of his body they did not paint. He wore a yucca apron. They made yucca horns for him and tied them on his hair. In each hand he carried a blade of broad-leafed yucca. His shoes were like those worn by the rest. He was called Solitary Hactcin.

The next was a single Hactcin and he was masked. The other Solitary Hactcin and this one always run up and down the line by themselves when the dancers go out. That is why they are called Solitary Hactcin. This one had his body painted entirely black. At the four customary places the yucca bands were tied and he wore the yucca apron. His mask was of mountain-sheep hide and like the masks of the eight Hactcin of the different colors. The mask was blackened. He carried broad-leafed yucca in his hand. He, too, was called Solitary Hactcin. Of these two who go by themselves, the one with the mask is allowed to go clockwise or counter-clockwise; but when they turn around the one with horns and no mask can only proceed clockwise.

Now came the two who represented the Two-Fighting-Stars Hactcin. They were painted red from elbows to fingers. Their upper arms and torsos to the knees were colored sky blue. A downy feather was tied to the top of their heads. Their faces were blackened with specular iron ore. From the knees to the toes they were painted red. They wore the yucca bands with spruce and the aprons. Their moccasins were of uncolored buckskin. These two were told always to dance forth and back.

The one who represented Thunder Hactcin and carried the groaning stick did not dress up at all. This was because he was told never to come in, but to stand outside the big corral and sound the stick.

[1] Soft spruce is Douglas fir.

[2] Hard-leafed spruce is white fir.

Now it was the turn of the deer. There were two deer, the first a male, the second a female deer. They were covered with the fur of the kind of deer they represented. Both were men, but one took the part of the female deer. They were both white-tailed deer. They held the hides over their bodies and their faces were colored with specular iron ore. They had sticks in either hand and walked as deer do. Their sticks were not of any special kind of wood. The horns were left on the hide and the man who represented the buck wore them. The male was a four-pronged buck. The one who represented female deer had no horns. But he held the sticks in the same way and his face was covered with specular iron ore.

Then came the Animal Leaders, two of them. They were dressed entirely in buckskin with leggings, moccasins, shirts, but no caps. Each had two eagle tail feathers hanging at the back of the head and their faces were painted black with specular iron ore. Each carried a mountain-lion skin quiver with arrows in it and held a bow and arrows in his hand. These were real arrows, the kind that people use on the hunt. They were not of any special wood or color. The arrows had flint points. The buckskin worn by Animal Leaders was plain, uncolored.

Now all were dressed. They did not dress up men to represent Truthful Hactcin and the others who drove evil to the north. They are the biggest ones, the most powerful. The people do not want to represent them. They mention them in the songs and prayers but do not dress up anyone to represent them. They are too powerful. They only use the small and less important Hactcin for that.

It was nearly dark when the men were all dressed and ready. Then the clowns ate their medicine. They gave it to each other. The leader was the first to take it. They motioned four times and put it in his mouth. Then the eight of them in turn had to swallow some four times.

Then the camp people were told to go into the holy place at once. The people went in. The Hactcin were in line and ready to dance before starting for the holy place. Talking Hactcin and the one who was being taught by him were there. They were going to sing for the dancers. After this time the Apache was going to do it by himself.

Before they started Talking Hactcin went down the line and shouted four times into the mouth of each dancer. And then he called four times into the mouth of the Apache to whom he was teaching the ceremony. When this was done Talking Hactcin and this Apache walked among those dancers and inspected them to see how they stood and how they were dressed.

Talking Hactcin said to the Apache singer and the dancers, "You must watch well, for this is the last time I am going to help you. After this dance I am going to leave you and go away."

Talking Hactcin spoke to the Hactcin dancers about the Apache whom he had been instructing. "This is the new man," he said. "He is going to take care of the ceremony for you after this. You must obey him. You people have to dance four times during this ceremony. If any of you should not be here, his place must be filled by another."

Then he spoke to Animal Leader, "Next time, when you make the deer, you must make the female and the child. Do it without the male deer. Have a fawn." They couldn't do this the first time because the male and female deer didn't have a child.

Then Talking Hactcin gave to the new man who was going to take care of this ceremony in the future a buffalo tail rattle which he had made during the day. Inside were kernels of that "sticky corn" to make it rattle. He handed it to the new man and then the dancers pranced in line. The man held the rattle up to the directions in turn. To the rattle was tied one downy feather of the turkey and one downy feather of the eagle. One side of the rattle had a design on it. It was a picture of a Hactcin holding a sun in his hand. On the other side was the same form, but he was holding the moon. The sun was made with rays. The images were incised on the hide.

When this rattle was held to the directions the singing and the dancing began. The Hactcin danced and then shouted. The groaning stick sounded and all the camp people who were outside got in the corral.

Talking Hactcin showed the dancers how to sway and dance until he was satisfied, then he let them go out.

The horned Solitary Hactcin was the leader of the dancers the first time. But Talking Hactcin did not wait for them. He went ahead and into the large corral.

He told the people, "You must give them an offering of pollen and corn-meal when they come."[1]

To the men and women assembled there he said, "If you have a headache, fan it away with your hand. Pray at the same time. Here is a new man coming to sing for the dancers. Next time he will do it alone."

Now the leader of the line, the single, horned dancer, came in. He came around the women's side. The single dancer with mask came along the men's side. They both shouted at the same time. Then came the clowns. They went straight to the center, "We are hunting," they said. And each of them said, "I am a good hunter. That is why I speak so."

The Hactcin of all colors started to come in. They all came in swaying. The last one to enter was Deer Keeper or Animal Leader. They all lined up and then faced the west.

---

[1] The people can't look at the faces of the Hactcin. When the Hactcin come in the people have to lower their eyes and bow their heads and throw pollen or corn-meal four times in the direction of the Hactcin. To look at the Hactcin would make your face crooked. (Inf.)

Then the singing started. The singer had the rattle in his hand. The Hactcin danced and made their call at the same time. All of them did it. The two Solitary Hactcin and the Two-Fighting-Stars Hactcin kept moving all the time. These four never stood still.

The first song was for the Hactcin. Then came a clown song. To it the clowns did that high step. The Hactcin danced too. The clowns acted as if they were drunk, for they had eaten their medicine. They danced ecstatically and furnished much amusement. After the clown song they sang a song that stood for both kinds of dancers.

Then the two foremost clowns walked out of line. They crawled to the deer, both of them. When they got near the deer they lay motionless. The Hactcin continued dancing. Then the clown leader motioned four times and "killed" the big deer. The second clown motioned four times and shot the female. Both deer fell down. The other clowns ran towards the place and rubbed their hands saying, "After this I will have good luck hunting deer. Wherever I go I will find many deer."

Then three of them helped lift one deer and put it on the back of the leader, and they went to look for a pretty girl. This would be the payment to secure the woman in marriage. They went around the women and chose a pretty girl whom they liked. Then the leader put his feet far apart and said, "Here is a deer. I'm a good hunter. You must marry me. Here is a fat deer. I give it to you for a marriage gift. Here is the arrow with which I killed the deer."

The rest of the clowns followed the two who were carrying the deer. They all chose girls saying, "After this if you marry me, you will eat deer meat all the time."[1]

Now the clowns started a joyous dance toward the Hactcin. They said, "We are glad because we are going to marry." They coupled up and made believe they were having intercourse. They had fun and amused the people.[2] Then this song and dance came to a close.

---

[1] Sometimes they choose a married woman and tease her; they can choose anyone. The feet are set wide apart because it is a funny posture. (Inf.)

[2] The clowns use backward speech. They say everything that people are not supposed to say, and this is true of the clown in the bear dance too. They are showing the people by action what not to do. Then the people are reminded of what they shouldn't do and tell their children, "See the clown. He is doing a shameful thing which you should not do." That's how they advise one another. The older people give advice to the younger when they are in the big corral. The clowns have intercourse (make-believe) with one another. One lies down and the other gets on top. And they give things to each other, making believe that they are paying and that one is a man and the other a woman. This should not be done by the people at the time of the ceremony either.

The clowns follow the Hactcin and pick up all the pieces of spruce that fall. They are imitating the Hactcin when they do this, but they do it for another purpose too. The reason is that it is dangerous to have anything lost in that holy place. If you drop something the clowns pick it up and give it to you. (In the bear dance the clowns do the same thing for the Tsanati.)

They all started out. The groaning stick was sounded. Animal Leader went back and picked up his deer. The two solitary dancers stayed till the last. Otherwise they went out as they came in. The last ones to go out before the solitary dancers were Two-Fighting-Stars. Then, when the others were already at their home, the one with horns ran out and then the one with the mask followed shouting. The groaning stick was sounded as they departed.

Talking Hactcin went among the people and said, "Now go home. Go to sleep. I'm not going to sleep. I'm going to sing and teach this new man for you. Get up early and prepare food."

The two singers went back to the Hactcin home, making a noise with the rattle as they went. They entered.

"All stay at home," they commanded.

No one was in the big corral now.

Then Talking Hactcin told Grey Hactcin, "Go around the camps clockwise but do not shout."

Grey Hactcin did so and came back.

"Did you see or hear anything?"

"No."

"All right. Let the people sleep."

Talking Hactcin spoke to the dancers. He told them over and over, "You have to obey this new man."

They all said, "We will do so."

The people had been told that in the morning when the Hactcin shouted four times, they must get up.

The dancers sat quietly in the Hactcin home and Talking Hactcin and the new man sang all night long and practiced until the morning came. Talking Hactcin was teaching the new man.

Then Talking Hactcin said to the others, "This is the man to whom I am going to give the ceremony for you. He will conduct it after this. We Hactcin will not be here, but we will listen from where we are. I will teach this man for you. This ceremony is not only for sickness. Sometimes make this ceremony in the springtime.[1] In the spring pray for the deer and for the coming crops. The deer will be changing their coats, and by that you will know it is time.

The clowns show mock fear too. They jump and act as though something has scared them.

Black Sky was the father of the original clowns and the mother was someone under the earth. No one knows who she was.

One who has danced as a clown can stop a rain storm which has been in progress a long time. He asks it to cease, and it does. He does not have to be dressed up like a clown when he does this. (Inf.)

[1] We use the Hactcin when there is something serious, like a great deal of disease, an epidemic. The ceremony can be held any time of year. It can be held in spring or fall for the crops. It can be held for the benefit of crops at these two seasons even if there is no sickness. It will make the rain come as needed if it is held in the spring and will assure a good crop if it is held in the fall. When we do it for the crops on either of these two occasions we wait till the new moon to begin the ceremony. Inf.

"Tomorrow morning you must all paint yourselves again. For the paint on some of you will fade.

"The other Hactcin will not be here any more. Some have gone into the mountains, some have gone up in the sky. But, though they are not here, they know what we are doing. Tonight the Moon Hactcin will see what we do. And Morning Star Hactcin and Two-Fighting-Stars Hactcin and Three-Vertebrae-Stars Hactcin and Pleiades Hactcin are going to pass and see what we are doing at night. Big Dipper and North Star will see us too. White Hactcin will be watching us. He is the one who wants me to tell you all this and show you how to do it. Tomorrow morning Sun Hactcin and Rosy-Cheeked Hactcin will pass and see us.

"All of you must remember Spring, Summer, Autumn, and Winter Hactcin and pray to them too. Remember what I tell you.

"Some day when there is sickness this man I am teaching for you is going to perform this ceremony for you, but without a corral sometimes. I will give him a groaning stick to use. He will use these prayers.[1]

"I am going to send all this sickness, all these Sickness People to the other side of the dipper, to the north. In one ceremony when we make a corral it is different, for then we have Bear Hactcin among those people, the one who steals the people.[2]

"You people will see me for just a little while and you will hear me for just a short time more. That is why I give you this talk."

The next morning came. All those Hactcin were painted anew. The deer were also painted again.

They started to paint about four o'clock in the morning. They shouted four times just before the morning light came and this was the signal for the people to get up.

Before they were painted, Talking Hactcin told them, "You must mix all the white clay and prepare all the different paints."

Then, when the sun rose, the women brought the food. Then the meal began.[3]

When breakfast was over the dancers began to dress up with spruce branches.

Now many of the dancers were already dressed. They sent four

---

[1] In the little ceremony now used for curing we sing and pray, using the songs and prayers of the big ceremony. But we don't have dancers dress up or anything like that. Sometimes when someone has a stiff or twisted neck, the man with the Hactcin ceremony can cure it in this way. (Inf.)

[2] This refers to the bear dance.

[3] In the Hactcin ceremony, when the men who dance are being fed, they always sprinkle a little soup or corn-meal on the masks first; they feed them too. In any ceremony something like this is done. When the people who are giving the ceremony serve something to eat, the singer always breaks off a little piece and, with four motions, throws it to the east. He is offering it to the power who is helping him. All the people present then do the same thing; they break off a little of the food given them and throw it to the east. (Inf.)

of the clowns to the camps of the people, and the clowns chased the people into the corral. These four made them all go to the corral. They shouted to the people to go in. The clowns can talk. Some of the people were too slow, and the clowns pretended they were going to shoot them, motioning toward them with their bows and arrows. It took a long time to drive them all in.[1] This was a big encampment with many people around. When all had been driven in there, the clowns came back to the Hactcin home.

Talking Hactcin asked, "Are they all in the corral?"

The clowns answered, "Yes, they are all there."

The dancers were all ready. They were all dressed. The Hactcin dancers, when they had come back to their own corral the evening before, had brought back all they wore and put it aside. Now it was all on again, and the man with the groaning stick stood at the door of the Hactcin home.

They started. One Solitary Hactcin, the one with the mask, was the leader this time.[2] He went out of the door four times and backed up each time. Then he went out, shouting as he left. The horned Solitary Hactcin was next. He went through the same ritual feint before leaving and called out as he went out of the door.

Next came the Two-Fighting-Stars Hactcin. They did the same ritual feint before leaving the Hactcin home. But these two did not shout.

Next came the two Hactcin children. Then came the eight Hactcin of different colors. They all made the ritual motion and shouted. Next came the four Spruce Hactcin. Next were the eight clowns. Last were the Animal Leaders and the Deer.

The man with the groaning stick went far ahead to the other corral.

The Hactcin swayed forth and back, dancing. The two corrals were about 150 paces apart. The Hactcin shouted as they went; the clowns were laughing. The people who waited inside the corral had pollen and corn-meal ready.

The dancers entered, following along the south side. The masked Solitary Hactcin was first to enter; the two Solitary Hactcin were far ahead. The line did not zigzag. Every now and then they went backward a few steps, then forward, then backward again and forward once more.

The eight Hactcin of the colors, the Spruce Hactcin, and Hactcin's Children did a double quick step, first with the right and then with the left foot. The two Solitary Hactcin did a fast four-forward and four-backward step, keeping their arms upright and moving. The two who represented the stars ran forward a few steps, moving

---

[1] If the people come quickly by themselves, the clowns don't have to chase them. If they do not come at once, the clowns chase them into the corral. (Inf.)

[2] The Solitary Hactcin with mask has a different call from the other dancers.

their hands in a forward circle as they went. Then they ran backward moving their hands in the opposite direction. The clowns did anything they wanted to; they went any old way because they were trying to be funny. They went over to the Two-Fighting-Stars and tried to join them. They imitated these dancers, using their hands in the same way. Then they tired of that and went on to imitate some other dancer. Some of the clowns were joking about intercourse, and some were making queer noises. The Animal Leaders and the Deer walked along; they made no special motions.

When they arrived inside the big corral the rest stood still, but the two Solitary Hactcin kept moving up and down all the time. The two singers with the rattle were standing there. When they first came in Talking Hactcin stood in front of the Two-Fighting-Stars Hactcin dancers. He was on the north side, facing north. The deer stood right on the north side, last in line.

Then they said to the Deer, "Dance, but do not do a high dance. Just keep moving all the time."

The man who was learning from Talking Hactcin had downy feathers on top of his head. His face was painted with specular iron ore as was that of Talking Hactcin.[1]

They started to dance and the clowns laughed. Their laugh is not a human laugh, but a fearful laugh that frightens away the sickness. They danced as they pleased.

The ceremony was being held in the daytime now.

After the first song, during which they faced the north, they turned around and faced the south. Then the clowns went on the other side and faced the Hactcin dancers. The two who danced alone stood at the side of the clowns.

Before Talking Hactcin sang he always talked to the people and explained what it stood for, so they would believe in it.

Before this they had had all kinds of sickness. The clowns saw some men and women who had signs of sickness, smallpox signs, pockmarks, for instance. They went right up to them and said, "Oh, we thought we had Sickness driven away, but here is his track." They pointed with their arrows, standing in line.

"Did they go to the east?" they asked.

"No," said one.

They talked about it; they argued about which direction the sickness had taken. They pointed and jumped around and then ran away. Then they jumped aside and started to dance vigorously.

They all said, "That sickness is not around here any more. We shall all enjoy dancing. Our country will be at peace again and crops will be plentiful."

And then they danced for a little while. Now the clowns went on

---

[1] Besides having the face painted with specular iron ore and having downy feathers on top of the head, the singer must be dressed in old time buckskin clothes.

a hunt. They looked for tracks and finally pretended they had found the tracks on the women's side.

They said, "We will hunt for these girls, for we want to get married."

Then the Deer tried to get away. The Deer tried to scare them. The clowns joked with each other about it.

One said to another, "He must be smelling you; you'd better go back."

Another said, "Don't scare away my deer."

Another, "You are in my way."

When they neared the deer the whole eight of them crawled. Then the leader motioned four times with the string and shot the big deer.

After both deer were shot the clowns put their hands on them and rubbed themselves saying, "Wherever I go there will be many deer after this. The deer will not run away from me wherever I go."

Then three of them picked up one deer and put it on another's back. Three of them picked up the other one and put it on another's back. They said, "We will take this for a present so some woman will give us her daughter."

They carried the deer to the women's side. The eight of them stood in line.

One said, "I know a girl who is always smiling at me. She is the one I am going to marry." When they saw someone laugh they said, "Here she is."

They put the deer down by her. "This is what I brought for your people. Eat it. I've been out in the mountains and I brought it for you and for them.[1] This is my arrow which kills many deer."

Some of the arrows they had were painted partly red at the end. Some were red all along the shaft. So they said, "See the blood." And some said, "My arrows went all the way through." These arrows were blunt and it was very funny to hear them talk so.

Because they had made the girls laugh they said, "Let us all laugh and be joyous too." At the same time they danced themselves, for the two singers had started a song for them now. They all turned and danced, jumping high and making the people laugh. The women, while the clowns were near, scattered corn-meal and pollen on the deer, praying as the singers told them to do.

When this one dance was over Talking Hactcin told the people all about this. "Watch closely," he said. "Next time you have this ceremony I will not be here. You must learn it properly. But if you need me or need something from me, ask for it and I will help you."

Then Animal Leader went to look for his Deer. When he found

---

[1] To bring gifts of food to prospective parents-in-law is one way of showing serious interest in a marriageable daughter of the household.

Deer, he hit him four times with his arrow and Deer arose. But those Animal Leaders said no words.

Then Talking Hactcin went to the men's side. The first time he had spoken he had been on the women's side. Now he told the men the same thing. "Look at these people. When they have another dance, perhaps one will be missing. Listen to the man to whom I am teaching the ceremony. If he asks you to fill up the place of the missing person, you must not say no."

They all promised they would help. Then he motioned to the two Solitary Hactcin dancers. They went around sunwise in the interior of the corral. The man with the groaning stick sounded it. Then they went out in the same order in which they had entered. The two who danced alone did not go first but stayed back. The clowns went out. Then Two-Fighting-Stars went. The clowns kept on saying, "Everything will be all right. Our country will be free from disease," as they went. Next the Deer went. The horned Solitary Hactcin dancer walked back and forth at the door four times and then ran out. The masked Solitary Hactcin followed the same procedure. The dancers went back. The groaning stick sounded as it always does when the dancers go out or come in. As they went the dancers called every once in a while.

The two singers stayed behind. They did not go out at once. Then they gave good advice to the people. "This ceremony is given so that you people will increase," they said, "so that you will have a long life and good food. If you have even a headache, pray to the Hactcin. If you have a fever, pray. They will help you.

"Tonight we will gather in this corral for the third time, and tomorrow will be the last time. Then I will talk to you again and you must listen closely. Then my body will leave you entirely."

The noise of the groaning stick stopped. That meant that all the dancers were back in the Hactcin home.

"All you people go to your camps, but tonight we are going to have another dance. Don't wait for anything."

The singers went out first and the rest of the people followed.

He told them, "When you get word to come you must get ready more quickly. Some of you are too slow." Some of them had to look for horses. He wanted them to do all their jobs and to be in readiness.

The two singers went back to the Hactcin home. It was late afternoon, almost evening. They had danced a long time this second time.

The Hactcin eat only once a day. This is in the morning, not early in the morning, but sometime before noon.

There are many songs to the ceremony. New ones are sung for the different dances all the time. It is just like turning pages to the end.

Now it was night. When it was growing dark Grey Hactcin[1] went

---

[1] This was the real Grey Hactcin; Grey Hactcin was still there. (Inf.)

around with his dog to inspect the two yucca leaves which had been placed at each of the different directions. He returned with his dog.

"How is everything?" Talking Hactcin asked.

"All right."

So Talking Hactcin sang and the Hactcin danced in their own home. That made the people hurry to go to the corral, for they knew they were nearly ready to begin the ceremony. The Hactcin shouted four times to warn the people and then they began to dance. The clowns did not go out to get the people in the corral this time. They did it only in the daytime.

Talking Hactcin and his pupil were at the Hactcin home. Talking Hactcin said, "This man is learning fast. Very soon I am going to let him sing by himself."

When the people heard the four cries they all started in. They were now all in the corral, and the dancers were ready.

This time the horned Solitary Hactcin dancer came out of the Hactcin home first.

Talking Hactcin told the dancers, "You must be very careful and follow my directions, for I won't be here next time."

Each time they go out they change the leader.

The groaning stick sounded. The single dancer with horns motioned forward and backward four times at the door and went out, giving a shout as he left.

Though the holes for the eyes were not large the masked dancers could see everything.[1]

The masked Solitary Hactcin dancer went out second. He also went forward and back four times and shouted as he passed the door.

This time the clowns were next. The man with the groaning stick got halfway between the corrals and stood there. The clowns were noisy. They talked loudly so that the others would hear and laugh. The people in the big corral could hear them, they talked so loudly. The people held corn-meal in their hands to sprinkle towards the dancers.

Then came the Hactcin children, then the eight masked Hactcin of the colors, then the four Spruce Hactcin, then Two-Fighting-Stars, and last the Animal Leaders and the Deer. They are always last.

As they were about to enter the dancers shouted. Solitary Hactcin with horns went in, going first along the women's side. Next to enter was Solitary Hactcin with mask. The horned Solitary Hactcin had gone as the sun goes, but the other entered on the north side and went counter-clockwise. Next the clowns entered. They went straight to the center of the corral. The others followed in order. They first advanced toward the women's side, where corn-meal was sprinkled on them. The two who danced alone went to the men's side where corn-meal was sprinkled on them also. When they were all inside the Deer entered too.

[1] The costume of the dancers gives them strength for the dancing. (Inf.)

The groaning stick sounded at the west.[1] The one who sounded it first took his station at the east, then walked to the south, and then on to the west where he twirled it, though he had not sounded it at the east and south. Those inside are not supposed to see this groaning stick, for the groaning stick is against the sickness. After he sounds it, the man hides it in his clothing. He must not let anyone see it. He stays outside with it.

This dance was to be the end of the part of the ceremony held at night. The old man told the people, "Tomorrow is the last day. Perhaps some of you dreamed something evil last night. Perhaps some have fevers. Perhaps some have headache. Now is your chance. You must blow away that sickness, just as you shake from you the dust."

They had fires built all around at night, four on each side and one in the middle. The singer had told the men from the camps to make these fires. Four young men were chosen to build the fires, but before they did it, pollen was put on their hands and feet. The singer kindles the fire in the Hactcin home first, using two flints and shredded cedar bark beneath. This ignites and burns. Then the young men take brands over to the big corral and start the fires there from the brands. The central fire and the others are not in pits but are on top of the ground.

Every time the dancers come in they face the north first, the line faces the north. The two singers stood at the west side facing the dancers.

First came four songs for the Hactcin and then one for the clowns, one of their own songs. The Solitary Hactcin were together in front of the line. The Hactcin stood there throughout the clown song, doing nothing. After four songs the two Solitary Hactcin came around to the end of the line. After four songs were sung these two rested. They were usually moving around. After resting, they moved around for four more songs. When it was time for the clowns to dance to their song, they had great fun, throwing themselves high in the air.

After that song, they sang for the deer. Then the clowns said, "Oh, they are singing for the deer, so we will be lucky in the hunt."

While the singing was still going on the clowns separated into two groups of four dancers each. The leader said, "My family is hungry. We'd better hunt." They crawled toward the Deer. The two Animal Leaders were dancing, meanwhile. They paid no attention to the clowns and their hunting.

The leader crawled up to one deer. The others were going to come too, but the leader said, "You stay there. Be quiet. You make too much noise and scare the deer. And the deer smell you."

---

[1] The first night it had sounded at the east, the next morning it had sounded at the south, and this time at the west. (Inf.)

He crawled near one deer, the leader of the other party of clowns crawled near the other deer. They "killed" both of the deer as before. The leaders were different each time. On the first night the real leader of the clowns and the second man killed the Deer. The second morning the third and fourth men did it, the third time the fifth and sixth men did it, and the last time the seventh and eighth men acted as leaders. When changing leaders they said, "You have enough meat at home. My family is hungry. Let me kill the deer this time." So the ones whose turn it was killed the deer.

As before they took the deer to the girls as a present; both hunting parties did this. They always chose different girls. They did not bring it to girls to whom it had been brought before.

The clown said, "Just a little while ago I sang for a deer, that is why I killed one so soon."

Two girls stood together. One laughed and one didn't; this one was bashful and turned away. She didn't want the clowns to choose her.

The clown said, "She is my mother-in-law, that is why she turns away and doesn't want to see me," and he jumped away as though he had seen his mother-in-law.[1]

Then the clowns who were getting married acted as though they were celebrating. When the celebration was over they acted bashful and danced laughing toward the Hactcin. So they went back to the place where the Hactcin were. They all danced. The two Animal Leaders looked for the deer as before.

Then the groaning stick sounded. They all started to move towards the door. On the way they shouted. When they formed in line they all shouted at once, when they were going out they did not all shout at once, but each uttered his call whenever he wished.

Each motioned at the door four times before he went out. The deer were the last to leave except for the two Solitary Hactcin dancers. The one with horns went first. They each motioned four times before they went out. The Solitary Hactcin dancer with the mask was the last of the dancers to leave.

The man with the groaning stick sounded it when they were all at "home." Talking Hactcin was still in the big corral, for he was going to give a talk to the people.

"This is the last night," he said. "Tomorrow is the last day of this ceremony. Let all the people know that this ceremony is nearing the end. Hereafter this man whom I am teaching is going to do this for you in spring and autumn if you need it.

"If you all believe in it, Night Hactcin will watch over you. I will help you too. Moon Hactcin will guide you at night. Evening Glow Hactcin will watch over you and Morning Glow Hactcin will watch over you too. These Hactcin stand on the side of Night."

---

[1] The Jicarilla practice mother-in-law — son-in-law avoidance.

This dance had continued nearly all night. It was late. So the old man said, "Go back and sleep for just a little while, then get up and make everything ready."

The people went out, led by these two singers. The singers went to the Hactcin home and kept praying all night. It was the last night. The people went to their camps.[1]

Talking Hactcin sent out Grey Hactcin[2] to the east, south, west, and north and told him, "You must bring back all those things which you put in those places. They will not be needed to guard us at night now, for this is the end of the last night's ceremony, and while you are there keep your eyes open."

Grey Hactcin[3] went to the east. Wherever he went there were flashes of light bright as a meteor flying. He found nothing to the east. He picked up the two yucca leaves. He went to the south and picked up the yucca leaves he had put there. He saw nothing evil to the south. He went to the west and to the north. After completing his circuit he returned.

Talking Hactcin asked, "What did you see?"

"I saw nothing."

Grey Hactcin took his place. The dance of the night was over. He put the yucca leaves he had gathered inside the Hactcin home. Putting these yucca leaves around was like putting up a trap. When they catch some bad spirit on them they throw these leaves to the north. That is why they were put there, for those bad people, Sickness People, go around at night. It was for ghosts, too, — to keep them away.

The man with the groaning stick came in.

Talking Hactcin said, "Look at this groaning stick."

All the dancers looked at it closely.

"I'm not going to give this to you," he told them. "I am going to give it to this old man whom I have taught for you."

So he gave the new groaning stick to the new man, saying, "The other one is still here, the one that Thunder Hactcin left, I am not going to leave it with you. I am going to take it back to him." Thunder Hactcin had left his groaning stick in the Hactcin home.

"This new one I will leave for you. But this old one I will send back to Thunder."

So he sent Grey Hactcin to Thunder Hactcin with the groaning

---

[1] When the ceremony is held to cure sickness, no fire is allowed at the outside of the camps, for such a fire could be easily seen. The reason fires are not allowed outside is that the Sickness People would see them and come straight to that place. It is all right to have a fire inside the tipi however. (Inf.)

[2] Grey Hactcin and the dog always stayed at the Hactcin home. They never went to the big corral. They were sent only to the different directions. (Inf.)

[3] The one who takes the part of Grey Hactcin does not dress up. He just puts yucca strips around and looks at the yucca from time to time. (Inf.)

stick. "Thunder will watch over the groaning stick," Talking Hactcin said.

To Grey Hactcin he said, "Stand right in the doorway."

Grey Hactcin stood there. "How am I going to take it back?" he asked.

"You know how you came back from above. Go up there the same way."

Grey Hactcin used his power. He made himself like a flash of light.

Talking Hactcin said to him, "Now say four times, 'My friend, I am going to take this back to Thunder.'"

Grey Hactcin did as he was told. At once he disappeared. Talking Hactcin continued to pray. In a little while they saw lightning flash in the distance four times. This was Thunder Hactcin lighting the way for Grey Hactcin who was bringing him his groaning stick.

Then four more flashes of light were seen at Thunder's home and almost at once Grey Hactcin was back. He came in again.

Talking Hactcin asked, "What did he say?"

"He said, 'I know what you are doing.' He put the stick against my chest, my sides, and my back. 'I do this because I know you hurried,' he said. 'Tomorrow evening when the people go to bed I am going to send a shower. Tell Talking Hactcin that that means I am happy because you conducted this ceremony. This shower will make the air fresh and sweet and the people will sleep well.'"[1] Thus Grey Hactcin told this message before these people.

It was almost morning now.

It was Grey Hactcin's turn to go back to Tcicnadjin, a mountain to the east.[2] He was going back there with his dog.

Talking Hactcin gave pollen to the new singer and some specular iron ore. "Now sprinkle this toward Grey Hactcin and pray, for he is going to leave you. Say, 'Thank you.' And everyone pray, saying, 'If sickness comes or anything evil, watch over us. Protect us wherever you are.'"

All the dancers offered pollen and specular iron ore to Grey Hactcin. They sprinkled it toward him four times and then put some in their own mouths and on top of their heads. He was going to take the rattle along with him, the real one of the first ceremony which had also been left at the Hactcin home.

Talking Hactcin picked up the rattle. He struck it four times against the bottom of the right foot of the new singer and then four times against the bottom of his left foot, then on the right and left

---

[1] This passage is indicative of the degree to which the Jicarilla had become interested in rain ceremonies.

[2] It is a mountain about thirty miles east of Alamosa, Colorado. There is a plain between Alamosa and this mountain. The spruces are very thick on this mountain and its name, Tcicnadjin, means "wood coming out black." (Inf.)

knees, then on the right and left hands, then at the center of the chest, then on the back, then on the right and left shoulders, then on top of the head. He touched him four times with it at each of these points.

Talking Hactcin prayed and the dancers all came to him. With the rattle he struck the chest, back, and top of the head of each dancer four times. He touched in this way all the dancers, even to the deer and Animal Leader. And he touched each of the clowns.

The dog was becoming excited. It jumped around. Then the wind came. It wasn't a strong wind.

Talking Hactcin said to the clowns, "You must say four times to Grey Hactcin, 'In our country everything is good. Let us all be like you. Do not let sickness see us.' Say this and then everything that opposes you will disappear. The evil things won't touch you."

All of them said these words. They all said to Grey Hactcin, "Thank you. We see that where we live no evil is lying in wait. And wherever you are we will pray to you."

Grey Hactcin and his dog went out. The dog barked. The wind blew hard suddenly. The next moment the dog barked again, a little farther away. Further on the dog barked for a third time. A fourth time the dog barked, and by this time they were so far away that the bark could be heard only indistinctly. Grey Hactcin and his dog were already at home.

By that time the morning glow was showing. The Hactcin dancers shouted four times to wake the people. Talking Hactcin stood aside. He was now the only one of the real supernaturals there. The dancers were painted anew. They wanted to start early, because this dance was to last a long time, for most of the day.

The sun rose. The women brought the food. The dancers were ready to eat breakfast. The night before Talking Hactcin had told the women, "You must bring bread, twelve pieces shaped like the full moon and twelve shaped like the crescent moon.[1] And also bring twelve downy feathers, six of eagle and six of turkey, and a basket. Bring these things when you bring food in the morning."

So these were brought in the morning. The downy feathers were for the two singers. The basket was before them. The rest of the food was passed around where the dancers were sitting.

The two singers were in the Hactcin home and sprinkled pollen on all the food.

The clowns picked up the ashes from the fire. "We are going to put pollen on too," and they threw ashes four times on the bread.

They stirred with their fingers anything liquid, like soup, that was brought them and said, "Oh, this will make it sweet." Then they ate it.

The two old men put the downy feathers in the bowl.

---

[1] Since each of the eight clowns is given six pieces of this bread to wear (p. 206), it would seem that twice as many as this number would be needed.

Then Talking Hactcin said, "These downy feathers are like bread too. After this, when you want to have a ceremony, you must bring feathers just like these which have been given to the singer, in a basket[1] like this one, and put it on his right foot. Before you put it down, motion to the directions with it clockwise. If you bring this, he will do it for you."

The women came after the dishes. He took out the dishes. He said, "You'd better hurry. Get back to your homes and get ready." And he said to them, "You must open your ears. When the Hactcin call four times you must go right into the corral."

He started to sing for the Hactcin, and the Hactcin began to dance in their home.

Then Talking Hactcin shouted. He said, "Soon I am going to travel to the mountain top."

He called out again, "I must travel to the cliff top. When I travel on top of the cliff my voice will fill Sickness with fear. When I go to the edge of the cliff, that will frighten all sickness away. At the meeting of the canyons, when I shout there, all sickness and evil will not be able to stand in my way." And he shouted as he said these things.

"After this you must listen when you hear the Hactcin call from the mountains, from the cliffs, from the four places I have mentioned. When you hear their call, you must pray to me."[2]

He asked, "Did you all hear? Will you remember? You must help this old man who learned this ceremony from me. You must all help each other with this ceremony.

"Next time when this new man makes the ceremony for you, two young girls must help this Hactcin ceremony. They must act as dancers.[3] But I did not do it that way this time for you."

---

[1] The one who asks for a Hactcin ceremony gives the singer a big woven basket. The feathers are placed in this. A design of one deer is woven into it. The deer is in red color; the rest is plain. Sumac is used for both the inside and the wrapping of the coils. The singer keeps it; it is not used in the ceremony. (Inf.)

[2] If a Jicarilla goes past a Hactcin place he prays and gives what he has. He might drop beads there. Or he might offer puffs of smoke. I heard a Hactcin call not long ago at my sheep camp. I prayed when I heard the call. (Inf.)

[3] When there was much sickness around they used girls as dancers in this ceremony. They really used two girls; not men dressed up to resemble girls. These girls do not get dressed in the Hactcin home or stay there, however. They help only in the dancing. Their faces are painted red all over. They are called Hactcin Girls. They have to be unmarried. They dance in the big corral, and when they dance they have their hands upraised and hold soft spruce branches. They dance up and down in time to the music. At night they go home to their own camps. They have great power. They can drive the sickness away too. One represents the daughter of the moon and the other the daughter of the sun. When they dance, they stand directly in front of the others. The clowns do not make fun of them much, but just call them, "my mother." (Inf.)

Then the Hactcin began to dance. The new man began singing by himself. Talking Hactcin was listening and he was dancing too. He listened closely to make sure that the singer missed no part. The singer finished one song. He made no mistake.

"That is all right. You know it well. Sing another song."

So the new man sang another song. Each song had four verses; each verse was from one direction. The songs are like a bowl. When you sing a verse, the seeds go in it. When four songs were finished all the Hactcin shouted.

Talking Hactcin asked the one with the groaning stick, "Did the people go in?"

"Yes."

Talking Hactcin asked for another song. He danced himself. He did not sing. The singer made no mistake. He sang the song for all the directions. He made no mistake.

"Now sing a clown song."

He did so and they all danced.

"Now sing for Deer."

He did so. He had the rattle in his hand as he did it. The Hactcin shouted. The clowns uttered their laugh.

The masked Solitary Hactcin stood near the door. He uttered his call so that the people would hurry. He went forth and back four times and then he went out. The groaning stick sounded once more. Then the horned Solitary Hactcin dancer went forth and back four times, and he, too, went out. Then the Two-Fighting-Stars Hactcin dancers went back and forth four times, but did not shout, and went out. These never called out. They are the only ones who don't.[1] Next came the clowns. They went out making a great noise. "I'm going back to my wife," each shouted.[2] Next in order were the Hactcin children. The man with the groaning stick was now between the corrals. Then came the eight Hactcin dancers of the colors and the four Spruce Hactcin dancers. Last came the Animal Leaders and the deer.

By the time they had filed out of the Hactcin home the one with the groaning stick was already at the door of the big corral. The masked Solitary Hactcin dancer entered first. He made the ritual feint before he entered. The horned Solitary Hactcin dancer entered next. Then the dancers representing the stars entered, followed by the clowns, and the Hactcin of the colors.

The clowns tried to stay close to the girl's side. They pushed each

---

[1] The Two-Fighting-Stars Hactcin dancers utter no call. The call of the Solitary Hactcin with mask is slightly different from that of the others. All the other Hactcin have the same call. The clowns laugh in a stylized manner instead of shouting.

[2] The dancers are under sex restrictions during the rite, for they must stay and sleep in the Hactcin home when they are not performing in the ceremony. The clowns are here indicating that the rite is coming to a close and that the sex restrictions will consequently be terminated.

other in their hurry to get there, and they acted jealous of each other over the girls.

The dancers formed in line finally. The Deer dancers came last. They all stood still. The two singers went to the end of the line. They all faced to the north except the clowns who stood in a line to the north facing south. They had come in and circled around and stopped at the north. The Deer went over there too, and the people offered them pollen. After going all around the interior they stopped at the north, facing the south.

The old men faced the women, and said, "All women, children, boys, and girls, listen. Today this dance is going to end."

To the new singer Talking Hactcin said, "You must use your rattle all the time."

To the people he said, "I give this ceremony to you. I have taught it to this man. Even though you are women, you must believe in the Hactcin ceremony.[1] In any of the four seasons, when the people need this, perform it for them. This is my last day with you. This is the last time I will be with you. The rest of my people, the Hactcin, have been away a long time.

"I am going to leave you today. I am going to stay at the Hactcin home. That will be my home. You must pray to me. Do not forget."

He went over to the men's side. The women all said they heard and understood what Talking Hactcin had told them.

Talking Hactcin said, "This is why I talk to you. There are Hactcin all around us, at the east, south, west, and north. Those people will all guide you. Don't get tired of this ceremony. Don't forget it.

"The new singer is going to sing by himself now. I am going to listen."

The rest were glad to hear what he said.

"Whenever this old man conducts this ceremony, you must obey him. All of you listen to him. When he sings it is just as though I were singing. I have sung for you one day and two nights during this ceremony, but now this old man will finish the singing."

So this man started to sing. The Hactcin gave their call. All began to dance. The man sang in a loud voice. After a while the song was ended.

Then he told the Hactcin dancers, "Turn around to the south."

Then the clowns went over to the south side. They teased each other and joked. One said, "I am a sturdy young man. That is why the women like me." They had some bones they had picked up. They used them like field-glasses. They looked up in the sky and made believe they saw night hawks. At first the people didn't believe it when the clowns said they saw the night hawk, but soon they saw the bird. The clowns were doing all kinds of tricks.

[1] This remark points to the slight ceremonial discrimination under which the Jicarilla women labored.

Talking Hactcin did not sing this time. He just listened. He was watching what was going on.

After four songs the new man sang one for the clowns. They acted very happy and danced vigorously.

After the song the singer said, "Now turn to the north." So they all gathered on the north side.

Then came the deer song. The clowns became excited when they heard this song, because when people sing songs for the deer they are lucky. So the clowns were happy.

After the deer song, the singer started another Hactcin song. He sang to the Hactcin of the different colors, Black, Blue, Yellow, and White Hactcin. He did this during every song, for each song has four verses. First the Black Hactcin is sung about, then in the second verse the Blue Hactcin is mentioned, and so on.

Talking Hactcin said, "Sing in a loud voice so everyone will hear."

He sang of the Yellow Hactcin and of the White Hactcin. This song was for the eight Hactcin. The next song was for the four Spruce Hactcin. The next song was for the Two-Fighting-Stars Hactcin.

It was late afternoon by that time. Talking Hactcin told all the camp people to arise. Then the clowns divided into two parties and began to hunt. They crawled to the deer. The old man was singing for the Hactcin. The clowns approached the deer. It was the turn of the last two clowns to shoot the deer. These two motioned four times and each killed his deer. Then all the clowns ran up and rubbed their hands on the deer and then on themselves and asked for luck in hunting. The three others in each hunting party helped the leader to carry the deer, putting it on his back. Then they chose from among the women the one whom they would have for wife. They found two girls standing together. Both looked pretty and one was laughing. They discussed which one to put the deer before.

One of the girls looked at the deer, so they said, "Oh, this one looked straight at the deer. She likes deer. I guess we will give it to her."

The other hunting party chose a girl in the same way. They said, "After she is married she will probably be a good housekeeper."

The clowns teased each other. One said, "Oh, this man! He never stays away from his mother-in-law. You'd better not marry him."

Now the marriages had been decided, and the clowns danced back towards the Hactcin.

Then Talking Hactcin whispered to the clowns' leader, "Pass your food around."

The leader of the clowns broke the bread. He motioned four times. He was on the women's side. A girl tried to hold it, and he pulled it away. He did that four times and then let her have it.

The clowns went all around to the camp people in a clockwise circuit and gave bread in this manner until all had some. They gave it to the men in the same way they had given it to the women, for this was the first time the people had eaten the bread of the clowns and it was strange to them.

Each clown had a necklace from which two pieces of bread hung down as well as the bandolier which had four pieces strung on it. They did not give away the yucca leaf strings though. While they gave the bread away they were dancing.

Talking Hactcin began to explain the meaning of the bread which was being passed around. He told the girls and women, "You must keep this bread and put it with the medicine of the clowns. Keep it for the children. I will explain to you what this bread is for. Whenever the children, boys or girls, have a stomach ache and vomit, you must give them this bread with that medicine. If that doesn't stop it, you must call one of these eight clowns, any one of the dancers. He won't have to dress up or paint himself, but he can come in his regular clothes. He will chew it himself, then motion four times and put it in the mouth of the child.[1] I am going to tell you now of the way of the clowns.

"Some day one of you girls may get married to one of these clown dancers. You will make corn mush for him to eat. When you make it, be careful not to burn it. Those who have danced as clowns must never eat burned corn-meal mush. And when you make corn bread or corn mush, don't use corn which has a black growth on it. All you girls must listen to what the clowns say. Each said he was a good hunter. Perhaps some day one of them will kill a real deer and bring it home to you. But don't cook the deer's tail bone. The men who have danced as clowns are not supposed to eat that.

"You must believe it; you must be careful. You must not feed such a man any of these three things. If you do he will not have power when he needs it.

"That is all I have to say now about the clowns. Now I will tell you about the rules for a man who has danced as a Hactcin. When these men who have represented the Hactcin kill a deer, refrain from eating the head of that deer.[2] At night when a man who has been a Hactcin dancer takes off his moccasins, do not make a pillow of them.

---

[1] Those who have danced as clowns or Hactcin can cure by coming to a person who requests it and pulling his hair on his head from each direction four times. This is good for any sickness. The one who cures does not have to dress up in any special manner to do it. The one who has danced as a Hactcin shouts as he does it, but the one who has danced as a clown makes no sound at this time. One who has danced for the Hactcin can also come to a sick person and shout four times and drive the sickness away. The dancer has done something for the Hactcin and now the Hactcin are doing this for him. (Inf.)

[2] The man who makes the kill can eat of the head, but others would get dizzy from eating it. (Inf.) Another informant claimed that a man who

"Never hit one who has danced as a clown or a Hactcin with a stick of oak, no matter how angry you are. Use something else.[1]

"This is what you are going to live by. I give you these commandments. With this you will live to the end of the world. I won't come back in a month or a year."

Talking Hactcin was speaking loudly so that everyone could hear. "I am going to give advice to these clowns too when we go back to the Hactcin home. I don't deceive you with what I say, because you are just like my children, just like my grandchildren. That is why I tell you the truth."

The sun was almost down by this time. Talking Hactcin said, "The Hactcin who are Night People are going to watch over us soon. Sun Hactcin has watched over us all day and he knows what I am doing."

Then he told the people, "All of you keep moving your feet, mark time as though you were dancing so that you will be moving with the Hactcin."

That was the end of his talk to the people. He addressed some remarks to the new singer now. Then, when the dancing started, he called on the leader of the clowns. He spoke to the leader of the clowns, saying, "Start at the east and go around the inside of the corral. Brush out all evil with your arrows. Start at the women's side and come around to the side of the men."

They had not started yet. The dancers and all were standing there.

Talking Hactcin told the people, "When these clowns finish brushing away all sickness from you and you go out, do not go directly to your home, but wait a little while till the clowns brush away all the sickness from your camps."

The Hactcin turned around; the Spruce Hactcin turned also. Then the one with the groaning stick started the sound and they all faced the door. They were all ready to go. They departed, the one with the groaning stick in the lead. The people all lowered their heads and did not look while the dancers went out.

First went the Spruce Hactcin dancers, then the eight Hactcin of the colors, then the two Hactcin Children, then Animal Leader and Deer, and then Two-Fighting-Stars Hactcin. The two Solitary Hactcin dancers were still in the corral.

These two had other work. They stood to the east, one behind the other. The one with horns came first. They shouted. Starting with the south and going around the corral clockwise, they chased

---

has danced as a clown, Hactcin, or Tsanati should never give away the head of any animal he has killed in the hunt for the same reason. It is also said that if a pregnant woman or the husband of a pregnant woman looks at the dancers in the Hactcin ceremony the child will be born with a skin blemish.

[1] This is a bit of unintentional humor.

all the sickness away from the people. They stopped at the door, walked forth and back four times and went out. The one with horns went first, followed by the one with the mask.

The clowns had also remained inside and now it was their turn. They went around whipping all the women lightly, saying, "We are going back to our own country now." They laughed. "Everything is all right in your country," they said. Then they went out. They did not go back and forth four times before the entrance. They rushed out like wild ones, running.

Talking Hactcin said then, "This is the last time I am going to speak to you. I am going back now. I am going back to the holy place. There I will stay and watch over you till the end of time."[1]

He went out of the big corral. The two singers went out together. They sang of the pollen path and the road of specular iron ore as they went.

The Hactcin went into their home. The clowns still stood outside. The camp people went outside but did not go straight to their homes. The clowns started to run to the camps. With their arrows they hit all the tipis. They made joking remarks as they did it, saying, "I guess right here is my wife's home."

The singers told the people, "When the clowns finish with the camps, do not look at them. They are going to chase the sickness and evil to the north. When they have done that and are on the other side of the hills you can look over there and go to your camps.

The clowns ran to the hills at the north. They put their arrows on the branches of young trees and their bows too.[2] They left there, also, the yucca strings from which the bread had been taken, the necklace and the bandolier. Then they went in a clockwise circuit and came back.

"After you come back you must not talk the way clowns talk," Talking Hactcin had told them. "After that you must speak in everyday fashion." So on the way back they were quiet. They returned to the Hactcin home.

The Hactcin took off all their branches, masks, and paraphernalia. When all the yucca and spruce boughs were removed, two took them to the north.

"If you see a rock there, put these things on top of it; if not, put them in a young tree of any kind," Talking Hactcin told them.

They did so. Then the dancers were not Hactcin any more. They came back.

Talking Hactcin asked them, "Did you do as I said?"

"Yes, we put them away.[3]"

---

[1] This holy place is at the center of the earth, where the first ceremony was held, where the corral of the first ceremony stood. (Inf.)

[2] They are put on any kind of young tree. (Inf.)

[3] The woven aprons of yucca are always freshly made. They are put away because they are unclean after the ceremony. New ones are made for

Then Talking Hactcin ordered all the clowns to take off their caps. They did so and handed them to the new singer. He was going to keep them.

"Now go to the river and bathe yourselves," Talking Hactcin said to the clowns, Hactcin dancers, and Deer.

They did so. They went to the river and bathed. Then they went back again to the corral, the Hactcin home.[1]

The new man had the groaning stick in his hand.

Then Talking Hactcin began to speak. "I am going to talk to you men," he said to the clown dancers. "You must dance together as clowns four times, all of you together."[2]

He spoke to the men sitting around. He said, "You must be Hactcin four times.[3] It is all right after that; if you get tired you can stop. But get another man to take your place. That will mean that you should take part for two years, spring and summer of each year."

Then he told them, "All of you get in line, where you are. Wherever I am I will help you when you have another dance.[4]

"You must go. Tomorrow come back to see me. I am going to stay here by myself. You must go home. Remember what I have told you. I will stay here for four days."

The next day when the sun rose, two came. He said to them, "Go back. You have seen me. Tell the others I am still here."

The next day four came to see. He was still there. They went back home.

The third day six came. He was still there, and they went back.

The fourth day four who had danced as Hactcin and four who had danced as clowns came.[5] The fourth time he was gone.

They went back to the camps. "Talking Hactcin has gone back to his home," they said.

---

another dance. They are put away with the sickness, so no one wants to bring them back. (Inf.)

[1] The corral is left until it falls from decay. It is not used again and wood from it would not be used. (Inf.)

[2] Possibly this is a dance society in embryo.

[3] A man must be a Hactcin dancer in four ceremonies, a total of sixteen appearances. (Inf.)

[4] After this, when the Jicarilla performed the ceremony by themselves, the people would begin to camp around a place when they heard that a ceremony was going to start there. They would have a big fire there and all gather around it. The Hactcin-maker would whirl the groaning stick and give the Hactcin call four times. Then all the men would come together and discuss what they should do. They would appoint dancers at this time. (Inf.)

[5] Those who came were always divided evenly between Hactcin dancers and clown dancers in this way. (Inf.)

III. MYTHS RELATING TO AGRICULTURE AND RAIN

A. THE MAN WHO FLOATED DOWN THE RIVER IN A LOG OR THE ORIGIN OF AGRICULTURE[1]

One time there was a man who gambled all the time. He played the hoop and pole game and every other game. But he had no luck and lost all he had.

He had a companion and pet, a turkey, and this turkey followed him around wherever he went.

One time when he was away his relatives were talking about him. The turkey was there lying around and heard all that was said.

These relatives said, "We'll give him one more chance. If he loses all we give him this time we'll kill him."

The turkey heard this and went straight to his partner. The turkey told him all that his brother had said.

The gambler talked to his turkey. "What are we to do now?"

The turkey said, "Let us go away and I'll help you in some way."

The man came home first. His brother wanted to give him some more things with which to gamble but he wouldn't take them. He went away without telling the others where he was going.

He went to the river. He asked Beaver for an ax.[2] "When I get through I'll bring it back. I just want to use it for a few days."

The beaver let him have it.

He went up the hill and he found a spruce tree close to the river. He tried to chop it down. He chopped and chopped. He had it almost cut down when the sun was about to set. He was very tired. He left it and went away. The next day he came back again. The ax was there. But the tree was just as it had been before he started chopping. He began to work at it again. He chopped all day. He nearly had it chopped down at sunset and he stopped, for he was very tired. When he came back the next day the tree was as before; there was not a trace of his chopping. It happened just the same the third day.

So he came back the fourth morning. He saw the tree was whole again. He started to chop once more. Then he heard a voice.

"What are you doing to my tree? Why do you try to chop it down?"

He was a little frightened. He looked around. Black Hactcin was there.

---

[1] Cf. Goddard, p. 214; Russell, p. 268.

[2] Beaver figures as the lender of the ax because he can fell trees.

"I want to use your tree to ride down the stream to the place where it runs into another river," he said.

Black Hactcin said, "How large do you want it?"

"Just large enough to fit me, just as high as I stand."

Hactcin said, "Let me have that ax."

He hit the tree and it fell at one stroke. Then he measured off the proper length and hit it again, and with one stroke it was severed there. Then he took the top part of the tree that was not wanted and placed it back in the earth, and the trunk and the tree grew as before.

That is why the Indians say you must not cut a tree without prayer to Black Hactcin, for all trees belong to him.

Then this man turned around. He asked Black Hactcin for further help. "Do you know how to hollow this log out for me?"

"I can't do that, but I can send someone who can help you with it."

So he called the woodpeckers, all the different kinds, and told them to help this man. And Black Hactcin told this man, "While they are working you had better go out and look for payment for them, for something to give them."

So the man went around looking for beads to give them. That is why people who do things for you must be paid today. He gathered up turquoise, narrow white beads, abalone, and assorted beads, jet beads, white beads, yellow beads, and varicolored beads. He collected them all there. He came back with them. By that time the woodpeckers were all finished. In a few minutes they had hollowed out the whole log.

Black Hactcin asked for cornflowers. That was going to be his pay. Now all the work was finished and the laborers sat in a row. The man began to pass out all the beads. That is why these birds have all these colors. Some received blue beads and became that color, some obtained red heads this way. He gave Black Hactcin the cornflowers too. When he had gone back to eat he had seen his pet, the turkey, and Turkey had the cornflowers. So he gave these to Black Hactcin.

Then when all was ready he said, "Now what am I going to do?"

He rolled the log down to the river. The woodpeckers went away. Black Hactcin went back too. But the turkey was with him and the turkey had power and knew things too.

Then the turkey said, "You must ask Spider to help you. You must call on Black Spider, Blue Spider, Yellow Spider, and Glittering Spider."

So he called on those spiders.

The woodpeckers had bored in from one side, and so this side remained open. That is the place the man was to enter.

The spiders were standing there. Then the turkey told the man to call on Green-Backed Swallow. The swallow came. Then the man went into the log. The spiders began to work. Each one made a web; the first was black, the second blue, the third yellow, and the fourth glittering. With these they covered the entrance. The swallow then brought mud and covered the hole so the water wouldn't leak through.[1]

Before he went in, though, the man returned the ax to Beaver. And he told Beaver, "When I get in, you must roll the log down to the water."

So Beaver did and the log began to travel down the stream. It floated for a long way. The turkey followed it along the bank. The log traveled for four days and was halted on four separate occasions by those in the water.

The first time it was Water Monster[2] who held the log back. It happened in the middle of the day. The turkey was there. These asked for some pay. Turkey had nothing but fruit. He gave them fruit and they allowed the log to continue. After traveling for a long time the log was stopped by Otter. He, too, wanted something before he would allow the log to go on. The turkey did the same thing as before and the otter let the log go. Then the log floated down till the third day. This day it was Beaver who stopped it. Turkey did as he had done before and the log was released. The fourth day something in the water called Kabaskin[3] stopped the log. Turkey again paid and the log was released. The water always wants a present; if you have pollen it wants some of it. It wants pay. That's why it held the log four times. The log went on till it met the whirlpool.[4]

When the log got to a certain place Turkey called, "Father, already we are here."

So the man got out. The log was in a whirlpool and was whirling around. It wouldn't go any further. So he got out. They left that log there and started to walk along the bank. The river was too wide to cross. On the other side of the river they saw a big mountain.

At this time Turkey gave this man his name. It was Man-Who-Floated-on-the-Water.

The man was wishing. "I wish we could have a garden here. This is a good place. I wish we had the seeds." He was just thinking this in his mind. But Turkey said, "Don't think that only. Why don't you say it? I can give you those seeds."

There was a fine level place there, a good place for planting. Turkey stood to the east of it. He shuffled along the east side of that field. On that side a great deal of black corn seeds were left.

---

1 Again Swallow is called upon to do the plastering with mud. See p. 139.

2 Water Monster is a supernatural who pulls people under water.

3 Kabaskin is the water being that symbolizes the waters around the earth. He is represented in a ground drawing of the bear dance as an elongated border figure. See p. 37.

4 In another version of the story it is told that the Pueblo Indians tried to pull the log out of the water but had to let it go. (Inf.)

Then he went around to the south in the same way. Blue corn seeds lay there. They came from the body of the turkey. Then Turkey went to the west in the same way and yellow corn seeds were there. He did it next at the north, and fruit and vegetable and tobacco seeds were there.

He told the man to get busy, and the man began planting the seeds with a sharp stick. After the work was over they made a camp by the garden. The man's bed was made of nothing but turkey feathers, feathers of his pet that had fallen out.

They stayed there till the garden was all grown. In those days the gardens grew more rapidly. The plants matured in twelve days.

Every evening after that the man was facing the east, sitting there with his companion. One evening he saw a light on the other side of the river. The next morning he thought, "Who can be making a camp on the other side of the river?" He went over there but could find nothing.

It happened in the same way the next night. But again he could find nothing the next morning. Then the third night he saw it again. By this time he already had tobacco in his pocket from the tobacco plants he had raised. The next morning he failed to find anything though.

The fourth night he saw the light again. This time he brought a forked stick and set it in the ground. He pointed the crotch straight to the fire. Now he was sure he could find it the next day.

He went over in the direction to which his forked stick pointed. As he approached the place he saw a young woman washing buckskin clothes at a spring. The cicada was sitting there in the leaves.

As he came to the woman, a point on the inside of his ear spoke to him. It said, "You must ask the cicada to let you have his flute."[1]

He spoke to the cicada and asked him for it. The cicada gave him the flute. It was divided along its length into the four colors.

He came to the girl with this flute in his hand and started to blow on it. He used it in the same way as the cicada does.

The girl looked around. She wondered what the peculiar sound could be. He had blown it the first time. Then he blew it again. She arose this time and searched about in the leaves and all over the place where she had sat.

"That is a sweet sound," she said.

The third time she was very eager to learn the source of the noise. She was delighted with it, but she could find nothing.

He blew it the fourth time.

She pulled her dress up then, for the music made her very much excited.[2] She looked and looked and looked, and finally she found him. There stood the man who had made the noise.

---

[1] Cicada and the flute are associated and both are connected with the practice of love charms.

[2] Her excitement was sexual in nature.

When she saw him she picked up the clothes she had been washing and ran straight for a rock wall. She went right in as though a door was there. The point on the man's ear told him, "You must follow closely." He did so. He went in the mountain also. He followed her.

After a while he found a camp. There an old woman and an old man were sitting.

The woman, as soon as she saw him, said, "Oh, here is my son-in-law. I'd better hide," and she ran away.

That is why among these people the mother-in-law cannot see her son-in-law and hides from him. It started at this place.

The old man who was sitting there was called Animal-Raiser. This old man, when he spoke to the boy, used the polite form. That is why the father-in-law uses that form now when he speaks to his son-in-law.

The old man said, "Come in, make yourself at home."

The young man sat down. He said to Animal-Raiser, "Give me a smoke of tobacco."

Animal-Raiser prepared some tobacco and put it in a pipe. He drew on it and then handed it to the boy. The boy took a puff of it, but he didn't like it. It was made of a big odorous plant called "big leaf," that grows among the rocks.

"How is it you do not like my tobacco?" He smoked it himself.

Then after a while the boy fixed his own tobacco.

The old man begged, "Won't you give me some?" He spoke in the polite form.

The boy handed the pipe to him. He took one deep puff and fell down. It was so sweet and good that he was overcome. It was just as it is with a child who has eaten too much of something sweet. The boy took the pipe out of his hand as he lay there and puffed on it and blew the smoke on the old man's right foot, then his right hand, then on the top of his head, then on the left hand, and then on his left foot. At that the old man recovered and arose again.

The old man said, "This is the best tobacco I ever have known."

The boy smoked it for a while and then passed it to the old man. They passed it back and forth like this till it was all used up.

The old man said, "Whenever you come here again you must bring tobacco like this for me to smoke."

Then the boy went out and went back to his turkey.

The next time he came that way he brought with him some corn, some tobacco, some pumpkins, and some bread. He gave these as a present to the old man. The old man was very grateful.

This family had never used those things before. Before this they had had no fruit nor vegetables. The young man gave them some of the products of his garden and they gave him some meat. They exchanged gifts and were friends. Soon after this he married Animal-Raiser's daughter.

The turkey was very proud because his father was being married.

He told all the people, "Now we'll have plenty of meat, for my father is marrying Animal-Raiser's daughter."

The people were all glad to hear what Turkey said.

Animal-Raiser had many animals of all kinds in that mountain. He let them graze, as they do sheep now, in a flock, and they were tame and gentle with him. There were animals out in the world at this time, but they were few and not enough for the people.

The men who know this story well are the ones who know Deer or one of the game animals. They are the ones who have the best success at hunting and always have plenty to eat. They have songs and prayers to go with this story.

The young man who married Animal-Raiser's daughter came to live with her people.[1] He showed those people how to use the plants and fruits, and they showed him how to use meat. That is why these Apaches use both now.

The deer and other animals there were very tame and gentle. They stayed around the camps of the people all the time and when the people wanted meat they had only to call the animals. Among the people there was one silly woman. She lived by herself. All the other people were careful about what they said to Deer and how they treated Deer and they advised her to be that way too.

But one day she made a shade out of fresh green brush. A deer came and ate of it. The next day she made another shade, but that night Deer came and ate the leaves again. This happened several times until she became very angry. The next time the Deer came she drove him away. She picked up a fire poker and hit him on the face with it. The marks can still be seen today. And she said, "After this you'd better smell me and keep away."

The deer ran away. The day after that it came back, but stayed a little while only. The second day it came but stayed some distance from the camps. The third day it came around, but not very close. The woman was hungry for meat now and called to Deer to come.

But Deer, too, was angry. "You hit me and drove me away," he said. "After this you will not see me around your camp. I'll smell you and stay away. And you, for what you have done, shall have a hard time. It will not be easy for you to get meat." And he went away.

The fourth day he did not come at all, and though she called to him she could not find him. After that the deer went away from that place and spread all over the mountains. Deer did not come near the camps of people again. After that deer were shy and could smell the people from a distance.

---

[1] Matrilocal residence is still the rule among the Jicarilla.

B. THE QUARREL BETWEEN CYCLONE AND THUNDER AND THE CEREMONY FOR RAIN

One time Cyclone and Thunder were quarreling. This was at the first time when they were on this earth. Thunder wanted to show his power, to show what he could do.

Cyclone said, "No, I don't want to see what you can do. I don't care. I want peace between us."

But Thunder kept on saying, "You have no power. I am stronger than you. You are no good."

Finally Cyclone said, "All right then, show what you can do if you are so strong."

Many pine trees were standing there. Lightning struck and broke all the trees down at one time. Thunder said, "You see now how strong I am."

Now it was the wind's turn. The wind used his power. He blew everything before him. He picked up pine trees, great rocks, everything that stood there. Cyclone won. Thunder lost the wager about his power.

They were both angry with each other. After that they wouldn't help each other. There were no storms, no rains. The mountain tops were burned. Sometimes you would see ashes on top of the mountain where fires had started by themselves. The fishes died right in the streams, it was so hot. The people began to suffer from the drought.

The men were talking to each other. They prepared a pipe (the men's type),[1] filled it with mountain tobacco, and offered it to the four who stand for the water.

One old man invited four people to meet him, and they all came. They all gathered around. The old man sent a messenger to them. They were all Jicarilla Apaches. They were men who knew a ceremony to bring rain.

When these four men had come together, the old man invited all the people of the camps to come and watch. This man was asking the people for buckskin. He said, "Let those of you who have plenty of buckskins give us some." Buckskins were gathered, and clothes, nicely decorated and fringed, were made of them. They had to have complete outfits of buckskin, shirts, leggings, moccasins; for they were going to dance for rain.

The old man talked to the women. "Hurry," he said, "help each other. Two of you work on one piece, one on each side, sewing, and finish it quickly. In four days it must be all finished, and then we are going to dance.

"You know what is happening. Many of our men and women are dying of thirst. That is why you must hurry."

[1] The men's type of pipe for ceremonial occasions is one with bowl and stem; the women use a tubular type pipe for ritual purposes. See p. 242.

Four days after this, at sunrise, these four men were going to begin the dance. Twenty-four young men and twenty-four girls were to line up facing the east. On the morning of the dance they stood in two parallel lines, twelve young men and twelve girls arranged alternately in each line. At the front and back of each line stood an old man. First these four old men puffed at pipes which each carried. The two to the east had the man's type of pipe. The two to the rear had the kind the women smoke. First they smoked. Then they began to sing. They were to sing eight songs; if rain came before the eighth they would stop. The songs were for rain, and the people danced in place for rain during the singing. The four old men stood for the people who control the water of the directions.

The leading old man said, "Here you are, all in line. You must all have faith and be of one mind, for I am going to sing for you, and you must dance for the water."

Then the man at the east said, "Everyone look at me. See this pipe. I offer a smoke for rain. I stand for the water from the east. I represent the black cloud. Old Man Salamander, I am he."

Now the old man standing to the south showed his pipe and said, "This is the one I give for the water. I am Old Man Blue Water Frog, I am he."

Now the one who stood at the west spoke. He said, "Everyone look at this pipe. They are asking for rain, therefore they gave me this. Old Man Yellow Crawfish,[1] I am he."

Then the one to the north spoke, "Look at me, everyone. The man gave me a pipe so that I should bring the rain. I stand for the water from the north, Old Man Red Turtle."

Then the first man, the leader of the whole ceremony, started to sing. He had no drum; he just used his voice. He danced too. And those in line danced. The whole tribe circled around, children, old men, women. The old man finished the first song. He told those standing around who were not dancing, "You must concentrate on one thought only; be thinking of rain." All the people believed it. They had one thought.[2]

They started to dance about eight o'clock in the morning. A little later the clouds had gathered above and they heard the thunder. The clouds began to grow larger and larger. In a little while rain was falling. They had sung about six songs, and the rain had already come, so they stopped.

---

[1] Crawfish is used now because he was used in this ceremony. When the lightning hits a person, he has to eat crawfish meat boiled. Crawfish are killed by having a rope tied around the neck until they choke. Crawfish take a long time to die; they are very tough. After they have been killed this way, they are roasted and the meat is taken out. (Inf.)

[2] This is the closest approximation to a Pueblo corn dance that has been recorded for any Apache group with which the writer is familiar.

The people stood right there in the heavy rain. They let their clothes get soaking wet. It rained for several hours.

In that way they brought back the rain. They used these four people that stand for the waters of the directions. These four people have the thunder and wind within their bodies and so they can bring the rain.

This ceremony was used for rain after this. But it's hard to get all the clothes now. They all have to be of deerskin. It doesn't make any difference whether the skin is from male or female deer.

All of us have wind in our hearts,[1] that is why we live and breathe; we are just like those four people in this respect. In this ceremony they always have to have the twenty-four men and twenty-four women dancing. Even now if people need water, the Jicarilla would dance like this and obtain it.

The clay to make the pipes for this ceremony has to come from the hole near Taos.[2] No other clay can be used.

The leader of the whole ceremony, this first time it was done, was not one of the four old men who represented the waters of the directions. He sat to one side. He was the one asking for rain. He stood for the rain. The man to the east knew the ceremony well too. He was the first to receive a pipe.

The pipes used were pipes that granddaughters had made. The leader handed the pipes to the four men in clockwise order according to the directions they represented.

All those dancing, and the four men, and the leader, too, have to have complete buckskin outfits for this ceremony.

There are still people who know these songs. If the buckskins could be obtained the ceremony could still be performed.

---

[1] Cf. footnote 1, p. 5.

[2] It is a place near Taos where clay to be used for ceremonial purposes must be obtained and can be taken only after certain prayers have been said.

IV. THE ORIGIN OF GAMES AND ARTIFACTS

A. THE STORY OF HOOP AND POLE[1]

When the people had come up from the underworld and everything was settled, two old men, brothers, were living in a certain camp. The old men had no games to play.

One day they had a visitor, who said to them, "What's the matter? You act rather sad and thoughtful."

"Oh, we have been thinking of some way to make a game, but we cannot think of any game we might play." And then the two old people said, "Father, you are the one who calls us your children."

The visitor just smiled and looked at them. "All right," he said, "after four days you must go to the east. There is a mountain. There is a canyon behind it running east and west. Wait for me by the level place there."

And then the old people heard a noise behind them. They looked behind them. They could see nothing. They faced forward again. The man was gone. He had disappeared. Both looked around but they could see nothing.

The older brother said, "I think this one who was before us was the one who created the earth and the heavens."

These two old men brought out "mountain tobacco." One sat on the north side. He said, "Let us mix together 'mountain tobacco' and 'big leaf,' for when a man needs anything he always gives an offering."

The other was sitting on the south side. He said, "Let us mix 'mountain tobacco' with 'narrow tobacco' and 'yellow tobacco' and 'red tobacco.' Let us mix together these four."

They mixed together these four tobaccos. They had two pipes, a straight tubular pipe and one with a bowl.

The brother on the north side said, "This is not enough. Let us put in one more, some kind of leaf to act as perfume. Let it be something with a sweet smell."

So they took some mint which the older man had in a bag. He untied the bag, took some, gave some to his brother, and they put it in the tobacco. Then they asked each other who would do it first. The older brother who sat on the south side said, "I will do it first."

Then he said to the younger brother, "Get some cedar bark."

The younger brother put down the pipe. He went and brought cedar bark. It was dry. They had a white flint and a black flint,

---

[1] For an introduction to this story see pp. 128—136.

and these the older brother struck together. The sparks fell on the shredded cedar bark and the fire was started.

The older brother first lit his pipe. He puffed at it four times without saying a word. Then he puffed a fifth time to the east and said, "I offer this to you who came to us, wherever you are. We want you to help us, watch over us, guide us. Do not let us have a hard time. This is 'mountain tobacco.' It is your own tobacco. The 'narrow tobacco' is yours too. And the 'yellow tobacco' is yours. I offer it to you. Bearberry, too, is your tobacco. Also we mixed in for you this perfumed leaf to give it a pleasant smell.

"Father, because you are responsible for the earth, the sky, the seasons, and the water, you must tell us about everything, all you know. Explain it to us before you hand to us what you promised to us. Explain it to us, explain what you are going to give us. Tell us what restrictions there are in connection with it. We are asking for your power, that we may live with it."

Then the younger brother spoke and said, "That is enough to say. You might make a mistake. Do not talk too much."

The younger brother lit his pipe. He puffed his pipe four times but said nothing. Then a fifth time he puffed to the sky and said, "You who were standing here a while ago, I offer this to you. This is your tobacco." And he gave the names of the tobaccos. "You told us you would wait for us at the other side of the mountain. You must remember your promise to us. These are your tobaccos we are offering. We want long life and healthy bodies. With this offering we hope to get these things. It is for you, this offering."

Then both were through with their prayers. The next moment the wind blew violently forth and back and shook these two people.

The older brother said, "I think our prayer has been heard and answered. I think that is why he sent this wind."

Then they went back to the camp. They said to each other, "Let us be sure to go to that place in four days."

They stayed in camp till the time appointed. The morning of the fourth day, both of them went to the river and bathed and washed their hair. They combed their hair and they painted their faces.

The older brother said, "My brother, go over to the home of my cross-cousin and ask him for red paint. If I go over myself he might kick me, so I'd better not go."[1]

The younger brother went over. His cousin gave him a very little. He said he didn't want to part with any, but he gave him some anyway. With this red paint they put marks on their foreheads and on both cheeks. Because they had so little red paint, it went no farther. Then they walked a little way.

The younger brother said, "I think that person is going to fool us. I guess we are going over there for nothing."

---

[1] Jicarilla cross-cousins engage in a rough and tumble joking relationship to which allusion is here made.

But they went to the place. They circled around the mountain. They came to the level place. Both sat together with their faces to the east. In the distance they saw someone coming. They pointed this out to each other.

"I believe he's carrying something," one said to the other.

They heard footsteps behind them. They turned quickly but could see no one coming. When they turned around again they faced a very old man with grey hair. The first time they had seen him he had been a young man.

This old man called the older brother by name. "Hanidji," he said, "get up." Then he called to the other brother too. "Tsatihi, get up."

The brothers smiled and looked at each other.

"Put your hands out straight before you, both of them," he said to Hanidji.

When Hanidji opened his hands, he saw they were red with paint.

"Now you, Tsatihi, open your hand."

The second brother opened his hand. He saw that his hands were red with paint too. Then both put their hands down.

Then this man said to the older brother, "Now put up your right hand toward me."

The old man held up a hoop to the four directions. Then he motioned four times to this man and put it in his hand.

"Give it back to me," he said.

The brother gave it back.

The old man motioned again in the same way and this time gave it to the younger brother. The younger brother received the hoop too in the same way.

The old man put it on the ground. Then he picked up the pole. He motioned four times as before and gave it to the older brother. This was the red pole. Then he picked up the one without paint, motioned four times, and gave it to the younger brother.

He told them, "You must hold them up from the right sides of your bodies." Then he ordered the older brother, "Lay yours to the south of the hoop." Now the brothers faced the east as directed. The old man spoke to the younger brother and said, "Hold up your pole in the same way. Lower it easily and place it on the other side of the hoop."

The hoop was already cut and designed. It was painted red, white, and black. The old man pointed out each band on the hoop. He told them the name of each and what each counted. "There are twelve all together," he said.

Then he picked up a pole. "Right on the butt is the part we call 'it lies within,'" he said. "There is a place called 'notch' too. This carved band is called 'bottom straight.' On the other side is a band called 'lying knotted.' The next is a band called 'head straight.' The whole pole is called *macka*. Another name to call it is 'it carries good.' This I give you, but you must pray to the east and the other directions. But don't pray to the north when you play.[1]

"Every new moon you must paint this red pole and the hoop anew and paint your face, too, at that time. Paint the black bands black again at that time. At the full moon do the same thing. If you believe and do what I say, every full moon and new moon you will gain toward a long life and good luck. And all the plants will be yours and all possessions will come to you with little effort."

Then he told the older brother, "Hanidji, pick up this red pole." He did so.

The old grey man picked up the uncolored pole. They played to the east and back twice, four throws in all. Then the older brother put down the red pole and the younger brother picked it up. He did the same thing.

Then the old man handed his pole to the older brother and said, "Now let me see you two play."

Before they started he showed them how the score was to be kept. He placed the hoop over the butt of the pole in different positions and showed them what the score would be in each case. "This position will score twenty; this one will count sixteen," he said. He put the hoop in all positions.

"You must believe it," he said. "This will help you. You must keep it. Don't get tired of this till the end of the world. Take care of it till the sky stands no longer. And through all the years you must take good care of it and believe it: to the end of the place where the waters stand you must believe it. You must live with it and then you will live in a good way with all your relatives and your family.

"You must offer something first. When I first came to you, you offered four different kinds of tobacco. And you prayed. I heard you, after I left. Use these same kinds of tobacco after this when you pray in this game. And pray in that same way. When you get too old to handle this game, hand it down to your younger relative. Show him how to make it. Stand around and show him how."

Then he untied the sinew which held the parts of the pole together. It all fell apart. Then he showed them how to tie it. "This is the way to do it," he said.

"After this choose a smooth place for playing. Throw the poles first four times to the east and to the west. After that start the game in earnest.

"When you play you must look around. It is all right if men or boys who are pretty well grown up come around. But do not let women or little children, little boys or little girls, see this game.

"I gave those girls the stave game. Some girls menstruate at the time of the new moon and the full moon. That is why, when you

[1] The inclination of the Jicarilla to avoid any reference to north in connection with the hoop and pole game has already been discussed.

play, you must not let them come near you. And do not go where the women play the stave game.[1]

"I'll come back in four days and see how you play."

They thought he really meant four days, but he meant four years. A year was as a day to him.

These two brothers were playing. Others came around and saw them. They watched and learned the game. Soon many were playing. They bet against each other.

Six pairs were playing with the same set. It took a long time to get around to the turn of the first thrower. So they talked about it. They said, "Let us make another hoop and pole set."

So these two brothers worked on it. They helped each other. They called out all the names and made the notches correctly. They did it as they had been taught. Then the younger brother took half the men and went off to play with them. He knew how to count and play too.

Whenever you teach someone, he must give you something from the inside of an animal, the intestine, liver, or heart from a buffalo, deer, or any big game animal. Then when you teach him he will remember it.[2]

Many were playing now and still it took a long time to get around and finish the games. They talked about it and decided to make two more sets. So they made four sets. They played in four places, but they were careful not to let the girls come near.

Four years passed. The two brothers were not staying together now. The older brother was playing the game on one side of the camps; the other was playing on the other side.

The older brother was sitting with seven men at the hoop and pole grounds. Then Killer-of-Enemies came.

He asked, "Where is your brother? You must tell him to come over and bring his hoop and pole too."

The older brother went over. He had been told to notify the younger brother to bring everything. He told his companions to wait till he got back.

The brothers went over where Killer-of-Enemies stood. Killer-

---

[1] The game played with three staves is meant. There is a game played with four staves in which the men may participate. For an account of the stave game see p. 225.

[2] Now the people do not know how to make these sets; some who have played this game all their lives do not know who made the first game, for no one pays anything from the inside of an animal. Killer-of-Enemies told them, "When you want to learn, pay this intestine and you won't forget. That is the only pay asked." Some of us know what the count is when we see the hoop fall, but we cannot make the set. I understand how to play, for I played for twenty-eight years, but I do not know how to make it myself, for I never paid for it. I know how to count and handle the set, but not how to make it. I waited too long and that is why I didn't learn from those old men. (Inf.)

of-Enemies examined the sets. He said, "This is all good. Who made these?"

"We did."

"Did they give you the intestines?"

"Yes."

"No wonder you made it just as I told you to do."

Then Killer-of-Enemies said, "There are some boys playing, some children. They have made themselves a hoop and are using sunflower stalks for poles. Take these away from them."

So these people went over and took away the game. One boy gave up his. The other cried and wouldn't give up his pole. It stuck right to his hand as if it were made of pitch. They brought this boy over to the old man. The boy couldn't get rid of the pole now. It stuck to his hand. He opened up his hand but it wouldn't drop.

The people all gathered around. They did not see Killer-of-Enemies standing there. Only the two brothers could see him.

Killer-of-Enemies said, "Hanidji, you motion four times toward that boy with your pole in your right hand, and four times with it in your left hand."

Killer-of-Enemies told the people, "You must not let the children play this game with any kind of wood. And you old people, when you play, do not continue the game long after sundown and till darkness comes. When the sun is four fingers above the horizon, when the sun is setting, stop all play. Do not play after this or at night. Early in the morning it is all right to play.

"Twelve children have played without permission. They will be punished for four days. For four days go to them each day, you two brothers, and press their bodies all over and blow their sickness away to the sun.[1] Those boys will be sore all over their bodies.

"When a girl makes a mistake and comes near while the game is being played, she will suffer too. Her body will pain her for four days. But the man who makes the pole can help her. He will go over there. He is the only one who can cure her of that sickness by pressing her body and blowing the illness away to the sun."

To the brothers Killer-of-Enemies said, "You must tell these people not to let the children play hoop and pole. This is not a game played just for fun. I gave you this pole and hoop game to live by.

"You must not bring your arrows near to the hoop and pole grounds. You can have them twenty-four paces away in any direction, but no nearer. It is all right to bet arrows on the game, but keep those arrows far away from the grounds. Put them somewhere else. Now I am going home. You must do what I say."

He clapped his hands and disappeared.

After this many old people learned the game and paid the intestine. They knew it well. But they have all died.

[1] The sickness is blown to the sun because Sun originally gave the game to Killer-of-Enemies and Child-of-the-Water.

The brothers had songs they sang when they made the hoop and pole.[1] They taught these songs to the ones who paid them something from the inside of an animal, and these men learned it from them.

B. ORIGIN OF THE STAVE GAMES

White Hactcin created everything. He was walking around. He came upon an old woman sitting down. Her hands were over her face.

White Hactcin asked her, "Why are you so sad?"

She looked up. She saw someone standing there. She said, "My grandson, where do you come from? What tribe are you from?" Then she said, "I am sad because I have nothing to do. There are no games, nothing is going on. I get very lonesome."

"What pleasure, what game do you want to have?"

"I have many relatives in my camp, many women, many young girls. We want to have a good game."

White Hactcin knew all about what this woman was wishing. He said to her, "You must gather some roots of the cottonwood; gather some of the roots that have been washed down by the river. Find dry wood of this kind."[2]

The old woman went at once and joyfully gathered an armful.

White Hactcin told her, "I'm going to make a game for you so that you will have much enjoyment."

White Hactcin picked up his knife of rock and began to cut and split the roots. He split three.

"Look closely at these," he said to the woman.

He picked up some dirt. He rubbed it on one side, and that side turned red.

Then he picked up another straight stick. He split it too. He chose three sticks altogether. He painted these three with a black band in the middle and left both ends red. This was the second set of staves.

He picked up another root and made a stave from this. He made two more like it. The round part, the back, he painted red. The straight side he did not paint. This was the third set of staves.

Then he split three more pieces. Those pieces which had a lot of knots on he threw away. He measured off about an inch and a half from one end and the same from the other end and painted the space between black on this set. The rounded backs of all three he painted red.

---

[1] The songs and prayers can be used for other purposes too. If a man uses the game well and then wants other things, like luck in hunting, he can sing and pray and the one who made the game for the Indians can give it to him. (Inf.)

[2] Maple is also used for staves according to informants.

White Hactcin told the woman, "You must turn the straight edges of all these staves down."

She did so and the rounded sides were up.

Then he asked, "Do you know how you have put them down?"

"Yes."

White Hactcin said, "You must take care of these four sets of staves. Don't mix them up. What I have made for you will make you laugh all day long and give you pleasure. You must believe in what I have made for you. This game is called *tsedil*.

"You must pick out rocks, altogether about forty. Make a circle of them. But at the east, south, west, and north you must have doors (spaces). You must have ten rocks between each two doors. You must get a flat stone about a foot square and put it down right in the center of this circle of rocks. Motion four times and then put it down."

Then he told her to pick up the first set of three sticks. He told her to motion with the sticks four times toward the central rock. "On the fourth time let them go," he said.

She did so. They bounced up and fell on the ground. The straight sides were all down.

He put a stick at the door to the east. It was to keep score. "You have made ten," he said and moved the stick to the south door. "Now do it again."

The staves fell as before.

"You have made another ten," and he moved the stick to the west door.

Again she took a turn and they fell as before. The stick was moved to the north door. Again she threw them, and he put her stick at the east door again. She had made forty in four throws.

"You have won," he said. "Now put back that set and take this one."

She began to play with the second set. She motioned four times and threw. The sticks came with the flat sides up.

"You have made five," he said and moved the stick to a point between the fifth and sixth stones.

He told her to take another turn. It came as before and she moved five stones ahead. Eight times she threw before she made her forty this time. But then she was back at the east door again.

White Hactcin said, "Now put that second set back and take the third."

She did so. She began to play with these, motioning four times as before. When she threw, two flat sides were up and one was down.

"You have made only three," he said and moved her stick to the third stone.

She was told to play again. Again it counted three. It came this way for her all the time, and it took her a long time to get around. She took thirteen turns before she was through. This counted only thirty-nine, but she was allowed to lose one.

Then she was told, "Put that set away and pick up the fourth and last one."

She did so and began playing with this set. She motioned four times and let it fall. Two flat sides were down and one up.

"That counts two," he said and moved the stick past two stones for her.

It was the same all through and it took her twenty turns before she was all the way around.

Then White Hactcin told her to put the set down. He told her, "Whenever the new moon comes and the full moon, too, paint these with black and with red paint. If you keep this rule it will make you happy and it will give you a long life too.

"This game is only for the women. The men should not come near when you play. If a man comes around, he will have an aching leg all night. You must follow these rules. This is only for the women, for their long life and good health.

"Now you must get some straight branches of ocean spray."

She brought it. He made four staves. One he marked with a cross on top.

He said to her, "Motion four times and throw."

All four fell with flat sides down.

"You have made ten," he said.

She did it again. The one with the cross on fell flat side down, but the flat sides of the others were up. That counted fifteen because that marked one was down. She tried again and it came the same way, the marked one was down on the flat side. The fourth time this happened again. She had gone around the circle of stones easily.

"Now you can start at the east again. This game, the one with four staves, you can play with the men and the children. But you must paint these sticks any time they have become faded."

What he meant was to paint that cross red when it faded. All the rest were plain. White Hactcin had marked it red when he crossed it.

"One more word I'm going to speak to you. If you play with someone who is winning all the time from you and you have lost two or three times, it is all right. But you shouldn't lose for the fourth time in succession. If you do, come back to these sticks. Take the first set and scold them, call them all kinds of mean words, for they understand what you say. Do this with the second set, for you lost with that one too. But the third is yours and the fourth. Don't scold them. Then you will be restored and win back all you have lost and more.

"You must pity your opponent. Take blankets or anything extra she has when she loses, but you must not take her clothes. That's not right. You must not take clothes. Other things are all right. The last two sets are to restore everything."

White Hactcin was standing there. He said, "Now put all the sticks with the faces down."

She did so. Then she looked around. White Hactcin was gone. No one was standing there. She stood up and looked around, but no one was to be seen.

She had a husband, an old man. There was a big camp towards the west, on the other side of the mountain. These two old people started to move and go to the big camp. They had only one horse, one which had been brought from the plains country and had been given to this woman. On it they loaded all their possessions and moved towards that big camp.

They built their camp on the edge of the big village. The people of the big camp came to see these old people.

After they had been there five days, three old women came to visit. They talked of how lonely they were, how no games and no amusements went on at that place.

This old woman spoke then. "Don't say that," she told them. "I have a game. Tomorrow bring some more women and I'll teach you the game." And she showed that bag with the *tsedił* sticks in it.

The next day that old woman, before anyone came, painted her face red.

After breakfast all the women came to see her. She took them out to the other side where there were no camps, for this camp was among the piñon trees. They cleared a place under the piñon trees at the direction of the old woman. They swept away all the needles. The woman made the circle. She sent for round stones. She asked for forty. She put them down.

She said, "You must watch very closely where I put them and what I do."

She took out the first set of sticks. "This is called *tsedił*," she said. But the other women did not understand what that meant.

The old woman chose three others who were wise. She told them, "Each of you bring a stick." One sat at the east door, one at the south, one at the west, one at the north. They asked the old woman who was to start first.

"The one who sits to the east starts first," she said.

The one to the east tried. She made five. She put her stick at the fifth stone. Then the one to the south tried. She made three. She put her stick at the third stone. Now the one to the west tried. She only made two. Then the one at the north side tried and she also made five. Now both the woman at the east side and the woman at the north side were on five.

Now it was the turn of the woman to the east. She made ten. She was now at the fifteenth stone. They kept on playing. Some were behind. Some were ahead. Whoever made forty first would win. They all sat there playing all day and laughing.

When you are lucky at this game and get all three flat sides down, you get another turn. Then if all three are up, it counts five. One might make twenty-eight while another made just five and so on. That is what happened. This woman who sat on the east side had a score of twenty-eight, although the others had small scores. Now it was the turn of the woman who had two. She got to five. Three people were at five. The next time she made another three and had eight. It was now the turn of the woman who made the *tsediƚ* sticks. She made three also and had eight now.

Now the first one, the woman to the east, had her turn. She made five. She had thirty-three now. She was far ahead. It was the turn of the woman to the south. She made three. These three women just stayed together; they were all at eight now. It was the turn of the woman to the west. She made three more and moved her stick to thirteen. Then it was the turn of the north woman, the owner of the *tsediƚ* sticks. She put the sticks down.

She said to the *tsediƚ* sticks, "I want you all to face down." She increased her score to twenty-eight.

The woman at the east was ahead of all of them. But now she made only two, and that brought her to the thirty-fifth stone.

This woman who learned the game from White Hactcin believed it. The rest of the women did not believe it and didn't keep the rules. They all thought that she was just telling lies.

Four women were playing. They were betting against each other. Each had a sack of corn.[1] They were not playing partners. They were not helping each other. They were all going around one way.

The rest of the women were sitting around watching. They didn't believe. They said, "Why pray to that wood? It has no power."

They had no faith. The woman who sat at the east threw the staves down hard on the flat stone. The sticks flew high in the air. As they did so a swallow flew under them. The three sticks fell under his wings. Everyone was waiting for the sticks to come down. They were afraid of being hit by them and were hunched up in their places with their heads down.

After a while they began to look up to see why the sticks did not fall down. There was nothing up there.

They asked each other, "Did you put those sticks away?" "Did you hide them?" But no one had those sticks.

Then the old woman took out another set of sticks and handed them to the four women who were playing. This time the woman was careful. She didn't throw them down so hard. She made three.

The second woman took them now. She thought to herself, "This wood has no power. It's all right to throw them any old way." She threw them down hard. The cliff swallow flew down in the same way and took them away.

The women were all sitting with their heads down, waiting for the sticks to fall. They were afraid. Nothing happened, however.

[1] Sacks of corn were a favorite wager of the Jicarilla women.

Then they looked all around but saw no trace of the sticks. The old woman took out another set of sticks.

It was the turn of the woman to the west. She took them and threw them down heavily. They all came down this time, but one of the sticks fell on the woman who sat to the north and gave her a severe blow.

It was this woman's turn again because she had hit someone with the stick. She took her turn again. She said, "I'm going to make a good score." She asked for a score and threw them down hard. Again the women hunched over with their heads down waiting for the sticks to descend. But the cliff swallow had come again and carried them away. So the woman to the west lost a set too.

Three sets were lost. Only one set was left. The old woman handed her last set to the woman who sat to the north.

This woman motioned with the sticks and then threw them down with great force. The same thing happened; she lost them too. They looked all over for the sticks but couldn't find them.

Everyone was sorry. This was the first time they had had the game to enjoy and now it was lost. They searched for the sticks. They shook out clothes and looked all over. But no one had the sticks. They stayed there all day. There was no game any more.

This old woman was sad. She missed her game.

At sundown the women began to go home and the sacks of corn used for the betting were taken home. The old woman went home. She was sad. She had only her empty bag to take home.

Night came. She took out her straight clay pipe. She put mountain tobacco in it. She blew four puffs to the sky. She said, "My father, I am praying for my game. You must help me and take it away from the one who has it, for it is my pleasure and my life." She prayed till the middle of the night. Then she went to bed.

She didn't feel sleepy for a long time. It was almost morning before she slept. She was dreaming. In her dream White Hactcin came to her.

White Hactcin asked, "Why do you want me? Why do you pray?"

Then White Hactcin told her, "Look to the east. See that swallow, see the others around in a circle. That cliff bird is playing with your game. Look to the south where the cliff stands."

She looked. Then she saw the cliff swallows having a good time playing with her sticks.

"Look to the west," said White Hactcin, and she looked. There at the cliffs were swallows having a good time with another set.

He told her to look to the north also and she did. There at a cliff near the river she recognized her own game. The swallows were playing and having a good time.[1]

[1] That's why Jay was after Swallow, because Swallow was a robber. The swallow is very pretty, but the Jicarilla do not like him very much. (Inf.) This refers to another story in which Blue Jay punishes Swallow. Cf. footnote 1, p. 349.

White Hactcin said, "If those sticks fall into the water, you might die. Those birds are having a good time with your game now."

The old woman said nothing. She thought with her mind, "Father, you must give it back to me; that's my body."

White Hactcin looked at her. He knew what she was wishing. He smiled. He told her, "You must get up at sunrise, exactly then. Take pollen and sprinkle it to the east, south, west, and north. After you have done that come in and take out your bag. I will give the game back to you just once more, but you must have faith and take good care of the sticks and pray to them. They are your body and your life. You must teach your people what I say and make all of them believe it." He clapped his hands together and disappeared. She didn't know where he went.

At sunrise the next day she arose. She offered pollen to the four directions. When she started it she was a little doubtful. She took out the bag. It did feel a little heavy. She put her hand right in that bag. She took out three staves tied together. She looked at them. They were new ones, recently painted red. She looked at the ends. She could tell they had never been used before. She took out four bundles like this. She untied them and examined them. They were all new; they had never been played with.

C. THE MOCCASIN GAME FOR DAY OR NIGHT

In the moccasin game played for day or night,[1] the road-runner and all the birds and animals who go around by day were on the south side. On the north side were the owl and all the birds and animals that go around at night. The owl was going back and forth on his side. The road-runner was doing the same on his side.

The road-runner said, "It is getting dark. Now what are you going to bet?"

Owl was pacing back and forth for a while. Then he came to the

[1] Cf. Goddard, p. 207; Mooney, p. 198.

This game is one of the "hidden ball" type. Sides are chosen and four moccasins are buried in a row on each side of a fire. A blanket is raised between the two sides and a member of one side hides a piece of yucca root in one of the four moccasins. The blanket is lowered and a member of the other side attempts to guess where the root is. According to the accuracy of his guess or the number of moccasins away from the one of his choice the root lies, he either obtains the root for his side to hide or obligates his side to pay out a number of yucca strips which act as counters. The side which first wins all the counters is the victor. The story of the first game of this kind ever played is long and important among the Chiricahua and Mescalero Apache, where it serves to explain how day came. For the Jicarilla the origin of day is adequately clarified by the creation of sun and moon under the earth. The Jicarilla moccasin game story degenerates into what is almost a trickster coyote tale, though its first part follows the Mescalero-Chiricahua version in outline.

road-runner. "I'll bet that the sun shall not rise. I don't want it to rise. That is what I will bet."

The road-runner answered, "All right, I'll bet with you on that. I want the sun to rise."

So they bet this against each other and either side shouted at the other.

The owl could see through the moccasins at night, for his eyes were very sharp, especially in the dark. The road-runner had red streaks under his eyes. He could see very well for the other side because of that.

They started to play. The game was played at Rock Nose, a place in the mountains below the Mescalero Reservation.[1] The owl's side hid the yucca root first. They put up their blanket and began to sing and have great fun. The road-runner came straight to the correct moccasin; he guessed the right one the first time.

Then on the road-runner's side Quail started to hide the root. The meadow-lark sang, for he knew all the songs. He clapped his hands while he sang.[2] The owl came out and got the root back the first time.

Then it was the turn of the owl's side to hide it, and the poor-will hid it for them. It is hard to see that bird; that is why he was chosen to hide it. If he doesn't move you just pass him by. The elf owl sang for the owl's side while it was being hidden. He continued to sing for that side till the middle of the night, then he got hoarse and couldn't sing well, so they pushed him aside.

The owl asked his side, "Who has learned to sing well? One of you who is a good singer come over here and sit in the owl's place."

Then one bird on the road-runner's side said, "Here I am. I'll sing for you. I'll help you sing. But I won't be on your side." Pine Siskin was the one who said this.

So Pine Siskin came over and sang on Owl's side. That bird helped with the songs on that side. After that, because he sang for those people, he knew just when it was going to storm and be cold so that everything would be frozen.

Gopher was on the side of those who played for darkness. He was on that side because he lives in the dark under the earth.[3]

The mouse was standing on the owl's side.

Road-runner scolded him. "After this the owl will eat you," he said.

That is why, even now, owls kill the mice at night. It is because this mouse helped for one song on the owl's side. He had two faces (i. e., was untrustworthy).

Turkey was not in the game.

---

[1] The Guadalupe Mountains.

[2] The informant here sang the meadow-lark's song.

[3] In the Jicarilla story they do not say that Gopher changed the position of the root by digging a hole under the moccasins. (Inf.)

Bear was on the side of those who played for darkness, for he buries himself in the mountains in winter.

Lizard played in this first moccasin game too.

After the game the road-runner said, "This game will be played only in winter. If someone plays in any other season, Lizard will get in his moccasins."

Lizard had no luck in the game. That is why he has a hard time getting his food now. All he has to eat are flies which he draws in with his breath.

Toward morning the owl's side began to lose. Before this the owl's side had almost won. The side which played for day had only two sticks left at one time and then they began to win them back again.

At that time Chickadee said, "It is my turn to sing now. He sang this song, "Chickadee came to life again and could not be tracked easily."

The owl began to be angry then and kicked at the fire because his side was losing. He kicked the stick into the fire. The chickadee was very happy. He clapped his hands and sang.

The owl went over to him and pushed him, saying, "Get out of the way. You must not sing any more."

The chickadee replied, "I thought you had such great power! What's the matter? We are gaining!"

Soon the morning glow was seen and the owl was sweating, for he could do nothing.

Rock Wren was the first one to see the daylight coming. He sang about it. Owl was very angry and twice pushed Rock Wren. The others had to hold Owl. That is why people fight in the game now and that is why they are advised by others not to fight.

The rock wren said, "The owl pushed me. Now I shall be able to go into holes and travel anywhere at night." And he can do so too.

The road-runner called to four on his side, "You must build a big fire. Make it very hot. Make them sweat even more."

They brought wood and built up the fire. The owl perspired freely and the sweat ran into his eyes. Then he could not see so well.

About five in the morning the light was bright.

The owl was angry again. He took the guessing stick and poked it in the fire. Then he rubbed it under the eyes of the road-runner where the red paint was. "You can see with this," he said.

The people on the owl's side were almost crying.

Those on the other side were celebrating. They were clapping their hands and rejoicing. They said, "We will turn over his hat!" (i. e., "We are winning".)

When some of those on the owl's side saw that they were losing, they started to run away. They didn't want to see the sun. But the sun hit them with its rays as they went, and that is why their fur is yellowish in places.

The moccasins were not picked up after the game. They are still there, turned to rock. The root with which they played is still there. It, too, became a rock.

The ones who were playing for day wanted to bet some more with the bear, but he didn't want to bet and ran away. He ran to a bushy place with the people of the road-runner's side after him, and that is why he is found in such places now. They were trying to kill him when they chased him.[1]

Snake ran away too and went right into a hole in the ground. He went through some rocks and they shot arrows in there after him. But no one hit him because he had power. He escaped into the hole.

Now it was getting rather bright. The owl said, "I thought the day would not come," and he began to fly for the shade.

No one chased the owl. He went to the shade after poking the road-runner with the burning brand under the eyes.

The road-runner and his side won. The sun's rays struck Towhee while he was dancing for joy over the victory of his side, and that is why he is multicolored today.

Those on the road-runner's side had their choice of colors. That is why there are so many beautifully colored birds who played on that side. The others ran away, but nevertheless the sun's rays hit some of them and colored them.

Pine Siskin came over on the birds' side and said, "I belong here. I was just deceiving those others."

Coyote was there, but he was quiet. He was sitting on the owl's side. The sun rose. Coyote was angry because his side had lost.

"I'll bet you about the stars," he said. "I'll bet that when night comes there will be no stars and no light at night."

Then Grouse stood up against the coyote. "You can't do anything," he said. "What can you do? What did you do in this game? What are you talking about?"

Coyote was so angry they had to hold him. He wanted to run over to the other side and fight someone.

On the road-runner's side was Fox. "Let him come over," Fox said. "I'll give him what he wants."

Coyote did nothing about it.

Those who had won day were very happy. The owl's side went to the shade, for they like the shade. Some went under the rocks, some under the ground, and some into all kinds of holes.

When all on his side had gone away the coyote went to the other side and asked the fox, "Why were you so angry with me?" He was the one who started it, but he was putting the blame on the fox.

Coyote said to the fox, "Let us go aside where there are no people. I want to ask you a question."

[1] In the Jicarilla story it is not told that the bear put his moccasins on the wrong feet. (Inf.)

These two went out to the north to a high mountain. They sat on the top under some shade.

Then Coyote asked, "My friend, do you know what the road-runner used in that game? Did he put on some kind of ceremony before we started the game? Or did he use some kind of plant? I thought the owl had more power, for with his eyes he can see everything in the night. Yet he lost."

The fox replied, "As far as I know, the road-runner did nothing. He didn't use plants, prayers, or ceremony. But he used the red streaks under his eyes, and he could see through the moccasins."

Coyote said, "I thought the day would never come again. At night when we travel it is very pleasant. We are fresh then. It is not too hot. My friend, Fox, you are foolish. Why did you stay on that side?"

Fox said, "Codi, you are more foolish than I am. That is why you are poor and thin. No wonder you are thin! It is best that people travel by day. By day people can find food easily. Even from a distance they can see it. No wonder you are thin! You want to go only by night. Look at me. I'm fat."

After a while Coyote said, "Do you know anything about some medicine? Give it to me, for I want to get fat."

Fox said, "I don't know anything about medicine. But when I go where people are having a celebration I eat all I can and that is the way I grow fat."

But Coyote didn't know what was meant by a feast of the people. He said, "Don't talk to me like that! You must tell me the truth. What do you mean by a feast? If you don't tell me the truth about how I may get fat I am going to eat you up."

Fox answered, "Tomorrow afternoon over here on the other side of the ridge they are going to have a feast and have good things to eat."

Coyote asked, "What is going on there? Will there be many people?"

"Yes, there will be many people. Some will beat drums. Some will blow flutes. Some will sing, some laugh. The people will enjoy it. I always get up on a tree and look down on what is happening."

So Fox showed Coyote how to do it. "This is the way I do it," he said.

Coyote said to Fox, "Tomorrow wait for me. Let's stay together tonight and tomorrow we will go together. What do people eat at the feast?"

"They eat soup, fruits of all kinds, and mush. That is their food."

Coyote didn't know what those words meant. He didn't know what mush was and didn't recognize the different foods Fox mentioned.

They talked all that day till sundown. They went to a place where oak leaves had fallen.

Coyote said, 'Let's sleep here where it is nice and warm."

The next morning they got up and started for the feast. The fox forgot and rubbed his eyes because they had mucous around them. Then they traveled all morning.

Fox told Coyote, "You must vomit out all you now have in your stomach. I know you have nothing but grasshoppers and insects in there. And defecate too. Have a good appetite by the time we get to the feast. You will find good food there."

Coyote said, "You stay here and watch while I vomit."

"No," replied the fox, "I'll go on a little way."

Fox took some dry juniper bark and wrapped it up to make a torch about two feet long. He was going to get away from the coyote. That was his thought.

He came back to the place where the coyote had vomited. Nothing but saliva was there. The coyote had forced himself to vomit until the tears ran. Coyote's eyes were red.

Coyote said, "What do you put on your eyes? It must be medicine." He was referring to the dirt the fox had in his eyes from rubbing them. "I guess these people put that in their eyes when they go to a feast. You had better do it to me too. Let me take it out of your eyes. I believe it is pinon pitch. I'll put some in my eyes too and we'll go to the feast."

And Fox said to Coyote, "When we get there you must eat all you can so you will get fat. When we come among the piñon trees I'll fix your eyes with pitch. Then I'll hold your hand and lead you to the feast. That is the way a person is always led into the feast when he comes for the first time. He has pitch in his eyes and is led by the hand."

So Fox took Coyote to a grove of piñon trees. They found some sticky pitch. Fox rubbed it on both Coyote's eyes, rubbed it on thick.

"Now you shut your eyes," Fox said. "Don't try to open your eyes. There are already many people at the feast. When you hear the noise of the drum and flute with your ears, when you hear the yelling and shouting, that is the first part of the feast."

Fox led Coyote along.

Coyote said, "My friend, you must take good care of me. Don't let me stumble."

Fox said, "At meal time your eyes will open by themselves."

Then Fox took him to the thick brush. "Stay here and wait for me," he said. "I'm going over and get my wooden spoon. I left it and I had better go back and get it."

Then Fox started to make a fire with a fire drill. The smoke was thick.

Then Jack-rabbit came over. "What are you doing?" he asked.

"Oh, come, hurry, help me!"

So the jack-rabbit helped and after he had twirled it a little while the fire ignited.

Rabbit asked, "What are you going to do with that torch?"

"Oh, I'm going to burn up someone who wants to eat me up."

Jack-rabbit said, "That is very good. I'm glad to hear that you are going to burn that coyote."

"Help me make another torch like this one."

They both worked and made another torch of cedar bark.

Then Fox went to Coyote and said, "Whenever you hear something, shout and laugh and sing."

Then they fired the place. Soon the fire was all around Coyote, for he was in the bushes.

Soon the noise of the burning brush was heard by Coyote. He started to laugh and dance. He said, "Oh, I'm going to have a great feast; that is why they are starting to celebrate."

The fire was coming nearer all the time. Coyote was getting too hot. He put his hand out on one side and it was burned. He put out his other hand and it was burned. Then his eyes began to burn, for the pitch was just like oil. Then he started to run straight ahead. He ran right through the fire. He was badly burned. Wherever he touched burning wood, he was burned. His tail was half burned and his fur was burned in many places.

The jack-rabbit looked at him. Coyote's burns were painful. It hurt him to sit down because of his burned tail. It hurt him to lie down on his side too. He stayed there about two days.

About noon he started to cry. "Oh, when I had my eyes I went all around and saw good country; I saw many things." He was suffering now.

Then the jack-rabbit came over. "What did you say? Why are you crying?"

"My friend, give me some medicine. I am very sick. Make my eyes well again. If you do that I will give you twenty-four prairie-dogs."

"I never eat prairie-dogs."

"What do you like?"

"I like to eat yucca fruit and prickly pears." Jack-rabbit asked for these two things. "If I make new eyes for you, you won't have to pay me."

"That is very good; you are just like Dios; you feel sorry for poor people."

Then Jack-rabbit broke some cedar wood. He split it and made some sharp edges. Then he went and picked up some hard pitch. He chewed it.

After chewing it, he went over to Coyote. "You must put your head down." He looked at Coyote's eyes and cleaned away all the burned part. He cut out all the burned part with a flint. The coyote almost cried, it hurt so much. Then Jack-rabbit motioned four times with the pitch he had rolled into two balls, and he put them in coyote's eye sockets.

"Now cover your eyes with your hands." Then after a while, "Now put your hands down." Then the jack-rabbit asked, "Do you see everything clearly?"

"Yes."

"Do you see those old trees standing to the east?"

"Yes, I can even see the roots." Then Coyote said four times, "Thank you. I never thought I'd have my sight again."

"Here are your eyes."

Coyote looked at what had been taken out. They were all singed.

Jack-rabbit had power. He made the fox and the coyote forget the trouble they had had. Coyote didn't even remember how it happened.

Coyote said, "I don't know what happened to me. Perhaps I slept in the bushes when they caught fire. After this I'll be careful. I won't go among the bushes."

That is why many coyotes are like this one that was burned. They have shorter tails where Coyote's tail was burned off. That is the way Coyote lost in this game. Fox beat him.

The fox went away. He saw many jack-rabbits in a certain place. Wildcat saw the jack-rabbits too.

Fox went over and told Wildcat what he had done to Coyote.

Other people came up and asked, "Why are you laughing?"

"I'm laughing about poor Coyote. I burned him because he wanted to eat me."

The people said, "That's very good. We don't like him. He robs and murders."

The rest of the people scolded the jack-rabbit when they found out what he had done. "Why didn't you leave him alone?" they demanded.

"No, Dios doesn't want it that way, "Jack-rabbit said. "You people standing over here, some day perhaps you will lose your eyes in some way. Then you can come over and ask me to help you. I will be willing to help you. I am not against any one of you."

The jack-rabbit is the only one who has power to do things for the eyes. A long time ago the jack-rabbit had power to hit the back of his head with his hand, make the eyes fall out in the other hand, throw them up in the air, and then make them fall back in their sockets again.[1]

D. THE ORIGIN OF CLAY POTS AND PIPES

In the beginning when no one was on this earth, there were created first one old woman and one old man. They went around; they had nothing to do. A Hactcin stood before them. They didn't know he was there.

[1] Throughout the animal cycle stories Jack-rabbit is depicted as being able to cure those who have suffered an injury to the eyes.

The man prayed to the one who made the earth. He said, "Give us something to live on."

Thus these old people prayed. They faced to the east and prayed.

Then the Hactcin stood there, but these old people did not see him. After they prayed they saw that someone was standing in front of them.

The Hactcin said, "I know what you are saying, and I understand. I know all the world. You are asking for something to live by. You are praying to me."

They arose.

He showed them a rock. "That is gold. It is worth much, but I cannot give it to you, for you do not know how to work it.

"The next is silver. That, too, is valuable, but you do not know of it or what to do with it. I cannot give it to you. Some day people will come from across the ocean, from the east. They will feed you, give you clothes and food. That is why I will send them. And they will like this silver and gold.

"And another people are coming from the south. They will give you all kinds of fruit."

He took them to the other side of the mountain and they stood together there. Two young trees were standing there. A big hole was there.

"Go over there and dig out that clay," the Hactcin said. "I will show you how to make pots and bowls with it. You will live by this means."

This was the first time Hactcin gave this clay to the people. Even now the people use the same clay.

"From the east, from the other side of the ocean, are people with eyes just like fish eyes, hair reddish, and skin white. Those people are coming. This gold and silver will be used then. They will come and show you how to use those things.

"When they come don't war against them. Don't fight with them, for I told them to come. Some day they will give you their possessions. They will cut the timber, work the mines, and use the metals because the Indians do not know how to do this. That is why I will send the white people over here.

"From the south will come another people. They will have a black mark around the lips (moustache, whiskers). But they will have eyes just like the eyes of the Indians.

"When they come into your country do not rise against them. They will be your neighbors."

Then the Hactcin called to the woman, "Come over here." He touched both her hands with his.[1] "Now work the clay from your own knowledge and with your own understanding."

[1] Special knowledge and health are often imparted by the supernaturals through touch.

Then both the man and the woman went up there and dug out the clay.

Then the old man said, "Now make a clay pot, for the Hactcin told you to do so."

And so she made a clay bowl and she did very good work. The old man was proud of that. The old woman made bowls of all shapes. But they had no names yet. They didn't know what to call them . They put mush in, but still they did not know what to call them. The two did not yet know how to name or properly use this work.

They said, "Let us pray again. We know someone is watching over us; that is why we did this work."

They prayed. Then they went to bed and slept. The woman dreamed of the Hactcin. In the dream the Hactcin told her how to use the pots and what to call them. "This one is for soup, this one for mush," he told her.

The next night this woman had another dream. The Hactcin told her, "You must teach the children this, and after that, when they make a pipe for you it will be worth much and the people will use these pipes for all good purposes."

They left the pots drying after fashioning them and then they went back to a big camp where there were many people. But they didn't tell the people about it. They stayed one night, then another, then another, then another. Then the fourth day, when the sun was just going down, the old man got up and called the people together and talked to them.

He said, "All my relatives, I'm going to tell you something important. Some day people are coming who have eyes like fish and bodies all white and reddish hair. When they come across the ocean they will give us all their possessions."

But some of the people did not believe what the old man said. They said, "He must be crazy! Let's tie him down and burn some medicine for him to inhale.[1] People such as he describes have never been seen."

The old man quieted them and went on. "From the south another people with black around the mouth are coming. They will come here and be just like close relatives, just like our own children. They will come to our country."

The other people didn't believe it. Twelve leading men came to the chief's home and talked to him about it. They said, "This foolish man! What does he understand? How does he know such people are coming? We ought to have a ceremony over him, for he must be crazy."

The chief said, "No, let us be quiet. I'll talk to him about it some time. It will not be right to go out and quarrel with him just

[1] The Jicarilla treat in this manner individuals who go mad and become violent.

because he speaks like that. Some day I'll call him here by himself and ask him more about it, about the country from which such people are coming."[1]

Now this old woman had another dream. The Hactcin told her, "The pot which you made is all dry. You must go back, build a fire, turn the pot upside down, and put bark over it."

When they went back they found the pot all dry. The woman went up to get pine bark. Twice she brought it on her back. The man went to pine and piñon trees and picked off lumps of pitch. Some of it was dry and he pulled it off the bark. All the pots were put upside down and they covered them with the bark and kindled the fire.[2]

When they were all through, while the pots were still hot, the woman dipped into the pitch with a grass brush and smeared the outside of the pots with the melted pitch.[3]

When all were finished, they wrapped the pots up and took them back to the camp of the people.

The people were astonished. They had never seen them before. They asked, "Where did you find such pretty pots?"

The woman said, "I made these myself."

The others did not believe her. "How could you make these? I guess you just picked them up somewhere," they said.

Then, since the people didn't believe, the old couple kept the pots for themselves. The others wanted them to give some away, but they kept them for themselves.

The old people had two married sons and one married daughter. They told their sons and daughter to come to them. They gave the pots to their children.

The children asked, "What are you doing? What are you going to do for yourselves if you give all these away?"

The old woman said, "I'm going to make more of them."

The children didn't believe it.

But the old people went back to the hole and dug out more clay. When they returned they made two bowls of every size and shape.

The old people were talking. Their daughter had an eight-year old girl. They said to each other, "Let's teach that girl. Let us do what the Hactcin told us to do. Let us use the knowledge for prayer. Let the girl make pipes for us and we will use them for a good life."

The grandfather then went over there and he returned with his granddaughter.

The grandmother said, "My grandchild, I want you to make pipes for us. I'll show you how first. Then you do just as I have done."

---

1 This is an excellent portrayal of the mediating influence which the Jicarilla chief is expected to exert.

2 The description of the firing of the clay vessels follows the usual Jicarilla method.

3 The inside of the pot is never pitch-covered. (Inf.)

She worked alone first and the girl watched her. The little girl had a hard time. She worked till sunset and couldn't do it. It broke every time.

The next day it went the same way. She worked with the same clay but to no avail. She did a little better that second day, but it was still far from what it should be. When the sun was going down the old woman, her grandmother, broke to pieces that pipe she had made. It was not good enough.

The third day came. The woman rubbed the girl's hand just as the Hactcin had done to her. This time the girl did very well. And the woman made the design then to show her how, for she had dreamed about it and knew the right way to do it. Then they threw it into the fire. Afterwards they rubbed it with pitch.

The man wanted to use it right away to smoke with. The woman put in the mountain tobacco. She used the fire drill to get her fire, and handed the pipe to the girl who puffed it four times and handed it back.

The old man said, "I'm going to make a pipe for myself too."

He went out and cut a big yucca leaf. He cut it about the length of a pipe. He rolled it up and tied it. He used this for a pipe. When they had no pipes they used these sometimes, but when you use this kind four times it is all burned, the ashes are too hot for it.

Then the woman said to the man, "You cannot use this pipe. The Hactcin who told me to have this made said, 'Some day when your husband needs it, some day when there is great need, then it is to be used, just that day.'"[1]

The people didn't know why the old people were doing this. Some people thought it was the idea of the old man and woman themselves, something they had made up.

The old man got angry about it because the old woman wouldn't let him use the pipe. He cut some sumac wood. He split it, shaped it, hollowed it out, and used this just like a pipe. But this was not much good either. And the old man was not satisfied.

So the grandmother said, "My grandchild, perhaps you had better make a pipe for your grandfather."

The old man said, "My grandchild, please do make me a pipe."

So the granddaughter made one like the men smoke today and puffed four times from it before giving it to her grandfather.[2] That's how the men came to use the kind they have today. Long before the people knew about the clay type of pipe they used one of sumac wood.

Neither the old man nor old woman had horses. Nor did their

---

[1] Cf. p. 217 for an instance in which the woman's pipe is used by the men for ritual purposes.

[2] Today every Jicarilla grandparent with grandchildren of the proper age is supposed to have a clay pipe made for him by his grandchild as is here described. This pipe is retained for ritual purposes.

children's families have any. When they moved camp they had to carry their goods on their backs. The woman had to carry all the wood on her back.

One day she was crying. She said, "I am getting tired of carrying wood on my back. My chest is beginning to ache. Some day soon I am going to die, I guess."

When night came she went to bed. She dreamed again and the same one who taught her how to make the pot said, "Tomorrow tell your two sons and their friends to go out and steal enemy horses and the enemy shall not see them."

The next day the woman sent her husband. She said, "Tell both of your sons to come over here."

He brought them.

The mother spoke to them. She told how she had been crying and for what reason. She told of her dream. "Someone told me, because he was sorry for me, that you should go out to Plains country and steal horses from the enemy."

The boys were glad to hear this, for they were without horses too and wanted some.

The woman said, "You must tell some others. Get four, or six, or eight in the party. Bring them over here before you go."

The boys found four men willing to go. Altogether there were six now. At sunset the four men and the woman's two sons came to the place where the woman was. They said, "Why did you ask to see us?"

"I am going to tell you something. I do not know whether you will think it good or not." She told them all about her experiences. She told how she had seen this Hactcin face to face the first time and had dreamed after that. She told how all her dreams had come true, about how she had been crying and what the Hactcin had told her to advise her sons.

The old man was sitting in front of them. The woman told it all. She had always kept her dreams secret, but now her husband heard it all.

The next morning he got up and went before the people and called aloud telling what his wife had dreamed. "These young men are going out and steal horses," he said.

When he came back his wife scolded him. "Where are you going?" she asked. "Are you the one who is going to steal horses? I guess what the people say about you, that you are crazy, is true."[1]

The next day many people gathered at the home of the old people. They said, "Those men must not go out. The enemy are numerous and fierce and our young men will be killed." They advised against the expedition.

---

[1] This excursion into domestic relations is highly realistic. The Jicarilla wife is not too timid to administer a sharp rebuke to her mate when it is necessary.

The old woman paid no attention to those who came around. Finally they all went off. Then she took out the clay pipe which her granddaughter had made for her and smoked and prayed and prayed.

Then she turned to the four men and her sons and said, "You must decide when you are going and whether you are going to leave during the day or the night."

That night she dreamed again. She dreamed that two of the men were going to change their minds because of the advice and words of other people.

She was right. Only two of the four came back with her sons.

They said, "Let us leave this very evening and get away from these people."

These four men had never gone out in Plains country before. That is why those two others had backed out. They were afraid that they would lose the way and not know how to protect themselves.

The woman gave advice to the four men. "Every one of you has a good mind with which to think. Go straight to the east. There you will find horses to steal. But you must take them at night."

The four started out and were already on the way when two other men started after them. These two were brothers. They knew much about war and how to go to the Plains. They caught up and so there were six again.

They walked all day and continued until ten o'clock at night. Then they lay down and went to sleep.

The woman stayed home, repeating her prayer. She said, "Let the enemy fail to see these people." She prayed for horses of the different colors, mentioning first the black horse of the east, then the blue (literally greyish) horse to the south, next the yellowish one of the west, and last the white horse of the north. First she called these four and then all colors in any order, sorrel, pinto, etc.[1]

The two men who had caught up, when they all arrived where there was some white clay, painted all of the men with white clay, all over the whole body, even the hair. This is because they are different on the raid or war-path. They speak a different language. They have different habits.[2] They obey restrictions such as one which forbids them to stretch their legs out at night. If they have to stretch them out at night when they get tired, when they draw them up again they have to say some words like, "A black horse (or the kind they like) I am drawing to me." Everything is different on the war-path, and so their bodies and appearance must be different too. Then nothing can happen to their real selves.

After they paint themselves this way they are not supposed to

---

[1] When a son or husband is on the raid the Jicarilla woman repeats such prayers.

[2] What follows is an account of a number of the rules, ritual observances, and behavior patterns of Jicarilla raiding and warfare.

look in back or to the left or right sides, for if they do they will see the enemy and the enemy will see them. They should go the way they are facing all the time, and the enemy will not see them even though they are right there.

This painting is called "white clay came."

The man who knows how to do it also makes a little stick for them with the horse's hoof on it. This is called "scratching," and is used for scratching the body after that.

They journeyed all the next day. Then they slept a little while. Then the one who knew the most about war told them to get up again.

They traveled all night and all day again. When the sun set they said, "Let us rest over here." And they all sat down and started to eat the dry meat.

After they had eaten supper the man who knew said, "Let us go again and keep moving until about ten tonight."

They did this. They were all very tired and slept through till the morning star rose.

Again they moved on. In a little while they came to a water hole. The men did not lie down and touch their whole lips to the water, for to do that would bring a great quantity of facial hair around the lips.

They started to walk to the east again. There, after going about four miles, they saw about twenty tipis of the enemy. All six of them went into some oak brush and lay there and watched the camps. No one went out.

The leader said, "Now be brave, be men. These enemies will take their horses to the tall grass."

The enemy did this. Two of the enemy watched the horses for a little while and then went back to camp. The horses were all alone in tall grass.

The leader chose the bravest of the boys and said, "You must get ready, for you are to bring the horses."

The boy went with him and together they drove back four bunches of horses. They drove them to the place where the four others were.

The leader said, "Now rope them and remember that the ones that turn toward you by themselves when you go to rope them are the best ones, the most gentle."

All of the six roped suitable horses. They mounted these. They did not plant spears at the place where they stole the horses because they had brought none with them; they had brought only bows and arrows.[1]

---

[1] It was the usual custom of the Jicarilla to bring lances and extra moccasins on a raiding expedition. Then, when the horses of the enemy were taken, the worn-out moccasins were tied to the lances and the lances were left conspicuously thrust in the ground as a gesture of contempt for the foe.

"Let us go quietly," the leader said.

This was about night.

The leader said, "Quietly, easily, so there will not be much noise. Don't let the enemy hear us."

They went some distance.

Then the leader said, "Now is the time. You all have grandfathers and grandmothers and many relatives. They taught you how to protect yourselves and how to be brave.[1] Our enemies would like to have our scalps and our lives. Now let us go fast and be ready for the enemy if he follows."

So they increased their pace. They didn't know how many horses they had. It was too dark to see, but they had a great many. They drove the horses all night and all the next day.

When the sun was going down they mounted other horses. Again they drove them all night and by that time they were nearing home. The first mountain of their own country was called "Edge crossed." There is a town near it now called Springer.[2] At noon they came to a spring near these mountains.

At noon the leader said, "I guess we had better not stay here long, for about this time people come to this spring to get water. Something warns me that we had better not go straight to our country. We must go by a different path."

They got on a high place, a slope, and looked around. Though they did not know it, ahead of them were two dead Utes, slain while hunting for antelopes. Seventy enemies had been on the war-path to the Apache country. On their way back they had found these two Utes and killed both of them. It was fortunate that the Apaches went another way, for they might have met these enemies.

The sun was almost going down when they got to the place which is now Springer. They drove the horses along the cliffs and got on the south side of the mountains. There was a hot spring there and they stopped and camped there over night. They took turns standing guard over the horses all night.

Early in the morning they started for the lake. About noon they got there, to "Dry Lake Bottom." It is east of Taos, about twenty-five miles east of Taos. There they camped. They counted and found they had sixty horses. They got them in a corral. Each of the six took ten horses.

The leader gave a horse to one of his relatives. He gave it to his mother's sister. The two sons had relatives too. There were three relatives, daughters of sisters of the old woman, their mother. These were grown girls but still single. They gave them horses.[3]

---

[1] The grandparents were the approved instructors of Jicarilla youth. Any Jicarilla who errs through ignorance is likely to be asked, "Did you have no grandparents to teach you?"

[2] Springer, New Mexico.

[3] This is an accurate picture of the feeling of responsibility to the larger body of relatives a Jicarilla would be expected to show.

The father's brother was dead, but he had two daughters living, and the boys gave them each a horse too.

The other men kept their ten horses.

The old woman was dancing all day long by herself, for she had a horse now. They dance in place, moving their arms when they are happy like this. Each of the sons gave the woman a horse, a mare.

After the horses were all divided up two Ute Indians came. They told what had happened to two of their own people who were out hunting antelopes. They told how they had not returned and how they had been tracked and found slain with their scalps, thumbs, and penises missing. The enemy took the thumbs and penis to use in naming their children. Then when the man who takes it has a child, he names him Thumb. These Indians do that too. The Jicarilla women I told you about in the other story who cut the arms of the men, named a child of the family Cuts-the-Arm after their deed. They do this if a child in the family has no name. Then they give him the name after their war deed. Or they save it and give it when a child comes in the family.

A man gives a name after his war deed to his child, his grandchild, or some other relative, but he does not ever change his own name because of a war deed.

One man in the fight of which I told you killed an enemy. They took off the enemy's clothes and saw that he had a sore on the anus. So one who was then an unnamed child was named Sore Anus after him.

The Jicarilla didn't take other parts of the body though, just the scalp. You can't take the whole body along!

The two Ute Indians came for help against the enemy who had killed the Ute hunters. And many of the Apaches went along to help. They went back to the place and saw the two dead men. But it was already too late to catch up with the enemy. Two days had passed. They came back to the Apache camps again the next day. The dead Utes were already all swelled up, for the days had been hot.

After they came back, the people talked among themselves. They saw what good horses these young men had brought back. The woman had prayed so hard that they got horses easily and not from so very far away. The others thought it would be easy for them also, and they wanted horses badly.

So they moved camp. Before this the old woman had had to carry her possessions on her back. This time she had two horses, one to ride, and one on which to carry her goods. The old man walked and carried his arrows.

All the camps were going to move to the place where the clay was dug. The old woman had a horse now and so could carry a great deal of clay. She gathered clay and made all kinds of dishes, about forty pieces altogether. Those in the other camps had no pots or dishes. She made all these and distributed them among her own relatives.

She called all her relatives. While she gave away the pots she told all about the Hactcin who had come to her and about her subsequent dreams. The next day many came to listen to her, and she told them all from whom she had learned to make her pots and pipes.

She said, "At one time my husband and I knew nothing. We prayed to rocks, to trees, to everything. We asked for one who had great knowledge and power to help us. Then a man stood before us. I couldn't make this pot out of my own head or by my own will. The one who stood before us told us how to make it and told us of the white people who are to come from the east and the south. He told us to use pipes. He said, 'Let your grandchild, when she is eight years old, make it for you. This will be the pipe for prayer.' Then once I cried for horses. I was tired and weary. That one came to me in a dream and advised me to send out my sons. Everything I dreamed has come true. The pipe I used for prayer."

Then after she had told the whole story all the people believed in this pipe.

The enemy from whom the sixty horses were taken in the story were the Kiowa.

The old woman's name was Wild Pony, and the old man's name was Smoke.

E. THE PLOW

One time a certain old man was dreaming. They do not say what his name was. It is a story of long ago. This old man was very tired, for the people had had a hard time planting. Because of this he was exhausted and lay down and slept. He dreamed that he passed along below a bank. Above, on the bank, grew all kinds of trees, and their roots were hanging down. He walked along watching these roots. He stopped before one which was very, very tough. He said, "This is one which will help us; it will make things easier for us." He looked up at the tree. It was the root of the oak tree.

The next day he woke up. He walked down to a bank like the one in his dream and dug a length of oak root. He cut a piece out of the trunk too. He sharpened the piece of root with a rough rock, just as is done with a file today. He took the trunk part for the handle and the attached root was jutting out to the side like a plow.

It took him about ten days to finish the plow. To complete it he selected a small oak whose roots were easily exposed. He cut the top branches off and the top of the trunk. Then he dug it out by the roots and sharpened a part of the root on one side. The rest of the roots he chopped off with a stone ax. A couple of branches he left on the other side of the trunk, on the part near the roots. They were for handles. Then he turned it over and used it as a plow. He went back and got a horse and tied it to this plow. It was not enough.

Then he got another man and another horse and both were able to pull it easily. Each man held a handle and guided it. At first the branches stuck straight up and the men had a hard time hanging on to them. So they stopped. They built a fire, heated the branches, and bent them back. Then it was easier.

Before planting they plowed up the rows where they were to plant. Then they put the seeds in, and the children came along and covered up the seeds.

The plow was about ten feet long. The plowing shield was about a foot and a half long.

The man planted in this way for two years. Then the others all said, "That way is better," and they also began to make plows. Some of them made plows of aspen, but these broke easily. The best ones were made of oak.

These were used in the beginning, before the planting, to prepare the ground. When the Mexicans came to our country they saw this plow of the Indians and made one like it, for in those days they had no plow either.

V. MYTHS CONNECTED WITH HUNTING RITUAL AND ENCOUNTERS WITH SUPERNATURAL ANIMALS

A. THE MAN WHO LIVED WITH THE BUFFALOES[1]

A certain man was out on a raid. He went out with a party to the plains country and became lost. He started back to his own country alone. He had his arrows with him.

He came to a big spring. Buffaloes were there for water. This man had nothing with him to eat. There was a small hill near the place. He saw the buffaloes going down the slope and he ran to the hill. There was a big bull there, followed by a female and two other females, and one small one, five in all.

He thought he would have a good chance to kill one of these buffaloes. He lay down about twenty-five yards away. The bull came up. He didn't shoot that one though. Now they came up to the sloping place. The bull looked around. Now the second passed and the third. He got ready to shoot the third female. He was ready to shoot.

Then the big bull turned and spoke to that third female. "Hurry!" he said. "Let's make a camp over here."

When the man heard the voice he didn't shoot. He let them go.

He stayed there and watched them. They were going up the canyon to the west. He waited to see where they were going to build a camp.

The bull was speaking again, talking to the females. "Have you people any food left?"

"Just a very little left," they replied.

The Apache let the sun go down. Then he followed the trail of the buffaloes. Darkness came. He was there at the western canyon He saw five tipis there just like the ones these Indians have. He never thought it was a buffalo camp. He thought it must be the tipis of his own people and that he was lucky to find them so near.

He came to the first tipi. He looked in. A young woman was in there. She was dressed in buckskin just like a real Apache. She was sitting in a corner pounding dry meat. A fire was burning in the center of the tipi. He went in.

She did not look up at him. She kept on pounding. After she had finished pounding the meat, she pounded fat in with it too. She put the meat before him. He didn't speak nor did she.

[1] There is a confused version of this story in Goddard, p. 221.

He thought, "This is surely one of my people."

She saved out a little for herself. The rest she gave to him. The man ate. Though he was very hungry he could not eat it all.

While the Apache was eating, the male, the bull, came out and spoke to his people. He said, "We must not sit up late. Early tomorrow morning we shall move and go to our own country." He was in the form of a bull, not a man.

The Apache ate; he didn't say anything. When he finished he went out and slept elsewhere.

Early in the morning, before the light, they all began to take the tipis down and roll the tipi covers up.

The man watched closely. When the dawn broke, he noticed that they were all buffaloes. He didn't know how they carried the poles and tipis. He tried to follow, but at a distance. He followed them all day.

At nightfall the same thing happened. They built a camp again. The Apache did as before. He came to a tipi, looked in, and recognized the same woman. Without speaking he entered. Again he was given the same food. He couldn't eat it all and handed the rest back. After the meal the bull came out again and told at what time in the morning the camp would be moved.

The Apache did not sleep in that tipi that night. He slept elsewhere and followed in the morning as before. This was the third day. When he reached the place where they halted he went in again and was served food as before. Nothing different happened this day from the others.

He followed the fourth day also. By this time they were getting near the buffalo country.

It was the fourth night. He came in as before. This time the woman spoke to him. "Why don't you sit close to me? Why do you sit far away and near the door?"

So he walked in and came near to her. He sat down.

They ate together this time from one food container. Then she said, "You must not go out tonight. You must stay here and sleep with me. I have plenty of blankets."

This woman had a husband, a white buffalo was her husband.

The next day the Apache went out early in the morning before daylight. He saw that to the west was a great encampment of people.

A chief, the white buffalo, was talking to the people. "In four days we are going to have a war," he said. "Let us have a war. A man took away my wife. Let us fight him. Let us get rid of him, my relatives, and let us war against her relatives who have treated me badly."[1]

1 This is an accurate presentation of one of the causes of family feuds and of the recriminations which are likely to pass between the antagonists, though the ordinary feud was scarcely so sanguinary as the one described

The big black bull was the chief of the other side. He spoke to his people. He said, "All of you, those eight years old and over, get out and get arrows. You children can gather the wood for shafts and help put the feathers on. You all know we are going to war in four days."

Some were at work shaping arrows, some were putting feathers on arrow shafts, some were weaving willow branches and making armor of them.[1] The men were doing these things. This work went on till everything was ready. These people had many horses too. After four days they got on good horses and put on their war-bonnets. The other side did the same thing.

On the other side were only adults. On the side of the black buffalo children were in the ranks too. The Apache put on a war-bonnet which the chief gave him.

The next day, before the sun came out, the fighting began. The white buffalo led his men around. Then the shooting began. The Apache was the only one not on horseback. The rest, even the children, were on horseback. They circled around for a while. Then the two sides formed into lines and faced each other.

The white buffalo chief came forward. "All right," he said, "who is chief of your side? Let him come out."

The Apache came out. "I'm chief," he said and came to the center to meet him.

They fought. After a while the white buffalo chief fell from his horse, dead.

When this happened, those on the white buffalo's side came out after him. Now the real fighting began. This man had many arrows and killed many of them.

They grew afraid. They said, "Let us stop. You have already killed our chief."

The fighting stopped. The side of the white buffalo picked up their dead. They were crying. They began to carry them to camp.

Then the chief next in rank to the white buffalo came out. "All right," he said, "you can have that girl, for you have more power."

The black buffalo came out now. To the men of the other side who were crying he said, "You are just like women; I hear you crying like women."[2]

The other chief came out again. "All right," he said, "we are not going to camp with you after this. We will separate." And they started to move their camps.

---

here. The practice of having the leaders of the opposite sides meet first in single contest was the Jicarilla manner of waging warfare. Note that the relatives of the woman are held responsible for the injury inflicted upon her husband.

[1] There are a number of references in Jicarilla stories to wooden armor. The writer could obtain no evidence that the Jicarilla themselves used such armor, however.

[2] The taunt is a common one which the Jicarilla level at enemies.

This Apache said that these buffalo people had everything. They were the richest people he ever saw. He stayed there among them for about a month.

His wife told him then, "I hear voices from your country. Your people are looking for you. They are very anxious about you and want to see you."

She gave him many things, many possessions. She gave him four horses belonging to the buffaloes.

"You go to your country now," she said. "Some day I'll see you again."

He started towards his home.

She told him, "When you go, do not go slowly; hurry. When these horses get tired, they will die."

He rode on one horse. Three other horses were ahead. He drove them toward his country. They all went fast. Just about sunset that horse on which he rode fell dead.

The girl, his wife, had told him, "I will see you tonight."

That night, after the sun had set she found him. "You are too slow in your travels," she told him. She stayed with him that night.

In the morning the dead horse had disappeared. He had gone back to his country. The man got on a second horse.

She told him, "Hurry! Don't wait; don't waste time."

He traveled hard all day. At sunset of the second day the horse which he had ridden died. Two were left. The girl found him again.

The next day the same thing happened. Now one horse was left.

The next day he mounted his last horse. The girl had again stayed with him the night before. She said to him, "Here I'll leave you. You must go on alone. I'm going to take these four horses back."

This was at the end of the fourth day. She went back. She was riding a horse too. His home country was near now.

At home, the others who had gone on the war-party had all returned. Only this one man had not come back. They thought he was dead. His relatives didn't expect to see him again. But now he arrived home on foot.

While he was among the buffaloes, his wife had told him many things: how to hunt the buffalo, what parts not to use, how to butcher the buffalo, the songs and prayers of the buffalo. All this he learned and when he came back he told the people. The Apaches knew about buffaloes after that and how to find them.

They don't say what the name of the man who lived with the buffaloes was. The name of the white buffalo is "mountain buffalo." They call the white buffalo, mountain buffalo, because they say it comes from the mountains.

When these buffaloes are in their own country, they are just like people. When they are out somewhere they are just like buffaloes. This man never found out how they carry their equipment, for they travel in the form of buffaloes.

B. THE WOMAN WHO CHANGED TO A DEER

This girl was out with her brother. They had separate camps.[1] This boy didn't know much about the deer (way). He killed many female deer, however, and brought home a great deal of meat. His sister jerked the meat.

One male deer wanted to kill those two.[2] He showed himself to the boy when the boy was out hunting, and the boy started to chase him. The boy followed for a long time. The deer kept just enough ahead to make him follow. Then the male deer turned and headed for the two camps where the boy and his sister lived. The boy kept following him, though he was exhausted by this time.

About noon the deer got to that camp. It stopped. The woman was sitting there, eating mush.

The deer said, "What are you doing here by yourself? Let us go to the west."[3]

She arose at once and started to follow the deer.

At every canyon to which they came, the deer shook himself. The sweat fell from him like rain and wiped out the tracks the two left.

When the boy got to his home he saw the deer tracks leading directly to his sister's camp. He called, "Where are you? Where did the deer go?"

There was no answer. He looked in. He saw the half-eaten mush. Then he saw her tracks following those of the deer. He looked for her tracks around the camp, but the only tracks of her he could find were those following the deer to the west. So he started to run after that deer.

Every time he got near to the deer, the deer shook himself and destroyed the tracks, making it hard for the boy to trail them. This happened three times, at three canyons. Each time the boy had a hard time to find the tracks again.

At the next canyon he was very near. He called. He said, "You stop and wait for me." He was tired and angry. He raised his bow and was about to shoot the deer.

But as he aimed, his sister said, "No, do not do it." So he didn't shoot.

She said to him, "You must come back when the deer have their young and find me at the place called 'where the pine trees are burning.' There you can find two of your little nephews."

He didn't go further. He turned around. He got back to his

---

[1] It is necessary to make plain that the sister and brother stayed in different camps because of the great restraint and sexual avoidance which are supposed to govern the relations of siblings of opposite sex.

[2] The male deer wished to destroy them because the youth was disobeying the rules of the hunt. The story is in reality a warning against hunting without the requisite knowledge.

[3] The story gains point because the deer is one of the elements connected with love magic.

camp. It was getting dark by then. He stayed over night. He left all his meat there and went to his people the next day. When he got there, he stopped at a close relative's.

The relative looked at him in astonishment. "Where is your sister? Where is the meat you went out to hunt?"

It was hard for him to talk. He didn't know what to say or how to say it. He just choked. "My sister has turned to a deer!"

"But," they asked, "how could she become a deer?"

Then he told the story. He told how he tried to kill that deer, how it had come to the camp and taken his sister away.

The people didn't believe it. They called in the chief to listen, and the boy told the same story over to the chief.[1]

The chief didn't believe it either. "You'd better go back with eight men," he said. He chose eight prominent men to accompany the boy.

So the eight men left with the boy. He led them to the place. They trailed the deer to the place where he had ceased to follow it. He showed them where the deer shook himself and obliterated the tracks.

He said, "Right here I stood and was about to shoot that deer when my sister spoke to me." He told all about what the sister had said, about what she had told him of when and where he should see her and his two nephews.

The men could do nothing more. They all turned around and went back.

He brought in all the meat then. He gave most of it away. He waited until the time his sister had mentioned came.

When the time came he went back to that place "where the pine trees are burning." When he got there he found two little deer. He did not kill them. He took them back home. When he got them home he heard a voice.

It told him, "When you get these two little deer home take care of them for four days. Feed them, but do not let anyone else, especially women,[2] touch or come near them. In four days these two will become real Apaches." They were both males.

He took care of them. He put them in a round brush shelter. At the morning of the third day, early on the third day, he heard voices. It sounded like two little children laughing and talking. It was almost like human voices. He went out there but saw nothing except these two little deer.

He went out somewhere. A silly girl came during his absence and found these two little deer and started to tease them. They both ran away and never came back.

When he returned, he found no deer.

---

[1] The advisory position of the chief is apparent in this matter.

[2] The inferior position of women is emphasized by making them responsible for the loss of the two fauns.

His sister had really turned into a deer. When she spoke to him the last time, at the fourth ridge, she turned away and started off with the deer. At that moment her body changed to that of a doe.

When the boy got back to his people finally, the older men and women had council about this matter. They asked each other why it was that this had befallen the boy and his sister. Those who had power performed their ceremonies to find out. They learned that it had happened because this boy had killed many deer without knowing how, without prayer or without handling the deer properly. After that the Apaches were careful. The young men had learned their lesson.

The story does not account for the ceremony of deer. That was all known before this. It just tells what happened to one who violated the rules.

The boy's sister was out hunting with him because the boy and the girl were all alone. Their father, mother, and closest relatives were dead. This boy was supporting his sister. They were just out to get meat, not to stay for any length of time.

C. HOW THE ANIMALS WERE TAKEN AWAY FROM RAVEN[1]

When the world was new there were many Jicarilla Apache living on it. There were many tipis in which the Jicarilla were living. There they played hoop and pole for the first time. It was a new game then. Many men, only men, were at the grounds where hoop and pole was being played.

Raven came. He had a quiver full of arrows. In it were also some intestines of a deer. At that time people were starving. They couldn't find the animals. They saw tracks but they couldn't find where the game lived. The raven was afraid that people would see what he had in the quiver, so he hung it on top of the tipi poles. Then he went over where the men were playing hoop and pole. He lay down and watched the game.

About evening the magpie came along and he took those intestines from the inside of the quiver.

The raven came back to his quiver. He intended to take out the intestines, but he discovered that they were gone.

The magpie took them and went to all the people. He said, "Raven brought intestines over here and I took them away from him."

Then the people learned that Raven knew where the animals were hiding. Magpie told all the animals and the birds. They all watched Raven.

Raven thought about what had happened. He didn't know what to do. Finally he slowly rose in the air, circling. All the people

[1] Cf. Goddard, p. 212; Russell, p. 259.

watched him to see which way he would go. He went so high they could hardly see him. It was his plan to get beyond the sight of all of them before he headed for the place where he knew the animals to be. He didn't want others to follow him.

At last Raven went to the east. Several of the Jicarilla watched, but they could hardly see him, he was so far away. But some saw that he was going to the east; a few could still see him. After a while no one but Bat could see him any more. He told the others. Bat saw that Raven went over to a certain mountain and lit on a cliff. Then all the Jicarilla talked and decided they would go over to the place where Raven had gone.

When evening came they were on their way and camped out. The next day they traveled. The third day they were still traveling. The mountain was near the place where they were camping that night. The next morning they moved again and came under the cliff.

Raven had his home there. He had many children. But there was nothing to eat at his home. The people could see nothing. The reason they could not find anything was that Raven had been killing wild game at night and eating it with his children all night. By daylight there was nothing left, nothing but the ashes of the fire. They even hid the bones. But there were stones there with spots of grease on them.

All the people were talking about what they were going to do. They had to give up.

There were two young fellows who had power. They turned themselves into puppies. The people left those little dogs in the camp and moved to some other place. After a while the people were all moved out and nothing remained at the camp where the puppies had been left.

Raven's children came around where the camps had been. They saw those two small dogs and picked them up, for they were fine looking puppies. The children said, "These are pretty little dogs," and began arguing about which ones would have the dogs. They brought the puppies to their home.

Raven didn't like the dogs. He said, "It's best not to keep these; they might be spying on us. You must get rid of them. I don't want you to keep those animals here."

The raven children didn't want to give up the puppies. They were crying. They wanted to keep them.

Raven said, "If you want to keep those dogs, you will have to hold fire before their eyes. If they don't blink you may keep them."

This was done and one of them blinked. The other did not. They didn't like it that the one blinked, and they chased that one way. But they kept the one who didn't blink.

At night Raven went hunting. He killed some animal and brought the meat home. So the raven children fed the dog some meat that was left over. The little puppy stayed there for four days and was growing up.

After the third day, when the father raven went hunting, this little puppy followed him. The raven came to a steep cliff. There was a sheer wall of rock. There was a door in it and the raven opened the door and went in. There were many animals in there. He killed one, a fat buffalo. Then he brought all the meat to his home. The puppy followed him and saw all this. The puppy watched closely. He saw how to open the door and enter.

Night came. The ravens ate all the meat. After eating they tried to sleep. The little puppy, when they were trying to sleep, went around and kept waking them up. The ravens couldn't sleep. About midnight the puppy stopped bothering them. The ravens were very tired now and fell sound asleep.

Once they were all asleep, the puppy went to the place where he had seen the raven go.

That little puppy changed to a man now. This man struck the rock four times as Raven had done, and the door opened. It was a rock door. When it opened, the man said to the rock, "Rock, don't move. Stay where you are."

That man went in. He had a white eagle tail feather. He came to the first buffalo and put the feather in the buffalo's mouth. He told the buffalo, "Go outside."

He said this to each animal he came to, and that animal had to go out as it was told. A whole crowd of animals was moving out.

Meanwhile Raven woke up and saw what was happening. He went over there. He began to shoot at the animals with arrows, trying to drive them back. But the animals were crowding out. He couldn't stop them. Mountain-sheep, deer, and buffaloes were coming out of there, and so were elks and all the other wild game. He tried to move the rock into place, but it was too heavy. He couldn't do it.

When many animals were outside and only a few were still in there, Raven had only one arrow left. The wild game animals were spreading out everywhere, all over the mountains. Raven kept his last arrow. He thought that the one who had caused all this was behind and would come out last. He kept that arrow so that he could shoot him.

The man arranged it so that the last buffalo to come out was a very old one, one in poor condition.

This buffalo said to the man, "Get between my toes and I will carry you out safely."

But the man said, "No, if you move your foot I'll fall out."

The buffalo replied, "Then go under my arm."

"No, if you move your arm I'll fall out."

"Then hang on to the hair of my head."

"If you move your head down I might fall off."

"Then go under my tail and into my rectum."[1]

So the man went in there.

The raven stood at the door. The old buffalo was feeble and had no hair on his skin. So the raven didn't want him and let him go out.

As the buffalo went through the door he fell down. He kept stumbling as he went along. He would go a little way and fall down, then get up and go on only to fall down again a little further on. When he was a short distance from the raven he ran slowly. There was a little hill ahead. When he got behind that hill and could no longer be seen, he ran faster like a younger buffalo. It was the power of the man that made this possible. A short distance ahead was another hill. The buffalo ran over to it. Then he came toanother hill. All the time he was gaining strength and speed. He came to a fourth hill.

Then the buffalo said, "You'd better get out."

The man came out. Now the buffalo was like a young one. He had fine fur and was in good shape.[2]

Meanwhile the raven was back at the door. He was looking around but couldn't find that man.

All the animals spread out over the earth.

That other puppy, the one who blinked and so was sent away, turned to a man also. He saw a trail. He went on and came to a place where the people had camped. He found a stick in the ground that had been left where the people had camped.[3] He asked the stick how long ago the people had been there.

The stick said, "About three days ago they left."

So he followed the tracks again. He came to a place where there had been a camp. Some bushes which had been used for beds were lying on the ground. He asked them how long ago the people had been there, and they told him the people had left two days before.

He followed along the trail. He came to another camp site. He saw a fire-stick that had been left. He asked the fire-stick the same question, and it replied, "Yesterday they moved from here."

He went on and at evening he caught up with the people.

He saw that there were already many animals around the camps. At that time the animals were tame, not wild. As soon as they were freed from the place where Raven had kept them confined they came around the camps of the people.

Some very old, poor women were living by themselves. They gathered brush of cedar and oak and made a shelter for themselves. Those animals were eating all the leaves of those bushes and leaving nothing but the sticks. The old women gathered the leafy brush every day, but those animals ate them bare by night.

---

[1] For a similar motif see p. 283.

[2] For another instance where a change accompanied travel over four successive ridges see p. 367.

[3] See pp. 287—288 for another case where objects around camp sites direct a traveler.

After a while these old women became very angry and cursed those animals. They called them all kinds of names. This happened for four days.

The old women said, "We have been gathering bushes every day." They were very angry.

Finally the old women picked up a stick and put it in the fire. When it was burning one of the old ladies struck the deer across the nose with it. She told them to inhale when she did it.

When day came those animals went far away. The next day they went farther. And the next day they were still farther away. The next day they were gone; no one could see them.[1]

In this way the animals spread over the world everywhere.

Because the old woman told the animals to inhale as she struck them with the smoldering stick, wild animals can smell very well, and when they smell the camp fires of man, they keep away.

After the game had run to the mountains, some of the leading men came together. The people were starving again and these leaders were discussing what was to be done. These men prayed to the animals. They called to them and asked them to come again. So the animals came closer. They stayed for a little while and then they fled to the mountains again.

That is why these people, whenever they want to hunt, pray first. They pray so that the animals will come and the hunt will be successful. That is our rule. We have to pray for what we want.

D. PRAIRIE-DOG AND RAIN

Prairie-dog is a leader for the rain too. One time a man was very thirsty. He didn't know where to get water. He had thrown away all his arrows, his quiver and everything heavy, for he was so thirsty he was ready to die. He lay down at a prairie-dog's hole and begged for water. After a while Prairie-dog came out with a very small cup and a little water in it. The man thought it would not be enough to help him. He took it however, and drank and drank. But he couldn't drink all of it though he drank for a long time. Now his mind began to clear and he was beginning to feel better.

Prairie-dog said to him, "Pick up your bow and arrows and blanket and start to walk. Go on and you will come to more water. The people are going to give you more water."

So he walked along. He came to a place where there had been a heavy rain. He knew that Prairie-dog had sent it. Now we believe that Prairie-dog has the power of the water.

---

[1] This motif is also found in connection with the story of the origin of agriculture. See p. 215.

E. THE MAN SAVED BY THE PRAIRIE-DOGS

Once forty-four men went out to the plains on the war-path. Forty-three died and the last was almost dead of thirst. He finally dropped right beside a prairie-dog hole.

Prairie-dog came out and asked, "Why do you lie beside my home?"

"I'm nearly dead of thirst. All my companions are gone."

"Then come with me."

Prairie-dog led him into his home and there gave him a small vessel filled with water. Although it was small, his thirst was quenched and there was some water left.

Prairie-dog said to him, "This will last you four days."

It did and he got back to his people. Prairie-dog gave him no songs or ceremony. He just took pity on him and saved him from death.

VI. THE COYOTE CYCLE; STORIES OF ANIMALS AND BIRDS

INTRODUCTION

The coyote cycle is a series of tales or episodes involving the travels and adventures of the trickster, Coyote. For any one story teller, these tales or episodes have a fixed order in respect to one another, though another story-teller's account may run somewhat differently. The manner of organizing these episodes seems to depend more or less on family lines, since the young of a given family group draw their inspiration from some venerable relative and carry on his version of the proper way to relate the antics of Coyote.

There are clusters of episodes which always are associated, however, and which usually appear in the same order in respect to one another. For instance, no matter who tells the story, one can be sure that the killing of the prairie-dogs by Coyote (p. 273) will be followed by the theft of these prairie-dogs by Wildcat, the attempt on the part of Coyote to retrieve the one which he has thrown away, and the revenge that Coyote visits upon Wildcat. Likewise the trick which Coyote plays upon Beaver (p. 312) is certain to be followed by retaliation on Beaver's part. The man who is sent up on the rock by Coyote (p. 286) will, without fail, reach the camps of the people by virtue of the direction which objects left at previous camp sites give him; and when he arrives at his dwelling he inevitably destroys the adulterous Coyote by forcing him to swallow hot stones. The reader will soon come to recognize these and many more episodic clusters as the means by which direction is given to the blunderings of the trickster and interest in the cycle as a unified whole is maintained. Another device to cement together the disparate episodes is the practice of interlarding references in one story to that which has gone before. Thus, after Coyote has burned a log to ashes in an unsuccessful attempt to roast the rabbit (p. 301) he meets Beetle. In order to escape, Beetle convinces Coyote that he must blacken himself with charcoal. It is to the log he has fired in the previous story that Coyote then repairs. Again, the story of the expanding meat is made to follow and depend on the tale of how Coyote slew his friend, Deer (p. 327).

Something should be said about the character of Coyote as he is presented throughout the range of Jicarilla mythology. Because Coyote is instrumental in obtaining and spreading fire for mankind, some may be led to think that he appears in the dual role of trickster-hero. This is one of the extremely rare occasions, however, where

Coyote is shown in anything that approaches a favorable light. And even in this episode he gains, in the Jicarilla mind, little honor, for his success is attendant upon theft and the deception of little children. Later he takes the bow and arrow away from the evil owl, but he immediately is responsible for quite as much havoc with the weapon as was its former owner (p. 290). In other words, Coyote is the epitome of the less desirable characteristics. "To follow Coyote's path" is a native phrase signifying gluttony, deceit, and foolishness. Jicarilla mythology is remarkably consistent in bestowing upon Coyote these characteristics whenever reference is made to him. It is Coyote who steals and hides the baby of the water being (pp. 266—267) and precipitates a flood and the first emergence. Later he joins two evil birds in acts that lead to the beginning of death for the people of the emergence (p. 45). It is he who deceives Child-of-the-Water into crossing the path of the infuriated cyclone, with the result that Child-of-the-Water is blown to bits (p. 95). He enters the arena for a brief interval in the story of the Spotted Enemy (p. 378) to claim falsely that it was his arrow which killed an eagle. There is really only one story in which Coyote appears as an unqualified hero and this is the account of the slaying of the monster bear (p. 338). Goddard recorded this story from the Jicarilla with the culture hero, Killer-of-Enemies, instead of Coyote as the chief protagonist, which would indicate that the Jicarilla, too, recognize the incongruity of Coyote's position in this myth.

Functionally, in respect to the culture, the coyote cycle serves a double role. The didactic use of it, the moralistic principles which are drawn from it for the benefit of the young, have already been discussed in the general introduction. The reverse side of the face is that it undoubtedly acts as a cultural safety valve. When people who cannot look at their mothers-in-law for fear that they will go blind, derive great amusement from a story of the violation of a woman by her son-in-law, the lesson is plain. Incest, sexual excess, adultery, perverse conduct, theft, falsehood, laziness, — all the frailities of man which cannot be attributed to one's neighbor with impunity, find frank expression in the tales which describe Coyote.

The other tales of this section which follow the coyote cycle represent an attempt to bring together separate stories in which Coyote is the chief actor and to include animal and bird stories of the same general flavor. The last story of the section, The Fight between Turkey and Eagle, is perhaps out of place in that it contains no trickster elements, but since I have no other stories of a like nature with which to put it I have allowed it to stand in this section. The latter part of the story of Phoebe illustrates well the tendency of the Jicarilla to use the stories of animals as moralizing agents.

A. THE COYOTE CYCLE[1]

1. COYOTE IN THE UNDERWORLD; THE ORIGIN OF THE MONSTERS; THE FIRST EMERGENCE

This coyote was just like a real person in the old times. He was two-faced; he was evil, but he was also good. He had power in both ways, in the evil way and in the good way. The people often use him in the evil way; and in the good way, too, they use him, for he has power to help as well as to harm.

Coyote was down below with the people. The chief down there, before they started to come up, had a wife who seemed to be very sick with rheumatism. This chief tried in every way to cure her. He had all the men with power perform their ceremonies for her, but it did no good. This woman was not really sick; she was only acting sick and making her husband believe it.

She said, "Take me down to the river. It is the coolest place and there I feel well."

A river was divided at a certain place and flowed from there in two branches. This place was called Divided Water, and it was here that she wished to be taken. The otter had spoken to this woman through his power; that was why she wanted to get to that place. He used his power as love medicine. Otter was a young man. The chief didn't know about this.

The chief carried his wife down there every morning and took a lunch for her too. Each evening when the sun was going down he called for her.

---

[1] Coyote traveled all around. The various tribes have different stories of him because he did other things in different parts of the country. We know only what he did among our people.

The coyote stories should be told only during the winter and at night. It is dangerous to tell the coyote stories while the snakes are out. These stories are told at night because Coyote ran around at night and slept during the day.

In telling the tales they always begin with Coyote down below before the emergence; then they tell about the race around the world for the two pretty girls; next Coyote gets fire; and from there on it is as I have told it. They don't say that the habits of mankind are due to Coyote. [The Mescalero and Chiricahua do. (M. E. O.)] Some things are due to Coyote. But some misfortunes are due to other animals. Baldness comes from the turkey buzzard. One who is bald belongs to the turkey buzzard people.

In the old days when the people were sitting around someone would begin telling the coyote stories and the others would help. One would say, "You left out this one," and he would start in. They listened to each other and helped keep it straight. Usually one man would not tell it all. He could stop at any point. The story did not have to be finished once it was begun.

You wouldn't tell "funny" coyote stories to your sister, your father-in-law, or to anyone to whom you use polite form. (See p. 15, footnote 1 for an explanation of polite form.) They wouldn't like it. You don't tell those stories when these relatives are present, even though others may be there too. A person is careful when he tells those stories, and if he sees that his sister is present, he skips that kind. (Inf.)

After a while he got tired of this and wondered why she always insisted on going to this one place.

The next morning he took her there as usual. Then he turned and went back as though he was going straight for his camp. But as soon as he got out of sight, he ran around a hill and approached from another side and lay there in hiding, watching. Within an hour he saw someone come swimming to that place.

She, too, saw that someone was coming. She took off her clothes and jumped in the water. She and Otter met right in the water. So the otter is our brother-in-law.

Now the chief had found out what that woman was doing. He went back to his home. He was not going after her any more. He had seen that she was not sick, for she had jumped up and taken off her clothes and plunged in as though she were very active and entirely well.

When the sun went down he did not go there as usual. He stayed in his camp.

At nightfall, after waiting for him, the woman came crawling in on her hands and knees. She acted as though she was very sick.

She said, "The old man doesn't feel sorry for this sick person. You see that I'm coming and having a painful time. See, here you are! You do not even come to get me any more."

The husband had a grindstone at his side. He said, "Yes, I feel sorry for you!" and he picked up the stone and hurled it at her. The woman leaped up and escaped it. She ran to the home of her mother.

The mother-in-law of the chief was very angry with him. She thought the girl was really sick and thought, "Why does that mean man treat her like that?"[1] She called him all sorts of names, though she did not come into his presence.[2]

She said, "The men are worthless! Look how this man has treated my daughter. I had a hard time to raise this girl and now he abuses her. The men think they do everything; they think they supply all the food and clothes and all the necessities. But the women work harder and do more than the men. The women know how to do things. They can do all the men's work too if necessary."

The chief came out when he heard her talking like this. He was very angry. He said, "All right! If you think you can do all the men's work, we shall see. We shall see who has more power."

He called all the men to him, even the boys, even the baby boys, and he told them that they were to separate from the women. Even the male dogs and male horses were taken on the men's side. The men and all male things crossed to the other side of the river.

---

[1] Another version relates that the girl's mother was cognizant of her misbehavior but connived at it.

[2] Despite her anger she did not violate the mother-in-law — son-in-law avoidance relation.

This chief had great power. He spoke to Kogułtsude. He dropped four beads in a whirlpool in the water.[1]

He said to Kogułtsude,[2] "I want the water wide, so that the women cannot cross over."

It was made so.

In the springtime the women and men both planted corn. They both hunted too. The women knew how to hunt too. That year the women as well as the men had plenty, all they wanted to eat. The second year the women had less. They were getting tired. They were afraid to go out and hunt as boldly as the men. They didn't sow enough seeds. The third year they had still less. The fourth year very few of the women had anything to eat. None of them planted crops that year. The men had plenty every year. The women were beginning to starve and suffer.

The women were standing on the bank calling to the men, saying, "Come back and take care of us."

But the chief would not let the men go. "Let them learn a lesson," he said. "Let them be punished."

All the older girls began to cry for the men now. They began to abuse themselves sexually. They masturbated with elk horn; and that is how the elk became an enemy of man. They used rocks also. That's how it happened that the rock became the enemy of man. And they used eagle feathers too. That is how the eagle became a giant and killed many of the people. The girls also used the feathers of the owl. All the things that afterward killed men, all the monsters, came into being because of what these girls did. For these objects impregnated the girls, and the monsters were later born from these unions. These were the monsters which Killer-of-Enemies was to destroy later on after the people came to this earth.

The men were affected in the same way as the women by the separation of the sexes. They became sexually aroused and unsatisfied. They tried to make vaginas out of mud and use them but they were unsuccessful.

This went on for a long time. Both sides were having a hard time of it and were punishing themselves because of what that old lady had said. The women couldn't cross that river; it was too deep and strong.

About that time Coyote came along. Codi is always funny. He went into the river. He found a baby in the whirlpool. He swam in and got it.

He said, "Oh, this is a nice baby! I'll take it and raise it myself."

---

[1] Four beads of different colors constitute a common offering to sacred rivers or springs for the Jicarilla.

[2] Kogułtsude, whose name probably can be translated "he holds in the water," is a powerful supernatural, the personification of the power of the water.

So he went back with it among the men. The child looked just like the babies of men, but it was the child of Kogułtsude.

Kogułtsude missed his child. He made the water rise so that his child would be brought back. He sent the water out to wash it back, to draw back his lost baby.

The chief was worried now. He said to the men, "We must go across the river and find out what has happened. Something has been done against this river that it acts this way."

So the men swam over and were now reunited with the women. They all went to the mountains to escape the water which was still rising. Some of the men and women were drowned. The rest got on the top of a big mountain.

They said to Coyote, "You must help us. Save us from the water."

So Coyote used his power to make the mountain grow. It grew and grew, but the water rose ever faster. All the time Coyote had the child under his cloak. At that time he had the same kind of fur that he wears now, only then he wore it as a man does a robe. No one knew that he had this baby under the robe.

The mountain rose and came right up to the present earth, this world. All the shamans were praying. But the water was still rising. All the people fell on this coyote. The water came right up to the edge of this world. It ran all over the country.

Now they were all getting after Coyote and scolding him. They said, "He is always the funny one! He must have done something."

So at last he said, "I have this baby. I thought he was not going to get this baby again."

The baby was almost dead; it was drying up. He took it out and showed it to the people, and then threw it into the water again. At once the water began to recede.

Before that there was no water on this earth, nor were there any mountains. The people didn't like this place. They wanted to go down below again. So Coyote made the mountain go down again, and it shrank. But the water which had spread over the earth stayed, and this was the water that was present at the time of the real emergence. Before that there was none on this earth.[1]

The people went down below again and stayed there for about nine or ten months. Then they started making the sun and moon down below after this.[2] These people were supernaturals.

By the time the emergence occurred, the girls who had abused themselves were already big with children. They had been impregnated from intercourse with the things they had used. These children they were carrying were therefore born here on earth, and they became the monsters that preyed on man, the monsters which Killer-of-Enemies had to destroy before men could multiply.

---

[1] See p. 20.

[2] Cf. pp. 10—14.

It was after the people went down below again that Hactcin's dog asked that people be made for him as companions.[1] So people of a different kind were made and these were the real Jicarilla. They intermarried with these first supernaturals who dwelt there, and so they were half human and half supernatural.

The supernaturals who were drowned when Kogułtsude made the waters rise, did not die. They turned to frogs and fishes.[2] There was no death in those days.

That is why Raven and Buzzard had to decide whether man would die.[3] It was half and half. In those days the dead were coming to life every four days. Then Buzzard threw a scraping pole in the water and said, "If this sinks man will die." It came to the surface. Then Raven threw in a mano and said, "If this sinks man will die." It sank; therefore man dies.

2. THE RACE AROUND THE WORLD[4]

Southeast of Santa Fe, sixty miles away, there is a little hill. It is just east of Estancia. There were an old man and an old woman living there who had two good-looking daughters. Some young men wanted to marry these girls, but the old people wouldn't allow it. They didn't like the men who wanted to become their sons-in-law. A number of young men were refused by them.

Twelve of the leaders of the people, the greatest men, met at a certain place. They talked about this matter and considered it carefully. They decided that the girls should be told to marry, even though their parents didn't want them to do so. So they sent word to the parents.

The messenger met the old people. "Why do you not let those two girls get married? Twelve of the most prominent men have decided that those daughters of yours should be married regardless of your wishes."

The old people said nothing.

The messenger said to them, "What's the matter that you do not talk? You have mouths. You must speak."

The old people said then, "Gather all the people who live under the sky. We are going to build a tipi to the east. Let all the people come over there, and from that place start to race around the world.[5] The one who wins the race will get both our daughters."

So on the appointed day all the people gathered around this tipi. Wood Rat was the first one there. Next came other animals who were slow runners. They came in all day long.

---

[1] Cf. pp. 6—10.
[2] Cf. pp. 111—113.
[3] Cf. p. 46.
[4] Cf. Goddard, p. 236.
[5] For another version of the race around the world see pp. 80—86.

The next day some who were faster runners came. The third day those who could run still faster arrived. The evening of the third day Coyote came and started to run. The others had started to run as soon as they arrived and Coyote ran after them. On the morning of the fourth day Sandhill Crane, Cliff Swallow, Hawk, and Fox started.

They started running to the south. Shortly afterward they caught up with Rat, the one who had started first. His face was covered with dust. The four were still together.

These four were sorry for Rat. They asked, "Who will carry this one?"

Fox said, "I'll carry him." And he put him on his back.

Many were still ahead of these good runners. When they arrived at the north and headed for the east, however, Coyote was the only one ahead of them. These four fleet ones still ran together. They saw the tipi ahead of them. This was the finish line. Here they passed Coyote.

After they had passed Coyote, Sandhill Crane took Rat from his back and said, "Now run to that tipi and win. Hurry, for Coyote is coming behind."

Rat ran over to that place as fast as he could. Coyote was coming behind and catching up. Rat ran around the tipi just a little ahead of Coyote.

Rat went in the tipi and stayed there four days with those two girls.

Four days passed and some people said to him, "Now go out." It was the four who had helped him who told him to go out.

Then Fox went in, taking his place with the girls. Fox continued to live with these girls and they became his wives. That is why the men had two wives in the old days.[1]

When Rat went out of the tipi all the people gave him gifts. That is why he always gathers everything together in his home and heaps sticks over it.

When Coyote lost the race he was very angry at Rat. "You didn't do it fairly," he said. He called Rat all kinds of names, but that didn't help.

This story explains how the September 15th race started. After this the people were told by Killer-of-Enemies, Child-of-the-Water, and others to hold a race like this so that they would have enough to eat and would have long life.

3. COYOTE OBTAINS FIRE[2]

When the people came up on earth, Coyote was the very last one of the animals to emerge.

When this world was made the trees wouldn't burn. The people were living without fire.

---

[1] The story in this form evidently served to explain the Jicarilla custom of polygyny.

[2] Cf. Goddard, p. 208; Russell, p. 261.

The coyote was running all over. No one knew where he would be the next day. He was running from place to place.

One time he found a place with great rock cliffs all around. In the bottom was a hollow place. A great spruce tree was standing there. The people who lived there were the fireflies. They came up in the cliffs by means of rock steps, so that no one could see their footprints and know the way to enter. The stones were laid one ahead of the other, so that the people, when they came out, could step on these rocks.

Coyote saw some little children playing on the other side of the cliff. He asked them, "Where is the entrance to this place?"

The children paid no attention to him, however.

He thought and thought, "What will these children like?"

He picked some cedar berries. He made beads out of these. He took four strings of these beads to the children. He colored them four colors, the first black, the second blue, the third yellow, and the fourth all colors. He went back to the children with them. He started to speak to them, but they paid no attention to him. They acted as if they didn't understand what Coyote was talking about.

He was trying to make a game for the children so that he could draw them to him. He wanted them to talk to him and laugh at him too.

Finally they noticed him. He said to them, "Now I'll give you these beads, but you have to show me the way to get in. I want to see the inside of this cliff place. If you show me the way, I'll give you these beads."

He put the beads around the necks of two girls and two boys. He said, "How pretty you are! You look nice now. You have on pretty necklaces."

The four children were pleased then and led Coyote to this entrance. They showed him the stones and said, "Right here is where you go down. Right at this tree is the door. We live beyond this cliff. This is the way we get in; this is the way we get out."

They spoke to the tree and said, "Come, bend down to us."

Then the tree bent down to each of the children.

"Now bend away from us," they said, and it took them across the cliff.

But Coyote didn't go in yet. He just learned how. The four children got on the other side and then had a tree which was standing there throw them on the outside again in the same way. Both were spruce trees. Now Coyote saw how to do it, but he didn't go in yet.

He asked the children, "What's going on down there?"

"We have great fun every night," they told him. "We have a big fire there each night and we dance around it."

Now Coyote knew all about what was going on on the other side. That's what he wanted. He wanted to get that fire and take it to his people. He wanted his own people to have good times at night too.

He went back to the people and told the chief. The chief gave commands to all fast birds and fast animals to help.

Coyote said, "Now I'm going to go to those people. When I get fire I'm going to hand it to one of you, and the one who takes it should run, and when he tires he should give it to another fellow."

Now everything was arranged. The fast running birds were notified too. They were told to stand all around the world and to be prepared to run. "The fireflies might prove to be good runners," Codi said. That is why all these helpers were picked out. These people were all around the world waiting. If the fireflies were not good runners, Coyote was not going to pass it on, but if they proved to be good runners he was going to do so. He explained all this to them.

Coyote then went and got some dry cedar bark. He shredded it and tied it around his tail. He made a regular torch.

When night came he went over to the place of the cliff. He went to the young spruce and spoke to it, and it put him over on the other side.

He saw the fireflies dancing with the deer and antelopes, with the white-tailed deer too. Flicker was there too. They were all having a good time dancing.

Coyote came up. He asked permission to join the dance.

Mountain-lion was chief there. Mountain-lion told him, "If you won't be too rough I'll let you join the dance."

"I'll try," said Coyote.

Coyote danced. He tried to dance close to the fire. But some were suspicious of him. Every time he got too close to the fire, someone got in between him and the fire.

After a while the people got tired of watching him and relaxed their vigilance. Then he approached even nearer to the fire and pushed his tail with the cedar bark into the flames.

Someone called to him, "Codi,[1] your tail will be burned!"

"No, I always do that without any trouble. I am a wonder worker."

He watched his tail. When it was ignited he started to run.

Someone called, "Codi is running!"

Everyone started to run after him. He lost his way. They all tried to circle around him, but he ran between them whenever he saw a space. Then he remembered where the place of exit was. He started to run that way.

He ran to the tree, crying, "Come, bend to me!" It bent down. Then he said, "Now you turn the other way with me." It did.

The people from that place were coming close behind him. They were gaining on him. He dodged about among the trees. Some

[1] Coyote addresses the other animals and birds and is addressed by them as Codi in these tales. The word cannot be translated but has the force of "friend."

trees he hit with his tail while he was running, and those are the ones which burn well today, like the oak and the pine. But he did not hit the rocks with his tail, and that is why they can't be made to burn now.

The fireflies and others were running after him still. Codi began to run around the world. On his way he set many things on fire; he spread it all over. Those who were running after him grew tired when they got about half way. They gave up, thinking, "Let him keep the fire."

The fireflies came back to one place. They had a council. They asked, "Who was it who told the coyote how to come in?"

Then the other children told on the four who had taken the beads from Coyote and given him the information. They said, "Coyote paid those beads for the fire."

The parents of those children got after them, but it was too late then.

Coyote had run far. He was tired by the time they gave up the chase. He fell right in the shade, his tail still burning. He rested and started running again. He went on until he had circled the world.

He meant to touch every kind of tree with his tail, but he missed one which was standing to the east. So all wood but this one kind will burn. Even if you put this one into the stove it will not burn.[1]

Coyote came back to the Indian camps. He said, "Now you can use this fire."

The people were all glad now that they had fire.

When Coyote ran around the world he went the way the sun goes. He headed for the east and then for the south, and so on. But he didn't run straight. He zig-zagged all around. The others took no part in the run. They stood around and just watched him.

4. COYOTE DANCES WITH THE PRAIRIE-DOGS[2]

Coyote went back to his home. From there he went to Prairie-dog Town. He had some red cloth and he put this on a stick and marched around with it held up, saying, "Let all of you circle around here." Then they all came.

Codi held a stone in the palm of his right hand. In his left hand he held the pole. He said to them, "You must all shut your doors tightly, for while we are dancing someone might steal your property."

The prairie-dogs all ran home. Quickly they shut their doors tightly and came back.

The dance started. Coyote began to sing. He sang, "Let the large prairie-dogs come near to me. Let the small ones form behind them."

[1] The informant did not know the name of this tree. According to Goddard, p. 209, this is petrified wood.

[2] Cf. Goddard, p. 230.

When a big prairie-dog approached him, he hit it with a stone. That prairie-dog would fall down dead.

Some cried out with alarm. But Coyote said, "That is nothing. They are just unconscious from joy and celebration. When the sun goes down they will all get up again."

The last prairie-dog to come out was a puny one. He was being carried on the back of his brother who was dancing in the rear. He caught sight of the rock in Coyote's hand.

He called out, "Coyote has a stone in his hand!"

Everybody started to run. Coyote started to run after them too. They ran for their homes with Codi after them killing them. A few escaped, but Codi killed most of them. He killed that little one who told on him too.

Codi went around collecting the dead prairie-dogs. He collected them in one pile. He carried them to a place where there was wood. He built a big fire and waited till he had a large pile of hot ashes. Then he opened them up. He put the prairie-dogs in the ashes in a straight line with only the tails sticking out. That smallest prairie-dog he put at one end.

This was in the morning. It was hot and he had been working hard. So he went to some shade and took a nap.

While he was sleeping Wildcat came along. He saw Coyote sleeping. He smelled cooking meat. He tip-toed around. He took all the prairie-dogs out, all except that small one at the end, which he left. He cut all the tails off and arranged them in a row just as they had looked before, sticking out of the ashes. He ate all the meat, for it was well roasted.

A few were still left and these he put up on the branch of a tree. It was hot weather and, since he had had such a good dinner, he went to sleep too.

Coyote woke up. He had been sleeping in the shade, but it was all sunny at that place now, and it woke him up. He stretched himself. There was a little pool of water near the place where he had buried the prairie-dogs in the ashes. He talked to himself. "I guess by this time that meat is done," he said.

He went over to the ashes. He pulled the tail of the first one. It was the tail of the small prairie-dog.

"Oh, that is a small one," he said. "I don't care for this; it's in my way," and he hurled it into the air without watching where it went. It landed on the branch of a tree.

He began to pull at the other tails. They came out of the ashes easily, but the bodies were not attached.

"Oh, I have burned the tails off," he said. He went down the whole line. All of them were the same.

He ran and got a poker and began raking the ashes. He couldn't find anything. Then he began to look for the one he had thrown away. He looked and looked, but he couldn't find it.

He gave up and sat at the bank of the pool, in the shade. Then he noticed the form of a prairie-dog in the water. He jumped into the water at once. But he couldn't find it down there. He got up and watched the water till it steadied again. He saw the prairie-dog again when the water cleared. Three times he did this. Then he gave up and lay down in the shade.

He was lying face upward. There he saw the prairie-dog up in the tree. He jumped up and got it. He ate it, bones and all, he was so hungry.

Then he called his name. He said, "I guess Codi took all my prairie-dogs."

He started to look for the tracks of the one who had taken the prairie-dogs. He finally found Wildcat. Wildcat was sound asleep.[1]

Coyote took out the rectum of the wildcat and started to roast it over a fire. He picked it up with a pointed stick. Then he woke up Wildcat.

"Codi," he called, "you must get up and eat. The people came with meat. This gut was all they gave me and I saved it for you."

Wildcat got up. He started to chew the meat. He had eaten all but a little of it when Coyote said, "Codi is eating his own rectum!"

Then Wildcat quickly took the remaining piece and thrust it back in place. That is why Wildcat has a short tail, for in his haste and excitement he pushed back part of his tail. Before this Wildcat had a long tail. Before Coyote woke up Wildcat, he pushed his face together and made it as it is now.

5. COYOTE VISITS KINGFISHER[2]

So Coyote started to go to the kingfisher. Kingfisher lived at the end of a cliff. Below his home was a lake which was covered with ice.

Kingfisher said, "Codi, did you come to see me? I have nothing to eat at home here, so I can't give you anything to eat."

Kingfisher went out and Coyote followed him. Kingfisher said he would get food and Coyote watched. Kingfisher went to the edge of the cliff and dove straight down at the ice. He hit the ice with his beak, shattered it, and went through. He came out with a fish in his beak. He returned and gave it to Coyote who ate it up at once.

Coyote said then, "Codi, you come to see me too sometime."

"Where is your home?"

"Directly across from your home, on a cliff on the other side of the lake."

The next day Coyote was waiting. Kingfisher came.

Coyote said, "Codi, have you come to see me? I have no food here to give you, but I'm going to get some for you."

So he went to the edge of the cliff and dove down to the ice. He

[1] Cf. Goddard, p. 230.
[2] Cf. Goddard, p. 231.

hit his nose on the ice and fell, half-dead, on top of the ice. The kingfisher had to come down and pick him up. His nose was all bloody. Kingfisher took him up on top again.

Kingfisher said, "You must not do what I do. I do it because I have power."

Kingfisher jumped again into the water and came up with a fish. He gave it to Coyote and Coyote ate it at once.

6. COYOTE VISITS BUFFALO[1]

So Coyote went to the buffaloes. Buffalo was lying there breathing heavily. He went, "Hahm!" And each time he did it Coyote was startled and afraid.

Buffalo said, "Coyote, do not be afraid of me. That's the way I breathe. I do that all the time."

Buffalo sat there, and Coyote sat there watching him. Buffalo reached under his armpit, right under his fur, and pulled out some dry meat. He began to pound this dry meat. When it was all pounded he took a sharp stick and pushed it into his nose. The fat fell down on the dry meat. It was just like grease. He handed this to Coyote. Coyote liked this very much and ate it all.

When Coyote had finished, he started to walk out. He turned and said, "Codi, you come to see me too."

The next day Buffalo went to see the coyote. He wanted to see what he would be given.

Coyote went and got some pine tree bark when he saw Buffalo coming. He sharpened some sticks too. Buffalo came up.

Coyote tried to breathe heavily. But Buffalo was not a bit afraid. Nevertheless Coyote said, "Codi, do not be afraid; that's the way I breathe."

Then Coyote put his hand under his armpit and pulled out the bark. The buffalo watched to see what he was going to do. Coyote pounded all the bark with a rock and then put the sharp stick up his nose. The blood poured out over the pounded bark.

Buffalo watched and finally said, "Coyote, don't do that. You'll put that stick right in your brain and kill yourself. Don't try to do what I do. I have power; that's why I can do it. I'll show you what I can do."

And for a second time Buffalo pulled out meat from under his arm. Buffalo started to pound that meat for Coyote. Meanwhile he said to Coyote, "Go out and get some sagebrush to put up your nose and stop that bleeding."[2]

As before Buffalo put a sharp stick up his nose and let the fat come out. This he put over the meat and he handed the meat to Coyote again. Then he left him.

---

[1] Cf. Goddard, p. 232.

[2] This is a Jicarilla specific for nosebleed.

7. COYOTE VISITS ELK[1]

So Coyote went to the elk. The elk was lying down. Coyote was sitting close by watching him. When the elk moved his head, Coyote jumped and started to run away.

He said every time, "The oak tree is falling on us!"

Elk told him, "You must not be afraid of me; those are my horns."

Elk put his hand down to his hind leg. He brought some meat out from there. He started to pound it just as Buffalo had done. He, also, put a sharp stick in his nose and let fat drop on the meat. This he gave to Coyote and Coyote ate it.

When Coyote had finished and started to go, he said, "Codi, you come to see me too. I'm a man too and I like to have visitors."[2]

Coyote got busy. On his way home he looked for some spreading branches of oak tree which would resemble horns. He found some and tied them to his head. He waited now for his friend, the elk.

Finally the elk came. As Elk approached, Coyote moved his head. The elk came on undisturbed, but nevertheless Coyote said to him, "Don't be afraid of me; those are only my horns."

Coyote had brought some rotten oak tree wood. He had it under his leg. He pulled it out and started to pound it. Then he put a sharpened stick up his nose and the blood came out. He stirred this up with the meat and offered it to Elk.

Elk said, "I don't eat such food, and you had better not do that; you might kill yourself. I have power and live on power, that's why I can do it."

And Elk did it again to show Coyote. He pounded the meat, drew the fat from his nose, and gave it to Coyote. Then Elk went home.

8. COYOTE VISITS FLICKER[3]

So Coyote started out to the home of Flicker. He sat near Flicker's home. Flicker opened his wings.

Coyote said, "Codi, your house is beginning to burn," and he started to run.[4]

But the bird said, "No, that is only my wings. Come back."

Coyote started back very carefully. He said, "You must come to see me too." Then he ran into the bushes.

He dragged a great quantity of dry brush around in the shape of a corral. He sat in the center. When he saw Flicker coming he set fire to it.

---

[1] Cf. Goddard, p. 232.

[2] "I'm a man" is a familiar Jicarilla phrase used by males in declaring their competency to perform a task. Conversely, "You're no man," is a grave insult, usually the prelude to a serious quarrel.

[3] Cf. Goddard, p. 232.

[4] The flicker is the red-shafted one, and Coyote mistakes the red under its wings for fire.

Flicker came up. "Codi," he said, "your house is on fire."

"No," said Coyote, "that's my wings."

He sat there. After a little while he got pretty hot. When the fire got too near he had to jump away from it. He burned up his whole home.

9. COYOTE AS EYE JUGGLER[1]

Then Coyote started out again. He met some Jicarilla Apaches who had power too. These Apaches were throwing up their eyes into the air, and the eyes would come back in place every time.

Coyote looked at them. "That's a good thing to know," he said. "You must teach me that."

"If you want to learn this trick, you must be careful."

"Yes, yes, I'll be careful. Show me how."

"If you don't keep the rules, you may lose your eyes."

So one Jicarilla Apache took Coyote's eyes out and threw them up in the air four times and showed him how to do it.

He told Coyote then, "You must be careful not to go among the trees, for these eyes may get caught on a branch."

"All right," said Coyote.

So Coyote went away. He was throwing his eyes up all the time. He had been told to keep near the plains, where there were no trees. But Coyote soon forgot and went right where there were many trees. He threw the eyes up. They stayed up there.

Coyote called, "Come back to my sockets!"

But the eyes stayed up there. Coyote shouted and cried.

The Jicarilla Apache heard him and came over.

Coyote said, "Codi, my eyes have stayed up there."

That man got up in the tree and got the eyes down again. He said to Coyote, "I told you to stay away from these bushy places."

But Coyote soon forgot. He went on his way and the same thing happened again. His eyes got caught. He shouted and the man helped him again. This happened for a third time. But the fourth time the man was good and tired of Coyote.

The man said, "No, I won't help. Those eyes will stay there, and the people will live on them. They will turn to plums."

So Coyote's eyes turned to plums.

The man then went out and gathered some pitch from the piñon tree. He rolled it into two balls and put these in the sockets.

He told Coyote, "Now keep out of the sunshine for four days. Stay in the shade during this period. If you go into the sun, the pitch will melt."

But Coyote forgot. He fell asleep in the shade. But he overslept, and the shade passed. It was sunny there and the pitch melted.

---

[1] Cf. Goddard, p. 229.

Coyote's eyes were spoiled. He called loudly for help again, and the man came to him. He fixed him again and gave him the same advice. But Coyote forgot as usual and the eyes melted again. They were fixed again, but for a third time Coyote let them melt.

Then this man said, "This is the last time I'm going to help you. If this happens again you will have to go without eyes."

It did happen the fourth time. Coyote fell asleep in the shade. Then it became sunny. His eyes started to melt and had melted just a little. But this time Coyote woke up. The pitch had begun to run down his face and that is why there are two black marks there running down from his eyes. The man kept his word and Coyote has had to stay that way. But it was not enough to spoil his eyes.

This Jicarilla Apache who taught Coyote learned the trick of throwing up the eyes from the jack-rabbit, for in those days everything talked. But it was the man and not the jack-rabbit who taught Coyote how to do it.

10. COYOTE LOSES THE POWER TO OBTAIN FOOD

Coyote went out again, and he saw another man. This man had power to make anything he saw fall into his hand. He would get food this way and then eat it. He could do this with anything.

He didn't see Coyote coming. Coyote watched him. The man was sitting in the shade. When he wanted something to eat he just asked for it, and it fell into his hands. Coyote watched very carefully. He was hungry. He wished he had that trick too.

He came out to the man. The man had something to eat in his hand. He felt sorry for that coyote, so he called Coyote to him. He gave Coyote something to eat.

Coyote asked then, "Who is up there? How is it that the food drops into your hand?"

"Oh, I have power; that's why. I used to live up there. I just came down to show the people where all the fruit comes from. That's why I'm doing this."

Then Coyote pleaded with that man. "If you want the people to learn this, you must teach me too, for I'd like to have something good to eat wherever I go."

So this man taught it to Coyote. "But you must be careful," he said. "You must not ask more than three times a day. If you ask every moment, they are going to stop feeding you."

Coyote went away. He asked for food at once. What he asked for fell immediately into his hands from above. Coyote was very much pleased with the food he had. Every few minutes he asked, even though he had had enough. He was already full. He would take a bite and throw the rest away. He kept asking for fruit and bread, anything he could think of.

Then he said, "I want all foods, all fruits."

After a while it was just as though a cloud gathered above his head. Then it began to rain fruits. All kinds fell, even watermelons. They fell on his head. When the watermelon hit him on the head, it splashed all over. He tried to protect himself but could do nothing. This happened on a plain and there were no trees under which he could find shelter. Coyote jumped around trying to dodge the rain of fruit.

"That's enough! That's enough! I want no more!" he cried. But it didn't stop for a long while.

Finally it stopped. He walked away from that place. He didn't try to pick up the fruit on the ground.

The next day he was hungry. He asked for something to eat. Nothing came. No one dropped anything into his hands. Then he called for different foods, but nothing happened and no one answered. He called for something four times, but no answer came.

He gave up. He went looking for the man who had taught him.

He met him again. He said, "I'm hungry. You must teach me again."

"I taught you once. I told you to be careful. I can't teach you again. You just wasted what you asked for. I can't help you again."

11. COYOTE IS FOOLED BY LIZARD AND VISITS HIS SISTER

Then Coyote started out to see his sister. He was traveling in the meadows on the way. He saw Lizard there running up the stalk of a sunflower. The lizard was afraid.

He said, "Coyote, don't bother me. I'm busy. I'm holding up the sky." The lizard knew that he was not on a tree and that Coyote could break the stalk and get him. So he said to Coyote, "I'm busy holding up the sky so it doesn't fall on us. That is my duty."

It was about noon and there were clouds in the sky. It was windy and the clouds were sailing to the east.

Lizard said, "Look at that sky! It's going to fall on us! I'm getting weak holding it; that's why. Don't blink your eyes; look right up. Keep looking and see if it isn't falling."

So Coyote looked and looked. Coyote got dizzy. His head was rolling back and forth as he held it up. The lizard saw that he was dizzy, so he got down and ran away. Coyote was still talking to the lizard, but the lizard was not there any more.

Coyote was very dizzy. Finally he noticed that there was no answer. He looked for Lizard, but Lizard was gone.

Coyote cursed himself. "Those little animals are smarter than I am; they can deceive me!"

Coyote went on a little way. He saw a small mouse.

The mouse said, "Codi, you must not bother me. The people never eat me."

Coyote said, "Oh, you are so cute, why should I not eat you? I have been traveling a long way. I have to have something to eat." So without waiting he swallowed that mouse without chewing it.

After a few minutes he began to break wind. It happened every time he moved, with every step he took. He got angry. He started to run. It kept on, even worse. It sounded as if he was shaking a rattle at every step he took. He stopped. He stood still. He was near his sister's house.

He called to his sister, "I have learned a new thing. Whenever I come to visit people, they pound a hide for me."[1]

His sister had a dry hide. She pounded it hard. He started to run and ran right into his sister's house, and there, as soon as he got in, he picked up his little nephew and put him on his lap.

But every time he moved he broke wind. Then he would say, "Oh, my little nephew, why do you make that noise? Why don't you sit still when I hold you?"[2]

His sister cooked for him. She offered him food, but he didn't eat much, for it was making too much noise. He stayed but a little while, then he said, "I must go. My family is so eager to see me. You must pound your hide again."

She began to pound the hide hard. As she did so he ran out.

He went back to the place where he had swallowed that little mouse and vomited it out. He stopped breaking wind at once. He jumped. There was no noise. He ran. There was no noise. He tested himself in every way. He was all right.

12. COYOTE MARRIES HIS OWN DAUGHTER

Coyote started back to his home. He had a family and among his children he had a grown daughter, just old enough to get married. He was getting tired of his wife and he wished he could find some way to marry his daughter.

He got back home. He told his family, "I'm feeling sick. I don't think I'll ever get well. This is the last time I'm going to hunt for you before I get very sick."

He killed a deer. In the deer's nose there are some worms called "deer's nose worms." He took out the worms. He brought the meat home. He put the worms in his clothes.

That night he told his wife, "I don't feel like staying home. Make a platform for me in a tree because I'd like to sleep in the open air. I'll be more comfortable there. You must watch that place. If some worms fall down, that means that I'm dead."

---

[1] Because of the restraint between siblings of opposite sex, especially in matters of sex, Coyote could not allow his sister to hear him break wind.

[2] The matter of blaming his nephew for his own shameful act gains point because of a joking relationship between these two kin in which they often banter and ridicule each other.

The platform was made for him up in a tree. He lay there. He kept groaning and sighing like a very sick man.

He told his wife, "After I die you must take no other trail but go right for the east. That's our custom. Stay there four days and then you can go anywhere you want to.[1] But you must give your daughter to the first man who meets you, no matter who he is, an old man or a young one. That man will then take care of you. I don't want you to have a hard time."

Coyote had a prominent wart on the back of his head between the ears.

They waited there two days. Then they saw the worms falling from that place.

The woman began to cry. Coyote had said before he died, "Don't bury me. I don't want to be buried. I don't want my body in the earth. I want it to stay in the open air." So when the worms dropped, the family burned the house and all the possessions and moved the camp to the east.

When the family was on the other side of the hill, Coyote got up. He put on fine clothes and painted his face with white clay. He combed his hair too. He tried to make himself look different.

Then he went over and met his own family. He stood there and asked questions. "Where are you going?" he said.

That woman answered, "My husband died just a little while ago; therefore we are moving." She was crying. Her hair was cut too.[2]

Coyote said, "Oh, how sad for you people! You have lost your good man. I was coming to help him, for I heard a couple of days ago that he was very sick. But I'm too late.

"What did that man say before he died? When a man has a family he always says something before he dies."

"He said nothing," answered the wife.

"No, I don't believe it. He must have said something. You must tell me what he said. You must not cover up his words. You must do what he said."

Finally the wife said, "He told us to go to the east and stay four days and then to go where we like. But he said I must give my daughter to the first man who met us."

"See, I knew it! Many times it happens that way. All right, here I am. If your husband said so you have to do it."

"All right, here is my daughter. You can have her."

They moved to the east and built a camp there.

Coyote lived there with his new wife. But he never stayed home in the daytime. He went out hunting every day and just came home at night.

---

1 It is the Jicarilla custom to move camp to the east after a death in the family.

2 Close relatives cut the hair as a sign of mourning for the deceased.

One time he overslept. When the sun came out he was still at home. His wife cooked and they ate breakfast. After eating he lay with his head on his wife's lap, and she looked for lice on the front of his head. When she tried to look at the back of his head he would say hastily, "No, no, it went in front; it's right on the front of my head." He didn't want his daughter to see that wart. After a while he forgot and he fell asleep.

She thought, "What's the matter that he won't let me look at the back of his head?"

She turned him over. She saw the wart. She recognized him as her father. She gently reached for a pillow and put it under her father's head.

She ran to her mother then. She said, "That man is my father! I know because I recognize that wart right between the ears."

"No," said her mother, "the owl has carried him away from us.[1] You must not say that. You must not talk about your father, for he is dead. It just makes me cry."

"No, it is my father! If you don't believe me, come over and look." Three times she told this to her mother. The fourth time the woman came.

Coyote was very sound asleep. She looked at the man. He was really her husband.

She got the scraping pole.[2] She hit him with it right on the back of the neck. This time he was really dead.

13. COYOTE AND PORCUPINE[3]

Then Coyote came back to life again. He was going along. He saw Porcupine in the distance. He watched to see what Porcupine would do.

There was a big river nearby and Porcupine was trying to get across. But he couldn't find a place to cross. He went back and forth along the bank without success.

It was a good thing for Porcupine that a buffalo came along. The buffalo said, "What are you doing over here?"

"I'm not doing anything. I just want to get across somehow."

Buffalo said, "Why don't you swim it?"

"I don't know how to swim. I might drown."

---

[1] "Owl has carried him away" is a circumlocution to avoid saying "He is dead," for death or the dead must never be mentioned. Owl was a monster who caught humans in the mythological period and carried them home in his basket. (See pp. 74—76.) Because the chance of escape was so small, being carried away by Owl was equivalent to death; hence the phrase.

[2] The scraping pole is the pole over which a hide is placed while the fur is being scraped from it.

[3] Goddard, p. 228; Russell, p. 263.

Buffalo said, "Well then, I'll carry you. You can sit right on my back."[1]

"No, when we get in the river you might shake yourself, and I might fall into the water."

"Well, you can sit close to my head and hold my horn."

"No, you might shake your head and then I would fall into the water."

"You can hold my tail and I'll pull you across that way."

"No, you might shake your tail, and then I would fall into the water."

"Well then, you can get into my rectum."

"All right." Porcupine agreed this time.

He went in. Buffalo started to swim across. When they got to the other side, Buffalo said, "We are already on the other side of the river. Come out now."

Then Porcupine knew that they were already on the other side of the river. He heard something moving. He looked up. He saw that the heart was above his head.

He started to think, "Well, I'll kill this buffalo."

He started to shoot with his arrows (quills). In just a little while the buffalo was dead and fell down. Porcupine crawled out again.

He had no knife and he wanted to butcher his kill. He said aloud, "I'm going to look for a flint with which to butcher this buffalo."

Coyote heard him. He jumped right out and came to Porcupine and said, "What did you say? You said something that sounded good."

Porcupine answered, "No, I didn't say anything."

"Oh, you said something. I heard you say something about a flint."

"Oh, yes. I did say I wanted a flint to make my arrow."

"No, you must tell the truth. You said something that sounded very good."

Coyote kept asking and would not be put off. Finally he said, "I heard you say something about butchering. What are you going to butcher?"

This time Porcupine told the truth. "I said I would look for a flint with which to butcher."

Coyote was glad when he heard this. "You don't have to look. I have a flint and I'll let you use it." Coyote had a little flint tied to him. "Let's go over there and see," he said.

They both started for the river where the buffalo lay.

Coyote had a good idea in mind. He was thinking of a way to take the buffalo away from Porcupine.

He said, "Let us have a contest. The one who jumps over the buffalo is the one to butcher him. The one who fails must just watch the other and get nothing."

---

[1] An incident like this is recounted in Section V, pp. 258—259.

Porcupine said, "All right."

Coyote said, "You go first."

Porcupine ran and tried to jump over the buffalo. It was a big buffalo. He couldn't clear it. Half way across he fell down.

"It's my turn," Coyote said and started to run. He jumped and went over the buffalo without touching it.

So Coyote started to butcher the buffalo. He said to Porcupine, "You must look at me. We must keep our word. The one who failed was not to butcher."

Porcupine was disappointed. Coyote butchered the buffalo. He was very glad, for it was a fat buffalo.

Coyote took the glands out from under the armpits and threw them to Porcupine. That's the only thing he gave Porcupine. Then he sent Porcupine to the river with the big stomach. "Wash this out at the river," he said, "but you must not touch it. You must not eat it."

But while Porcupine was washing it, he kept eating it all the time. He returned with just a little piece. Coyote was very angry about it. Coyote looked for a stick and knocked Porcupine down with it, he was so angry.

Porcupine was half dead. Coyote pushed him away. Coyote butchered all the meat and piled it up. He went to get his family. Before he started he defecated near the meat. Then he started off.

He had gone only a little way when Porcupine came up and began to touch the meat.

Then Coyote's excrement called, "Father, he is going to take the meat."

Coyote came running back. He chased Porcupine away again.

Again he started off. He got only a little way when Porcupine came again and made ready to eat some of the meat. The excrement shouted a warning, and Coyote came running back. He picked up a stick and hit Porcupine.

This happened for a third time.

The fourth time Coyote started off. Porcupine got up. This time he picked up some dirt and threw it on the excrement. "Excrement shouldn't talk," he said.

Coyote heard no warning. He thought he had killed the porcupine with the last blow and that that was why he didn't touch the meat.

Porcupine got busy in Coyote's absence. He carried the meat to the top of a tall pine and cut it into thin slices there. He took it all up there. He even covered up the blood with dirt.

After a while Porcupine looked down and saw Coyote coming with his family, dancing toward the place where they thought the meat was. All were calling the names of their favorite pieces. One said, "I'm going to have the hind quarter," another, "I'm going to have the front quarter," and another said, "I'm going to take the liver."

When they got to the place they didn't find a thing.

Coyote said, "It must be that codi that did it."

The whole family looked all over. They found the porcupine's track.

When they discovered Porcupine, he said to them, "You all lie face downward under this tree. I'll throw meat down to you." He threw down the buffalo hide to them. "With this cover yourselves up," he said.

The youngest coyote was suspicious. He was the only one who did not obey. He looked up through a little hole in the hide. He saw Porcupine cut off all the meat from the backbone.

The youngest coyote[1] saw Porcupine throwing down the backbone on them. He jumped aside, crying, "He's throwing a backbone down on us!"

He was the only one who was saved. The others were all killed.

That porcupine said to this young coyote then, "You must come up." Porcupine stretched out the intestines and lowered them. The little coyote tied the end around his waist, and Porcupine pulled him up. He got up there.

The little coyote sat there on the branch. Porcupine gave him some glands to eat. After a while he got full. He wanted to relieve himself.

"Where is your toilet?" he asked.

"Right over on the branch."

Coyote went out on the branch. "Right here?"

"No, farther out."

"Here?"

"No, a little farther."

He kept Coyote going out until he was right at the very end. Then Porcupine kicked that branch, and Coyote fell off. When he hit the ground he burst and the glands scattered all over.

14. COYOTE BURNS HIS CHILDREN.[2]

Coyote went along again. He met some deer. It was the mother with her two spotted fauns.

Coyote said, "What do you do to make your children so pretty?"

"Why that's the way they are born."

"No, don't tell me a lie. Tell me the truth. You must do something to make them spotted like that."

"No, that's the truth. They are always like that when they are young."

But Coyote didn't believe it.

After a while the deer got tired of his questions. She said, "All right, I'll tell you. I dig a hole. I put my children in there and tie

[1] The youngest and smallest child is often represented as the most wily. Cf. p. 273.

[2] Goddard, p. 227; Russell, p. 265.

their arms so they can't get away. In front of that I make a big fire of cedar brush."

Coyote said, "See, I knew you did something!"

He started to run to his home. He was very much excited. He wanted to have his children pretty like this.

He came to his family. He said, "You must help me to dig this ground."

They all helped him. But he didn't tell what he was going to do.

Then he said, "Every one of you bring some cedar branches now, old ones."

He took the little coyotes and tied their legs. He put them on the other side of the hole. And on this side he built a big fire of the cedar brush. Some of the children began to cry.

"Don't cry," he said, "I'm making you pretty."

He kept making a big fire. When it popped Coyote was delighted, for the deer had said that every time it popped it hit some fur and made a spot.

At first the children cried. After a while they were all dead. Then they started to burn. Their lips were drawn away from their teeth by the heat. When the fire had died out, Coyote saw this. He thought the little ones were smiling.

"Oh, you are laughing because you are pleased at being so pretty," he said.

He said to the youngest, "Come out. You're so pretty."

No one moved. So he reached down and took hold of the arm of the youngest. "Come out," he said, and he pulled the arm right off the body of his child.

Then he began to pull at the others. They were all dead.

Now he was very angry. He knew that the deer had gone in a clump of willows. He thought she was still there. So he set fire all around that place.

He watched that place. The willows always make a noise when they burn. He thought the deer was crying.

He said, "You talk now, but you lied before."

15. COYOTE STEALS ANOTHER MAN'S WIFE.[1]

So Coyote went out again. He saw some people hunting, some Apaches. He saw a man near him.

Coyote said to that man, "Get up on this rock."

The man got up on it. Coyote made that rock grow. It became very tall. The man couldn't get down. Coyote went away.

This man had a wife. When the sun went down Coyote went to her.

He said to her, "You, whose husband went up on the rock."

---

[1] Goddard, p. 224.

He tried to stay there and marry her. He sat right in the doorway. He tried to jump and catch that girl. But she changed to a red flower. Every time she turned to a flower he would urinate on her. That's why some girls have an odor under the armpits; it smells just like Coyote's urine.

Meanwhile the man on the rock saw a bat woman carrying a basket.[1] He called to her. She heard him. She knew already where he was, but just for fun she looked around the earth, making believe she was looking for him.

He continued to call, "Grandmother, grandmother, take me down!"

She almost went into the woods past the place, but then she turned and, shading her eyes with her hands, looked in his direction. She came over.

She started to sing while she climbed up to him. The words she sang were, "Stick to the rock, stick to the rock."

She got on top.

He said to her, "Coyote sent me up on this rock. I called to you so that you would take me down."

The string of her basket was of spider web. He didn't think it was strong enough.

"I will break it," he said.

"No, it's tough string," she answered. "I carry big mountain-sheep in it."

But he didn't believe it. "You must put some rocks in it and let me see how strong it is," he said.

She did and danced with those rocks in the basket. The web was strong and held.

"Now get in. But keep your eyes shut while we are going down."

She assured him it would not break. She jumped up and down with him in the basket to show him it would not break.

"But shut your eyes when we start," she warned him.

"My vulva sticks to it," she sang as she went down.

The man thought, "That's a funny song," but he couldn't help it.

When they got down, she jumped and jumped. "We are already down," she said, but he kept his eyes closed. After a while he got out.

He started for his former camp. When he got there he asked the fire poker, "How long ago did these people move away? Which way did they go?"[2]

"This way."

He went in the direction indicated, following the tracks.

He got to the next place where they had camped at sunset. There he found a scraping pole.

"How long since those people left?" he asked it.

---

[1] A similar incident is told as part of the origin myth, pp. 63—64.

[2] Cf. p. 259.

"Two days ago."

He went on again. He came to another deserted camp site.

He asked the bedding, "When did these people go?"

"Yesterday."

He continued his journey. He found another deserted camp site.

He found a corral there and asked, "When did they leave?" He asked about noon.

"They left this morning," he was told.

This man had arrows with him. On the way he found a deer and killed it and carried it. At sunset he got there and went to his home.

Coyote was out hunting at the time. When the man got home the whole house smelled.

He said to his wife, "This is a bad smell. Take your clothes out and throw them away."

The woman had to take off all her clothes and throw them and many other things away. They washed things till dark. They burned all kinds of weeds and smoked the house to rid it of the smell. The woman didn't clean well under her armpits though, and it still smelled there.

After dark Coyote came back from his hunt. He came straight for the house. He saw the man in the corner and stopped at the door.

He said, "Did you come back?"

The husband did not answer.

He told Coyote then, "Get four small stones."

The man cut a slice of meat and roasted it. Coyote brought the four stones. The man threw them into the fire and let them get red hot. Then he rolled them up in the meat and threw them that way to Coyote.

Coyote swallowed them. "You think you are going to kill me with those marbles," he said.

He sat there. Nothing happened for half an hour. Then Coyote began to run. He ran and ran in circles until he fell down dead.

16. COYOTE PLAYS TRICKS ON OWL; THE VOMIT EXCHANGE.[1]

In those days the people were much afraid of the owl, for the owl had arrows and had a club too.

It was about noon when the owl was coming down from the mountains to the plain. He was coming among the trees.

He was saying, "Hoo, hoo, hoo, hoo! I'm hunting for man."

He met Coyote.

Coyote said, "Where are you going?"

"I am hunting for a man."

Coyote said, "Let us vomit, and the one who can vomit meat of humans is a real man. Let's both shut our eyes and vomit. I'll vomit in my left hand, and you vomit in my right hand."

[1] Goddard, p. 225.

As soon as Owl had shut his eyes, Coyote crossed his hands. Coyote vomited nothing but grasshoppers. Owl vomited the meat of all people. Then Coyote changed his hands back again.

Then Coyote said, "Now open your eyes and see what we have done."

Owl looked at what was before him. "Where did I ever eat grasshoppers? I must have drunk them with my water. I sometimes see things in the water but I swallow it anyway."

Coyote said, "Well, I'll teach you to be a good runner. I'm always teaching people things."

He took Owl out to a smooth place.

"I'm a man," Coyote said. "I ate the people. I did it because I can run so fast. I'll teach you how to be like me. You must take off your leggings. You must shut your eyes while I take them off for you. But first watch me."

So while Owl looked he ran and ran at his top speed. "See how fast I run," he said.

So he cut the flesh off Owl's legs.

He said to Owl, "While I'm cutting you must say, 'Aiii, aiii.'"

He cut off all the flesh, leaving just the bone. Then he made Owl sit down facing the east. He brought two stones.

He said, "You must lay your arrows and bow aside, for they are sometimes poison. They make it painful."

Now Coyote put one of the two big stones under Owl's legs, and one he held in his hand. He had Owl put his legs on top of the first stone. Then, while Owl's eyes were closed, he hit the bones and broke both legs.

This time Owl was angry. The quiver was far away and he couldn't get to it. But he had not given Coyote his club. He started to hit at Coyote with his club. He threw it at Coyote. Coyote dodged and it missed him.

Owl called, "Club, come back to me."

It came back. Three times he hurled it at Coyote and missed but got his club back every time.

The fourth time Coyote shouted, "Club, stay where you are thrown!"

The club failed to return to Owl that time.

Coyote said, "After this you must live in the shade. Don't build yourself a home like a man any more."

That is why Owl's legs are thin today. Coyote cut all the flesh off. Coyote took the arrows and bow and went off then.

Sometimes this story is told a little differently. Some say that Coyote took Owl into a sweat-house and tricked him into allowing the flesh to be cut off his legs. Coyote pretended to do it to himself first and let Owl feel a bone, which he had brought in, as proof. Then he claimed to restore the leg and said he would do the same thing for Owl.

17. COYOTE LOSES HIS BOW AND ARROWS TO THE ANTELOPE.[1]

After Coyote got the arrows from Owl he killed everything he saw. He wasn't afraid of anything.

The people talked about him among themselves. Some wise people said, "Let us not get after him in a fierce and direct way. Let us be crafty and in some clever way get his arrows. Let us make antelopes.

They took two men and turned them to small antelopes. They put the two on the path through which Coyote went. This was near the plains country.

The next time Coyote went that way he saw the antelopes in his path.

Coyote called to them, "My little nephews, let us race. I know you are just little children and can't get away from me." He kept saying this over and over.

After a while they got up. Coyote put the quiver on the back of one. On the other he put the bow. He tried to drive them away from him. They tried to walk, but they stumbled and fell down.

Coyote thought it very amusing. "Oh, my little nephews, what's the matter that you can't run fast?"

The people had given the two antelopes a good talking to. They had said, "When you race with Coyote, do not run together."

So now they separated and went in different directions. They were running. Coyote ran after them. He ran first towards one and then towards the other. When he would nearly get to one, he would look back and see that the other one had almost fallen down. So he would start after the other and give up the first one. Coyote soon got tired running back and forth. When he had all but caught the first one, the second one would cry out and Coyote, looking back, would see that one fall and act weak. Then he would run after him.

So Coyote became very tired. He called to the antelopes, "Wait, my little nephews. I must tell you something. There is one thing I have not told you." But they wouldn't stop or listen.

So after a while Coyote gave up. He was very angry. He said, "Whenever I see you, I'm going to get rid of you, my young nephews."

Coyote went to the chief's home. He told what had happened to him. He asked for help. He said to the chief, "You must tell your people that they must help me. They must circle around and catch the antelopes."

The chief called his men and told them. They said they would help, and they circled around. But they were deceiving Coyote. They did not want him to keep his arrows.

They said to one another, "Whenever you see those antelopes, do not stop them. Let them pass through the circle."

---

[1] Goddard, p. 225.

So the people went on the hunt. They surrounded many antelopes and killed many antelopes. But the two with Coyote's bow and arrows they let pass. So the day passed without the capture of these two antelopes.

Coyote asked for help the next day too. The people hunted, but they agreed among themselves not to kill the two antelopes with the quiver and arrows.

After four days Coyote got tired of it. He said, "All right, I'll give up my quiver and arrows. I'll let them have it. The bow will turn to horns."

18. COYOTE AND TURKEY.[1]

So Coyote went along. He saw Turkey. Coyote had a basket with him. He had been picking choke-cherries and yucca fruit, for his family was hungry. He had lost his arrows now and had no way to kill deer.

He spoke to the turkey. He said, "Now I want you to go to my home."

"Where is your home?"

"Over here," and he showed him. "You must go over there and tell my wife to kill you and let the children eat you, but tell my wife to save the hind leg for me, for by that time I'll be hungry and will come home."

"All right, I'll tell her."

This was before noon. Codi went on and picked fruit.

The turkey went over to Coyote's home. He told the coyote woman, "Your husband sent me over here to tell you to kill his youngest child and eat him. But he wants you to save a hind leg for him."

So the woman did it. She killed her youngest child. They ate him but saved a hind leg for Coyote.

The turkey flew on top of a nearby tree before the coyote came home.

Coyote came home with the fruit. He was excited, for he expected a good meal of turkey. He came in and looked around. He missed his youngest child.

"Where's the little boy?"

"I killed him; here's his hind leg for you," answered Coyote's wife.

"What did you do that for?" Coyote flew into a rage and scolded his wife.

"It's not my fault," his wife said. "I did what you ordered. That's what you sent a man back to tell me."

Coyote hurried out with an ax. He went to the place where he had first seen Turkey. Turkey was not there.

"I shouldn't have given you a chance," he said.

---

[1] Goddard, p. 233.

He looked for Turkey. He followed the tracks. He trailed him to a pine tree branch. He tried to call Turkey down, but Turkey was not afraid and wouldn't come down.

"I told you to go to my home and tell my wife to kill you, but you didn't obey. So now I'm going to do it myself. You'd better come down."

"I did what you told me; I told your wife what to do."

Coyote was very angry. He chopped at that pine tree. Just as it was about to fall down, the turkey flew to another pine. Coyote chopped at that one too. Turkey did the same thing.

Coyote got tired. He gave up.

19. COYOTE AND GEESE

So Coyote went over to the place where the geese lived, because the geese are good flyers and have been all over the world.

"Where are your people preparing to go?" he asked when he got there.

"Oh, we are the inspectors of all the world. If everything is all right, we come back."

Coyote said, "I'd like to help you. I'd like to go with you."

"How are you going to go with us? You have no wings."

"One of you let me have your clothes and I'll go with you."

"No, we have no extra clothes. You can sit on top of us."

"Oh, that's fine!" said Coyote.

Two geese flew together, and Coyote sat partly on one and partly on the other.

The geese told him, "You must honk as we do, and shut your eyes." They started to travel. Coyote was sitting there. "If you open your eyes, you'll fall off. That's why you must be careful," they told him.

They flew up above the camps. The camp people saw Coyote and yelled, "Coyote is on top of the geese! Look at that!"

They yelled at him. He forgot and opened his eyes. He began to fall down. He struck the ground. He was unconscious.

When he regained consciousness, he said, "Why did you call me? You made me open my eyes."

"We didn't call you. We just talked to each other," they said. "We can't help it."

20. COYOTE AND DUCK'S CHILDREN

They say Coyote fell right by the camps. He went along. He came to some people living at the other side of the lake. He started to go home. Then he saw the lake. He looked at it from a distance.

Then, right on the lake, he saw a mother duck swimming. Behind her, right in line, he saw all the little ducks following her. They came out to the edge of the lake. They were walking in line at the edge of the lake.

Coyote thought, "Oh, this is very good!"

He went over. He asked the duck, "What do you do with your children, that they stay in a line just as though they were helping each other?"

"I did nothing. We are like that."

"No, you must have done something! I don't believe you."

Duck was telling him the truth, but Coyote wouldn't believe her.

So Duck said, "I use an eel. I put the eel right through the heads of all the children and it comes out of the mouth of each one. That is why they stay in line."

"See!" said Coyote, "I knew you did something. You told me a lie before. Now I have made you tell me the truth."

Coyote left the duck and started to go home. He wanted to show his family.

When he got home he asked his wife about sinew. She gave him some, and he made it long, just like a bow-string.

Coyote had two children. He didn't think that that was enough. So he said to his wife, "You put your head down too. I'm going to fix you in a nice way so that you'll follow me wherever I go."

He took the awl and pushed it through the back of his wife's head to her mouth. She was bleeding from the mouth and crying.

He said, "Don't toss around so!"

In a moment she lay down, for she was dead. He put the string right through the hole. He did the same with his two children. He tied a stick in back of the head of the last one, the youngest, so that the string wouldn't come out.

Then he said, "Now let's get up. Let's go!"

But no one moved. He tried to pull them, but they were all dead. He tried in every way to make them move. He lifted them up and kicked them. But they just fell back.

He left them. He was very angry. He said, "I'm going to eat up that duck. She fooled me and made me kill my children."

He got over to the lake. The duck was in the center. He could not get to the duck. He tried to make the duck come to him, but the duck wouldn't come.

21. COYOTE STEALS TOBACCO FROM CROW

Then Coyote went on his way again. It was in the early morning.

Crow had been eating some dead animal. He was sitting under the trees. Coyote stayed on the other side, a little way off. He looked at Crow. Crow was smoking after his meal. Coyote looked at it. He thought it was very peculiar.

Coyote asked, "What are you doing? I saw you with some smoke in your mouth. Is your mouth smoking?"

"No, that's not smoke coming out of my mouth. That's just my breath. It's early morning and my breath shows."

"No, it's not your breath."

He kept asking and asking what it was till Crow told him. The crow said, "Well, I'll tell you. I was smoking."

"What kind of plant did you use?"

"I have some over at my home. I have just a little bit here."

He took it out and rolled a cigarette for Coyote, using the oak leaf as a wrapper. The tobacco was bearberry. Crow had two kinds of tobacco, this kind and the Mexican tobacco (cultivated tobacco). They both sat there and smoked.

Crow told him, "Whenever you want to pray, you should offer this smoke. This is very holy. When you smoke, the girls always like you too."

Coyote asked him, "Where is your home?"

Crow said, "I have no home. I sit right on top of the old trees."

Coyote kept asking him. He said, "I know that every bird, every person, has a home. Some live in a hole, some in a cave, some in a nest. But all have homes."

So Crow finally said, "Yes, I have a home."

He took Coyote to his home. He showed it to him.

He showed Coyote his tobacco. "This is real tobacco," he said.

The coyote watched and saw where Crow kept his tobacco. They smoked.

After a while Coyote said, "I have to go home. I have many things to do at my home."

He made Crow believe he was going straight home. But, though he left in the direction of his home, Coyote stopped on the other side of the hill and waited in the bushes until he was sure Crow had left his home.

About noon he saw Crow fly away to the place where he had left the dead animal. Coyote saw him go and knew that he wouldn't be back for a while.

Coyote ran swiftly to the crow's home. He ran right in, for he knew where the Crow had put away the tobacco. He gathered it all up and started to run back. That's how he stole Crow's tobacco.

With the tobacco Coyote went to his own camp. He was smoking all the time. People from other camps asked him, "What are you smoking?" He wouldn't tell them. They asked him for some, but he wouldn't give any away.

The people wanted to smoke too. Coyote had had tobacco for seven days and was smoking all the time. He was very proud of his tobacco.

The people talked among themselves. They said, "Let us fool him. Let us take the tobacco away from him."

So they dressed up a young boy in girl's clothing.

One man told Coyote then, "I'll let you marry my daughter.

But we don't want deer for a present. I want tobacco, for a supernatural power has asked me for some. I heard that you have some and I need it, so I'll let you marry my daughter."

Coyote remembered that Crow had told him how the possession of tobacco makes a man lucky with the girls. He was greatly excited. He gave away his tobacco.

The people built a tipi for him. They said, "You don't have to wait for anything. Just go right in with your wife."

He hadn't given all his tobacco away. He kept a little bit.

When the sun went down the people went in again and sat around. They asked him for tobacco, saying, "You are my son-in-law," or "You are my brother-in-law, give me some tobacco." He couldn't refuse.[1]

He tried to get rid of them. He said, "You people had better go and let me sleep. I want to go out hunting very early in the morning."

But the people stayed until the tobacco was all gone. Then they all went out. But instead of going away, they stayed outside the tipi and listened.

Coyote said to his new wife, "You'd better put all this fire out. You must make a bed for me. I'm very sleepy. I'm going to hunt tomorrow."

He began to do it himself. He put out the fire and made the bed.

Then Coyote put his arms around the girl. He put his hands on the girl's hair and ran them down her body.

"Don't bother me," she said. "I'm menstruating."

But Coyote was so eager that he said, "Oh, that won't hurt me!"[2] He just fell on her, saying, "Why won't you let me? You're already my wife."

Then he grabbed at her genitals. He got hold of them. It was not a girl.

Coyote ran out and called to the people. "You must give me back my tobacco!" he shouted.

But some had already smoked it. Others had divided it with other people. He never got it back.

That's how he lost the tobacco. Coyote went away ashamed.

22. COYOTE AND GRAMA-GRASS

Then Coyote went over to Grama-grass. He asked the grass, "Why do you just stand by yourself? You are very straight too. What are you waiting for?"

---

[1] This passage mirrors the obligations of assistance and generosity which the Jicarilla owes his affinities.

[2] The impatience and foolishness of Coyote are emphasized by this remark. Rheumatism is supposed to be the certain penalty for attempting intercourse before the menstrual period has ceased.

After a while Grama-grass answered, "The people use me sometimes. When the people have wounds, they come over and then they use me. I have power.[1] But sometimes they do not use me and I have to stand here in one place for a long time. Sometimes I stand all summer and all winter unused."

Coyote said then, "I was going to take your place, but now I have changed my mind. I don't want to stand in one place all day all year around. I don't think that's much fun."

So he went away.

23. COYOTE VISITS THE RED ANTS

Then Coyote went to the fields. He came to the ants. He sat and watched them. They were scurrying all over. Some went far away, but they did not lose their way. They came back after a while. Coyote thought it peculiar.

He said to the ants, "You are a small people, yet you never lose your way. How is that? You must teach me what you know so that when I go away from my family I shall not get lost but will be able to go straight back to my home."

The ants told him, "If you want to learn this you must not step on us whenever you are going along."

Coyote asked, "What are you doing? I see you people run to a place and then come back. I see you carrying little stones and sticks to your hole. I don't know why you do that. There must be someone in there who tells you to do it. Can you let me go down and see?"

The ants told him, "There is not room enough for you. You'd better stay away. And it's too dark down there. If you go in there, some other ants might bite you."

Coyote said, "Oh, I'm not afraid. You are small. Even if you bite me it won't hurt. Come on, bite me. My body is all tough." He let his tongue stick out for the ants. "My tongue is tender; bite it," he said.

"You'll swallow us when we get on your tongue."

"No, you can get on my lips. Get on the edge of my lips."

The ant said, "All right." He got up and bit Coyote on the tongue.

Coyote put his hand up and scratched at the ant. Then he jumped and kicked and ran away. The ants were all around and he was afraid he would be bitten again. It was the red ants that he had visited.

24. COYOTE AND MOSQUITO

Coyote met Mosquito and saw that he had a bag right on his back. It was filled with blood, for he had been sucking at someone.

"What are you carrying?" asked Coyote.

Mosquito said, "Why, that's blood."

[1] Grama-grass is used as an arrow wound medicine.

"What are you going to do with that blood?"

"Oh, that's our food. We have no teeth, so we have to eat blood."

"How do you hunt? Where do you get blood?"

"When the people sleep I suck it out."

"How can you suck it out?"

"With this beak."

"Oh, you can't do it with that. You must have some kind of awl."

"No, I've told you how I do it."

Coyote just kept bothering Mosquito and asking him again and again. Mosquito kept telling the truth, but Coyote didn't believe it.

So finally he said, "Oh, I carry along a big thorn and I punch the man with it in the hands and face. Then I gather up the blood in this bag when it flows out."

"See! You lied to me before. Now you have told the truth. What do you do with the blood?"

"Oh, I take it home and feed it to my little children. They have no teeth and cannot eat anything tough."

So Coyote left Mosquito and went to his home.

He said to his wife, "Give me a water bag and an awl. I'm going to get some good food for the children. They have no teeth and can't eat solid foods." He told his wife, "Some people got deer and want me to gather up the blood."

It was about evening. He stayed at the other side of the camps. He approached. Some of the people were snoring. He crawled to one of these. The chief was sleeping soundly.

Coyote felt the chief's face and decided upon the spot where he was going to get the blood. He stuck the awl right into the man's face.

The chief woke up and ran after Coyote. "What did you do that for?" he shouted.

Coyote ran away. He didn't get any blood.

The next morning the people asked each other, "Whose awl is this? Who came around last night?" But no one claimed the awl.

Coyote was looking for the mosquito who had fooled him, but he couldn't find him.

25. COYOTE AND SANDHILL CRANE

This happened at a lake. Coyote was going along there. He saw a bird at the lake. He didn't know what this long legged bird was. He thought it was a tree, and he went and sat under the shade. The bird didn't move his legs, though he moved his head around.

Coyote looked at the bird's foot. He said, "How does it stand up? The root is right on top of the earth. And it looks as if it has claws."

A little distance away there was another crane sitting. Coyote looked that way. He went over there and asked the crane why he was sitting that way. The crane had his feet up and his claws out.

"Oh, I sit over here to rest," the crane said.

"You sit in a queer way."

"That's the way my people sit."

So Coyote tried to sit the same way. He sat facing the crane with his feet out against the crane's. Coyote didn't like sitting that way. So he changed and sat as he was accustomed to sitting.

Then Coyote said, "You must teach me in some way to sit as you do."

"How can I teach you this? You are a different person."

"Oh, many people teach me different things. This should be easy."

"No, I don't know how I can teach you."

But Crane tried. "Stretch out your feet close to me." Coyote did so. The bird began to work Coyote's leg with his claws. He tickled him at the hip.

Coyote said, "Why are you tickling me? Instead of teaching me anything you are making me laugh."

After a while the bird got hold of Coyote's penis. Coyote started to laugh. The bird closed his claws tightly and Coyote began to change his face. Very soon the tears were coming from his eyes.

"What's the matter? I thought you were laughing. What are you crying about now? I guess you are crying because you can't learn my ways easily."

Coyote was crying because it hurt so much.

Coyote said, "I don't want you to teach me any more. I'm getting tired. I'd better sit my own way."

So Crane let go of the penis. Coyote moved hurriedly away. He was afraid to sit close to the bird.

Coyote's penis was all swollen up. He started to go home. He had to walk with his legs far apart. He was afraid to go in during the day. He didn't want his wife to see him. So he stayed away from his home till night.

When night came he went in. He acted in a peculiar manner. He didn't want to lie down.

His wife said, "What's the matter with you? Come to bed."

After a while he lay down. But he wouldn't lie close to his wife.

Then his wife said, "Now let's have intercourse."

"No," said Coyote, "I'm too tired. My legs are too stiff. I've been traveling all day and my legs and body are all sore. How am I going to do it?"

His wife tried to tease him and get him excited. She tickled him.

He said, "Don't bother me. I'm stiff all over."

"There's one place that isn't too stiff," she said and she tried to tickle that.

He pushed her away, "Don't! I'm too tired."

So his wife let him sleep. When he was asleep she felt him all over. She felt that place. As soon as she touched it he woke up. But she already knew what was wrong.

She got right after him, "You have been around with other women! That's what you do every time you go away, I believe!"

He tried to excuse himself. "I fell on a thorn," he said.

"No, you fell on some woman."

"I sat under a tree and a big bird scratched it for me."

But she didn't believe it. She told him, "Stay away from me. I don't want you to sleep with me. I don't want that sickness from you."

So Coyote had to sleep by himself.

That is why, when men go out with other women and get this sickness, they always make excuses when they come back.

26. RABBIT SCARES COYOTE AWAY

Coyote went on the side of an arroyo. It was a place where the sagebrush was plentiful. He saw a rabbit there. Rabbit started to run. Coyote made after it, and the rabbit jumped into the arroyo and into a hole, a prairie-dog hole. But is was an old burrow and so the rabbit couldn't get far into it.

Coyote jumped down and tried to dig Rabbit out. He put his hand in the hole and started scratching around inside.

Coyote was getting near the rabbit. So Rabbit tried to fool Coyote. He yelled, "Hey, you people, come over here! Coyote just put his hand in the door. Now is your chance to hold him."

He tried to make Coyote believe that others were in the hole. He was just talking to himself. No one else was in there.

"Shall I hold his hand?" he asked.

He grabbed hold of Coyote's hand, saying, "I'll hold it. You cut it off."

The coyote was frightened and pulled his hand away before someone could cut if off. He ran right up the bank. He looked down. He saw that no one was coming. He had thought they were all after him.

27. COYOTE CHASES THE ROCKS

Coyote started to run on the other side. He said, "No one is going to fool me again." He saw another rabbit. But he was a little afraid to chase it. He thought it might be going to lead him to his enemies.

But after a while he started after this cottontail. The rabbit ran to a place where he knew there were many rocks. He kicked the rocks so that they would roll down the slope. Coyote saw a rock rolling down hill. He thought it was the rabbit, for it jumped like a rabbit. He ran to head it off, and when he got to it he found it was only a rock.

The rabbit, who was on top, sent another rock. Coyote chased that too but found it was a rock when he came to it. But he didn't believe he was being fooled. He kept chasing rocks. When he found that they were rocks, he thought the rabbits had changed to rocks.

"Oh, they are nothing but rock rabbits," he said. "I'm not going to chase rock rabbits."

So he urinated on the rocks, saying, "I don't care for rock rabbits," and then he went away.

28. RABBIT ESCAPES

Coyote went in the meadows. There he saw a rabbit, a small cottontail. Before the rabbit had a chance to run Coyote thought, "I've missed my rabbit twice. This one I'll trick."

Coyote stood there for a while, thinking. He walked around on his tiptoes. When he got near to the rabbit he made a noise with a stick he held in his hand.

The rabbit woke up and looked.

Coyote pointed to the plains and said, "Hush! Don't run away. Don't make any noise. The enemy are all around us. They chased me here. Keep silent and come here and I'll tell you something. You must help me in some way, for these people are after me. If you run away they'll be after you too."

The rabbit believed him and came near. Then Coyote jumped on him.

The rabbit said, "Why do you jump at me? What are you going to tell me?"

Coyote was pushing Rabbit down. He held him tightly.

Rabbit said, "Don't bite me before I tell you something. One time the wildcat got me. He put me right under his arm. That's how he took me home."

Coyote asked, "How?"

"This way. I'll show you. You are stepping on me too heavily. How can I tell you or show you if you don't let me breathe?"

So Coyote relieved the pressure on him.

"I'll show you. Put your arm this way." And saying this, Rabbit ran right between Coyote's legs and ran into Prairie-dog's home. So Coyote missed his rabbit for the third time.

Coyote cursed himself. He called himself, "No-good Codi, always letting the people get away from me."

29. RABBIT FOOLS COYOTE

So Coyote went along, for he knew he couldn't get the rabbit out of the prairie-dog hole. He went around in the woods. He tried to catch some chipmunks, but they just ran up the trees and he couldn't catch them. He saw a squirrel, but the squirrel ran up a tree and escaped too. He was cursing himself and hating himself because the people were afraid of him and ran away wherever he went. He was getting hungry.

Then he saw a rabbit in front of him. He started to run after it. The rabbit ran for a hollow log which he knew about and ran right through it. Coyote almost caught him, but the rabbit ran in the log just ahead of him. Coyote was smelling in that hole. He put his head right in. The rabbit was far ahead by this time in some bushes and looking back.

Coyote got some rocks and filled up the hole at one end of the log. Then he walked around and did the same at the other end. Then he sat down for a while and rested, for he had been running and was out of breath.

He said to himself, "Codi is going to have a good dinner. He hasn't eaten in a long time. At last I've caught a rabbit."

He had a flint tied around his neck. He always carried this. He picked up a rock and struck the flint against it and built a fire in this way. He started to burn the log. The fire made a popping noise. "That's the rabbit's eye popping," he thought. The other end of the log popped. "That's the other eye. Now you can run around without eyes." Then there was another popping noise. "That's your glands. Now there you are!" Coyote was glad. He listened to the popping. "I'm going to have a nice dinner," he said. He sat in the shade and watched until the log was reduced to ashes.

When it was all burned he looked for a long stick and pushed aside the ashes to find the rabbit. He was very happy at first. But he could find nothing.

He stopped. He said, "What is the matter with me? Here I had a rabbit and I have burned it all to pieces!"

30. COYOTE AND BEETLE

Coyote went away from there and came to a beetle. He thought he was going to eat this beetle. He tried to approach it from the side where its head was, but every time he got near, it put its head down and tipped up with its back toward him. So they went turning around in a circle this way.

The beetle told him, "Don't bother me. If you bother me I'm going to kick you and break all your teeth."

Coyote said, "Oh, why shouldn't I eat you up? You look so pretty that I guess I'll eat you anyway."

"No, don't bother me. You go on your way. Don't bother me. I'm looking down through the earth. Someone is speaking to me from under the earth. That is why my head is down."

Coyote looked down. He couldn't see anything. He couldn't see through the earth.

Coyote said, "I don't see anything. How can you see through the earth?"

"Because I have power."

"Teach me how. Then I'll be able to see through anything."

The beetle said, "You have to go off and get some ashes and paint yourself all black like me. I'll wait for you."

Coyote knew where there were some ashes; there were some where he had burned that log. Coyote ran over there and painted himself black. He was happy and excited.

Meanwhile the beetle hid himself in the grass.

Coyote painted himself all black. His face was blackened too. He came back. He couldn't find the beetle.

"Maybe I'm at the wrong place. Maybe I've lost the place." He looked for his own tracks. "I was standing here. No, that's someone else's tracks."

He walked all over. He followed all the tracks he saw. He tracked himself back to the place where he had painted himself. Then he gave up.

"Oh, a lot of people have been around here. Anyway, that power is no good. A good many people probably know that by now."

So he gave up.

31. COYOTE AND THE BEES

Coyote went on his way. He was very hungry by this time. He came to a rocky place where there was a shelf of rock. Right under it the bees were living. They had a hive there. The bees were sitting on the edge of that shelf of rock.

Coyote said, "What are you doing up there, Codi?"

The bee said, "I am not doing anything. I just sit here and watch the people who pass by."

Then Coyote asked him for something to eat. "Can you give me something to eat, old man?"

"I have no food to give you. Why do you ask me?" the bee said.

The bee had honey on his lip.

"If you have nothing to eat, what is that around your lip?" Coyote asked. "It looks like some grease to me."

The bee said, "My lip is like that all the time."

"No, I don't believe you. Look at my lips; there is no grease around them. I never see grease on people who have no food. You must have a lot of fat food up at your home."

After a while the bee felt sorry for Coyote, for he knew he was very hungry. The bee walked under his hive. He told Coyote to come over. The hive was too high for Coyote to reach, so Bee flew up there and shook the hive, and honey dropped down. Coyote ate and ate. He liked it very much.

Bee asked, "Is that enough?"

"Yes, it's enough."

An old hive which the bees had thrown away when they made a new one was lying there. Coyote picked it up and put it under his armpit.

He called to the bee, "Codi, you come to see me. I'm a man too."

"Oh, I'll come and see you some time. Where's your home?"

"Just a little way from here, over at those rocks."

So Coyote went over there and put up the old hive; he hung it from the rocks. He sat on the rock shelf just as the bee had done.

The next day the bees came in a swarm to the place where Coyote had said he lived. They saw Coyote sitting up there.

"Coyote, what are you doing up there?"

"Oh, I watch the people who pass by."

Coyote had put mud all around his lips.

"What's the matter with your lips?" They are very dirty."

"Oh, they have been like that for a long time."

"No, it looks as if you have fallen in the mud," said Bee.

"No, I didn't fall in the mud."

Coyote got down. "I'll show you what makes my mouth dirty," he said. He shook and shook the hive. A little old dried honey fell down.

The bees looked at it. "Oh, that's old dried stuff! We don't eat that. There's nothing in there," they said, and they returned home.

32. COYOTE EATS GRASSHOPPER

Coyote went down to a field then. He saw a grasshopper there. Coyote tried to catch him.

Grasshopper said, "Codi, don't bother me. The people don't eat me."

The coyote didn't believe it. "You just say that," he said. "It must be that you are very sweet tasting and that's why you don't want anyone to eat you."

"When people eat me they have to jump up in the air every once in a while. That's why they don't use me for food."

"Oh, I'll eat you anyway, even if I have to jump up in the air."

Coyote had been warned. He went toward Grasshopper. "Oh, I guess these people lie," he thought. He ate the grasshopper. Then he walked a little way. Nothing happened. "I guess these people lie," he said to himself again.

Suddenly he jumped. He looked back. "Why did I jump? There is no arroyo there. Why did I jump?"

He walked a few steps. Again he had to jump. "There are no rocks here. What did I jump over?"

That's the way he went, jumping every time he moved.

He cursed himself. "You always get into trouble," he said. "You always try to do everything."

Every time he moved he had to jump up. When he looked back there was nothing there. He had to jump higher and higher. He was getting frightened, for he knew that he would get hurt coming down to earth. He wanted to move, but every time he moved he went up in the air.

He looked at his body. "It must be that I have wings to fly with." He couldn't see any wings. He was still more frightened. He didn't move. He held tightly to some brush. Then he moved. But he went up in the air, grass and all. The grass broke right in his hands. Every time he jumped he went higher and higher. Finally he broke one arm. It hurt him badly.

He spoke to himself, "What have I done? Did I eat anything?"

Then he remembered that he had eaten that grasshopper after being told not to. He made himself vomit. That is why, after that, whenever Coyote ate grasshoppers, he vomited them out. They won't stay in his stomach. After he vomited he stopped jumping.

This was the first time Coyote ate grasshoppers. Before that he never did. Now he eats them. In the spring he can be seen chasing them.

33. COYOTE AND THE WHITE WOOD WORM

Coyote was going along. He lay down in the shade. The white wood worm was eating inside the tree. Coyote heard a noise. He got up and looked on the other side of the tree. No one was standing there. Then Coyote put his head close to the tree. He heard a crunching noise in there. He didn't believe there could be anyone in there. He looked at himself. He felt his teeth. They were not moving. His ears were listening to someone in there.

"There must be someone in that tree," he said to himself.

After a while he lay down. He didn't move. He listened. Then some chewed wood dropped on him. He looked up in the tree but could see no one up there.

"Who dropped this corn-meal on me?" he asked. The wood was yellow like corn-meal.

He looked up in the tree, to the very top. He saw no squirrel or bird there at all. He moved closer to the tree and another ball of this material dropped on the top of his head. He didn't know that just above his head the wood worm was sticking his head from a hole in the tree.

Then Coyote heard a voice. "What are you doing here, Codi?" it asked.

Coyote got up and looked on the other side of the tree. He could see no one.

Then the voice spoke for the second time, asking the same thing.

Coyote looked and looked. Then he saw someone in front of his nose.

"Codi, you scared me," Coyote said. "What are you doing in that tree? Are there some people in there?"

"Did you come to see me?" the worm asked.

"Yes, I came to see you. Now I am here."

The worm went in there and brought some more of the chewed wood. "You can eat this," he said.

Coyote tried to eat it, but he didn't like it.

He said, "I don't care for this. It doesn't taste good without salt. You must come to see me."

"Where do you live?"

"Oh, right at the next tree."

This next tree was an old rotten tree. It had a hollow in it. So Coyote went over there and got on the inside. He made little holes in it and stuck his head out from them. He tried to chew some of the wood.

The worm came. Coyote stuck his head out and said, "Codi, what are you doing over here?"

"Why do you ask? I thought you wanted me to come and see you."

Coyote ducked his head back. He threw out some rotten wood. "Eat that; you're hungry."

"Oh, I don't eat this kind. I eat the fresh kind. This is too old."

So Wood Worm went back to his own home. Coyote got out of his hole.

34. COYOTE AND WATER DRAGON

Coyote was getting very thirsty. He went down to the brook. He drank and as he was drinking he saw some water dragons fly by. They flew to the water and came down on it just as if they were sliding on it. He watched them. They all came around and hit the water in the same way again and again.

Coyote thought there must be something in the water. He thought that there was some girl in the water and that they were trying to have intercourse with her. Every time they flew they did the same thing.

Coyote went back a little way and ran forward, jumping on the water the way they did. He didn't find anything there but the water. He came out and looked back. He saw nothing.

But the insects were still doing it so he thought someone must be there. He tried it again and hit the water as before but could not find anything.

Water Dragon came around. "Why do you jump in the water?" he asked.

"I thought you were having intercourse in the water, and I tried to do that too."

"You must not do that. You'll hurt yourself. There are rocks sticking out of this river."

"You show me how to jump in so I won't hit the rocks in the water. I want to do it too."

"You must not do it."

They didn't teach him; they just let him sit there. He waited for a while. Then he went away.

35. COYOTE IMITATES WILDCAT

Coyote went to the woods then. He went to sleep under a tree. He woke up after a while. He saw that on the other side of the tree someone was sitting on the branches. A little rabbit was coming. It was Wildcat sitting up there, but Rabbit did not know it, for he didn't look up in the tree. So, as Rabbit passed, Wildcat jumped on him and killed him. Then Wildcat took the rabbit up on a branch and ate it.

Coyote thought to himself, "What a good idea! What an easy way to get the meat!" So he went over to Wildcat.

"Codi," he said, "I know how you catch the animals. I saw you. No wonder you are so fat! You must teach me to get on the branches like that and catch my meat too."

"Codi, you must not try it. You might just hurt yourself."

Coyote went away. He had a hard time doing it, but he finally managed to get up on a tree. A deer was coming along. Coyote was tired and sat on the limb. Deer came along and scratched himself on that very tree.

"Oh," thought Coyote, "it will be easy to get him."

He mentally counted the members of his family and divided the deer among them. "This boy will get a hind quarter, this one will get the ribs." He already had the deer all divided.

Then he jumped on the deer, right on his back. The deer was frightened and jumped away from him, sending Coyote to the ground. Coyote bumped his nose and lay there unconscious. The deer ran away.

Coyote regained consciousness and looked around. No deer was to be seen. So Coyote got up and went away again.

36. COYOTE AND WILDCAT

Then Coyote went back looking for Wildcat. Wildcat had killed a squirrel and was eating it on the branch.

Coyote said, "Codi, come down and bring down what you are eating. Eat it right here and while you are eating I'll tell you something."

Wildcat came down and put down the squirrel. Coyote told Wildcat what had happened, how he had jumped at the deer and lost it. He looked at the squirrel. Some lice came out from the squirrel's fur.

The wildcat picked up a louse. He knew that he could scratch any spot on his back but that Coyote could not reach the center of his back.

He put the louse in the middle of his back between his shoulders and said, "Whoever can scratch the place where this louse is in the middle of his back will eat this squirrel."

"All right; that's good."

He put a louse on the middle of Coyote's back. After a while the middle of Coyote's back itched. Coyote tried to scratch that place. He tried to reach it with his leg but he couldn't do it. He tried and tried but couldn't reach it. Finally he had to roll to get relief.

Wildcat said, "Don't roll around on the ground. Watch me."

Coyote got up and watched. Wildcat put his hand right to the spot and scratched out the louse. He put it before Coyote saying, "See, here it is."

So Coyote lost the squirrel.

Coyote couldn't stand it. He tossed himself around. The itching was bothering him. He scratched among the bushes. He ran far away. That's how Wildcat chased Coyote far away from him.

37. COYOTE AND MOUNTAIN-SHEEP

Coyote was going along. He saw a big cliff that extended all around. He was rather afraid for he saw Mountain-sheep there with big horns, and he was afraid of them.

"Codi, why have you those big rocks on your head?" he asked.

"Oh, it's like that all the time."

"No, you must put something there. You must have done something." Coyote just kept asking about those horns.

After a while Mountain-sheep said, "It wasn't like this in the beginning. Then I rammed my head against the cliff, and each time I did so some of the rock stayed on my head."

Coyote said, "Let me see you do it and I'll believe you."

Mountain-sheep walked back and then ran at the cliff. He hit it with his head lowered and a great noise arose, for it was in a corner of the cliffs and the echoes began to ring.

Coyote fell back from the noise. Every time there was an echo he said, "There's another one! There's one over there! There's one on this side!"

Coyote became very much afraid. He got up and said, "The rocks must be falling. I'd better run away before they fall on me."

He ran away and stood for a while at a distance. Then he went away.

38. COYOTE DECEIVES SQUIRREL

Coyote went on his way. He found a dead deer. He carried it among the trees, the piñon trees in the direction of his home. He was going to take the deer home to have the hide tanned.

The squirrels sat in the tree and laughed at him. They made fun of him saying, "Poor Coyote!"

He tried to get them to come down. "Come down. We'll have a nice time over here," he said.

But they wouldn't come down. They were afraid of him.

After a while he said, "Oh, come down and get me something to eat, for I'm almost dead of hunger. I'm ready to die. If you don't take pity on me I'm going to die."

They wouldn't do anything for him. He sat there for a while. Then he fell over, just as though he had died.

The squirrels called to him. They threw cones at him. They talked to him.

"Oh," said some, "he's just trying to fool us."

"No," said the others, "he must be really dead, for he doesn't move."

They threw more pine cones at him.

Some said, "Let's hit him with little rocks. If his hide gives off a rattling noise he must be dead."

Some of them came down and got fairly near. They threw rocks at him. Coyote had the old deer hide he had found over himself on that side. So the rocks made a rattling noise.

So they were satisfied. They said, "Let us all circle around him and dance as though we were having a scalp dance, for you all know he is our enemy.[1] Let's do it before his body begins to smell bad."

So they danced and kept getting nearer and nearer Coyote. Coyote lay still. After a while they were not afraid. They walked around and walked right to him.

Finally one took a long stick and hit Coyote. "He's dead all right. He's all dry. Don't be afraid. Come, everyone, let's dance."

So they started to dance around him. Coyote was getting tired of it. He leaped up and ran for them. He killed one, but the others got to the trees safely. Coyote ate his kill right away.

The others were all afraid of him and stayed at a distance.

39. COYOTE NAMES THE MEMBERS OF HIS FAMILY

Coyote went to a prairie-dog town. He saw a badger there.

He said to Badger, "Friend, help me to get something to eat."

Badger asked, "What do you want? Is there anything that is a favorite food with you?"

"No, I eat any meat."

So Badger went into a hole and came up with two prairie-dogs.

"Do you want any more?"

"Yes, I need three more, for I have four children and a wife."

The badger went in two more times. Each time he came out with two prairie-dogs. So Coyote had six prairie-dogs. He carried them to his home.

---

[1] The Jicarilla took scalps and had an important scalp dance ceremonial.

He built a fire there and made plenty of hot coals. Then he buried these prairie-dogs in those coals. He stayed there till they were roasted, a long time. He had a long stick and he took them out. Twelve pieces came out, more than he had put in. They had broken in half in there. He was near to his home. He called his wife and children.

They got to the place. Coyote's children had no names.

He said to his family, "We must all have an equal amount to eat. One must not get more than the others."

They all agreed to this.

Then he said, "I must make names for all of you so that I can call you by name and give each one the same amount. I, myself, will be called Codi. You, my wife, will be called Codi's Woman."

He didn't know what to name the four children. He began to make up funny names for them. The oldest he called Anus; the second he called Buttock; the third he called Penis. The fourth was the youngest, so he called him Youngest.

So he was going to divide the prairie-dogs. He put two aside. He began to count. He said, "This one is for Codi; this one is for Codi's Woman; this one ...." There he paused for he had lost track of those counted. He started over. He got half way and the same thing happened. He forgot which names he had already called.

He started to scold his wife. "You must help me keep track of these," he said.

He tried once more. It happened as before. Then Coyote gave up. "Oh, go ahead and eat them," he said, and they all began eating them without any counting.

40. COYOTE PRETENDS TO GO HUNTING[1]

Coyote and his family went home after eating the prairie-dogs. After a while they were hungry again.

Coyote said, "I'm going out to hunt."

He had no arrows, he had nothing to hunt with. Since he had brought in plenty of meat the last time, however, his wife believed him. Coyote had it in mind to beg some more meat.

But he couldn't get anything. He brought back nothing but grasshoppers. He had some excuse. This happened several times.

The first time he said, "I killed a deer. While I was looking for a flint with which to butcher it, someone stole it and put these grasshoppers there instead. Tomorrow I'll try hard and get another deer."

His wife believed this excuse.

Before he started out the next day he asked all the members of his family what they wanted to eat. One said deer meat, one said rabbit meat. He promised them all they wanted.

---

[1] Goddard, p. 235.

This time he again came back without meat. "I killed an antelope," he told them. "I brought it half way. Then I had to defecate. It bothered me too much. I put the meat down and went a little ways away. When I came back the antelope was gone and only these grasshoppers were there. That's why I have come home late. I looked and looked for the antelope again."

Every time he came home late.

The next day before starting out he again asked his children what they wanted to eat. But when he got home again he claimed that something had happened to him to deprive him of his meat.

By this time his children were getting very hungry. But he himself went out each day among the camps where the people were eating well, and he got his meals there.

But after a while Coyote's family got tired of him. His wife didn't believe his excuses any more and his family would not listen to him.

41. COYOTE AND THE PITCH BABY

Coyote knew his family was hungry, so he went down to the corn patch and stole some corn. He did this several times. The people, every time they went to the corn patch to work, missed some corn. They asked each other about it, but no one knew who was taking it. The people talked over how they were going to find out who was the thief.

Coyote always went after midnight, for he knew that by that time the people were all asleep.

After a while they found tracks there. Some said it was Dog who was taking the corn. The tracks looked like dog tracks. Some said it was Codi. They tracked him to his home. Then they knew.

"Let us punish him," they said.

Some went out to the oak trees and gathered pitch and some went among the pine trees and got some. Coyote always took one trail to the corn patch and the people had discovered this from his tracks. So they made a figure of pitch, just like a little baby standing up.

Next time Coyote came down he saw a figure there. He thought someone was watching.

"Oh, someone will find out I'm stealing the corn," he said.

He came up quietly. He thought that he was discovered.

So Coyote spoke up to this figure. "What are you doing over here?"

There was no answer.

"Are you lost, or are you waiting here?"

He asked many questions, but got no answer.

"All right, if you won't talk to me, I'm going to slap your face!"

He slapped at the face of the figure. His hand stuck there.

"You won't talk to me and then you hold my hand! Let it go, I say, or I'll hit you again."

There was no answer. So Coyote hit at the figure with his other hand. This hand stuck fast also.

"Now you are holding both my hands! What does this mean? If you don't let me alone, I'll kick you."

He kicked with one foot.

"Oh, so you're holding my right foot now!"

Now he was caught in three places.

"Oh, I have another leg. If you don't let me go, I'll kick you hard with it."

And he kicked with his other foot. This too was caught. So Coyote was caught fast by both arms and legs.

At first he was angry. Then he began to plead. "I didn't mean to frighten you. Please let me go. I was just playing with you. My children are waiting for me."

Finally he became angry again. "Now if you don't let me go, I'll bite you."

He bit at the figure. Now he was caught by the mouth too and he was helpless. He had to stay there till morning. When the people came around that morning they found him.

Four people came and put a rope around his neck. They pulled him from the pitch figure. They started to take him back to the camps, to the chief. The chief acted as judge.

They asked questions. "Why do you come down and eat our corn every night? You have two hands; why don't you plant corn yourself for your children?"

He said, "I didn't steal your corn. My wife wanted me to go and get some leaf. I was going that way for the first time. I didn't know someone was standing in my way because it was so dark. So I walked into him and he caught me."

But the chief didn't believe him. "We saw your tracks there many times," he said. "The next time you steal corn you will stay right on that figure, for no one will take you away and save you."

Then they released Coyote.

He started to go home. His hand was all covered with pitch. He picked up some grass, and it stuck to his hand. He tried to bite it off. But his face was the same way. Grass and thorns and everything that touched him stuck to him.

When he got home his wife asked him, "Where have you been? It looks as though you have been eating by yourself. Look at your face and hands! They are all sticky. Why don't you tell us and invite us when you have something to eat?"

He was quiet. After a while he said, "Oh, you bad children! You sent me away and I fell in the mud. The mud was very sticky and that's why I am like this."

So they helped clean him off. They cleaned off his mouth and his feet too.

Then his wife told him, "Go down to the river and wash yourself.

I don't want you to come in with your face and hands that way. You might get the children dirty and sticky."

So he went down to the river.

42. COYOTE AND BEAVER[1]

Coyote got to the river. There he saw Beaver sleeping.

He spoke to the beaver. "Codi, what are you doing?"

The beaver was so sleepy he gave no answer. Coyote kicked Beaver. Beaver was so sound asleep that he did not stir.

Coyote said, "He must be dead. I'll pick him up and carry him away, for the people drink this water and don't want dead things in it."

So Coyote picked up Beaver and took him far from the water.

"You're dead; you stay over here," he said, and put him down.

Then Coyote went back to the river and washed. He washed his hands and feet and face thoroughly.

This was in summer, and because the sun was so hot, Beaver woke up. He didn't know where he was or who had brought him to that place.

He said, "It must be Codi who put me here."

Then he started to go back. He tried to find his way to the water. When he was almost dead he got back to the water. He got back sometime in the afternoon. He saw someone sleeping there. Coyote had bathed himself and was now taking a nap at the edge of the water. The beaver went in the water and refreshed himself and rested for a while.

A little distance from shore there was an island which Beaver had made when he built his dam. Beaver brought a log over and made a bridge to that place.

Then he went to Coyote. He talked to him, but Coyote was so sound asleep that he didn't hear. So Beaver picked him up and carried him to the island, taking him over the bridge. Then he pushed the log away. Beaver went back to his home and watched.

When the sun was just about ready to go down, Coyote woke up. He stretched himself. He didn't realize where he was. After a while he got up. To his surprise there was water all around him.

"How did I get here?" he thought.

He yelled for help. "Someone help me! Someone take me to the other side of the water!"

Beaver heard but he didn't care.

Then Coyote thought, "I guess it is because I put Beaver off there away from the water. Perhaps someone is punishing me for it."

Then the beaver came along. He was on the shore across from the island.

Coyote called, "Codi, come and help me."

---

[1] Goddard, p. 231.

Beaver asked, "What are you doing over there? How did you get over there?"

"I don't know how I got here. Come over and help me."

Beaver said, "No. How can I help you? I might get drowned. I didn't put you over there, so why should I help you?"

The sun was going down by now. Coyote jumped in the water. He swam and swam. He had a hard time to reach shore. He nearly drowned. The bank at the edge of the river was steep and he had a hard time getting out. It took him a long time and he was exhausted.

43. COYOTE AND HIS MOTHER-IN-LAW

Finally Coyote got out of the water. He was cold and tired. He went to the oak trees and lay down among the dead leaves. He stayed there over night, for he was too wet to go out.

The next day he went home. That day his mother-in-law came over to visit with his wife.

Coyote saw that his mother-in-law had a big bottom. He thought, "She is better than my wife." He tried to think of some plan by which he could have intercourse with her.

He went out and chased a rabbit towards his home. He chased it into a brushy place, and it was right in the corner there. He crawled in after it, but he couldn't reach it; his arm was too short. He went over and spoke to his wife. His wife did not have long arms, but her mother did.

So Coyote said, "Tell your mother that she can get that rabbit, for she has long arms."

So his wife went over to her mother and said, "My husband wants you to reach a rabbit under some brush. He can't reach it, but you have a long arm."

The mother said she would do it and started for the place.

Coyote said to his wife, "You stay here and watch your food so that it won't burn. And watch your mother's camp too so that no one goes over there in her absence."

Then he left and ran to the place. The old woman had just got there and had crawled in that narrow, bushy place. Her head and her body down to the hips were in there, and her buttocks were sticking out. She couldn't look behind her, for it was a narrow place.

So Coyote came up quickly and had intercourse with her from behind. He did it hurriedly and then ran off before the old lady could get out and see who it was.

The old lady got the rabbit and went home. She called her daughter then and told what someone had done to her.

The two women went to that place and looked at the tracks. They measured them with a stick. They tracked the person and saw the tracks lead to the other side and then to Coyote's house.

Coyote was in there singing and happy as though he had done nothing. Then his wife came in with the stick and tried to measure Coyote's foot as he lay there.

"What are you doing?" he asked. "Get away. Don't measure my foot."

Then his wife asked, "Did you go over where my mother was and have intercourse with her?"

"No, she's my mother-in-law. I wouldn't do such a thing!" he said. "If you talk like that about me, perhaps the bears will run after me sometime when I am in the mountains. If you say such things, Bear won't pay any attention when I say, 'My mother-in-law, don't look at me.'"[1]

So Coyote stayed at his camp for a few days. And then he became blind.[2] Then his children had to lead him wherever he wanted to go.

He went over where Jack-rabbit was, for Jack-rabbit makes eyes for people.[3] He was led to Jack-rabbit's home. He asked Jack-rabbit to help him.

Jack-rabbit asked, "What did you do to make your eyes like this?"

"I slept right in the sunshine with my head up and my eyes were all burned. I want you to help me."

Jack-rabbit looked for a stick and then opened Coyote's lids with it. There was something covering Coyote's eyes. Jack-rabbit took it away from one eye and then from the other.

"Can you see all right now?"

"Yes, my eyes are all right now."

"You must not sleep in the sunshine."

Now Coyote could see once more.

44. COYOTE MAKES AN OLD COUPLE FIGHT

Some old people had just two daughters. The camp people were going out to pick berries and these two girls went along. Both were grown-up girls. One was a married woman. She was boiling some corn and so she took a potful to these old people and asked them to take care of it for her.

The old man was taking care of the pot. He was running a stick over the top of the pot so that no corn would boil over and be lost. The old woman was making some bread in the ashes.

The old woman could see just a little, but the old man was totally blind.

---

[1] Since the mother-in-law was avoided, a man who met a bear in the mountains addressed the bear as his mother-in-law. The bear was expected to become very much ashamed at meeting one who called it by an avoidance term and to run away.

[2] A film over the eyes and ultimate blindness are the penalties attached to purposely facing or becoming intimate with one who stands in an avoidance relationship to a Jicarilla.

[3] Again the jack-rabbit is associated with the cure of the eyes.

Their work was just about done when Coyote came to visit at this camp. He saw that all the people were gone; only children were there playing.

He asked, "Where are all the people?"

The children said, "They are all out picking berries."

"Who is staying here?"

"Just two old people are staying over there, but they are blind."

Coyote went in. He saw these old people. The old man was running the stick over the outer rim of the pot.

Coyote went and got a stick for himself. With his stick he lifted up the old man's stick, and the old man kept running his stick across Coyote's stick, thinking it was the rim of the pot. In the meantime, Coyote lifted the pot from under with his other hand. When Coyote was ready to go he threw his stick in the direction of the old woman. The old man was looking around for his pot.

He said to his wife, "Why did you take away my pot? I can't find it."

"I didn't touch your pot. I'm taking care of this bread."

The old man felt all over. He couldn't find it. He began to be angry.

"I guess you did it," he said. "You put it somewhere. Why do you tease me like that? There is no one here but the two of us. I'm not a child; I don't want to play with you. My daughter, when she comes back, will get after me. You'd better give it back."

He kept talking that way to his wife. At first she just said, "No, I haven't got it." Then she, too, became angry. After a while she became very angry and picked up a stick and threw it at him. She missed him.

The old man didn't even know that his wife had hit at him, for he couldn't see.

Then Coyote picked up a stick and hit the old man.

Now he was angry and said to his wife, "What did you hit me for?" and he struck her.

She found a stick and began hitting him too. Pretty soon they were beating each other with sticks.

Meanwhile Coyote sat outside eating the food. He finished in a little while what they had been cooking all morning. Then Coyote left. He put the pot back in the tipi but on the other side.

The old people stopped beating each other. Both sat there quietly, angry at each other.

When the sun was low the people came back.

They asked, "What's the matter?" for they saw that the two old people were angry with each other.

The old man said, "This woman took away the pot I was supposed to take care of. She's been teasing me."

The old woman said, "This man started saying I took his pot. I didn't know anything about it. We've been fighting."

The old man said, "She hit me first with a stick and we've been hitting each other since then."

The daughter called the children who had been playing there. She asked, "Did you go in there where the old people were?"

"No."

"Well, who went in and ate my corn?"

The children said, "No one but Coyote went in where the old people stay."

So the woman knew what had happened then. She washed the pot out thoroughly, for Coyote had touched it.[1]

45. COYOTE SHOWS HOW HE CAN LIE

Coyote came around to a group of camps. The men were sitting around. They knew that Coyote was always telling lies.

They called to him. They said, "Codi, you are the biggest liar we ever saw."

"How do you know I lie?"

"Oh, you always make trouble in the tribe and then you lie about it. Why don't you teach us your power to lie so we can lie successfully too?"

"What I learned is from my enemy.[2] And I paid a big price for it."

"How much did you pay for it?"

"One good horse. And it had to have a rope on too."

"Is that all?"

"Yes."

In those days one man had a lot of horses. He brought out a white horse.

"Yes," said Coyote, "this is a pretty horse. This is the kind I mean. It is one like this I paid for my power."

Then he said, "Let me try it. If this horse doesn't buck I'll tell you, I'll explain to you all about the power to lie."

So they pushed him up on top of the horse. He got up. Coyote had never ridden a horse before. He stuck his claws into the horse's back. The horse started to buck.

"Oh, this horse wants a blanket on; that's what's the matter."

They put a blanket on the horse.

Coyote had sharp claws. He stuck his claws right through the blanket, and the horse jumped again.

"Oh, he wants something over his back; he wants a good saddle on."

So they got a good saddle and helped Coyote put it on the horse. Coyote mounted again.

---

[1] Anything that a coyote touches is thereby rendered unclean for the Jicarilla.

[2] That is, he learned it from an Arapaho Indian. The Jicarilla called the Arapaho "enemy."

Coyote put his head up to the sky. He made believe he was listening to something. Then he said, "That voice, my power, wants a whip too."

They gave him one.

He said, "I'm going around now and try this horse to see if it still bucks. I'll come back and tell you all about it."

He rode a little way. Then he shouted back, "This is the way I lie! I cheat people and get them to give me good horses, blankets, saddles, and many other things!" Then he rode away.

The people couldn't do anything about it.

So Coyote went back. He was riding this fine horse.

He told his wife, "See, I have this good horse from my enemy, from the plains country." He got off the horse.

He didn't know how to take care of it, however. He let the reins go, and the horse started off. It ran back to its owner.

46. COYOTE HIDES IN GOPHER'S MOUTH

An old lion[1] built himself a little corral and acted as if he were becoming blind. He told the people to pity him because he was getting blind. He was trying to deceive the people, for his sight was really good.

He told the people, "Now three times a day someone must come in to see me and I'll teach him something."

All the animals went in there and he ate them. That was his plan. They never got away from him.

Coyote came around. He stood at the door of the corral.

The lion said, "Come in to see me."

Coyote knew that the lion was eating people. He said, "I'll tell you something before you eat me." He stopped at the door. "I have a man here for you; I'm going to bring him first."

"Whom did you bring?"

"Oh, one who wants to come to see you."

"All right," said Lion, "but put down something before you go."

Coyote said, "I have nothing with me."

Lion said, "Anything will do."

Coyote put down his excrement there. That was to assure Lion that he would be back. He was lying though. He didn't intend to come back.

Lion waited and waited. Then he decided to go out and look for Coyote.

Coyote saw him coming. He was frightened. He went into the bushes. He was still afraid of being found. He came out and ran in a hole. But he didn't like that either and came out.

---

[1] The informant insisted that not the mountain-lion but the African lion, "big head," was meant.

Then he saw Gopher there. Gopher had just come out of the earth. He pleaded with Gopher to save him.

He said, "You must help me some way. The lion is following me and wants to eat me."

All the while Lion was following Coyote's tracks.

Gopher said, "Go in my home. Right here is the hole."

Coyote answered, "No, he might see me if I go in there."

Lion was very near now.

Gopher said, "Well, get in my mouth."

Coyote went in. No sooner was he out of sight than Lion came along.

Lion asked, "Where is that fellow? Where is Coyote? Did he pass this way?"

Gopher said, "No, I can't talk. My cheek hurts. Don't talk to me."

His mouth pouch was full and looked swollen. He just motioned with his hands that he had not seen Coyote.

Lion looked around. He couldn't find tracks any more. He went back. Then he thought that Gopher might be hiding Coyote somewhere, so he returned and asked Gopher all kinds of questions.

As soon as Lion turned back Coyote got out and ran away. When Lion returned Gopher's swollen jaw seemed to be all right.

"What happened to your toothache?" asked Lion. "I thought your jaw was swollen."

Gopher said, "I found a good medicine for it. I just bit once on it and the sickness was all gone."

Then Lion went back to his corral. Coyote had already escaped.

47. COYOTE MARRIES THE CHIEF'S DAUGHTER[1]

A man who was the chief over some camps had a very pretty daughter. He was proud of her and wanted to be very careful in choosing a husband for her. The young men kept coming around and asking for the girl.

So he said, "I want my daughter to marry a very strong man, one who will be of service to me. I want him to have large muscles in his arms and in his legs."

Coyote heard of this. He made his muscles swell up by pounding them with a stone. He pounded his arm muscles and his leg muscles. Then he went over to see the chief.

He said, "I heard that you were looking for a man who has big muscles."

"Yes, I am looking for a youth or a man with big muscles. He will be the kind of man who can help me."

"Here I am," said Coyote. "I am ready to marry your daughter."

---

[1] Goddard, p. 234.

The chief agreed to the marriage.

But Coyote didn't want to stay around in the daytime after his marriage. He just wanted to stay around at night.

One time when he came back the girl said, "Where do you stay every day? Why is it you never stay at home?"

"I've been out hunting. I have been making a fence around the deer so that they will be easy to get. That's why I've been away in the daytime. I'm doing it so my father-in-law won't have to work hard to get deer."

He went away the next day. Then, when he had gone, the girl went over to her father.

She said to him, "My husband says he is making a corral around the deer for you so that you won't have a hard time getting them. He says it is nearly finished."

The old chief was happy about it. He called some servants who were taking care of horses for him.

He told them, "You must go over and help my son-in-law. He is making a fence over there."

The boys got on horses and rode over there. They couldn't find anything.

They came back and said, "We went over there and looked all around but couldn't see any fence at all."

That night Coyote came home and said, "The corral is all finished."

So the next morning the chief and his servants went over there. They couldn't find anything. Coyote had gone before and was hiding.

The chief came back. He stayed at his daughter's house until Coyote returned.

Coyote came back after dark. He saw his father-in-law at his home.

The father-in-law said, "Why did you lie? Where is the fence? If you lie I don't want you to stay with my daughter. Get out of this camp. You are not going to sleep here any more."[1]

That's the way Coyote lost his wife.

48. COYOTE COMES TO LIFE FOUR TIMES

Coyote had a plan which he knew he could carry out by means of his power. He took his heart out and cut it in half. He put one half right at the tip of his nose and the other half at the end of his tail.

Having lost his wife at one group of camps, he went to another. He asked the brother of a certain girl if he could marry her.

Every time the brother went out hunting, Coyote would go with him and try to help him. He chased the deer towards this man and

[1] This speech is indicative of the degree to which the son-in-law was governed by his wife's parents and relatives among the Jicarilla.

did everything he could to assist him. So the brother brought in meat all the time and was very much pleased.

He said, "I guess this boy ought to have my sister."

So he went over to the place where his sister was. He talked to her. He said, "This man wants to be my brother-in-law. He wants to marry you."

She said, "I'm not going to marry him."

But Coyote stayed there. He tried to help all the time and acted like a servant for these people.

The brother kept talking to his sister. He said, "My sister, you should marry this man. He's good to us. He's not lazy."

Finally the girl said, "All right, I'll marry him. But he must let me kill him four times. If he comes to life each time, I'll marry him."

Coyote said, "All right, come and kill me."

So this girl picked up a stone ax and hit Coyote on the head. He fell. Then she pounded and pounded and broke all his bones. She felt all the bones to make sure they were broken.

Then she said, "He's dead."

But the next day Coyote walked in looking just as he used to. There was no sign that his bones had been broken.

"Here I am," he said. "Come and kill me again."

So she hit him again with the ax. She chopped and chopped till he was all in pieces.

But the next day he came back again.

So she tried again. This time she cut his arms and legs in pieces and scattered them in far places.

But the next day Coyote came back.

She thought, "That ax is no good. I'll use my flint knife this time."

She hacked him to pieces with this and scattered the parts.

But the next day he was there as before. So she had to marry him

49. COYOTE LOSES HIS FUR[1]

On one side of a river lived the beaver people and on the other side the otters. They were playing a game. Badger and Prairie-dog were playing too. They were all playing hoop and pole together near the river.

The water animals had pretty good fur. It was all clean. The land animals had dirty fur. Their fur was not so good as the fur of the water animals.

Coyote came along and saw the game in progress. He sat there and watched.

The beaver and otter people lost all they bet.

Then the otter said, "Now I'll bet my fur. Who wants to bet with me?"

[1] Goddard, p. 208.

Coyote looked at Otter. Otter had pretty fur. Coyote had pretty fur too at that time.

Coyote said, "I'll bet my fur against yours."

They took off their clothes and put them in a pile. The game started. The beaver and otter people began to win back what they had lost.

So Coyote lied and tried to fool these people. He said, "Someone sent me on an errand and wanted me to hurry back."

He grabbed at the pile of fur that lay at the river's edge. The otter tried to take the fur away from him, for Otter was ahead and had almost beaten Coyote.

Otter said, "I won't let you have it." He pulled it to one side and tore it in half.

The others started to run after Coyote. Coyote ran with the torn fur in his hands.

Coyote ran into a badger's hole. They all came after Coyote, but they were afraid to come in the hole. They stayed on top. Coyote hid this torn fur in the hole.

He had no clothes on, so he called to Badger and said, "You must give me some clothes. I want to get out."

Badger had some old clothes, greyish in color. He let Coyote have them. Coyote put them on but they were a little small. He stretched the fur out at the arms and legs until it fitted. Coyote looked at it. It was not so good, but he couldn't help it. The other one was torn right in half.

Coyote came out. He stood around where they were still playing. But Otter didn't recognize him. The coat was different and Otter thought it was someone else. Coyote was afraid to stay around there. He went away. He didn't come back.

That is why Coyote's coat is something like Badger's today.

50. COYOTE VISITS THE NAVAHO

A little bird saw Coyote coming. The little bird did not recognize him because his fur was not as it used to be.

Coyote called, "Codi, why are you so frightened?"

But the bird flew a short distance away.

Coyote said again, "Why are you so frightened?"

"Because you are not Codi; you must be someone else."

"I'm Coyote."

"No, your fur is not Codi's."

Every time Coyote approached, the little bird jumped a little ahead or flew a short distance ahead. Coyote kept following behind. He kept on like this. Pretty soon Coyote got out on the plains, away from mountain country. He did not know his way there. He was lost. He had thought this bird was trying to lead him.

At first he said, "I guess this bird wants to show me something." Then he thought, "I guess this bird wants to feed me somewhere.

I guess this bird wants me to come this way." Coyote said things like this. He didn't realize that the bird was afraid of him.

When they got to the plains the bird hung to the end of a bush and Coyote lost sight of him too. Coyote was lost. He didn't know where he had come from. He continued toward the plains country. He finally got to the Navaho country. He had been going west, not east.

He went to a Navaho woman. She was making a blanket. He sat there and watched her. At first this old woman twisted the wool into yarn. Some she made red, some black, and some she left white. Those were the three colors she used. She put the strings through something and pounded it down.

Coyote thought it was easy. He asked her, "What are you making?"

"I'm making a blanket. Some are for covering yourself when you go to sleep; some are for the horse."

Coyote was glad to know that, for Coyote and his family had no blankets. He thought that he would make himself some. When he had made a lot of them, he thought, he would carry them back to his family and surprise his wife.

He watched the Navaho woman for a whole day. Then he asked her, "Where did you get this wool?"

"From the sheep."

"Sheep?" Coyote had no sheep. He had to look for places where the sheep had died and wool was scattered. He remembered places like this which he had passed on the way. So he went over there and picked up the wool.

He went right into the woods. He looked for string and he found wild hops. "Oh, this is lucky!" he said. "Here is plenty of string." Then he looked for the sticks. He twisted the wool and made a large ball of yarn. He started to work, but he didn't know how to start. He just kept trying. He said, "I thought I knew how." He sat and tried to think it out. He tried all the ways he could think of but he couldn't get the blanket started. He sat there trying all morning and all afternoon. So finally he gave up in disgust. He threw the wool away.

That is why when Coyote kills a sheep, he scatters the wool all over. He has no use for it. He never learned to make a blanket.

When the sun went down, Coyote went over to the camps of the Navaho. He went in there and the people took off their moccasins. Coyote took off his moccasins too. They were going to bed.

They told Coyote, "You go over on that side and sleep."

He went over there.

Coyote's moccasins were not good. They were all worn out. The others had fine moccasins. He was jealous and decided to burn their good moccasins.

Coyote said to them, "Your moccasins are getting too hot over there. Put them over here."

The others said, "No, our moccasins are all right. Leave them where they are."

But when Coyote thought they were all asleep he reached over and got the moccasins belonging to one of the Navahos. He drew them near to him and lay down again. He tried to kick them in the fire. But he had become confused now that two pairs of moccasins were in front of him, and he kicked the wrong pair, his own, into the fire. He didn't know this, however. Then he made believe he was fast asleep and snored.

The next morning he got up early, before the morning light, and put on the moccasins that were beside him. They belonged to the other man.

At daybreak the Navaho got up and looked around for his moccasins. Then he saw them on Coyote.

"Coyote, give me back my moccasins," he said.

Coyote had not looked to see what moccasins he had on. Without looking he answered, "No, these are my own moccasins that I have on."

"No, they are mine."

Coyote looked. He saw that he had on the other man's moccasins. He had to take them over and return them.

Coyote sat there. He was angry. He thought he had burned the other man's moccasins. And he was somewhat ashamed of himself too.

He started for home. He had a hard time for he had no moccasins now, and his feet hurt. People he passed laughed at him. He had to go slowly for he stepped on prickers every now and then.

51. WOLF FOOLS COYOTE

Then Coyote went back towards his family. He found Wolf.

Coyote said, "Codi, you must give me something to eat."

The wolf knew all the things Coyote had done. He had heard many times about what a foolish man Coyote was. He didn't want him around.

So Wolf said to his wife, "You must cook something in a hurry for Coyote."

Coyote tried to tell him a long story but Wolf wouldn't listen. "I have work to do somewhere," he said.

Wolf scolded his wife. "Hurry! Give Coyote something to eat quickly," he said.

Coyote asked, "Where are you going? What is your business?"

"Codi, don't talk to me so much. I am thinking of something else."

Wolf's wife cooked something hastily. Before it was well cooked she gave it to Coyote.

Wolf said, "Coyote, hurry and eat. I must be going soon. Someone is coming and wants me to go with him. Hurry! Finish that and leave."

Coyote believed it. He ate as fast as he could and went away.

52. COYOTE AND ROLLING ROCK[1]

Then Coyote came to a rolling rock. It was a round rock up on top of a cliff.

The rock said, "Codi, don't urinate on me."

"I can urinate on anything I want to."

"Codi, be careful. I'll run over you if you do that to me."

Coyote didn't believe it. "How can a rock roll up hill?" he asked.

So he urinated on that rock.

"I don't care if you run after me!" And saying this, Coyote ran straight for the plains. The rock rolled after him.

"Oh, that rock can't climb up hill," Coyote thought. And he started up a hill. The rock rolled up hill easily, however, and was soon at Coyote's heels. It was up to Coyote now. Coyote dodged around, but the rock kept following.

So Coyote headed for the place where he had first seen the rock.

"You stop here," he said. "I'll clean you off."

Then he licked it all off. The rock didn't run after him any more.

53. COYOTE AND THE BEAR CHILDREN

So Coyote went over to the other side of the ridge. There he saw Bear's children. Bear had power. He had cut a log from a tree trunk and had given it to the children to play with. Coyote saw the children roll down the hill on top of the log. Then they all helped carry it up the hill again. Then they rode down on it once more.

Coyote watched for a time. Then he came over.

"Oh, that is a great thing!" he said. "You show me how to do that."

"No, you'll kill yourself. You'd better not try," the little bears said. "Our father gave us this to play with."

"Oh, it's easy. I can learn that," Coyote answered.

The little bears said, "You must not try. You will hurt yourself."

He helped them carry up the log. "Now you children watch me do it by myself," he said.

So he got on. The log rolled slowly at first. When the hill became steep, it started to go faster. Coyote got dizzy then and fell in front of it. The log ran over his legs and body. It hurt him.

The bears ran up. They threw the log to one side and picked him up. He was unconscious and it was a long time before he came to. Then he got up. He began to walk. But he limped because his leg was badly hurt. He limped away.

---

[1] Goddard, p. 234.

54. COYOTE AND THE TALKING TREE

There is a tree far away that whistles when you pass by. The people were talking about this tree, saying, "When you pass this tree it goes, 'Whist!' When you turn around you can't see anything."[1]

Coyote heard the people talking about this. "What are you talking about?" asked Coyote.

They told him they were talking about this tree.

"You tell me what tree this is."

They told him the location of the tree. But Coyote didn't believe it. So the people thought, "This is a funny man." They began to tell him lies. They covered up the real story. They told him, "This is the tree. That is the tree." Coyote hadn't believed the truth but he believed these lies now.

So he went to the trees pointed out. He would stop in front of one and say, "Are you the tree that talks?" He would get no answer. "I guess you don't understand what I say. I heard you were a talking tree," he would say.

He went around like this. He talked to all the trees but they did not answer him. So he gave up finally, for not one answered.

So he started back.

55. COYOTE STEALS SKUNK'S CLOTHES

Coyote came to a hollow log lying on the ground. He saw someone's clothes lying outside it. It was Skunk's clothes. When Skunk had come home he had taken his clothes off. Just as people do, Skunk takes off his coat when he comes home. He thought no one was around.

Coyote thought, "Someone has gone to the toilet and has left these clothes here." He looked and looked around and then took the clothes. He decided to run away with the clothes. He didn't know that the tail which had a hole in it was full of Skunk's water.[2] He had the skin over his shoulders as he walked.

By and by he felt some water on his back. He thought it was a water bag leaking, that the skunk had had a water bag in his pocket. He shook it. More water came down. He looked all over. He could find no water bag. Then he pulled the tail, and the liquid ran out. It had a very bad smell and he threw it away.

The skunk who had lost his coat discovered the theft and was tracking Coyote by now. He came up just as Coyote pulled the tail. The bad smell frightened the coyote and he started off at a run.

---

[1] The Jicarilla talk of a kind of tree like this in Chiricahua country.

[2] The Jicarilla believe that the pungent smelling liquid that the skunk emits is his urine.

56. COYOTE AND THE QUIVER OF BEARSKIN

The coyote had a quiver, but he got tired of it. He saw the bear's fur and he thought that that would make him a better one. So he began to think about how he could kill a bear and get a bearskin.

He had a hard time killing a bear. He brought some arrows from a camp and came back and tried to kill the bear. The first time he only struck the bear a glancing blow, and the bear was warned.

Bear said, "Codi, why do you try to shoot me?"

Coyote said, "I didn't try to shoot you. I was shooting at a chipmunk, but I missed it and my arrow hit you. I didn't know you were there."

Then Coyote went off and scraped his flint arrow point on a rock to sharpen it. He came towards Bear again. He crawled nearer this time and shot. The arrow hit the bear but not hard enough to do much damage. The bow-string was not tight and that is why the arrow did not do much more than penetrate the skin.

The bear was very angry this time. He got after Coyote. "Why did you shoot at me?" he demanded.

"I didn't shoot at you. I was shooting at a little bird, but Wildcat came and pushed my, arm, and that's how it happened."

Coyote went away again and tightened up his bow-string. He crawled toward Bear from a different direction, for Bear was moving around eating berries. He came up to the bear the third time, motioned four times and shot. This time he killed the bear.

He went over and took the skin off. He took home the bear's hide but left it far from his home. His own arrows were hung up in their quiver in the branches of a tree. He had used someone else's arrows. He put the bearskin far from home so his wife wouldn't scold him. He took back those arrows he had used to the person from whom he had borrowed them.

The arrows had a bad odor from Bear,[1] and the man said, "What did you do with my arrows? They smell of bear."

"Well, while I was sleeping Bear came along and slept on these arrows as they lay at my side. That's why they smell that way."

But the man found blood on his arrows and said, "You must have shot a bear."

"No, this bear was wounded and that's why he lay on the arrows. His blood got on the arrows."

But the man wouldn't keep the arrow with the blood on it. He threw it away. But he kept the other one. Coyote had borrowed two arrows.

Coyote went back to take care of the hide. He brought it home. He first went back to get his own arrows. Then he threw away his

[1] The animals of which the Jicarilla have supernatural dread are said to have distinctive, unpleasant odors. The bear is much feared and avoided by the Jicarilla. The skin, odor, tracks, excrement, or even the sight of a bear — any one of these is capable of causing sickness.

old quiver. "It's no good any more," he said. He was going to have a new quiver made.

When he got home with that skin, he told his wife, "Now you sew up a quiver for me."

His wife didn't know Coyote had brought a bear. When she turned and saw what it was she jumped aside.

She said, "I won't do that! We are not allowed to touch bears. You take it far away from this home. The children might touch it."

So he took it far from his home and made the quiver. He sewed it himself. He came back to his home with the quiver. His wife wouldn't let him have it in the house.

"Take this out! I won't have it in this house!" she said.

So he had to take the quiver out.

The next day he went out among the camps with it, but the people were all afraid of him. The people chased him away wherever he went or tried to visit.

He sat down and said, "What's the matter? Everyone is afraid of me."

One woman said, "If you have that bearskin quiver, you have to keep away from my home."

He knew now why they all chased him away. So he threw the quiver of bearskin away and started to look for the one he had thrown away before, the one made of deerskin. But he couldn't remember where he had thrown it and he couldn't find it.

57. COYOTE KILLS DEER WITH HIS CEREMONY

Coyote was on friendly terms with a deer.

But the deer's wife said to him, "Don't go around with this coyote. He will kill you some day."

"No, Coyote is my best friend. How is he going to kill me?"

"All right, you'll see some day whether he is your friend."

Coyote liked to hunt with this deer, for every time he went with the deer, the other deer would come right up. Coyote would sit behind this deer who was his friend and kill the other deer when they approached. He killed a deer every time. This deer acted as a decoy to draw the deer to Coyote. That is why Coyote was such a good friend of his.

One time they went out hunting together. They couldn't find any deer anywhere.

Coyote thought, "Perhaps this deer has told the others not to come near again. Perhaps he has tricked me."

Coyote's family was hungry, so he decided to kill the deer whose friend he pretended to be.

The next time they were out, Coyote said, "You must go ahead of me. Go to that hill. I have something to do before I go. I'll catch up to you."

Coyote turned off and the deer kept going. Then Coyote ran to the other side and crawled near to the deer. He shot his friend. The deer was badly hurt. He started to run back to his home.

Deer got home. He said to his wife, "Pull this arrow out of my body."

They pulled it out. They saw that it was Coyote's arrow. So they sent for Coyote. Deer asked him why he had shot him with his arrow.

Deer asked, "Why did you shoot me? I thought you were my best friend."

Coyote made an excuse. "I didn't mean to shoot you. I thought you were another deer. I was a little afraid to shoot, but I did shoot. But don't be frightened. I'm going to cure you right away."

The female deer said to her husband, "I told you he was going to kill you some day."

Then the deer was taken near to Coyote's home. The deer was very sick and was lying down.

Deer said, "You must cure me in some way."

Coyote said, "Yes, don't be afraid. I can cure you right away."

Coyote's wife was a little deaf. The children were making a noise too. So she couldn't hear Coyote's directions very well. Coyote sang and sang. Then he asked his wife for something. He tried to motion to her to come to him. She didn't see. Then he whistled to his wife, but the children were making so much noise that she didn't hear. Coyote chased the children away.

He sang and sang and then he said, "Give me the medicine, my wife."

He had two different things which he called medicine, one that would cure, and one that was an arrow poison.

He said, "Give me the medicine." Then in a low voice, "That arrow poison, I mean."

But Coyote's wife didn't hear and asked, "What did you say?"

So Coyote said in a loud voice, "That medicine for arrow wounds."

But the deer and his wife had heard what he said the first time. The female deer was very much frightened.

"Don't eat what Coyote gives you," she told her husband. "I heard him ask for arrow poison."

"No," said Coyote, "I asked for the medicine that cures."

Then the coyote woman picked up the poison and handed it to Coyote.

Coyote sang and sang. He said, "My power tells me that Deer will get better about the middle of this night. The voice tells me to give this medicine. It is not a poison."

He rubbed it on the wound. It began to pain the deer.

Coyote said, "That's all right. Just lie down. A good medicine always gives you a pain at first."

At about the middle of the night the deer was dead.

Coyote said, "He is sleeping."

Deer's wife came and looked at him. She knew he was dead.

The next day the deer's family moved camp.

Coyote said, "I'll take care of this dead body."

As soon as the deer's wife and family were gone, Coyote started to butcher the body instead of burying it as he had said he would. Coyote's wife jerked the meat. They all got busy.

58. COYOTE AND THE EXPANDING MEAT

All the meat was dried now and Coyote packed it up. He moved his camp. His wife was carrying this bundle of meat right on her back. The woman heard something moving in that pack.

She said to her husband, "My husband, something is moving in this pack. It is just as if something alive is in there."

Coyote said, "It's because I know how to make a ceremony over deer. I guess we are going to have more meat. That's why you hear that noise. You must not open the bundle wide or some of the meat might jump out.

They built a home at another place.

"Now don't open this package wide or the meat will expand," Coyote warned.

So his wife opened the pack just a little and picked out a piece just large enough for a meal.

But Coyote forgot his own directions and opened up the bundle wide, and the meat spread out all over. It swelled up. He couldn't push it back into the parfleche. He tried to push it back, but it kept growing.

He called to his wife, "Why do you stand there? Why don't you help me push it back?"

Even when all the children tried to help, they couldn't push it back.

After a while Coyote was tired and angry. "You can expand as long as you like!" he said. "I don't care."

The meat grew and grew till he couldn't see the end. That's the way Coyote lost the meat. They ate just a little and then they gave up. They couldn't handle the meat and so they went away.

59. COYOTE AND YELLOW JACKET

One time Yellow Jacket was coming along carrying his children in a bag. Coyote met him.

"Codi, what are you carrying in that bag?" Coyote asked.

"I carry my children in there."

"No, that can't be true. I never carry my children that way. You must have something else."

"No, I am carrying my children. Come close and you can hear them."

Coyote still insisted that Yellow Jacket did not have his children in the bag. He kept asking what was in it.

Yellow Jacket then said, "I'll tell you. The people have had a feast over there and they gave me fruit of all kinds to carry home. This is the fruit."

"See, I said it was something good!" Coyote said. "I'll help you carry it." He wanted some of the fruit too.

Yellow Jacket got tired. He said, "All right," and he handed Coyote the package.

Coyote told him, "I'll go ahead. You rest and when you want to, you can catch up to me."

Coyote went ahead. He looked back. Yellow Jacket was still sitting there. So Coyote ran off to the side and made straight for his home with the bundle. He thought he was bringing his children something good to eat.

The yellow jacket rested and then came on. He couldn't find Coyote.

Coyote got home with his bag. He called his children. "Now all gather around. We are going to have a feast on something good."

The children were very eager to eat. They gathered around and his wife came close too.

Coyote put in his hand. One wasp stung his hand.

Coyote said, "I must have laid this bag on a thorn. One pierced my hand."

He still didn't know what was in there. He put in his hand again and another one stung him harder. This time he pulled his hand out so fast that the bag broke and the yellow jackets flew out. They attacked the whole family. The children ran to the bushes and so did Coyote and his wife, but the yellow jackets got in their fur and kept on stinging them.

After a while the yellow jackets flew away, for they heard their mother calling them.

Then Coyote and his family gathered together. Their faces were all swollen. Coyote couldn't see. His eyes were swollen shut.

60. COYOTE AND DOG ARGUE

One time Coyote and Dog barked at each other.

Dog said to Coyote, "Don't come around here near my people. Every time you get near you do some trick to my people."

"How do you know I trick them? These people are all my friends. They are just like my own people."

The dog said, "No, one time these people were without dogs for a long time. At night they had no way of knowing who was coming or what was happening. That was your fault. They said you were a good friend. So we dogs got angry and went away and were wild for a long time. Then the people missed the dogs. After a long time they found some little puppies in the woods. They took them home and raised them. Since then they have kept them and raised them."

"Don't try to lie about me," said Coyote. "Don't tell me that these people are against me or that they speak badly of me. I always have been a friend of these people. You are the one that does wrong. When visitors come you bark and bite. That is why they chase you away. That's what you are talking about. I never bite the Indians. I always try to help these people and be good to them."

"Why, you big liar!" said the dog.

Coyote said, "You're a big liar!"

The female dog came over. "What are you fellows talking about?" she asked. She scolded the male dog. "Get away from that coyote. He's a sorcerer.[1] Don't speak such words to him!" She made Dog get away from that coyote.

61. COYOTE KILLS HIS WIFE AND CARRIES HER BODY

Coyote was going along and met Robber Fly. Coyote noticed the hump on his back.

He said, "Codi, what are you carrying on your back?"

"Why that's the way my back is. I have a hump there."

"Codi, you must not tell lies. You must be carrying something there." Coyote didn't believe that he had been told the truth. He kept insisting, "You must have something there."

So the insect finally said, "That's my wife. She died a long time ago. I don't want to throw her away because I love her so much."

"See, I told you that you were carrying something there!"

Coyote believed it. He started home. When he got there, he fell against the scraping pole and pushed it against his wife. He did this on purpose. In that way he knocked her down and killed her.

He told his children, "You have to go away and not come back."

They all went out.

Then he put the body in the bag and carried it. He went out when the sun was hot and the body began to have a bad smell.

The people where he went asked, "What have you got on your back?"

"I have nothing there. That's the way my back is."

No one would believe him. After about three days the body began to have such a bad odor that wherever Coyote went the people said, "You smell bad; you must be carrying something dead."

"No," answered Coyote, "that's just the way my back is."

Finally he said, "That's my wife. She's dead, and I didn't want to throw her away, so I carry her on my back like this."

---

[1] To anger one suspected of practicing sorcery is most dangerous, since it may induce him to use his evil power on you.

They all chased him then. "Get away from these camps with that dead person!" they cried.

Coyote carried the bag for a little longer. Then he got tired of it and threw it away.

62. COYOTE DIVES AFTER THE MOON'S IMAGE

Coyote was going along at night. It was the time of a full moon. He was going to cross some water. He didn't know the reflection of the moon was on the water. He passed over. He turned around and saw something yellow in the water. He thought of a stone about which he had often heard.

He thought, "That must be the 'yellow bead' about which the people are always talking.[1] They say it is very valuable. Someone must have lost it. I'll get it and wear it."

He jumped in the water. He put his hand down but couldn't feel anything.

"I must have the wrong place."

He came out and sat on the edge. He marked the place with his eye carefully. Then he dove and tried to find it. He stayed under a long time. He couldn't find it. He felt a stone. He picked it up and arose with it. He looked at it. It was a common stone, and the one he had gone after was still in the water.

He went away and returned with a stick. He put the stick down at the right spot and reached down with the other hand to be sure he wouldn't miss it. But he couldn't find anything. He kept this up with first one hand and then the other till his hands were cold. Then he gave up.

63. COYOTE GETS DRUNK[2]

This is a story about a house dog and Coyote. This dog always stayed in the house. Once he went out in the yard and saw Coyote there. They barked at each other.

Coyote said, "You mean fellow! Why don't you invite me in and give me something to eat. You're too fat. Here I am, thin and hungry, and you don't feel sorry for me."

"I never see you near, so how can I feed you? You can come over tonight. They have a dance hall in town. My master is going to the dance tonight, so you can come over and we'll both have a good time too."

---

[1] The confusion depends upon the similarity of the Apache words for "big bead" and "yellow bead," *yutso* and *yutsoi* respectively. The word *yutso*, "big bead," is the name given to a sea shell used by the Jicarilla in the girl's puberty rite and other ceremonies. Coyote, who has never seen the shell, has misheard the word and taken its name to mean "yellow bead." The moon's reflection must be this "yellow bead," he thinks.

[2] Goddard, p. 236.

Coyote said, "All right."

He went away till night. Then he came back.

The dog was looking for his friend. He told him to come in. They stayed there.

The dog said, "My master with his wife and family have gone to the dance. I am staying by myself. Instead of giving you something to eat, I'll give you something to drink."

"What is it?"

"I'll show you what it is."

He opened a drawer. He took out a pint bottle. He filled a glass and handed it to Coyote. The dog had another glass, but he put tea in it from another bottle. It was tea that the children had been playing with. The coyote thought they were both drinking the same thing. But the dog drank nothing but tea.

After finishing the bottle the coyote felt good.

"I feel that I must sing and yell." he said.

"No, please don't do that. You'll get me in trouble. They will get after me and chase you away, for coyotes are not allowed to yell around here."

But Coyote talked in a loud voice and said, "I must yell!"

Dog pleaded with him not to do it. "They will all be after you and they'll chase you and kill you or put you in jail."

But Coyote yelled anyway. He couldn't help it.

They all heard him and came after him. They caught him and killed him.

64. COYOTE AND THE BADLY-TREATED DOG[1]

Coyote found a dog. The dog's master had gone away to town, and so Coyote approached. He saw that the poor dog was lying down almost dead. Coyote was very sorry for the dog.

He said, "Say, my friend, what is the matter? You're too thin. Why is that?"

"Oh, my master hates me. He doesn't feed me anything."

Coyote said, "I'll help you some way. It must be that you have not proved of use to your master and that's why they treat you that way."

The dog said, "All right, if you want to help me, that will be fine. Show me what to do."

Coyote said, "Where are the chickens kept?"

"In the yard on the other side of the barn. They are loose there, and they scratch for the worms."

"You must be there. You must watch them. I'll come around and make off with a hen. Then you must come over there when the chicken screams and try to save the chicken and chase me away. After that your master will be proud of you and will feed you."

[1] Goddard, p. 236.

"I guess that's a good idea. Let's do that."

The sun went down. The dog's master came back from the town. The next day the chickens were let loose. They were looking for worms. The dog lay in the shade watching the chicken yard. The master was working in the garden nearby.

The master heard the chickens screaming in a little while. Coyote had caught a hen. The dog started to bark and ran after Coyote. The dog caught Coyote and took the hen away. Coyote had not bitten the hen very badly. Then Coyote and the dog made believe they were fighting, and finally Coyote acted as though he were driven away and ran off. The master saw all this.

"That is a good dog after all," he said.

He went home and said to his wife, "You must feed that dog. He is a good dog and just saved a hen for us and drove off a coyote."

After that the dog was well treated.

One time the master went to town again. The coyote came again. He said, "My friend, you look different now. You are well fed and well cared for."

"It is because of you," the dog answered.

65. COYOTE IMITATES MOUNTAIN-LION

Coyote saw a rock rolling down a hill. It rolled toward some deer. Coyote wondered who had rolled that stone down. He looked up. Then another stone came rolling down toward the deer. The deer ran both times. Then a third stone rolled down, but this time the deer were not afraid and paid no attention to it. They knew it was just another stone.

The next moment Coyote saw another stone rolling. But this was a soft rock. It was Mountain-lion who had rolled himself up like a ball and was rolling down the hill.

"What a funny rock!" thought Coyote. "It doesn't make a noise."

Rolled up like this, Mountain-lion came close to the deer, who were not suspicious by this time. Then Coyote saw the mountain-lion get up, leap at a big deer, and kill it. The mountain-lion picked up the whole deer and carried it right on his back. He carried it to a cliff and ate it there. The rest of the deer ran to the other side of the hill.

Coyote thought, "That's a good idea. I'll get a deer that way too."

He rolled a stone down the hill. The deer ran off. Coyote did this three times, and each time the deer grew less suspicious. Then Coyote thought it was time for him to get one, so he rolled himself up just as the mountain-lion had done and rolled down.

He rolled to the bottom of the hill, jumped up, and tried to leap at a deer that was near him. But he was dizzy and missed, and all the deer ran off unharmed.

66. COYOTE AND KILLER-OF-ENEMIES

Killer-of-Enemies had killed all the monsters on the earth. He came back to the people and talked to them. He told them how to pray and conduct ceremonies and how to live. Coyote was there. He heard it. He heard Killer-of-Enemies teaching these people. Killer-of-Enemies wanted them to know all of it well, for he was not going to stay there longer.[1]

But Coyote continued to make fun of what was said.

Killer-of-Enemies said, "Codi, you must believe it. This is not just fun. This is not play."

Coyote thought, "This is just a man; he has no power. He cannot do anything."

Killer-of-Enemies told him, "You must not think that way. You must behave yourself."

But Coyote didn't care; he acted like a naughty child.

So Killer-of-Enemies went to him and said, "All right, Codi, if you can't get along with me, go your way. But do not get in my way. Do not stay where I'm teaching."

Coyote continued to disobey.

"All right," said Killer-of-Enemies, "I shall take away all of the power you have." He took away Coyote's power. He said, "After this you must stay away from the people. When you want food you are going to have a hard time."

Coyote said, "All right. After this whoever sits where I have sat will become crooked in the body. These people are not supposed to touch my fur. Whenever they touch it they will go mad."

"I don't like that," said Killer-of-Enemies. "Be quiet! Go on your way!"

"All right, these two things will be my evil way, but there are songs and a plant which will cure these things."

Killer-of-Enemies said, "All right, sing your song."

Coyote sang the song. He said, "If someone is sick he must send for one who knows this song and then he will get better. And here is the plant too. Burn it for the sick one and let him smell it."

Then Coyote went away from the people. Since that the people have been afraid of Coyote.[2]

B. COYOTE AND THE TWO RUNNING ROCKS

When the people had just come up on this earth there were two rocks which were very kind and helped the people. They went

---

[1] Cf. the version of this episode in the origin myth, p. 78.

[2] At the conclusion of the coyote cycle the informant said, "I have heard a story which tells how Coyote let the light out of a bag someone was carrying, but I don't know who had the bag; I've forgotten."

A coyote tale not told to me was recorded by Dr. Harry Hoijer. It recounts how Coyote, while crossing a bridge with a piece of meat in his mouth, mistook his reflection for another coyote. He tried to obtain the other animal's meat and dropped and lost his own.

around the world with the people. If you asked them to kill a deer for you or to run over a buffalo's leg, they would do it for you. But then Coyote put his excrement on them and angered them. It happened this way.

Coyote never did anything very good. He went over to the running rocks.

The rocks said, "Coyote, get away from us. You are foolish."

"You pretty rocks! Why should I not come around you?" He circled and came around.

"Coyote, get away. You are ignorant."

But Coyote didn't pay any attention. He came nearer. Suddenly he jumped over them and defecated on the rocks.

Then Coyote started to run around the world. He ran to the north. The rocks followed him. He pleaded with the rocks to stop.

"Friend," he said, "stop and I'll clean it off with my tongue."

He was just pleading with the rocks to stop so he could get away. Coyote started to run to the center of the world. The rocks rolled on top of Coyote and flattened him.

Those rocks are over near Taos still. There is a black mark on them even now where Coyote defecated on them. The center of the world is very near Taos, about three miles east of the Pueblo. That is where the rock is. Both rocks chased Coyote. They are joined together now. The story says they are tied together, but when I saw them they were joined together.

The heart of the world is also near Taos Pueblo. Some time, at the end of the world, that place will start to burn. The fire will spread to all the world.

The running rocks had been around the world before Coyote defecated on them. After that they would not help the people.

C. COYOTE AND BEAR[1]

The little children were playing in an arroyo. One little girl dug into the bank. She dug out a big hole, big enough for her to get in and stay in.

Then she came out. She said, "Let's play bear. I'm a bear."

The children liked the new game. They thought it was great fun. They played this way for a while. The children would run to the hole and say, "Where's the bear?" The little girl would run out at them, and they would retreat, laughing.

The little girl who was acting the part of the bear said to them finally, "I know that you aren't afraid of me. But I'm sure that I'm turning to a bear."[2]

---

[1] This story has been recorded by Goddard (p. 203) with Killer-of-Enemies as the hero. In a version recorded by Russell (p. 262) Fox (probably Coyote) figures as the slayer of the bear.

[2] Cf. p. 113.

She went into the cave again. She came out. Her feet and hands had sprouted fur. She chased the children away. She went in the hole again. When she ran out this time she was furry to her knees, and her arms were furry to the elbows. She ran in again. As she came running out the third time, her body was all covered with fur, but her face was still human.

The children thought she was just fooling them and doing this for a joke. They continued to play.

The fourth time the girl ran out, her face too had changed. She started to run after the children. She killed many of them.

Her sister, when the girl had come out for the second time, realized that something was wrong. She knew the girl was not as before.

She ran home and told her parents, "My older sister is changing to a bear! Her feet and hands have already become furry like those of a bear."

The older people came running to see. When they saw Bear Girl they too were frightened and all ran away.

The bear girl killed many men and women as well as children. She became very mean. She went to the east. She went all over the world. She took her heart out when she was somewhere on the present Navaho Reservation.[1] She buried it under some oak leaves.

In those days Coyote had bows and arrows, for he had taken them away from Owl.[2] Coyote also had a war-club made of wood.

Coyote came to visit at the Indian camps. The people begged him to help them and told him what was wrong. They gave Coyote food and Coyote ate. Then the people saw that Bear was coming to the camps. They were frightened and pleaded with Coyote to help them.

Coyote paid no attention to the approaching bear. "Let her come," he said to the people. "I'll take care of her."

He gave his arrows to the people, saying, "Hold these arrows for me."

He started to go to the north. He knew where the heart was, because a little mouse had found that heart and had told him.

Coyote had come upon that mouse once when he was hungry. He had caught the mouse and was about to eat it. Mouse called out, "Don't kill me! Spare me and I'll tell you some great news." Then the mouse told about the heart.

Coyote asked the mouse, "At what place did you find it?"

The little mouse named the place. The mouse said, "When I came near the place where the heart is, when I got near to it, the bear was after me. So I ran away from the bear. That's why I've come to tell you."

---

1 In Goddard's version the location of the heart is given as Navaho country also.

2 See p. 289.

Coyote approached the place. He saw the leaves move. The heart was pulsating. The leaves were going, "Sha, sha, sha, sha!" Coyote went around that place in a clockwise circle beginning with the east. He motioned four times when he was once more standing in the east, and then he started to hit that heart. He had a hard time with it. Every time he would hit it, it would jump around like a ball. He hit it about six times.

By that time the bear felt what was happening and came running to the place. The bear was nearly there when Coyote hit it for the twelfth time with his club and then he killed the heart. At that instant the approaching bear, too, fell dead.

Before this the people had tried in vain to kill the bear with arrows, for the bear was without a heart in her body.

Then Coyote cut the heart into pieces with his flint knife and threw them in the air in all directions. He said, "After this you will not be a monster."

That night, when Coyote was asleep, the bear came after him in a dream. "Why did you kill me?" it asked.

Coyote said, "Because I feel sorry for the Indians. If I hadn't killed you, perhaps you would have killed me too. Therefore I destroyed you."

Bear said, "I shall not die forever because of this. Where the wind blows my fur, other bears will come to life."[1]

After killing the bear Coyote went to get his arrows from the people. He said to them, "Why don't you be brave and be a man like me? I killed that bear."[2]

The people were all happy again. Whenever Coyote came around their camps they gave him food. The people treated him well after that.

They call Coyote *codi* in this story, but it is not one of the cycle. Coyote cut the heart in pieces. This is why the bear is not so mean as it used to be before this.

D. ANTELOPE STORIES

1. THE RACE BETWEEN ANTELOPE AND WHITETAILED DEER.

The antelope came around and said to the whitetail, "What's the matter? You don't run fast."

The deer said, "Don't speak that way to me. I'm a good runner."

The antelope kept saying over and over, "You are not a good runner. Let's race and see."

---

[1] The continued existence of animals of evil omen is explained by saying that whenever they are killed they come to life again in any locality to which their fur is blown.

[2] This story is unusual since Coyote seems entirely out of character in it. Hitherto, even when he has succeeded, as when he obtained fire, it has been by stealth and deceit.

The whitetail said finally, "All right, I'll race you and I'll choose the end of the race track myself. I will let you know where it is."

The antelope agreed. "All right. Let's each bet something against the other before we race. Let us bet our fat against each other. And let us also bet our dew-claws. And we'll bet the hollows under our eyes." So they bet.

The whitetail said, "I'll choose the place, and it will be the end of the race track."

So they went off. They went to the top of a big mountain, to the steepest place. They agreed to race down the mountain side, through the brush and the rocks where it was hard to run.

Antelope asked, "How shall we start?"

Whitetail answered, "Let us count to four and then run."

After that the people, when they raced, always counted to four and then started.

Whitetail began to count. "Now look out," he said and began, "One, two, three, four!" he said. And at four they started to run down the mountain.

The whitetail jumped over all the small brush and oak trees. The antelope tried to run where there were no bushes. The antelope lost the race. He fell far behind. Even though he was a fast runner, he lost.

He had to pay the winner. He turned over all that he lost. He gave Whitetail his fat, his dew-claws, and the hollows under his eyes. That is why he does not have the dew-claw. He lost it then. All the other animals have it. He alone does not. And he has no hollows under his eyes now. It is smooth there.

The whitetail felt sorry for the antelope. He said to the antelope, "Oh, you poor thing! I'll give you back half of this fat. I don't want you to be so thin."

He gave back half of the fat, gave him fat around the stomach. And that is why, when you play a game with a man and win everything from him, you often feel sorry for him and give him back something which you have won. And this is why the antelopes, even in summer when they eat good grass, do not get fat. They just get fat in the stomach. The rest they had to turn over to the whitetailed deer.

2. THE RACE BETWEEN ANTELOPE AND FROG[1]

Sometime after the race with Whitetail the antelope was going around. He came down to the water to drink. There he saw Frog sitting.

He said to him, "You can't run fast. What is the matter with you that you go so slowly?"

---

[1] Cf. Goddard, p. 237.

The frog answered back, "Don't speak to me like that. I'm a fast runner. Don't say it again, for I am very speedy."

The antelope said again, "You're the kind of a fellow who never will run fast. You just hop around."

Again the frog said, "You have told me enough. I tell you I am a fast runner."

The antelope liked moss very much. It was just like salt to him. He said, "I like this moss very much. It is my food. You like it very much also. It is your food too. Let us race and bet this moss against each other. If you win, I won't eat this moss any more."

The antelope showed what a fast runner he was. He ran and jumped and showed off in general. While he was doing this Frog said to a number of other frogs, "Now let us help one another and beat that fellow."

The frogs arranged themselves in a line along the track.

To the last one, the one nearest the finish line, the first frog said, "When the antelope comes up say to him, 'I told you I'm a good runner and you wouldn't believe it. Now here I have beaten you.'"

This frog said he would repeat these words and took his place by the finish line.

The frog said, "We'll race over to my house. Now stand beside me."

The antelope looked at him and said, "Do you think you can hop that far?"

Frog replied, "You'll have to be a fast runner to beat me. I'll beat you anyway." Then Frog said, "I'll say one more thing to you. It is about water. What do you say to this: If I beat you, you will have a hard time to get water and you will get water only once in three or four days. Will you agree to that?"

The antelope said, "All right. I know you. You can't win."

The antelope then spoke to the frog and said, "If I beat you, you have to get up out of this water and go into the desert where there is no water at all. You will be thirsty there, yet you will have to wait for a storm and rain. You will not be able to eat moss any more."

"All right," said the frog.

Now everything was agreed upon.

The antelope said, "Who will be the one to count?"

"You," said the frog, "for you are the one who asked me to race."

The antelope counted to four. They both started.

All the frogs began to jump in the same direction at the same time. It was just like a string being pulled.

The antelope ran with all his might. But he lost. When he got to the finish the frog who was there said, "I told you I am a fast runner. Now you see how I have beaten you."

After that the antelope never touched the moss. He has to go out and stay away from water for several days.

3. ANTELOPE AND HORNED TOAD

The antelope was walking around. He found the horned toad.

He said to Horned Toad, "I guess you are one who runs fast too."

Horned Toad said, "I'm the fastest runner in the whole world."

The antelope asked the horned toad for power to make him a good runner. "If you are a good runner give me power that will make me a fast runner."

The horned toad said, "If you want to be a fast runner, rub my legs, all four of them, and rub your hands over yourself. Then go back to the one who beat you and race with him again."

The antelope then told the story of what had happened to him. He said, "If I rub your leg you must listen to what I say. I went to Whitetail. I thought I was a good runner, but he beat me by a good deal. He took me on top of the mountain and beat me down to the bottom."

Horned Toad said, "You are very foolish and ignorant. The whitetail is the best runner in the whole world."

"When I lost that race, I walked out and met Frog. He beat me too. I guess you are just like the Frog People. I guess you are a good runner just as they are."

"No, I am better than those two. I am the best runner in the whole world."

The antelope said, "You must teach me in some way and give me some power so that I can go back and win what I lost. I lost my fat, my dew-claws, the hollows under my eyes, and the moss and water."

The horned toad asked, "Do you know the names of all these plants? I know the medicines. I know the one which will make you run fast. You must come to see me at a place to the east. There is a mountain there called Standing Mountain. That is the place where I live. I'll get a certain plant, the small sunflower.[1] That is the medicine I'm going to get for you. In four days I'll have it at my home. Come to see me early the fourth day."

The horned toad had the medicine ready to give Antelope on the appointed day, but the antelope did not come. The day after that Horned Toad kept one of the plants for Antelope and took the others and put them back in the holes. Two days after that, on the sixth day, Antelope came.

Antelope said, "I was far away. That is why I couldn't get here the day you wanted me to come."

"This plant is all you will get now," said Horned Toad. "I guess you don't want to run fast; that must be why you came late. But you can take this one plant anyway."

The antelope put the plant in his mouth and swallowed it.

---

[1] The small sunflower is used to impart speed to the boys who run in the ceremonial race which now takes place on September 15. See pp. 80—86 for an account of this race.

The horned toad asked, "Did you swallow it?"

"Yes."

"Let me look in your mouth." He looked in Antelope's mouth and didn't find the plant so he knew that Antelope had swallowed it. Then the horned toad said to the antelope, "Now you must just walk around for about two months. When the time comes you go to see the swallow. This bird always flies above the earth. Try a race with him. Let's see whether he can beat you. And race with the night-hawk too. They fly close to the earth at sundown. Run a race with them and see whether they are going to beat you."

The time came. Antelope was on a level place that was good for a race track. He watched the swallow flying. When the swallow came by, he started to race with it. Antelope won.

The next day he went out to that same level place and waited for the night-hawk. He started to race with the night-hawk and he won that race too.

After beating these two he went back to tell the horned toad what he had done. "I won from those two whom you told me to race."

"Well, now go back and race with those who beat you before. But I want first to see how fast you really can run, so I'm going to call another fellow, Fox, because he is the one who is the leader of running for the whole world. I want you to race with him."

Three days passed. Antelope was practicing at a level place. Coyote came along.

Coyote asked, "What are you doing around here in the plains?"

"I'm practicing. Tomorrow I'm running a race against Fox."

Coyote said, "You had better not run against Fox. I'll take your place and run for you, because I'm the best runner."

Antelope said, "No, I'm going to run myself. I want to see how fast I can run. One time I lost all I had, and I want to win those things back."

Coyote asked, "Where is the race track going to be made?"

Antelope said, "At the mountain ("Mountain Leaning Toward") which stands to the east."

Coyote said, "I'll go up there and watch. If you are losing, I'll help you out."

Coyote went away. Antelope stayed there over night. The next day at daylight Antelope went to the place where the race was to be held and saw that Coyote was already there.

The door of Horned Toad's home was to the east. He came around to the east and saw Fox already there. When he saw Fox, Antelope's heart was filled with fear. Antelope stopped at the door of the horned toad's home. Horned Toad came out.

"Are you here?"

"I am here."

"That is the one you are going to race. You must go to the level place about a mile away."

Old Man Horned Toad picked up some grass and weeds and laid them down, one bunch on one side, one on the other. "Between these is the finish line. You must run through here. Now go back a mile and run to this line."

So the two racers went out for about a mile. Coyote was sitting there watching. He was eager to run, but he had to watch and see who would win. He wanted to challenge the winner.

The race began. All that the people could see was dust. They could hardly distinguish the bodies of the runners. Those two crossed the line at exactly the same time. It was even; neither won.

The horned toad said to Antelope, "You must race once more, for you have raced three times without winning."

The coyote jumped up and asked permission to race. "Oh, Grandfather," he said, "let me run with him."

Horned Toad asked, "Can you run fast?"

"Yes, I'm a good runner, better then these two fellows."

Permission was granted. They went back to the start again. Coyote was hard to see for his color was grey.

The race started. The dust arose. The three of them were running, for Fox was in the race again too. It was hard to see their bodies.

In just a little while they passed the finish line. Fox won, but just by the length of his head. Coyote was about two hundred yards behind the other two. They all came together.

Coyote said to Horned Toad, "Grandfather, give me some medicine. Make me a good runner. I know you gave something to these two fellows. That is why they ran such a good race for you."

"No, you must just practice by yourself. Practice hard for two months and then you will be just like these fellows. I have no medicine for the race."

The horned toad spoke to Fox. "In two days come back again. You, too, Antelope. You fellows must have another race."

Coyote said to Horned Toad, "Grandfather, shall I come back too?"

"All right, you may come back. But I'll bring another fellow to race with you."

"Who is he?"

"Oh, when you come, you will see him."

Coyote asked, "At what time shall I come, noon or morning?"

"In the morning when it is still cold."

The antelope was very eager to run. He practiced and felt fine.

Coyote also practiced day and night. Coyote, though Horned Toad had not given him permission to do so, told all the people he met about the race and invited all the people to watch it.

The time for the race came. Early in the morning, at daybreak, Coyote came to see Antelope.

"I'm very fleet now. I'm eager to run," he said. "How long before you are going?"

"I'm going right away."

The antelope started out. He walked ahead. The coyote came behind. They came to the race track. When they got there they came around the mountain clockwise to Horned Toad's home. Fox was already there and on the race track. Horned Toad came out again.

"Did you come ?" he asked.

"Yes, I'm here."

"This time you must go out about twice as far."

Coyote was standing there. He said to Horned Toad, though no one asked him, "I came too."

"You sit down for a while. These two are going to run. You'll be next."

The racers went back about two miles. They could hardly be seen. The people watched. First all they could see was dust. In a few moments the two passed the line. They passed at the same time. They were equally fast.

"You'll have to race again."

They went back again. Again the dust rose. Then they passed the line. Again it was a tie.

Horned Toad told them, "Both of you sit down and rest a while. Watch while two others race. Coyote is going to race."

He called out Cottontail Rabbit and told him where to race Coyote. They were going to race only a very short distance, about twenty-five paces.

"You two must start to run at the same time," they were told.

Horned Toad said to Coyote, "Run with all your might, for you say you are the best runner. But I know that Cottontail is the best one."

Coyote said, "I'm going to beat that rabbit by five paces."

The two went out twenty-five paces.

"Who is going to count for us ?" asked the rabbit.

Coyote said to Horned Toad, "You count for us."

Horned Toad counted, "One, two, three, four," and clapped his hands, and they both started.

The coyote lost. Cottontail won by the length of Coyote's body.

Coyote said, "What is the matter with me ? I thought I was the best runner, but here I have lost. I must have swallowed something in my water, for I am very careless. Even if the water is running with all kinds of dirt in it, I swallow it. That's why I don't run fast."

Horned Toad spoke to Coyote, "Go home. Some day when you are to run a race with some fellow again, I'll call you."

He just wanted to get rid of Coyote so he could say something to the other two fellows which he didn't want Coyote to hear.

The coyote went off. The two other racers were called up.

Horned Toad spoke to the antelope. "You are improving now. Before this you lost, Antelope, but now you have not lost. Yet Fox is still the fastest runner at more than two miles' distance. For he is the best runner all around the whole world. He is even faster than the fastest bird."[1]

Coyote went all over the country. He told the people, "One of these days I'm going to be called and I'll race." It wasn't true but he spread the news all over.

Jack-rabbit heard that Coyote was going to race. He said, "I never heard that Coyote was a good runner. Let me run against him."

So they went out to a level place. All gathered round to see these two race. It was a race of about two hundred paces. The coyote lost again. He lost by about five paces.

The race against Fox was the last time the antelope tried. But the antelope was more eager to run now than before, for now his grandfather, Horned Toad, was helping him to be a faster runner.

The first time, when the birds and animals were racing around the earth, Fox ran with the fastest. Now the antelope is just like Fox at a shorter distance, but after two miles the antelope gets behind.

E. STORY OF PHOEBE

There were many people camped together. The men brought in elk, and all these people said, "They are bringing in elk."

This bird was hopping around the edge of the camps. "I'm going to use that name," he said. "After this I'll be known by that name."[2]

This bird was very spiteful. He was fighting all the time. Wherever he went, when he saw another bird's nest, he broke it up and destroyed the eggs just for spite. Sometimes there were little birds in the nest just about ready to begin to fly. This phoebe would break open the little birds' heads, destroying the brain and killing them.

He was malicious not only to the birds but even to the cottontail rabbit and the chipmunk. When he found their young, he would break open their heads also.

He continued doing this, killing all the young of the little creatures. He made this his business every day and did nothing else.

One time he went to the woodpecker's nest and killed six of the woodpecker's young. Woodpecker didn't know who did it; he found the children dead when he got back. He had been out looking for worms and had not seen it happen.

The chickadee came to the woodpecker and told him, "You must come over here where the people are having a meeting, for many people have lost their children, and they must find out who is doing this."

All the little animals and birds gathered around and held council. The little birds were there, and each stepped out and told how many children he had lost and how they had been treated.

[1] The reference is to Fox's part in the race around the world, p. 269.

[2] Phoebe's name is "He Carries Elk."

Then Pygmy Nuthatch stepped out and said, "I know who did it. It is Phoebe. I saw him killing the woodpecker's children."

The people talked among themselves. They asked whether anyone else had seen Phoebe at his work. Then Goldfinch came out and said, "I saw him do it once. I saw him kill two little rabbits."

Another bird came up, a small bird, like Nuthatch, but with a little longer tail. This bird said, "One time I saw him kill Magpie's children."

Now Black Tree Squirrel spoke, "I was busy eating nuts in a tree. Below I saw that bird destroy a nest."

That made four people who had seen what Phoebe had done.

All the people complained of how many children they had lost. Over five hundred children had been destroyed by this bird. Then all the people who had lost children were very angry. One said, "Promise me his body!" Another said, "Promise me his head."

Say's Phoebe, who was a friend and partner of Phoebe, heard all this and listened closely to what the people said. The people did not know that Say's Phoebe was Phoebe's friend. The people who had lost children were much aroused.

Say's Phoebe hurried away as soon as the meeting was ended. He told his friend, "Tomorrow all the people are going to form a circle around this mountain and advance to the top. They are going to get rid of you. Before they come you had better hurry to another mountain to the east, to Black Mountain. Come back in eight days, and I'll tell you what to do."

Phoebe had been staying on a mountain at the center of the world called First Mountain. The next morning, before daybreak, Phoebe left his home. Soon after all the birds and animals circled around the place and searched over the whole mountain. They looked among the rocks, in the grass, the holes. They searched everywhere till they reached the top of the mountain. The mountain was covered by people searching for Phoebe, all the way to the top.

Say's Phoebe was the only one they found. He was on top of the mountain. "Did you see Phoebe?" they asked him.

"No, I never knew the one of whom you speak. He never came to see me. I don't know who he is."

The people searched once more. They looked in every hole and in all the hollow trees. They searched all the way down to the bottom again. Then they went away.

Crossbill came up to Say's Phoebe then, and Say's Phoebe told him what he had done. He said, "These people tried to kill my friend, but I warned him and sent him to another mountain. In eight days he's coming back."

But Crossbill was opposed to Phoebe too. He went at once among the people and told what Say's Phoebe had said. Crossbill had once had a fight with Phoebe and that was why he was opposed to him.

Say's Phoebe heard that this bird was informing the others of what he had done. He was frightened himself now. He went to Black Mountain. He told Phoebe, "You had better go to Blue Mountain to the south. I'll go with you, too, for the people know what I have done."

Meanwhile all the people, the good runners first, circled quickly around Black Mountain, the mountain to the east. Now the people were against Say's Phoebe too, because he had two faces. They searched on both these mountains. They searched for two days, but they found nothing and had to go back.

Myrtle Warbler heard the two fugitives. They were sitting on the top of Blue Mountain and laughing. Phoebe was saying, "I killed all those children, but these people will never find me. They think I am in the east."

There was another bad-tempered bird, Pine Siskin. He sent a message to these two birds. "Tomorrow the people are going to surround you and destroy you." He went there and said, "Tomorrow they are going to catch you and kill you before a great crowd."

Both of them were frightened. They flew to the west, to Yellow Mountain. They sat on top of that yellow mountain and said, "No one will ever catch us. This world is large."

But another bird, Goldfinch, heard them.

Meanwhile the people had circled around Blue Mountain and could not find them. But Goldfinch notified the people, and they came toward the yellow mountain in the west.

By this time Phoebe was very much frightened. He said, "Let's hurry to Spotted Mountain in the north." They were both worried and troubled, for they had no way to save themselves. They were being chased from one place to another.

Buzzard was at Spotted Mountain in the north. They found him there, and he said to them, "What's the matter? You two seem to be sad."

They asked the buzzard for help. They said, "Grandfather, do you know anything that can cover and protect us? We were at the mountain in the center of the world. Then we had to flee to Black Mountain in the east, but they surrounded that. In turn we fled to the mountains of the south and west, and now we have come to the north. They will probably follow us here too."

Buzzard said, "You must stay here two days. Do not go away to any other place."

Buzzard went to the place where all the people were meeting. He heard that they were going to circle around Spotted Mountain. He came back and said to the two birds, "Tomorrow the people are coming. But stay where you are, and they will not see you. You must do as I say."

The next day the people circled around the mountain. The buzzard came to the birds. "You must come with me," he said. He took them to the cliff, to his nest, where he had some sticks. His children were there. "They won't see you in there," he had said to the phoebes.[1] The people looked all over. They peeked in every hole. They passed by the buzzard's nest. Those two birds sat there and were not seen, though they saw the people pass by.

The people couldn't find them, so they said, "Let us look all over the world for them." They spread out all over the world.

The buzzard said, "Let us go to the east, to Black Mountain. Let us go through the mountain, right through the center." The buzzard went first; the two others followed. They motioned four times at Black Mountain and then went right through, just as though it were a doorway.

When they were on the other side of the mountain Buzzard said, "Let us go to Blue Mountain." When they got there they motioned four times and went through that one too.

Then the buzzard said, "Let us go to the yellow mountain in the west." They motioned there four times too and went through it.

When they were through that mountain, Buzzard said, "Let us go to the north, to Spotted Mountain." In the same way they went through this one also.

When they got through that mountain they went to Buzzard's nest. Buzzard said, "Now this time you must do as I tell you. You must go to that little hill. In the canyon below the crowd is looking for you. When you get on top of that hill, Phoebe, you must shout and call your name and that of your friend. Let them circle around you again. Don't go away. Just stay where you are. They won't see you."

They did this, and though the people came and looked all over the little hill they could not find those two.

The people grew tired and went off. The two birds went to Buzzard and told him. Buzzard said to them, "You must go back and do this again. You must do it four times, staying right there each time."

The next day the people were looking all over again. These two birds were sitting right on top of the hill though. This day Say's Phoebe said, "Let us go to another place. Perhaps the buzzard is fooling us." He wanted to separate and hide. But Phoebe said, "No, let us not do that. The people are looking for us all over the world. We had better stay right here and do what Buzzard says."

The next day Phoebe did the same thing. He called out and mentioned his own name and his friend's name. This was the third day, and the people, though they searched again, failed to find them.

The next day Phoebe did the same thing. He stood up and shouted, "I am the one called Phoebe. This is my friend, Say's Phoebe." All the people heard, and from all over the world they

[1] The connection between the buzzard and the ability to hide or steal has already been mentioned.

hastened to search, but the two birds sat on their flat rock at the top unseen.

Now the directions of the buzzard had been followed for the four days. They went back to Buzzard and said, "You told us the truth; they never saw us."

"Yes, I tell the truth, but they are not through looking for you. I'm going to show you another way to hide yourselves."

The people were gathering around and holding council again. They talked among themselves. "One of us must have some power to find this bird," they said. Many people there had power, but it was not very strong power.

The woodpecker said, "I know who has power. I will go and see him and ask him. Perhaps he will agree to help us with his power."

So the next day Woodpecker went up to see Steller's Jay.

"Hello, friend," Woodpecker said. "Two people have been murdering children, and we have been looking for them all over the world. That is why I come, to ask you to help. Perhaps you still have power."

Jay said, "Why couldn't you have come around before, when I had power? Now it is too late. Once White Hactcin gave me his power. Now it is too late. I have given him back the power."[1]

The woodpecker pleaded with him in all ways, but Jay said, "I have no authority now. If I should see those two I will fight them; I'm strong and can claw and peck them, but I have no special power anymore."

The woodpecker just kept asking him to help.

Jay finally said, "All right, go home now and come back in four days and see me again."

Woodpecker went back. Jay stayed where he was all day, thinking of how he might help the people. At noon of the second day he went out to where White Hactcin was.

Jay went up to the place where White Haçtcin was. He asked him for power once more. "There are two who have been murdering all the children," he said. "The people have no way to get rid of them. One man came to ask my help. He begged me for nearly a whole day, but I have no way to help."

White Hactcin asked Jay, "What do they plan to do with those murderers when they find them? Are they going to hang them or are they going to burn them to ashes?"

---

[1] This is a reference to a long tale, not included in this collection, in which Jay is given the power to ordain a way of life for all the birds and animals. One after another the animals and birds are brought before him and he serves them much as he does Phoebe in the latter part of this story. The story attests to the detailed knowledge of the Jicarilla concerning the habits and appearance of the wild life of the region, but because of its length and its lack of importance in other directions it has been omitted, and this story of Phoebe is allowed to stand instead as an example of its type.

"When they catch them they are going to kill them. After they are dead they are going to burn them."

White Hactcin said, "Yes, I have power and authority over all the living creatures. Whoever believes me will go in a straight path. For them there are no arroyos. I stand for long life.

"You have come and asked me to help you get rid of these birds. You want to kill them. That is not right. It is all right to punish them severely until they change their ways, but there is no need to kill them. I will give you my authority and power once more, but you must do as I say. Hereafter I shall never give you my authority again. After you catch these two birds you must make them get rid of their wicked ways."

White Hactcin spoke once more, "Listen carefully to what I say. Here is my hand. You think the world is large and that there are many people. But you can fit it all into the palm of my hand. Here is my heart. There is sorrow in it for all of you because you are fighting and killing each other. I do not like a man who murders. You must come close to me." He held out his seventh finger[1] and rubbed it behind Jay's right ear after putting it in his mouth and wetting it. "Wherever you go now you will be able to hear me all the time and receive my directions."

The jay came back to his home. This was the third day after Woodpecker had left him. He was thinking of what he would do. In one more day Woodpecker was returning.

The next day was the fourth day. Early in the morning of that day the woodpecker came again.

Jay asked him first, "What do the people say? How are they going to dispose of those two birds when they catch them? Are they going to burn them?"

The woodpecker said, "Yes when they catch them they intend to hang them up until they are dead and then burn them, or else they will kill them some other way and then burn them. Another way they talk of doing is to put them on a grinding stone and grind them to pieces."

After Woodpecker had told this to Jay, Jay said, "If you talk like that I'm not going to help you. I'm not on the side of death. My name stands for long life."

Then Jay said, "I went up where White Hactcin is. He told me all about this. He showed me his hand. He said, 'All of you live in my hand, all the animals under the sky and all the people live in my hand. I feel very sorry for you people. If I want you all to die, you'll all die the same day, but I am very sorry for you. I don't want any of you to die. I will help you to catch the two birds, and they will be caught easily, but then I don't want you to kill them.'" That's what Jay told Woodpecker.

[1] The index finger of the right hand.

Jay sent Woodpecker back. "Go back and tell the people what White Hactcin said, that he didn't want anyone to die. You must hurry back and get here before noon, and then I'll go after the birds at once. When I catch those birds, I'll just get rid of the evil in their hearts, that's all."

Woodpecker went back to the crowd of people. He stood in the middle. He told what Jay said. "Jay is willing to help us, but he won't kill those birds. If you will let them go, he says he will catch them and make them get rid of their wicked ways."

And all the people put up their hands to signify that they agreed. "It's a good idea," they said.

Woodpecker came back to Jay, and Jay said to him, "You must bring four hawks to help me."

The hawks came.[1] "Why did you want to see us?" they asked.

"I'm going to take you to get two birds who are very malicious."

The four birds all smiled.

Meanwhile Buzzard knew what was happening. He took the two birds to the east, to Black Mountain, and he put them inside the mountain. They lived in there. There was no way to get in that mountain.

Jay and the four hawks went. Jay called the name of each of the hawks and his own name last. He said he wanted five to go because he had five fingers on his hand. They started out. When they came to the mountain, one hawk stood to the east of it, a smaller hawk stood to the south, another hawk was standing to the west, and the red-tailed hawk stood to the north.

Jay stood to the west. He faced the east and pushed at the mountain after first motioning to the east four times. He pushed the mountain away, and there sat those two birds.

One big hawk caught the phoebe, and a smaller hawk caught Say's Phoebe. Then the others came up and helped.

Jay said, "Don't scratch them. Don't be too rough with them."

They brought them away. Jay motioned four times from west to east, and the mountain came back in the same position as before. The two prisoners were held on both sides and were taken to the place where the crowd of people was waiting.

After they had brought the two birds to this place, Jay said, "I'm going to take them to my home. You must come and see me tomorrow at noon."

Jay took them home. At sunset he tied their feet and arms with ropes of spider web. "Don't be frightened," he told them. "Stay here quietly until tomorrow. I shall not harm you." Jay fed both of them. The two birds said nothing.

The next morning a great multitude of people gathered around Jay's home.

[1] These hawks were Sharp-shinned Hawk, Cooper's Hawk, Prairie Falcon and Red-tailed Hawk.

Jay spoke, "Now those of you who have lost your children come near and see what I'm going to do with these birds."

Jay untied both feet of the phoebe. Jay sat facing the east. He spoke to Phoebe. "Stand near to me," he said. The phoebe came to him. Then he asked Phoebe questions. "Is it true that you killed all the children of the people? My heart knows the truth. If you did it you must say yes, if not, no. I know you."

Phoebe was trembling violently. He tried to speak. All he could do was cry, "It's true; it's true. I did kill many and ate eggs and children." He said at last, "I did it because no one was taking good care of the eggs, and I thought they had been abandoned. And I saw many children who looked thin and weak. I thought they were starving to death and had been abandoned. So I did eat them."

Jay said, "You must stand still." To the people he said, "This one has told the truth. I believe what he said. He explained all about it. If people want their children they should stay around and watch them and keep them clean. Those of you who have four limbs, you have two hands. Why don't you stay around and watch your children? I t's true, what this little bird says; many of you do not take proper care of your children. They are dirty and uncared for and are as badly off as if they were thrown away. So let us not be against this bird. I don't blame him."[1]

Then he turned and spoke to Phoebe. "Do you think you'll get rid of all your wicked habits? You must tell me before all these people."

"Yes, I'll give up all my evil habits."

Jay picked Phoebe up in his hand and pushed him down, making him small as he is now. He picked up the black dirt and rubbed it on the bird's head. He reached up and motioned to a grey cloud and rubbed some of it on the body of the bird. Alternately he painted one tail feather white and one black.

He held the bird up and said, "You all see him. Before he was your enemy. Now he is your friend. He is transformed, his whole heart and body. When he comes around you, do not hurt him. I'm going to send him up to the top of the mountains. That's the only place he will live."

Then all the people thought about it, and they said, "This jay is just like White Hactcin."

He held the bird before the people and said to it, "Now after this you must go to the top of the mountains. Your food will be the insects from the inside of the bark. With moss hanging from the trees you will make a nest for your children. You will lay eggs. Your children will be warm in their nest. Keep them clean. Don't be like the people whose children you killed before."

Then Jay put Phoebe down on his left side. He untied Say's Phoebe and told him, "Stand near me."

---

[1] This is a sample of the didactic and moralizing use to which Jicarilla tales are often put.

Jay knew that this bird had not done anything wrong but that he had only acted as messenger and had therefore turned the people against him.

Jay asked him, though he knew the bird hadn't done it, "Did you kill children? You must tell the truth. Don't lie about it."

The bird said, "I didn't do anything wrong. I didn't kill children. The people want to kill me because I heard what they said and notified my friend."

Jay picked him up and put him on his hand. He pushed the bird down and made him small. He made the feathers stick up on the top of his head. He put some greyish cloud on the little bird. He rubbed some black dirt on the tail feathers.

He spoke again. "Phoebe is your friend. You must live near him. When you are going to have children, make a nest of moss too. After your children come, one of you parents must hunt for food and the other must watch the nest. Then change off. The squirrel or some animal may step on your nest if you don't watch your children. Hunt for ants, bugs, butterflies, and things like that.

Then Jay[1] spoke to the people, "Now these two birds are going to the mountain tops and will dwell there. They will not come among you anymore. But you people must be good and not fight. Stay around your homes and take good care of them. When enemy birds come you must protect your nests and your children. Feed your children enough, and then they will not cry from hunger. If you have four or six children, feed them all the same amount. Don't give more to one than to the others. That is why children fight; it causes trouble.

"Children are not all the same. Some may have evil thoughts. Give them advice. Train them in a good way. Don't let them fight with each other.

"I am not speaking only to those who have lost their children. I am talking to all. You must all go back to your country and tell all those who are not present what I say. Every one of you sees these four helpers of mine, these four big birds who brought these two guilty birds to this place. If some day you make a mistake and kill someone, they'll bring you over here to me too, and I'll change your body like this. That's why you should not fight. If you hurt anyone, you'll get into trouble the way these two birds did. And husbands and wives should refrain from fighting too.

"All of you can hear. You know what these people confessed. They told the truth. Phoebe said he ate up the thin birds because he thought they had been thrown away. All of you know you tried to catch these two birds. Though there were many of you, you

[1] When a jay comes to visit you, don't kill him. Give him something to eat. That's what the old Indians did. If they needed the feathers or any part, they had to ask for it. They prayed and told for what purpose it was to be used; what part was needed. Then they could kill it. (Inf.)

couldn't do it. They stayed right in the middle of the east mountain until I pushed the mountain away. That is the end. You must remember my advice. Now go home.

"I forgot to say one thing. High up on the cliff is one called Buzzard. Don't go over there and make friends with him, for he is one of the worst of birds. Keep away from him and let him stay by himself."

The people went back to their homes. They told the others what Jay had done. They said Jay was just like White Hactcin, that he changed these two people and gave them different bodies.

Jay gave the four hawks who acted as policemen the right to eat small birds.

F. THE FIGHT BETWEEN TURKEY AND EAGLE

One time a man went out to hunt. He was among the piñon trees. He heard the turkeys making lots of noise. He watched and saw three male turkeys walking around talking among themselves. The man hid in the bushes and watched. He saw two eagles, then, a male and a female. The female eagle swooped down. That eagle killed one turkey. She shot at the turkey. The end feather of the wing of the eagle is called "eagle's arrow." The turkeys shot too. They shot with their wattles. The two sides fought. At the end of the battle all five were dead.

The man went to the bodies and opened up a turkey. He found an eagle feather in the turkey's heart. He was afraid then to take the feathers; he didn't dare to after seeing that. He went back and told the people.

Many came to see. They opened up an eagle, and through the heart of the eagle they found the wattle of the turkey. None of them dared take the feathers, though they were good ones.

So these two sides had a war and both proved they were good fighters.

VII. STORIES OF FOOLISH PEOPLE, UNFAITHFULNESS, AND PERVERSION

A. THE TRAVELING PEOPLE[1]

1. ORIGIN OF THE GROUP

There was once a group of Jicarilla Apache composed entirely of foolish people. They were called Traveling People. This was a long time ago when the different groups of people didn't know each other. When these foolish people tried to go around with the people who had sense, they couldn't get along. They wandered by themselves from the various camps and met with others of their kind. That is how the group was formed and after that they traveled together.

2. THE TRAVELING PEOPLE WISH FOR FOOD

One time these people said, "Let's get on top of the hill. Let's all wish. Let one say, 'I wish I had this to eat,' another, 'I wish I had that.'"

So they went up on the hill and sat there wishing. Some wished for fruit, some wished for all kinds of edible berries. Each had his turn. Some wished for meat. Some wished for deer, some for buffalo. Animals of all kinds were wished for. They stayed there all day wishing for things.

The next morning they started in wishing again. They kept it up till they were tired. Then they went away.

3. THE TRAVELING PEOPLE HUNT BUFFALO

One time these people went out to the plains country on a buffalo hunt. These people had no horses.

One man who was very strong said he would get a buffalo. There was a buffalo bull sleeping. They all crawled near to this buffalo.

---

[1] These stories of the "traveling people" were told as an object lesson — to warn the young against foolishness and misbehavior supposedly — and for amusement. The straits into which the traveling people get themselves are reminiscent at times of the scrapes in which Coyote involves himself. Indeed, one informant from whom I recorded myths and tales included several of these traveling people episodes in his version of the coyote cycle. It is noteworthy that these tales evidently furnished a vicarious release from inhibitions decreed by the culture. Various subjects treated in these tales, such as the eating of human flesh, the retention of a corpse for any length of time, the handling and consumption of a snake, the cursing of a son by a parent, and perverse sexual conduct are among the most repugnant to the Jicarilla Apache in the traditional sense, and are taboo in ordinary conversation.

While the buffalo was still sleeping, this man tied a rope around its neck. Then he tied the other end around his waist.

The man said, "I'll choke that buffalo to death." He thought that when the buffalo started to run he could brace himself and throw the animal back.

The others woke up the buffalo and told the man, "Choke him!"

The buffalo woke up and started to run, for it was frightened. It dragged the man along. The rest of the foolish people ran along the trail after it.

They said, "He will probably choke that buffalo to death further on."

They came to a place where the man's clothes had been torn from his body.

"Our friend has taken his clothes off. He must have been too sweaty," they said.

Then they came to a place a little further on where the man's arm had been torn from its socket. It was lying there.

"Well, he must be holding on with the other arm," they said.

A little further on they came to a leg which had been torn off. They didn't pick it up; they just passed by. They looked only for the dead buffalo.

"Well, he's still holding on with the other arm and leg," they said.

They came to the other leg then.

"He is still holding on with one arm," they said. "It must be that these two legs were in his way and that is why he threw them away."

A little farther along they came to his hair.

"He must still be using that one arm," they said.

Then they came to the other arm.

But they said, "He is holding on some way with the rest of his body."

Then they came to the entrails.

"He must have let these go, but he is still holding on with the rest of his body."

The rope had broken by now and they came to the rest of the body. They found it and looked at it.

They said, "Our partner must be very tired, for he is lying down."

The buffalo had run away, and they never killed it.

They picked up this body and started to carry it back home. They retraced their steps and picked up the arms, the legs, and all the parts.

They said, "These were just in his way; that's why he threw them away."

The man's wife was expecting a buffalo. Then the men came in with the wrong meat. They didn't say anything to her about it, but just piled up the meat. So she began to cook her own husband. She roasted some of the meat.

The others came over, for they smelled it cooking. Some thought, "She must have buffalo meat."

They all visited and sat around and ate this man.

The next day the woman was cutting some more meat to roast. She saw the penis. She realized what it was and recognized it as her husband's. She thought that some enemy had killed her husband.

She went out to the people and said, "This is my husband. It must be that the enemy killed him."

So they didn't eat any more of the meat after that. They threw the meat down an arroyo.

4. HORSES ARE OBTAINED

Then these people started out to hunt for more buffaloes. They traveled and traveled until they got to the country where the Plains people were. They didn't know these were their enemies. They just kept going among them. They built a camp near the camp of the enemy.

Some of the enemy people came around and said, "These are Apaches. Let's kill them."

Some others said, "No, let's not kill them. They must belong to some other tribe."

So they began to make friendly advances. The traveling people stayed there for a little while. But these people never stayed in one place all the time. After a while they were going to move. So the enemy people gave them some horses, for they felt sorry for the women who had to go on foot. They gave them some gentle horses which would not buck and also gave them saddles.

They told them, "You must take these along wherever you go."

But these people didn't know what the horses were for or what the saddles were for. The enemy watched them to see what they would do.

The Plains people told them, "Put your saddle on the horse and ride it." They told them this is sign language, for they could not speak the same language.

So these people put the saddle on, but put it on in reverse fashion. They didn't even put a saddle blanket on the horse first. They didn't tie the cinch. They knew nothing about saddling horses. The enemy people laughed at them.

Then the enemy said, in sign language, "Sit on it!"

So one of them tried to put his foot in the stirrup and mount, but the saddle fell on him.

The enemy people laughed and laughed. "These are funny people," they thought.

They came and showed them how to put the saddle on the right way and then told them, "You sit on it now."

But the man who tried it did not sit the right way. He sat on backward, facing the tail. He didn't put his feet in the stirrups, but let them hang down. Then he started off, but his face was turned the wrong way. He couldn't stop the horse. The horse just carried him around. They tried to stop it in different ways. One pulled the tail, one tried some other way, but the horse walked around. Some who were not on horseback ran around in front and put sticks in front of the horse, thinking to stop it this way, but the horse stepped right over the sticks. The reins were dragging. One man finally tried to catch the rope. He succeeded and held it. This time the horse stopped. But they didn't know how to take the horse and lead it home. They had the horse stopped but didn't know how to make it go the right way. Every time the horse moved they pulled the rope, but they didn't know how to turn it around. So they waited till some of the enemy came and led the horses back. At the camp one of the enemy rode a horse and tried to show them how to manage it.

Another one of these men sat on the horse then and tried to do as the one who was instructing them had done. He started to kick the horse, but he didn't put his feet in the stirrups and therefore fell off as soon as the horse started. The horse walked off. The man from the enemy tribe caught him.

He brought the horse back, but now the traveling people were afraid and didn't want to get on.

They said, "These people must have pitch on their buttocks. This is plains country without trees and pitch. Let's lead these horses back to our country and get pitch and put it on ourselves. Then we'll all ride."

So they turned around and started back. Each had a horse. They went along leading the horses.

The enemy thought, "On the other side where no one will see them, they will probably all get on the horses."

One of the horses had never been ridden before. It was a bucking horse. All the other horses were gentle.

These people finished half their journey. They pitched their camps. The horses were all in the center of the camps, sleeping.

One fellow was visiting. He came back towards his home in the middle of the night. It was dark with no moonlight. He didn't know that this wild horse was right in front of him. He stepped over the horse, and just then the horse got to its feet. The man found himself sitting on the horse, and then the horse bucked till he threw him off.

The man got up. He said to himself, "I've been saying for a long time that I must ride this horse." He acted as though he had done it on purpose. He got up and went home. After that he was afraid. He never went out to visit other camps at night.

All the men in the group went over to the woods and took their horses along. They were going to surprise their wives. They gathered pitch. They covered their buttocks with the pitch. The horses were standing around in all positions while the men were doing this.

The men then helped each other and pushed each other up on the horses. They were not using saddles. Some men sat facing the horses' heads and some sat facing the horses' tails. Some were sitting up on the horses' manes, and some were far back near the horses' tails.

They said, "Let's start home."

The horses moved off in the directions in which they were headed. Some went one way, some another. The horses didn't know where they were supposed to go. The men didn't get home that night and not the next day either. They couldn't get off the horses; they stuck to the horses' backs.

The women missed their husbands and went out looking for them. One found her husband in one place, another in another locality. The horses were grazing, and the men were stuck to their backs. Each woman found her husband, picked up the rope, and led the horse to her home.

They told the men, "Get down and have something to eat."

But the men didn't get off. The men didn't tell what was the matter. They just sat there unable to get off the horses. The women tried to pull them off, but the men said, "Don't! That hurts!"

"What's the matter?" asked the wives.

Some of the women said, "They must have defecated on the horses' backs and so are stuck there."

Since the men couldn't get off, the women led the horses to the river to see if they could clean off the horses and get the men down. They filled the water bags with water and then threw it underneath the men's buttocks.

The men had sat on the horses two days and one night. It took a long time to clean it up and get the men off. But finally all were off. The men were afraid then. They didn't want to get on the horses. They said it was dangerous.

They began to talk about the horse. They didn't call it by the word that is used today. One called it a deer.

Another said, "No, it's not a deer. I know the deer has horns. It must be something else."

One called it a buffalo.

They looked at it. "It's not a deer; it's not a buffalo," they agreed. They didn't know what it was.

Some said, "We have heard a story. This animal must have come from the water. That's what we have heard. His hooves are just like water boulders."

So they all agreed and said, "That's true."

Then one said, "I guess this animal has come to pound meat for the people; that's why he carries these boulders from the water."

Some had meat. They said, "Let's try it."

They put down a rock. They put a pile of meat on it. They led the horse to the meat. He stepped on the meat and stood there.

They tried to lift his foot and use it like a pounding stone, but they could not lift it. The horse wouldn't move. They were disappointed, for they had expected the horse to use his foot like a pounding stone, moving it up and down rapidly.

So they said, "That boulder must have pitch on it to make it stick to the other rock."

They couldn't move the foot, so they took the rope and led the horse away from this rock.

Then they talked among themselves about the horse. They didn't know how they could use it.

Finally they said, "One thing the enemy tribe didn't tell us. They didn't say what they feed the horse."

Some said, "That's true, but it's too far to go back. Let's see whether we can feed it something."

They ground some corn and fed the corn-meal to the horse. The horse liked it and ate all they gave it.

Someone said, "Why do you give corn-meal to it? Why don't you give it mush?"

So they made a thick mush.

Another said, "Mix it with soup. I guess he will like it that way."

So they did that. Then they put it before the horse, but he wouldn't eat it.

They said, "What's the matter? We must have forgotten to put something in it."

They took it and ate it themselves.

Then they gave some water to the horse. He drank that all right. One man had been boiling meat. He offered it to the horse, but the horse wouldn't touch it, though the man held it close to the horse's mouth.

"I guess he doesn't like meat. He must like something else."

Then they said, "Oh, let the horses go. They don't want us to take care of them."

They turned the horses loose. The horses went at once to the grass and started eating it.

The people said, "They must like that grass, for they are eating a lot of it. Grass must be good."

So they, too, started to pick grass and chew it. They liked it.

Each day they tried to ride the horses, but they didn't know how yet. The men knew how to ride but not very well. The women didn't know how at all. The men could guide the horses a little.

They moved camp. The men sat on the horses with all their goods in front of them. The women walked behind dragging the tipi poles. When they came to an arroyo the women would get on the horses behind the men and hold on to the men. One woman did this first. The others thought that was very good. So every time they moved camp they went this way. They rode the horses on the level places, but they didn't know yet that they could get over mountains or high places with the horses. They didn't use the saddles; they found the saddles too much in the way and so threw them away.

Finally they said, "Let's move to the other side of the mountain."

It was a steep place to cross. They started on horseback. The women were holding on to the men, and because the incline was so steep, the men, who had no saddles, kept slipping back. They tried to hang on to the manes of the horses, but slipped anyway. The men and their wives slid off down the horses' tails and fell on the ground.

The men said, "It must be that this mountain does not want us to cross him."

So they all went on foot and crossed the mountain leading the horses. When they got to the top they mounted double again. All went well for a while, for it was level right on top. But when they started down the other side, they slipped off over the horses' heads and fell to the ground again. They all got up and walked till they got to the level ground. Now they were afraid. They had fallen off twice and didn't want to get hurt again.

Every time they moved camp they lost another horse, for they didn't know much about caring for horses. This went on till all their horses were gone. After they lost their horses, they traveled on foot once more.

5. THE RACE BETWEEN THE RUNNER AND THE MAN ON HORSEBACK

One time some members of an enemy tribe came from the plains to see these Apaches.

The enemy said, "Let's have a horse race."

The foolish people had no horses left now, but one of them could run very fast, just like a horse. The enemy were going to fight if they wouldn't race horses, and the enemy were more numerous.

So these people said to the enemy, "We have a man who will race on foot with your man on horseback."

The enemy just laughed.

They were to run about five hundred yards. Everybody gathered around the race course. There was much betting. The enemy were very wise. Their plan was to win all the Apaches' arrows and then start a war. That's why they wanted to race. So this enemy went out with a horse. Someone watched along the course to make sure there was no cheating.

They threw a blanket up, and when it hit the ground, they started to run. The foolish man was far ahead of the man on horseback. He beat that horse by about thirty yards.

The enemy were ashamed, for they had thought they were going to win easily. They had bet all their arrows and many possessions too. This is how this man saved his people.

6. THE LICE

These people were so foolish that, although their heads itched, they didn't know they had lice in their hair. They never searched their hair for lice. They had lice in their clothes, but they thought it was black ants that caused the itching.

They said, "We lie on the ground and that is why it happens."

They saw the lice, but thought they were ants and just brushed them off. They didn't kill them. They shook their clothes out every once in a while and many lice fell out.

Once they looked at one closely. It had a hard shell. Someone said, "I guess you couldn't kill those even with an arrow, they have such a hard shell."

Once they found two lice, one on top of the other. A man found them right on the back of his neck. The others saw it. They thought it was another kind of bug because they did not recognize the two together.

They said, "We had better kill that for you. It might bite and be dangerous."

So they got a big stick. "Stand still!" they told him. And they hit him right in the back of the neck at that spot. They killed the man. They didn't know what to do, for they had killed their friend.

7. RATIONS

When the white people first came to this country they gave the Indians hats, pants, shoes, and coats. Dishes and blankets were also given out, and food, such as flour, sugar, and coffee.

These foolish people received some too. They heard the other people say "buttocks bag"[1] and they asked, "What is this bag for? What do you put in it?"

"Why, you throw your buttocks in it," was the answer.

So they decided to do it. They put the pants in a low place and got up on a cliff above them. They hopped in place, getting ready to jump. Then they tried to get in the pants. Their feet missed, and they fell. Then they tied the pants around themselves, but the leg part hung down behind. Some put the pants on backward; some had the legs hanging down in front. That's the way they went around. They put the shirts on. Some wore them in the right way; some put them on backward. The hats they used for carrying water. They didn't know what hats were for. They thought a hat was some kind of dipper. They didn't know what all those things were.

They wouldn't keep gloves. They said, "This must be Bear's hand." The shoes they wouldn't keep either. "These must be the bear's moccasins," they said.

---

[1] Pants were called *tlatsizis*, "buttocks bag."

They didn't know what flour was either. They just threw it away. They kept nothing but the sack and emptied out the flour. All the Indians did this, even those who were not foolish. And the baking powder they threw away too.

At first they tried to eat bacon. They made soup of it and ate too much of it. A lot of them died from eating it.

At first they tried to make the flour into a mush. They tried to use it like corn-meal. But it was too sticky, and they threw it away. The brown sugar they liked though. Some of the children ate it like candy. They tasted the salt. They knew what that was. The white people gave them beans too. The beans they recognized. They knew how to eat them.

They were all given green coffee. This is what all the Apaches did with it, not just the foolish ones. They boiled the green beans for two days. They didn't get any softer. The people couldn't eat it. So they pounded it up and thought they would make a mush of it. It didn't taste good even though they stirred sugar into it. So they tried to make bread of it after grinding it. That didn't taste good either. They gave it up then and threw it away. They thought it was some queer bean. They called the coffee "owl quiver" after some plant by this name that they thought was the same thing. Every time coffee was issued to them after this they gave it to the Mexicans. They had no use for it.

8. BLASTING

These foolish people saw the white people working on the railroad. This was the first time the railroad had come through. They saw them put powder in the rocks to blow them up. Two of the foolish people watched this. They learned what it was for. So they stole a chisel with which to make a hole and a can of powder. They hid these things under some buckskin.

They went back and showed five others what they had learned. They said, "This is just like thunder."

Two of the five worked digging a hole under the rocks. The other three sat on the rocks with their legs hanging down talking to each other, telling a story. The other two were reporting what was going on, saying, "Now they are doing this." and, "This is what they are doing now," and so on. The ones above paid no attention.

The two men threw the powder into the hole. They stuffed an old piece of cloth in and set fire to it. Then they went up and stood on the rock with the others, laughing and talking. The fire reached this powder. The rock went up in the air with the explosion and killed all five of them.

The others heard the explosion. They all ran over to the place to learn what had caused the noise. They saw rocks all over and found pieces of their friends.

They said, "Oh, lightning has hit these poor people!" They didn't pick up the bodies; they were afraid.[1]

9. THE MEXICANS COME

In the days when the Mexicans first came to the Apache country, these Indians fought the Mexicans all the time. The Mexicans came around and were fighting all the Indians, not only the Apaches.

One time they came on the plains somewhere with their covered wagons, for that was the way the old-time Mexicans used to travel. They always made a circle of the wagons when they stopped in case the Indians should attack.

These foolish people didn't know what people these Mexicans were and so that night they went near them. They went right in the circle of wagons. Both men and women went in. The Mexicans were all sleeping. They thought these people must all be dead. They didn't know they were sleeping. They stayed there until morning.

When the Mexicans woke up they were frightened to see all these people standing around. They thought these people must be brave to stay there like that. Neither understood the other's language.

The Mexicans tried to scare away the Indians. But these foolish people thought the Mexicans were playing with them. They kept on talking in their own language. The Mexicans poked guns at them, but they didn't care.

Finally one Mexican killed a man, then another killed a woman. Still these foolish people thought nothing of it. Then another man was killed, and now they began to be frightened. They started to run. Even the girls among them could run very fast.

10. A FOOLISH MAN ESCAPES FROM BEAR

One time one of these people was on a mountain and killed a rabbit. He took the skin off and threw it behind him without looking. He didn't know the bear was coming close to him from behind. He opened the rabbit now and took out the entrails. He didn't know the bear was right behind him. He threw the entrails back, and they hit the bear right in the face. He looked back and saw what he had hit and began to run. He got away. If he hadn't thrown the entrails, he might have been killed by the bear.

11. THE FOOLISH WOMAN KILLS HER BABY

There was a woman who gave birth to a little baby. She was a very silly woman. She was looking over her baby's head for lice once

[1] If an Apache is struck by lightning, no one will touch the body but one who knows lightning. They send for such a man, and he will sing over the body. Sometimes he can bring the man to life. If he can't bring him back to life, if the man is dead, the one who knows lightning buries him. The others won't do it. The idea is that if you touch the body, you will be hit by lightning yourself. (Inf.)

and she noticed the soft spot. She was so stupid she thought it was a boil and she made up her mind to open it.

She took an awl and stuck it into the soft spot. Sure enough, a great deal of matter came out. She pressed the baby's head and more came out. She thought it was pus and never guessed it was the baby's brain. The baby had been crying as babies do when they are hungry. She had not fed it. So when she opened up the head she said, "No wonder the baby cried! He had this in his head. But now he is sleeping."

When this happened the husband, who was not foolish like his wife, was out hunting. After four days he came home.

When he met his wife she told him, "My husband, our baby has been sleeping since you left."

"Oh, you foolish woman! Perhaps you have killed the child. Where is it?"

Then she showed him the body. It was still in the blanket. She had been sleeping with it even though it was dead. It was all decayed and putrid.

"You foolish woman, why do you keep this evil-smelling thing? Throw it away!" And he scolded his wife. They threw the body away and they left that place.

12. THE BUFFALO

The man was going along with his wife again. He wanted to do some hunting. So he said, "You go in a straight line down this canyon till you get to the spring. Stay there until I come back. While you are waiting grind some corn for me on your metate. If you see some buffaloes call to me."

"What color is a buffalo?" she asked.

"Black." But he didn't explain how big a buffalo is.

The husband went away. He didn't get very far before he heard his wife shout, "Here's a buffalo!"

He came running. When he got near he looked around for the buffalo.

"Where? Where is it?"

"Here. Right here."

He looked down to the place where she pointed. All she had seen was a black beetle.

When the husband saw it he smiled. "This is not what I meant," he said. "I meant a big one, a big black one."

13. THE SNAKE

The man was ready to go hunting again. It was the time of year that the little deer are born. It was summer-time. He told his wife that the fawns were likely to be around.

"Look for them," he said. "There will be two together sleeping. Do not shout to me. Catch them yourself and kill them and make soup. You will know them for they are spotted."

He went to the woods again.

The woman went in the bushes and there she saw a rattlesnake. She thought she had come upon the spotted animal described by her husband. She had a hard time with it. She thought it would be best not to wake up the little "deer," so she jumped on it as it lay asleep. The rattlesnake woke up and started fighting and biting. It bit her all over her face, body, and hands, but she killed it, cut the body to pieces, brought the meat to the spring, and made a soup of it. She put her finger in the soup and tasted it. It tasted good to her.

14. GRINDING THE CORN

After making the soup, the woman started to grind corn. She did it at the spring and with her stone right in the water. As fast as she ground the corn, the meal was washed away by the water.

Now the husband was getting thirsty and came down to the water to get a drink. He was far below the place where she was working. He noticed that the water tasted of corn-meal. He started to run to her as fast as he could. "That foolish woman! Maybe she has wasted all the corn," he thought to himself.

He came up and stopped her. Then he saw the soup.

"Husband, I have done what you told me," she said. "I saw the deer and killed it. But I had a difficult time. It bit me all over."

The wounds were beginning to swell up by this time. Her husband took one look at the wounds and knew what was the matter. He ran for some plant which was a medicine for snake bite. He brought it back and rubbed it all over her. He made her chew some of it. The swelling and pain stopped.

Then he threw away the soup. "That is not good to eat," he told her.

Then he showed his wife how to make corn-meal mush. He ground up blue corn, and when the water boiled dropped the corn-meal in and stirred it and let it boil down till it thickened a little.[1]

"This is the way to do it," he told her. "Why did you waste all that corn?"

Then they both ate.

15. THE MOTHER WHO ABUSED HER SON

This story is of a foolish woman. She had a son. She was not treating him right, and so other relatives, seeing this, took the boy from her and raised him until he was growing to manhood.

[1] The Jicarilla used to eat corn-meal mush. Even now they like it very much. It should be made with blue corn. (Inf.)

The relatives always told him, "That is your mother," but she paid no attention to him. She acted as though she had no son.

One time, after he was grown up, he came to visit her. He called her mother.

She said, "I do not know you. I do not know whose son you are. You don't belong to me."

The boy tried hard to explain that he was her son, but she wouldn't believe him. He called her his mother again. She grew angry now and cursed him.

"You go out! I don't know you. Why do you call me mother?"

He called her mother for the third time. This time he was becoming angry too. He was nearly crying.

She shouted at him, "I don't know whose child you are. I hate men and have had nothing to do with them."

Now the boy was becoming angry too, for he had tried hard to make her recognize him. He called her his mother for the fourth time, and she rejected him again.

This time the boy was very angry. "All right," he said, "we'll see about it."

He went away. He said, "Very well. If you don't want me, you must look out for your life."

He was angry with his relatives and friends too. He went to the east, away from his mother.

It was rolling country marked by little hollows and rises. He was but one person when he went down into the first hollow, but then two men emerged and went down into the second hollow. Three came from it and went down the third. And then out of the fourth came a multitude. The boy had changed to all these men. There were so many that you couldn't count them. They were armed with spears and bows and arrows and all weapons.

At the other side of the hill they all turned around and started to run back and fight with the Apaches of these camps.[1]

Then the old woman, the boy's mother, remembered her son and began to cry and say, "My son, my son, don't kill me!"

But he no longer heard her. He no longer spoke her language. He had changed to the enemy, to the Arapaho, and killed her and all these Apaches.

That is why, when you have children, you must love them and be good to them. You must talk to them and advise them from the time they are little babies so that they won't grow up to be enemies.

16. THE OLD MAN WHO WAS ALWAYS BEHIND IN TRAVELING

The people were traveling from place to place. They always have to move when the grass gets poor where they are. So they were off

[1] This is why we have enemies today. (Inf.)

again, looking for better grass. There was one old man who was always far behind.

All those who were ahead talked it over. They discussed why he was always behind. This man had five good-sized boys.

They said, "Let us paint our horses."

They painted them with white clay and red ochre and different colors. They changed the color of all the horses, made them look like the enemy (Arapaho) horses which were always spotted. They had to do this, for the old man knew the Apache horses. And they painted themselves on the body and face and disguised themselves so they would not be recognized.

The old man was behind again. He hadn't left the place where the people had been last, though the people were moving and were far away by now.

The boys made long spears and stone axes. Out of willow from which the bark had been stripped they made whips. The crowd waited at a certain place, in the woods, with the horses.

In the distance they saw the old man come. When he was near, they all shouted. The five boys ran out. They encircled him with their horses, while they shouted, just as is done in war. They hit him with the whips, but not hard, for he was their father. They did this until the old man fell down and played dead. They shot arrows at him but missed on purpose. Then they rode off. They watched from a distance and saw him get up. They went over to the other side of the hill and washed themselves and cleaned up the horses.

Then they all looked for the old man. Finally they saw him coming on foot, running as fast as he could. He thought he was escaping from the enemy. When he got home he was all worn out.

He called the people together and told them what had happened. He said, "When I started to go, they followed my tracks. They tried to kill me but couldn't do it. One of them looked just like my oldest boy." He had seen one of his boys.

But the people knew what had happened.

After that he traveled near to the people when they moved. This went on for some time. Then he began to get careless again. He was always behind as he used to be. He had forgotten all about his experience.

17. THE OLD MAN FOOLED BY A GIRL

When the old man began to lag behind once more, the people talked it over again. They decided to teach him a lesson. They wanted to frighten him.

They selected a girl this time. She was not his daughter. They told her, "You must take along an ax. Go on the trail and lie down as though you were dead. Pull up your dress and expose yourself."

She did as they had told her and lay without any clothes on up to her neck.

The old man came along, late as usual. He came to her and looked at her and said, "I guess the enemy killed her." He picked up the ax. "I guess they hit her with this ax," he said.

Then he thought, "I wonder how long ago it happened." He put his hand to her genitals and then smelled his hand. He said, "It smells pretty strong. I guess she's decayed already. It must have happened a long time ago."

He was frightened again. He ran to tell the people. He remembered how the enemy had nearly killed him.

He found the people and told them about it. "She has been dead a long time," he informed them. "I smelled her and she smells pretty rotten already."

The people didn't laugh in front of him. They laughed after he was gone.

So after that he was afraid and never stayed behind. He was afraid that he, too, would be caught and left dead in the road.

He didn't know who that girl was because she had had her dress pulled over her head and he didn't see her face. He was talking to himself as old people do, and she had heard him. Afterward she told the people and they laughed privately at the old man.

18. THE WOMAN WHO ABUSED HERSELF WITH CACTUS

Now the people were again moving to another place. Many people were moving. They would select a place and live there for eight or ten days and then move on. There was a man in the group who wanted to marry a certain woman. In fact, many men wished to marry her. Her relatives wanted her to marry too, but she always refused the men. She wouldn't marry anyone. This girl was very good looking. The people wondered about it.

At the place where the people were living at this particular time there was a great deal of brush. About evening this girl picked up a rope and went out to get wood. The man who wanted to marry her was hiding in the brush, but she did not see him.

She began to gather some dry wood. She piled the wood up in good order. Then she stood up and looked around in all directions. Near her was a small round cactus plant. She had had it covered with pine bark so that no one would see it. When she was sure that no one was around, she sat down on the cactus and masturbated. She had peeled off the spines and outer covering from the plant so that she could use it like this. The man saw what she was doing. He knew now why she would not marry.

Later this man came to the place and cut around the bottom of the cactus with a knife. Now it was very weak and ready to break off, though it still looked strong.

The next day at evening he watched her. She went out as before to get wood. She went over to the same spot and looked around as before. She was going to do the same thing. She gathered dry wood, piled it well, tied it up ready to carry, and then stood there looking around.

Soon after she sat down on the cactus, it broke off and stayed in her vagina. She tried to get it out but couldn't reach it.

The man came forward then. He said to her, "What is the matter that you stand here? Can't you walk?"

"Something is wrong with me," she said. She had to tell him what was wrong.

So the man said, "I'll cure you."

He made a small bow and some small arrows. He had her sit with her legs outspread. He shot two arrows into her vagina, one crossing the other. He held the arrows and pulled them out, and the piece of cactus came with them. Then this girl got better.

B. THE WOMAN WHO DISLIKED THE MAN WITH THE FINE SUIT OF CLOTHES

There was a man in one group who had a very fine suit of buckskin clothes with fringe hanging from it and rattles on it that made a jingling noise when he walked. He was well liked among the people too. There was, however, one woman who claimed she could not stand him. This woman was continually telling her husband that the man with the fine suit of clothes made her positively ill every time she saw him.

The husband listened to this for quite a while. He thought about it. "Why does she feel so strongly against him when everyone else likes him and he has done her no harm?" he wondered.

He decided to test her. He said to his wife, "I am going out on a hunting trip for four days. Take care of the children and wait for me here."

He got ready what he needed and started off. But as soon as he was out of sight he reversed his tracks and went toward the home of the man with the fine suit of clothes.

"My friend," he said to him, "would you let me take your suit of clothes for a short time?"

The man was surprised at the request, but he agreed to lend his clothes.

The husband took the clothes and put them on. He waited until it was nearly dark and then he started towards his own home. His wife was there with the children. She had a fire going in there.

The husband approached and stood in the doorway. He did not come so near the fire that his features would be visible. The woman recognized the sound of the jingles and knew the suit. She thought it was the man whom she always claimed to dislike so much. The man motioned to her to follow him.

Immediately she arose, threw the water out of her water jar, and carried it and a blanket outside. The man led the way, the woman followed him.

When they had gone only a little way she asked eagerly, "Shall I put the blanket down here?"

"No, a little farther on."

They went a little farther.

"Is this place all right?"

"No, a little farther."

The man walked for a short distance and then the woman asked, "Is this the place?"

"No, just a little farther."

The man stopped now, right at the edge of the stream.

"This is a good place," he said.

The woman put down the blanket and lay down, waiting for the man.

But the man picked up the blanket and the woman together and threw them into the water.

Then he went back to the man from whom he had borrowed the clothes and returned them, thanking him for their use.

He waited a little while and then made his way home again. His wife was there, drying her wet clothes, when he came in. He made some excuse for returning so soon, saying that he had changed his mind about the hunt. Then he asked what had happened to her that her clothes were all wet.

"Oh, the children bothered me until I went to get them fresh water. It was dark and I fell into the stream." She blamed it all on the children.

The husband said nothing. But he heard no more about her dislike for the man with the fine clothes.

C. THE FOOLISH WOMAN WHO PLAYED SICK

This woman had two little sons. She had a good husband too. One time she tried to fool her husband. She made believe she was very sick. The husband went out to look for a shaman who could cure her. He had many ceremonies for her, but they could not do anything for her. They gave her many medicines but she got no better.

She said, "I'm going to die, my husband. When I die don't bury me entirely. Leave my head sticking out of the ground. If you bury my head too, I'll be nervous."

Then a little later she acted just as if she were dead. He did as she had asked him to do, buried her with her head sticking out of the ground. Then, according to custom, he killed all her horses, broke all her pots, and burned the home. They moved camp too. He had done all he could. He was lonesome, alone with his two sons.

Just as soon as her husband went away, this woman got out of the ground. She was having an affair with another man. That is why she did all this and fooled her husband.

Every morning and every evening after that the people in the camps heard the music of the flute on the top of one of the hills.[1] They knew that a certain boy was playing up there, but they didn't know that he had this woman with him. He had been carrying her food every day too.

One day those two sons of this woman were playing in the brook. The mother and that man were coming to the brook just then. They were thirsty and were coming for water. The little boys recognized their mother.

They began to call, "Mother! Mother!" and ran to her.

The mother said, "You get away! I don't know you. Your mother has been dead a long time."

The little boys began to cry. "We know you are our mother. We know you."

"No, I look like your mother but I am not your mother."

So the woman went off and left the children crying. The children ran to their father. They told their father.

"No, don't talk about your mother," the man said when they tried to tell him. "Your mother has been dead a long time."

But the little boys insisted. "We saw our mother today. She was down by the water with a man."

"No, no, my children. Don't talk like that. The owl has taken her home."[2] He tried to explain to the children that their mother was dead.

The boys were crying bitterly. They couldn't stand it. They knew they were right. They made their father come with them to the water's edge.

"Our mother stood right here," they told him.

He saw the track there. Then he believed it. Then he remembered how he had been requested not to bury her head.

"I guess it's true," he thought. "I guess she got out of that place."

Just then he heard that music up on the mountain again. He picked up his bow and arrows. He went on the other side and came up the hill.

He found them. But they did not see him approach. He came closer and closer. He recognized his wife.

He started to shoot, and he killed both his wife and the man.

Then he came down to tell the relatives, the woman's mother and father and close relatives.

---

[1] This is another case of the familiar association of love magic and the flute.

[2] For the meaning of "Owl has taken her home" see footnote 1 p. 282.

He said to his father-in-law and mother-in-law, "Your daughter is really dead now. The first time she just deceived us."[1]

Then they all went up to see. They found the two dead people, the girl and their new son-in-law.[2]

D. THE GIRL WHO HAD INTERCOURSE WITH DOGS

There was a good-looking young girl who was not yet married. Different men wanted to marry her but she always said no. She said she hated men and wanted nothing to do with them.

This girl always had many large good-looking dogs around. She had about five of them. And she would never stay with the others when they broke camp or were moving away. She always left the trail and went off in the hills by herself with these dogs.

There was one boy who wished very much to marry her. He brought meat and many presents to the parents and relatives of the girl,[3] but when the girl came she refused to marry him. He tried again and again in this way. He had given her people a great deal to eat and many presents. Still she refused to marry him.

He began to get a little angry now. He watched her. Soon after that the people started to travel to some other place. He saw her leave the others and go into the woods with her dogs.

"I wonder why she always goes off with those dogs," he thought. He quietly followed her and watched.

After she was some distance from the others, he saw her stoop down and lift up her dress. The dogs came and had intercourse with her.

"No wonder she wouldn't marry me!" he said. "She has five husbands already!"

He drew his arrows and shot. He killed her while she was having intercourse with one of the dogs and he killed the dog while it was still on her in the position of sexual intercourse. Then he shot all the other dogs too.

He came back to the people and told her relatives about this. They came and saw for themselves. The one dog was still on her. They all wept.

That is why people say, "You must be proud of dogs and treat them well, for they are relatives-in-law to you."

---

[1] According to Jicarilla social conventions the aggrieved husband had a legitimate complaint against these people, since they were responsible for his fair treatment at the hands of their daughter unless he proved unworthy. They could not take any action against him, therefore.

[2] The last phrase is ironic.

[3] This is a characteristic way for a young man to show interest in a girl he wishes to marry.

VIII. MONSTROUS ENEMY STORIES

A. THE SPOTTED ENEMIES

Once a long time ago a man and his wife were out hunting deer. They were living near some enormous mountains. At that time when the world was new, they saw a dangerous thing. It was a man with a spotted body.

The man went out hunting. He left his wife at camp. The woman was pregnant and had two babies in her womb.

When the woman was alone this great spotted man came to her. That man came to that woman and killed her. He cut her breast. He took the two unborn babies out of her body. One of the babies he took to a place where there was a spring. The other baby he put under the ashes of the fire place.

When the hunter came home his wife was dead. He saw how she had been cut. He felt great grief. He did not know who had killed her. He tried to carry her on his back. He took her to some caves in the mountains where they had been burying people.

He returned home by himself. He saw that something had been buried in the ashes. He used a stick and dug out the baby that had been buried there. He looked all over the body of the child. It was not burned.

When evening came he was still with the baby. They had been talking to each other. They slept in one bed together. They slept together four nights. The baby boy was already playing out alone by now.

Sometimes the man stayed inside the tipi. Once he heard a sound; he heard the child talking to someone. He didn't see who it was. Evening came. Then he heard the baby talking outside again.

A voice said, "Tell our father he must make some arrows for us."

The man made arrows for his boys. The babies used the arrows in playing. The father didn't know where that other child came from, and he wanted to know. The children had been playing together for three days.

When evening came the one child said to the other, "Take these arrows inside the tipi."

The next evening the man was talking to his child. He told him, "If you play together tomorrow evening and your brother tells you to take the arrows in, then in the morning go out with him to show him some place and put your arms around him and hold him."

This happened. The second child was crying, trying to get away from his brother. The father went out to see the child who was being held. He came up to him. He took both of them. He took the second one inside.

He saw then that the second boy was just like a frog; he had long fingernails and toenails too. The man cut all of those nails. He didn't know that the baby had been down under the spring. The child had been getting ready to be a frog and was nearly spotted as the frog is. The father had caught his child just before he turned into a frog.

At this time both children had arrows. The second child was kept there for four days.

The next day those children asked their father, "Where is our mother?"

He told the children, "You must not mention that. Your mother is dead."

The children said, "You must tell us. We want to know where our mother is."

That man told his babies, "You must not say that. Your mother is dead."

The children repeated, "We really want to know where our mother is."

"You must not talk that way. Your mother is dead."

Those boys said to him, "You had better bring our mother to us."

The man remembered the place where he had buried his wife. He went there, got her out, and brought her back to his children.

The babies told the father to lay the body with the head toward the east and with the face up. One of the children then stood beside her head, and the other stood at the west, beside her feet. Both of them shot arrows upward. The arrows, as they came down, fell near her feet.

Then the woman moved her feet. The two children shot up arrows again. The arrows came down on both sides of her body, one on each side. As the arrows were falling, the boys called to their mother, "The arrows are coming down; you must get out of the way!" As the arrows fell the middle of the woman's body began to move and relax.

The children shot up arrows again. One arrow came down near her feet and one came close to her head. The boys told her, "You had better get out of the way. Arrows are coming down."

Once more the children shot arrows up. As the arrows were falling, they called, "Run away from that, Mother!"

The woman arose and jumped away. She was as well as ever again. The children had given back life to her.

They all lived right there for a long time. The boys were growing up. They were getting grown up enough to leave their mother and father.[1] They moved off together, a long way off, about eighty miles.

[1] These sentences reflect the relative independence of Jicarilla men before marriage. The girls are expected to stay with their parents and to attract sons-in-law to the parental encampment to compensate for the boys who leave it.

There they met a man. That man said to them, "I saw some dangerous things over there at the mountains. Let us go over there."

Those two boys did not want to go. He urged them to go. So they all started off to see some dangerous thing.

They went to the place where Thunder was living. Many dangerous things lived around there, but they kept away from Thunder's place.

When they came to the place a great storm started and the bodies of the two boys were blown to pieces. The pieces of the bodies were scattered and could not be seen. There was no more life in them.[1]

There was an old woman, married to Rattlesnake, and she saw blood splatter. That old lady was starting out to get some water. She was going along the trail to get the water. She saw a leaf beside the trail and it was stained with blood. She picked the leaf and looked closely at it. She was pleased, thinking she was going to have soup. She carried the leaf in her hands, brought it to her home, and built a fire. She took a clay cooking pot and put water in it. She put the leaf in the pot.

After a while the water was boiling. She heard sounds; it was the baby crying in there. She went to get a stick. She was going to dig it out from the water. Something just jumped out from the pot, and there was the boy. That is the way he got back his life.

One of the boys still had no life.

The boy who had come to life stayed right there. But he didn't see the snake.

The boy had been there about a week. He told his grandmother that she would have to make some arrows for him. The old lady made arrows for her grandson. The boy used them; he played outside with them. He learned how to shoot well with the arrows.

The next day in the morning the old woman said to her grandson, "Let us go and get some water."

The old lady went out first. The boy got out then and saw something. He saw the snake's head. He was looking around on the left side. The snake's tail was there. The boy didn't tell his grandmother. Instead he ran after her. He saw her a little ahead. He ran home. He saw the snake's head. He tried to shoot it with the arrow. The snake was almost dead when the old lady came back and saw him.

She was crying and said to her grandson, "You have killed my husband!"

The old lady was sorrowful. The boy left her at once. He was going somewhere else.

He went far from that place and saw an eagle's nest. He saw where it was and went there.[2] About noon he saw the eagle bring

[1] Cf. p. 95.
[2] Cf. pp. 100—104.

in a jack-rabbit. The eagle took it to the nest and told the boy he had to eat it up. The boy didn't want to eat the meat because it was not cooked.

The eagle told him, "You must strike it four times and eat some of it."

Then the giant eagle went out and brought in a deer. He told the boy, "You must eat it."

The boy didn't want to eat it raw. "It will make me ill," he said.

The giant eagle replied, "Strike it four times and then eat it."

He struck it four times and ate it just as the eagle eats it.

The boy was kept there for four days.

Evening came. It was growing dark. A stone wall was there, and the eagle opened a door in it. The boy went in with the eagle.

When they got in, the eagle took off his coat of feathers and hung it up. He was dressed just like a man then. Many feathered skins of eagles were hanging around there.

The next day the eagle told the boy to pick out one of those skins, the one he thought best. The boy looked them all over. He picked out one that fitted him best. The tail of it was white.

The eagle told him, "Strike it four times and put it on."

He did so and put it on. Then he looked just like the eagles. He had a curved beak just like theirs. He had talons. He stretched his wings.

He went out and tried to fly that morning, a short distance at first. In the evening he tried it again, he exercised this way. After a while he flew around to the eagle's nest. The giant eagle and the little eagles had been watching him fly around.

He kept this up for two weeks. Now he could fly far. He turned back and was close to the eagle's nest when he began to feel weak. Each morning and each evening he tried to do some flying. The eagle thought he was getting strong enough.

The next day he went out about a hundred miles with those eagles. The next day they went out for a long way in another direction. When the eagles had taken him a great distance he began to feel weak and he turned back. Then they went to other places. They took him again. He returned again and when he was near the nest he became tired again and was beginning to drop. The next day he had to go out to another place. That time he did not tire.

He stayed there for four days more.

The giant eagle told him, "You are going up in the sky. You are going to circle upward. We are going up to about the middle of the sky. Some eagles are up there and they will meet us."

They started upward. That eagle was getting weak and tired and was falling down. The eagles of this earth supported him from beneath and pushed him upward when he began to tire. He was going up toward the sky. There was a world up there. There were people living there.

The eagle boy met his grandmother. He met some people, and they said, "We'll have to scout for something. You'll have to come with us." These people were in the form of eagles too.

He said, "All right, I'd like to go with you."

There were enemy bumble-bees up there. And there were yellow-jackets there too.

He returned to his grandmother. He told his grandmother, "Tomorrow I am going to be a scout."

These women had buckskin dresses they had made. His grandmother made lances for him. He was ready to start in the morning. He met the others who were going.

The bees had been going inside the eagles' feathers and stinging them and killing them. The boy had buckskin clothes that his grandmother had made for him and the bees could not get in and sting him. He picked them off his clothes and stuck them on the lance when they came for him. He filled up two sticks with them. He did the same with the yellow-jackets, covering the length of two sticks with them. By this time many of the eagles were dead, however. All the eagles who were left were scattered and fleeing. The boy was still there, and the people who returned thought he was the first one killed in the battle. Many of his companions returned home. They thought the boy was dead. He had been left over there by himself. But he was still catching bees.

He was the last one to return. He took the sticks of bees and brought them to his grandmother. He had been scalping the bees and he brought these scalps to his grandmother. The old lady was happy. She uttered the woman's cry of victory.[1] He stayed there four days.

He told the people with whom he had been, "I'm going to leave you. I'm going to return home."

He started to come down to this world. At about the middle of the journey he tired. He got back to the eagle's nest. He stayed there for four days. He took off his clothes and went inside the stone wall to give back the clothes. Then he was just like a man again.

He came out again and he was going to some place across a river. He was going to a certain mountain and there he saw a certain tree, and some eagles were on that tree. He shot at them with an arrow. He struck one and killed it. He didn't know that Coyote was looking at him from a hiding place. The coyote had an arrow at this time. He ran to the dead eagle and put his arrow in the wound in place of the boy's arrow, and he hid the boy's arrow in the ground.

The boy was looking for the eagle he had shot. He came up to it and the coyote was standing there.

Coyote said, "This is what I killed with my arrow."[2]

[1] The same call the attendant utters in the girl's puberty rite. See p. 90.

[2] This is a typical coyote trickster element which has been introduced here.

The boy looked at the arrow. It was not his. He said, "I killed that eagle with my arrow."

"No," answered Coyote, "I killed it."

The coyote took the eagle away from the man. Coyote carried the eagle a long way. Then he tried to take the feathers off.

The one who had killed the eagle was getting angry. He returned home, to the place where his mother had been given back life.

His father asked him, "What did you do with your brother that you have come back by yourself?"

He replied, "The storm swept him away and broke his body to pieces. I have come back alone."

Then he said to his father, "Let us go to some other people."

They went to a place where many people lived.

The father told the people about the one who had killed his wife. He said, "I buried my wife at the mountain. I went back there and brought her out. Now she is alive again."

The people did not believe him.

The man said, "It is true."

Now the boy got married. His wife had a sister. He lived there for one month with his wife. The woman was saying that she wanted some meat. So the boy and the two sisters went to another place, to a place where there were high mountains. There he killed many deer.

He was butchering the deer and they were drying the meat. The boy said it was almost time to go home and that he would try for a kill just once more.

This locality was the hiding place of the spotted enemy, and he tried to kill this boy. Only the women were left at home. The next day came, but the husband was not back. The women thought the husband was coming back. But the boy had not come home by the next day.

The spotted man killed the boy, took off his clothes, and put them on himself. And the next day the spotted man came to the women.

The spotted man did not know how to talk to the women. He just motioned, "My stomach is getting hungry."

The tipi was small. One of the women was boiling something to feed the spotted enemy. When the meal was boiling and nearly ready the women took the meat from the fire and built a big fire there. The spotted enemy was getting ready to eat. After a while he began to perspire from the heat of the fire. All the clothes were getting tight on him.

After a while he got so hot he motioned to the women to help him take off the clothes. One of them began to pull the buckskin shirt over his head. She saw that it was not her husband.

She said to her sister, "Come, you must help me. Get a butcher knife and cut his stomach."

They cut his stomach open and the intestines hung out. The spotted enemy died right there.

That spotted enemy had been killing many of the men when they were out hunting.

Those women left the tipi and returned to their own people. They were on the way two days. The women told their people what had happened when they got back.

None of the people believed the man's wife.

She said, "It is the truth."

All the people were telling each other about it. Then some went to see the dead spotted enemy.

The women came with the people, for they knew the way. They went right to the place. Those people who had not believed them saw it with their eyes. It was the truth. The woman did not know where her husband had been slain by the spotted enemy. People were still coming to see the spotted enemy as he lay dead. There were many people there, about two hundred. Those people were talking and looking for the boy. They said, "Maybe we will find him somewhere." They went about looking for the home of the spotted enemy; they looked for his tracks. They looked all around one big mountain for the tracks of the boy or the spotted enemy.

At the top of a mountain, at a spring, many had been drinking water. They separated and went around the mountain looking for the boy. Two old men were left at this spring. After a while one of the men got up and looked around. He wanted to think about it, to find out.

From that spring a double row of stones led out. It formed a trail. The old man said, "Perhaps the spotted enemy got his water from this spring." At the edge of the spring there was a flat stone. That old man sat on this stone. At the edge was moss, and it looked as though the moss had been pushed aside to make it easier to get water. The old man started back along the trail. His companion followed.

After going a little way they saw some crags on the hills. That was the home of the spotted enemy. Tall grass waved around it so no one could see it. It was a fine hiding place.

The old men stood at the door. They listened to something inside. The spotted enemy's wife was in there with her baby. She was singing to it. The old men listened very carefully. Then they divided, one went one way and one the other, so they would be sure to meet the people and tell them they had found the spotted enemy's home.

One of them saw the people and told them. All the people were calling to each other, giving the command to meet at one place. They met at this place near the home of the spotted enemy. Tall grass was waving before the door.

These two old men told them, "Get some of this tall grass and bring some wood too."

They brought wood on their backs and brought grass in great quantities. The wife of the spotted enemy stayed inside.

Two men opened the door and got inside where the wife of the spotted enemy was. They saw many children in there. These two men saw that the spotted man had been killing men and bringing in their heads. The heads were hanging around the walls with the tops of the skulls cut off. Spotted Enemy had used them for water carriers and they were filled with water.[1] The spotted enemy's wife and children were frightened. The two men went out.

There was an old spotted enemy in there staying with the wife and children. He was the spotted enemy's father. The woman there was his wife. It was his oldest son, his tallest boy, who had killed the woman and who had been slain.

Outside the people were talking of what the spotted enemy had done. They were very angry about it. Those people took the dried grass and wood and set fire to it and threw it into the spotted enemy's home. The spotted enemy's home had a hole in the middle of the roof which was covered by a flat rock. The people moved the rock and threw down burning grass and wood.

The spotted enemy's children were crying and wanted to get out. They were trembling. After a while the crying of the children ceased, for the fire was flaming up. The smoke was rising in a great column from the burning fat of the spotted enemies. The fire was kept burning for about five hours, and the spotted enemies were all burned up.

The next day there was an earthquake around the home of the spotted enemy, just around that place. That was the end of the house. It was all gone after that. And that was the end of the spotted enemies.

B. THE ORIGIN OF THE KIOWA APACHE[2]

Formerly the Jicarilla people were very numerous. Now there are just a few left. The Jicarilla were living in separate groups at that time. Some were living far to the north.[3] They stayed there a long time.

There were enemy people who had been killing bears, cutting off their paws, and using the bear paws as moccasins. These enemies had been part of our people once, but they had turned against the Jicarilla and were killing them now. They hid in the brush and killed the Jicarilla. The people were scouting after these enemies. These enemies had been weaving together pieces of tall grass and had been putting on clothes made in this way so that they wouldn't be seen.

The Jicarilla would find their tracks around the bodies of the dead. These enemies had curved, sharpened sticks, and when they

[1] For a similar theme see p. 114.
[2] Cf. Goddard, p. 212.
[3] Cf. p. 117.

killed the Jicarilla, they pulled flesh and skin off with these.[1] The Jicarilla would go out hunting. When one was killed his relatives would find the slain man and see the tracks of the people who wore bear paws.

About twelve families of Jicarilla moved away to gather choke-cherries. Those twelve families were gathering the fruit. These enemies came to that place. One girl was saved; all the rest were killed, even the children. That girl escaped to the top of the mountain. She saw that all her people had been killed. She sat up there all day. She was grief-stricken at the murder of her relatives. She came back to see whether any of her relatives had got away. She looked among the bodies. No living person was there. She reached the place where they had been picking choke-cherries before the attack. She was trying the trees to see which was the strongest. Finally she climbed to the top of one. She was afraid and looked around every once in a while. She saw moving forms coming from the mountains to the west. They were running toward her. She ran away to the mountain and hid near the top. She looked back to the place where she had been. She saw that they were some of the enemies and they were going around among the choke-cherry trees. They were after her. They wanted to kill her. But they couldn't find her. At evening the girl ran away to the south where many people lived.

When she arrived at the camps of the people to the south she told of what had happened. All the people came together to decide what to do. The girl came forward to tell what was wrong. She said, "Those are not bears who are killing our people, but men wearing bear paws."

They all went to the place where the killing had occurred. The people then began to follow those bear paw moccasin tracks. They saw the trail. After a little way the tracks divided. Then, after some distance, the tracks came together again.[2] At that place the enemies had put on their own moccasins and had gone on again. Further on the tracks divided again and scattered. The Jicarilla followed just one set of tracks. Later on the tracks came together again. Once more they scattered and came together, this time at the foot of a big mountain. Here there was a great deal of brush encircling the mountain. There, in holes in the ground, these enemies were living.

It was near sundown when they came to the homes of these people. The Jicarilla left the homes of the enemies and went some distance away for the night and slept there.

They got up very early, before sunrise. They returned to the

---

[1] The flesh and skin were pulled off in this manner to create the impression that it had been done by the claws of the bear.

[2] To scatter and meet at an appointed place farther on was one of the most frequently used Jicarilla devices to confuse and delay pursuing foes.

place where the enemies were living. They circled around the place. Two men went close to one of these holes. They heard a voice down there. It was nearly day then.

After a while one of the enemy, an old man, came out. Then his wife, an old woman, came after him. The man stood and urinated. The woman was sitting, urinating. The two Jicarilla shot their arrows and killed both of them right there as they urinated. The Jicarilla then gathered a great deal of wood and set fire to it and threw it down the holes. When the fire was over an earthquake occurred which shook the land all around there.[1] Just four big holes were left. They looked in the first of these holes. Nothing was inside of that hole. The four holes were in a row.

The Jicarilla thought all those people were dead. They didn't look at this time into the other three holes. But when the Jicarilla were ready to return, one of them looked in those other holes. At that time, when the Jicarilla got up in the morning, they went to urinate the first thing. A certain man was doing so and saw those other three holes. He looked in them before he came back. He saw then that many enemies were sleeping there, armed and ready for war. He went back to tell the others.

The Jicarilla were afraid to fight them any more, so they were ready to return home. At daybreak they left their enemies. They counted the days it took them to get back. It took them twenty days. They met with others and decided to return to these enemies. Most of them said they were going to the holes again.

About fifty men started to the enemy's home. They came close to the holes and slept right there. At sunrise they met and circled around. There was no one there. All the enemies were gone. All the fifty men went down in the holes and looked inside. There were many bear paws there. Some of the Jicarilla put on the grass clothes which they found there. "These fit us," they said.

The enemy traveled to the east and looked for a place to settle. The fifty Jicarilla men returned to their people. They told the other Jicarilla that they could not find any enemies at the place where they had formerly been. "There was nothing but the bear paws and the woven grass clothes in the holes," they said.

The enemy had taken home the arrows, quivers, and other equipment of those they had slain, and so the Jicarilla had also come upon the possessions of their own slain relatives in those underground places.

The enemy had been hunting for a place to live. They settled in Oklahoma. They speak our language; the language is just about the same. We call them Wet Feet, our name for the Kiowa Apache. They were part of our people before they turned to enemies.

---

[1] Cf. p. 381.

IX. STORIES OF THE WINNING OF WIVES

A. DIRTY BOY[1]

One time there was a young man who was staying with his grandmother. The two lived alone. This boy was training at night for running. During the day he was very tired and slept.

A neighbor woman came by in the morning when the sun was already up and saw this boy sleeping soundly.

She said to the grandmother, "Why don't you train that boy in the right way? Make him get up early before sunup and run and look after the horses."[2]

The grandmother said, just to please this woman, though she really did not mean it, "I keep telling that boy to get up early but he won't listen." All the while the grandmother knew that the boy was practicing running every night, that he was training to be a good runner and that he would know how to use arrows and bring plenty of meat home.

After that the grandmother always had fresh meat in her home. Her grandson brought it home to her late at night when he came in from his running. But the people did not know who gave her that meat. She always had buckskin too, but the people did not know where she got it.

The boy's hair was bushy. He never combed it.

One time the boy went to listen to a council. The chief was having a council because some men were going to the enemy's country after horses. The boy listened. He heard them say they were going to start in four days.

The boy went home to his grandmother. "Grandmother," he said, "I want you to make me two pairs of moccasins with soles of double thickness. Make them of two pieces of rawhide sewed together instead of using just one piece."[3]

He got his club ready. He always had a club; he used it instead of arrows. His grandmother worked on the moccasins. He didn't ask her for provisions.

In four days when the men started off he followed them.

The chief spoke to him. "Go back. We are not going for a short distance; we are going on a long journey. We know you do not get up early. Go back to your grandmother and stay there."

---

[1] This is a much shortened version of the story of Dirty Boy. In the longer form it is related how the boy subsequently went on a number of raiding expeditions, and the details of his rivalry with a jealous uncle are given. A hint of this rivalry will be found in Goddard, p. 195.

[2] Jicarilla youths were subjected to a period of strenuous training, part of which consisted in rising early and caring for the horses.

[3] Moccasins of this description were carried on raid and war-path.

The older men tried to chase him back. They all hated him.

But the boy wouldn't pay any attention. He kept following. They tried to hide from him. But he kept on the trail. He stayed far in the rear because they all disliked him and treated him badly.

They went for a day and a night and for another day and night. Then they felt sorry for him. They said, "Well, let's wait for him and take him along." They waited until he came up and let him walk among them.

The party went on for three days, then a fourth day, and then a fifth day. Now the party was out of food. The provisions they had brought with them had been used up. They were out on the plains by now. Far off they saw the buffaloes lying down.

Then they all began to voice their wishes. One said, "I wish I could eat some buffalo tongue." Another said, "I wish I could eat buffalo meat."

The boy listened. He was sorry that his own people were without what they wanted.

The boy had a blanket, an old-time one. He had moccasins, too, an extra pair. He said, "You must hold these for me." He gave them to someone to hold and then he started off, but not in the direction of the buffaloes.

The people didn't know he was a good runner or that he intended to run after the buffaloes. He went a little way and then turned and ran toward the buffaloes. Upon reaching them he killed a number of them with his club. He ran for a long way and then walked back to his party.

They saw him in the distance and began to be afraid. They thought an enemy was coming. When he was near they recognized him.

He went to the old people and said, "I have killed some buffaloes. I had a hard time to kill them. You must go and butcher them and take what you want of the meat."

They all went to the place he indicated. There they found a number of buffaloes slain. They were all surprised. They began to butcher the meat and took what they wanted of it.

The boy said, "You must not take too much with you. It will be too heavy. If we sight some more buffaloes later on, I will kill them."

So this boy saved the people from starvation. They stayed at that place preparing and drying meat. They stayed there one day. Then they traveled east for two days more.

He said to them, "Make a smoke signal over here as a sign for me."

Again he left the blanket and his moccasins and started to run toward the camps of the enemy. There was no moonlight and he started to run at sunset. About the middle of the night he came back.

He said, "The camps of the enemy are near."

They stayed there over night and slept. The next morning they journeyed to the east again. They went on for a day and a night. They continued for three more days and nights. That boy had run a distance as far as from here to Santa Fe and back in the same night. He was just like an automobile.

One more day they traveled. Then he said to the people, "You must stay here and be ready. Prepare rope, for I shall return with the enemy's horses." And he started to run.

The people were all ready. He ran and ran. About the middle of the night he returned, chasing the horses before him. The horses were all sweaty, but he was not tired though he was running on foot.

He said to the chief, "Let each man rope a horse." And he added, "All the rest of the horses are for you. You can be responsible for them, but I want just one mare for my grandmother."

He said to the other men, "You must wait here for me, for the enemy are near."

The others went on ahead driving the horses. This boy and one other man were watching the rear for enemies.

The enemy were coming. A great cloud of dust was sighted. So the boy got on his companion's horse with him. They sat double. He tried it several times, but each time he fell off. The enemy were advancing rapidly, shouting. They thought they were going to slay that boy. He was on foot now.

He said to his companion, "When the enemy are near, you must make your horse run. Get away as fast as you can and save your life."

The boy had only his club. When the enemy were very near, the boy made believe that he was trying to get away, that he was running as fast as he could and trying his best though he was tired.

The chief of the enemy came close. He thought he was going to kill the boy easily. But the boy turned on him and ran after him. With a burst of speed he reached the chief's horse, took him by surprise, and killed him.

The second man of the enemy was close too, and the boy ran after him and killed him also.

The others stopped. They were afraid and stayed at a distance.

The boy began to scalp the chief. The other members of the enemy party were afraid to come near. They stayed where they were and cried. The boy ran with the chief's scalp in his hand.

The boy was running after his own people who were far ahead by this time. All the horses of his people were sweaty and tired. The boy caught up and said to the men, "Take your time. There is no need to hurry now. Take your time and rest the horses. I will go ahead." So he ran fast and reached home in one day.

When he got home he shouted first to his grandmother, and she uttered the woman's cry of victory.[1] Both were very happy.

[1] This is the call, signifying applause, which has been mentioned before.

She said, "My grandchild has been away a long time and now he has returned to me."

The next morning all the people came around to the old woman's house and asked questions of the boy. They asked him, "Where did you leave the others?"

The boy said, "I lost them because of my sleepiness. I was left on the way, so I came back."

They all believed him because they knew that the boy slept late in the morning. They said to the grandmother, "Why do you make the call of applause when your grandson comes home? There is no need for excitement. He hasn't done anything."

About four days later those other men arrived with the horses. When they got home they gave a mare to the old woman.

They waited another four days and then the chief told the people about the boy, about what he had done for them.

The chief was wealthy. He built a tipi and put everything in it. He sent some men to the boy and told him to come over and marry his daughter and his niece. He gave the boy two girls.

The boy didn't go right away. He waited a day while he dressed up and combed his hair and washed himself. Then in the morning he dressed. He did not look like the same boy. He was a fine looking young man.

He came to the chief. He said, "What do you want of me?"

"You have done a great thing for us. I didn't think you were worth anything when you lived here before, but now I see you are a good man. You saved us. I thank you for all you have done. Now here is my daughter and here is my niece. They are both pretty girls. I give them to you. They are going to be your wives."[1]

B. HOW A POOR BOY WON HIS WIVES

When the world was new there were only the Jicarilla Apache living; there were many of them then.[2]

At that time an old man and woman had two attractive daughters whom they would not allow to marry any of the young men. Many young men wanted to marry them, but the old people refused every time.

Many were moving to the south from the east and continuing to the west. They were taking their time. Several young men came to these two old people and asked whether they could marry their daughters. But they were told no. The old man and woman continued moving with the others. This was at the time the people

[1] This passage reflects the Jicarilla custom of polygyny.

[2] The episode described in this tale is supposed to have occurred at the time when the people of the emergence were traveling around the earth. Cf. p. 47.

were going around the world. They kept going all the way to the north. At every place they stopped to camp, the old people received offers, but they wouldn't let the daughters marry. They continued moving. Now they were approaching the east again.

Every evening when they stopped to rest young men came to ask for the girls, but they were always sent away. In this way they approached the east, and the girls were still unmarried. The people were now approaching a place that is now called Cimarron.

There were many people there at Salada. The old couple and their daughters stayed there for a while, but the old people still would not allow their daughters to marry. The young men came to the tipi, but they were refused as usual.

For twenty-eight years from the time the young men began to ask, the old people would not let the girls marry.

One time a poor young fellow who had nothing, who was just like a tramp, came along. It was summer. The water of the streams was warm because of the hot weather.

The people wished they could get some cold water. The mother of the girls expressed a wish that she could have some.

The old man said, "I wish I could get some cold water from the high mountain stream. I wish I could drink it from the leaves of the skunk cabbage and make my teeth cold."

Later the old woman was sitting out in the doorway of the tipi. She looked to the south. She saw a high mountain peak in that direction and there was snow on it. She said, "I wish I could have some cold water from the melted snow."

That poor young fellow was sitting there.

The old lady said, "I wish I could have that cool snow to melt and use for water. If someone would get it for me, I'd let him marry both my daughters."

The boy didn't say anything. He just got up and left. He went to another tipi and took some rope and a buffalo robe. He went to another place where the horses were grazing, stole one, and went toward the snow-capped mountain.

When he arrived there, he got plenty of snow and carried it back in the buffalo hide. He let the horse go and carried the snow on his back, though it was a long way.

He came in with it and put it before the old woman saying, "Here is the snow you wanted someone to get for you."

The old woman cried out and stepped back. She said, "Yes, I asked for it. I made the agreement myself. I'll keep my word. Here are my daughters now. I won't say a word against it."

The woman said to her husband, "Drink the cold water."

He dug a hole and put the robe in there where the snow would keep fresh until it was all gone.

The young man seemed to be very poor. He had no horse, no arrows, no blankets, nothing. All the young men in the group were jealous that this worthless fellow was given the two girls after they had tried in vain. They cursed him.

When night came the old man got out. He knew that the young fellow had many relatives. He called all these relatives of the young man together. The old woman went out too and went around speaking to all the close relatives of her son-in-law.

The young fellow was sitting in the tipi with his two wives. They had a big fire in there. The two old people were outside. Now all the relatives of the son-in-law came, many people.

The old people said to them, "Each one of you must go in and see that boy with our two daughters."

The old man built a fire outside too.

The relatives of the boy went in one by one, smiled, and came out. They all had a turn to see that their relative was married.

They all got together then. Some liked it that the boy was married to the two girls, some didn't like it. They separated. Most of them thought it was all right. After a while all agreed that it was all right to let the boy marry the two girls.

The old man said to his son-in-law's relatives, "I wish you all would give my son-in-law something, a bow, some arrows, a blanket, a horse, so he can live well with my daughters."

So they all gave him something. Each relative gave him three buffalo hides.

The old man's brother's son gave him a good quiver full of arrows. The old man had three brothers. One of these gave the boy a pony. Another gave him leggings. Another relative gave him a buckskin shirt.[1]

There were a few relatives of the girls who didn't like the boy. "He is a poor man; he just had good luck," they said.

The girls didn't say anything. Their mother told them what they had to do.[2]

The young man lived with these two girls for a year. He was a good hunter. The old man was blind by this time. The young man was helping him take care of his horses.[3]

At the time they married, one of the girls thought, "How am I going to go among my people? I have good clothes and this boy has nothing but rags." She said nothing, but she thought this way.

Five years passed. The old man had died. The old woman was blind by this time too, but the young fellow took good care of her.

---

[1] This generosity is an accurate picture of the economic assistance which the body of relatives is expected to extend to any needy member.

[2] Such acquiescence and obedience are traditionally required of the girl.

[3] The young man is obligated to care for his parents-in-law and is judged by his fellow Jicarilla according to the fulfillment of that duty.

C. THE FOUR-LEAFED CLOVER

One man, a chief, had a wife and a daughter. The daughter was a pretty girl. There were a number of young men who wanted to marry her. They were all fine looking boys, and the man liked all of them. He didn't know which one he should choose for his son-in-law.

He asked his wife, "Which one shall we have for a son-in-law?"

"I don't know. It's up to you."

So he turned around and asked his girl. He asked her, "Which one of these four boys would you rather marry?"

She didn't know. They were all the same to her.

So he went out with these men to a nearby field where clover grew.

He said, "You four boys have to look in all this clover. You see these have three leaves. But you must look for a four-leafed one. The boy who finds it first is going to marry my daughter."

One of the boys found one after they had been looking for a while. He picked it and handed it ot the father, and the chief said, "This is the boy who is going to marry my daughter."

The others gave up. They couldn't find any.

X. MISCELLANEOUS

A. MUSCULAR TREMOR AND INVOLUNTARY NOISE[1]

One time these two had a quarrel. One said, "You know nothing." The other said: "I know a great deal more than you do."

They were quarreling about a war that was going on between the Jicarilla Indians and their enemies, the Arapaho.

Involuntary Noise said, "I'll be the first one to try to tell what is going to happen. I say that the Jicarilla are going to be beaten, every one of them." As he said this that sound escaped from him, warning him that he was wrong. He tried it again; he repeated the same thing, but again the sound escaped from him. Yet he was still against the Indians, the Jicarilla, and called for their defeat.

Muscular Tremor said, "No, I can see that you are wrong. The Jicarilla are not going to be beaten."

But the other kept trying to prophesy that the Jicarilla would be the losers, and kept trying to bring it about. Yet every time he would say it, the sound would come from him. Finally he had to give it up.

Now it was Muscular Tremor's turn. He sat down. He said, "Every one of the Apache is going to be saved. Not one of them is going to be hurt."

By this time the fighting had started. These two sat there and watched it. After the war was over, it was apparent that Muscular Tremor had told the truth. The enemy was beaten. None of the Apache was hurt.

Then Involuntary Noise said, "Even though you have won, the people will use me."

That's why some of the Indians still believe Involuntary Noise. I think that sometimes it tells the truth, sometimes not.

B. HORSE STORY[2]

One time a man was treating his horse badly. He hit the horse needlessly and threw around the horse's bridle and rope carelessly. He didn't care what he did. He would hit the horse with rocks too. That man was very mean to his own horse. When he rode his horse,

---

[1] According to the part of the body affected, muscular tremors are considered diagnostic signs, warning of danger or suggesting good luck to come. When an involuntary noise escapes from the lips while a person is speaking, it is considered that what he says is erroneous.

[2] This story was told to the children.

he would always make it run. He never took good care of it. And that horse got very thin. It was just bones.[1]

There was another man who took good care of his horse. He didn't throw rocks or sticks at it. He treated it well. And this horse was always fat and strong and helped him a great deal.

One night these two horses met each other.

The one who was well cared for spoke to the thin one, "What's the matter? You look thin and hungry and unhappy."

The badly treated horse said, "It's because my father doesn't take good care of me. He always chases me and hits me with rocks and strikes me with big sticks. And he whips me with the bridle and ropes. When he puts the saddle blanket on me he never makes it soft first. When he puts the saddle on me he always throws it. Always he says harsh words to me. He never gives me a kind word. That is why I'm thin, miserable, and unhappy. That's why, when I'm taking him out riding, I am heavy-footed and slow."

The other horse said, "My father is always kind to me. He always takes good care of me and calls me his child. He takes care of me as he would of his own baby. He never hits me with rocks or sticks. When he puts the saddle blanket on me he always brushes it and softens it so that it will not make my back sore. That's why I'm happy. I eat all I want and I'm fat. I'm very proud of my father. That is why, when I take him out anywhere, I am always light and dancing in front of all the people. I make him proud of me too."

C. THE CHILD THAT CRIED

One time a baby was crying and crying. The mother became very much worried. She thought something was the matter. She sent for a shaman to cure the child. She thought some ghost had frightened it.

The shaman came and sang and tried to chase the ghosts away, but the baby continued to cry.

The mother didn't know what to do next.

The child was growing, that is all. That is the reason it was crying. You see, when the child grows, it has fever and cries. When the teeth are growing, they hurt and the baby cries then too.

The baby spoke out then and said to the mother, "Why do you worry? Don't bother me. I like to cry. If I cry, just let me cry as long as I want to. That will make my heart brave and strong. When children cry a great deal they will be brave. They develop their voices."

After that when the child cried the woman paid no attention to it. She just went about her work.

[1] To treat a horse badly or to throw the saddle and bridle carelessly aside might bring on sickness or misfortune with horses, the Jicarilla believe.

Some of the people, when they hear this story, let their children cry as long as they want to.

D. HEN AND CHICKENS

One time the hen had little chickens. She told them not to go away. "The hawk might catch you," she said. The hen told this to her children over and over. She kept telling them not to go far away. She told them of other dangers that awaited them. "The hail might come in a big storm and hurt you," she told them.

But one little chicken thought, "I wonder why my mother always tells me those things. I am old enough to take care of myself. I know what the world means."

He went out. His mother tried to call him back but he kept right on. He thought he was old enough to take care of himself. He wandered away. He went so far that he could no longer hear his mother's voice. He got under the trees and looked up. There a big cat was lying asleep in the fork of a tree. The chicken was very much frightened. That was the time he needed help and he started to cry for his mother, to cry for help.

He turned to run. But he was lost. He couldn't find the way back. His mother, too, was worried. She was looking for the young child. She was calling and calling. After a while he heard his mother's voice and ran quickly to her. He was happy again and thankful that he was saved. He promised his mother right there, "I won't run away any more. I thought you were just joking with me."

INDEX

(n = footnote)

A CATALOG OF SELECTED

DOVER BOOKS

IN ALL FIELDS OF INTEREST

A CATALOG OF SELECTED DOVER BOOKS IN ALL FIELDS OF INTEREST

STICKLEY CRAFTSMAN FURNITURE CATALOGS, Gustav Stickley and L. & J. G. Stickley. Beautiful, functional furniture in two authentic catalogs from 1910. 594 illustrations, including 277 photos, show settles, rockers, armchairs, reclining chairs, bookcases, desks, tables. 183pp. 6½ × 9¼. 23838-5 Pa. $8.95

AMERICAN LOCOMOTIVES IN HISTORIC PHOTOGRAPHS: 1858 to 1949, Ron Ziel (ed.). A rare collection of 126 meticulously detailed official photographs, called "builder portraits," of American locomotives that majestically chronicle the rise of steam locomotive power in America. Introduction. Detailed captions. xi + 129pp. 9 × 12. 27393-8 Pa. $12.95

AMERICA'S LIGHTHOUSES: An Illustrated History, Francis Ross Holland, Jr. Delightfully written, profusely illustrated fact-filled survey of over 200 American lighthouses since 1716. History, anecdotes, technological advances, more. 240pp. 8 × 10¾. 25576-X Pa. $10.95

TOWARDS A NEW ARCHITECTURE, Le Corbusier. Pioneering manifesto by founder of "International School." Technical and aesthetic theories, views of industry, economics, relation of form to function, "mass-production split" and much more. Profusely illustrated. 320pp. 6⅛ × 9¼. (USO) 25023-7 Pa. $8.95

HOW THE OTHER HALF LIVES, Jacob Riis. Famous journalistic record, exposing poverty and degradation of New York slums around 1900, by major social reformer. 100 striking and influential photographs. 233pp. 10 × 7⅞.
22012-5 Pa $10.95

FRUIT KEY AND TWIG KEY TO TREES AND SHRUBS, William M. Harlow. One of the handiest and most widely used identification aids. Fruit key covers 120 deciduous and evergreen species; twig key 160 deciduous species. Easily used. Over 300 photographs. 126pp. 5⅜ × 8½. 20511-8 Pa. $2.95

COMMON BIRD SONGS, Dr. Donald J. Borror. Songs of 60 most common U.S. birds: robins, sparrows, cardinals, bluejays, finches, more—arranged in order of increasing complexity. Up to 9 variations of songs of each species.
Cassette and manual 99911-4 $8.95

ORCHIDS AS HOUSE PLANTS, Rebecca Tyson Northen. Grow cattleyas and many other kinds of orchids—in a window, in a case, or under artificial light. 63 illustrations. 148pp. 5⅜ × 8½. 23261-1 Pa. $3.95

MONSTER MAZES, Dave Phillips. Masterful mazes at four levels of difficulty. Avoid deadly perils and evil creatures to find magical treasures. Solutions for all 32 exciting illustrated puzzles. 48pp. 8¼ × 11. 26005-4 Pa. $2.95

MOZART'S DON GIOVANNI (DOVER OPERA LIBRETTO SERIES), Wolfgang Amadeus Mozart. Introduced and translated by Ellen H. Bleiler. Standard Italian libretto, with complete English translation. Convenient and thoroughly portable—an ideal companion for reading along with a recording or the performance itself. Introduction. List of characters. Plot summary. 121pp. 5¼ × 8½.
24944-1 Pa. $2.95

TECHNICAL MANUAL AND DICTIONARY OF CLASSICAL BALLET, Gail Grant. Defines, explains, comments on steps, movements, poses and concepts. 15-page pictorial section. Basic book for student, viewer. 127pp. 5⅜ × 8½.
21843-0 Pa. $3.95

FRANK LLOYD WRIGHT'S HOLLYHOCK HOUSE, Donald Hoffmann. Lavishly illustrated, carefully documented study of one of Wright's most controversial residential designs. Over 120 photographs, floor plans, elevations, etc. Detailed perceptive text by noted Wright scholar. Index. 128pp. 9¼ × 10¾.
27133-1 Pa. $10.95

THE MALE AND FEMALE FIGURE IN MOTION: 60 Classic Photographic Sequences, Eadweard Muybridge. 60 true-action photographs of men and women walking, running, climbing, bending, turning, etc., reproduced from rare 19th-century masterpiece. vi + 121pp. 9 × 12. 24745-7 Pa. $10.95

1001 QUESTIONS ANSWERED ABOUT THE SEASHORE, N. J. Berrill and Jacquelyn Berrill. Queries answered about dolphins, sea snails, sponges, starfish, fishes, shore birds, many others. Covers appearance, breeding, growth, feeding, much more. 305pp. 5¼ × 8¼. 23366-9 Pa. $7.95

GUIDE TO OWL WATCHING IN NORTH AMERICA, Donald S. Heintzelman. Superb guide offers complete data and descriptions of 19 species: barn owl, screech owl, snowy owl, many more. Expert coverage of owl-watching equipment, conservation, migrations and invasions, etc. Guide to observing sites. 84 illustrations. xiii + 193pp. 5⅜ × 8½. 27344-X Pa. $7.95

MEDICINAL AND OTHER USES OF NORTH AMERICAN PLANTS: A Historical Survey with Special Reference to the Eastern Indian Tribes, Charlotte Erichsen-Brown. Chronological historical citations document 500 years of usage of plants, trees, shrubs native to eastern Canada, northeastern U.S. Also complete identifying information. 343 illustrations. 544pp. 6½ × 9¼. 25951-X Pa. $12.95

STORYBOOK MAZES, Dave Phillips. 23 stories and mazes on two-page spreads: Wizard of Oz, Treasure Island, Robin Hood, etc. Solutions. 64pp. 8¼ × 11.
23628-5 Pa. $2.95

NEGRO FOLK MUSIC, U.S.A., Harold Courlander. Noted folklorist's scholarly yet readable analysis of rich and varied musical tradition. Includes authentic versions of over 40 folk songs. Valuable bibliography and discography. xi + 324pp. 5⅜ × 8½. 27350-4 Pa. $7.95

MOVIE-STAR PORTRAITS OF THE FORTIES, John Kobal (ed.). 163 glamor, studio photos of 106 stars of the 1940s: Rita Hayworth, Ava Gardner, Marlon Brando, Clark Gable, many more. 176pp. 8⅜ × 11¼. 23546-7 Pa. $10.95

BENCHLEY LOST AND FOUND, Robert Benchley. Finest humor from early 30s, about pet peeves, child psychologists, post office and others. Mostly unavailable elsewhere. 73 illustrations by Peter Arno and others. 183pp. 5⅜ × 8½.
22410-4 Pa. $4.95

YEKL and THE IMPORTED BRIDEGROOM AND OTHER STORIES OF YIDDISH NEW YORK, Abraham Cahan. Film Hester Street based on Yekl (1896). Novel, other stories among first about Jewish immigrants on N.Y.'s East Side. 240pp. 5⅜ × 8½. 22427-9 Pa. $5.95

SELECTED POEMS, Walt Whitman. Generous sampling from *Leaves of Grass*. Twenty-four poems include "I Hear America Singing," "Song of the Open Road," "I Sing the Body Electric," "When Lilacs Last in the Dooryard Bloom'd," "O Captain! My Captain!"—all reprinted from an authoritative edition. Lists of titles and first lines. 128pp. 5$\frac{3}{16}$ × 8¼. 26878-0 Pa. $1.00

THE BEST TALES OF HOFFMANN, E. T. A. Hoffmann. 10 of Hoffmann's most important stories: "Nutcracker and the King of Mice," "The Golden Flowerpot," etc. 458pp. 5⅜ × 8½. 21793-0 Pa. $8.95

FROM FETISH TO GOD IN ANCIENT EGYPT, E. A. Wallis Budge. Rich detailed survey of Egyptian conception of "God" and gods, magic, cult of animals, Osiris, more. Also, superb English translations of hymns and legends. 240 illustrations. 545pp. 5⅜ × 8½. 25803-3 Pa. $10.95

FRENCH STORIES/CONTES FRANÇAIS: A Dual-Language Book, Wallace Fowlie. Ten stories by French masters, Voltaire to Camus: "Micromegas" by Voltaire; "The Atheist's Mass" by Balzac; "Minuet" by de Maupassant; "The Guest" by Camus, six more. Excellent English translations on facing pages. Also French-English vocabulary list, exercises, more. 352pp. 5⅜ × 8½. 26443-2 Pa. $8.95

CHICAGO AT THE TURN OF THE CENTURY IN PHOTOGRAPHS: 122 Historic Views from the Collections of the Chicago Historical Society, Larry A. Viskochil. Rare large-format prints offer detailed views of City Hall, State Street, the Loop, Hull House, Union Station, many other landmarks, circa 1904–1913. Introduction. Captions. Maps. 144pp. 9⅜ × 12¼. 24656-6 Pa. $12.95

OLD BROOKLYN IN EARLY PHOTOGRAPHS, 1865–1929, William Lee Younger. Luna Park, Gravesend race track, construction of Grand Army Plaza, moving of Hotel Brighton, etc. 157 previously unpublished photographs. 165pp. 8⅞ × 11¾. 23587-4 Pa. $12.95

THE MYTHS OF THE NORTH AMERICAN INDIANS, Lewis Spence. Rich anthology of the myths and legends of the Algonquins, Iroquois, Pawnees and Sioux, prefaced by an extensive historical and ethnological commentary. 36 illustrations. 480pp. 5⅜ × 8½. 25967-6 Pa. $8.95

AN ENCYCLOPEDIA OF BATTLES: Accounts of Over 1,560 Battles from 1479 B.C. to the Present, David Eggenberger. Essential details of every major battle in recorded history from the first battle of Megiddo in 1479 B.C. to Grenada in 1984. List of Battle Maps. New Appendix covering the years 1967–1984. Index. 99 illustrations. 544pp. 6½ × 9¼. 24913-1 Pa. $14.95

SAILING ALONE AROUND THE WORLD, Captain Joshua Slocum. First man to sail around the world, alone, in small boat. One of great feats of seamanship told in delightful manner. 67 illustrations. 294pp. 5⅜ × 8½. 20326-3 Pa. $4.95

ANARCHISM AND OTHER ESSAYS, Emma Goldman. Powerful, penetrating, prophetic essays on direct action, role of minorities, prison reform, puritan hypocrisy, violence, etc. 271pp. 5⅜ × 8½. 22484-8 Pa. $5.95

MYTHS OF THE HINDUS AND BUDDHISTS, Ananda K. Coomaraswamy and Sister Nivedita. Great stories of the epics; deeds of Krishna, Shiva, taken from puranas, Vedas, folk tales; etc. 32 illustrations. 400pp. 5⅜ × 8½. 21759-0 Pa. $8.95

BEYOND PSYCHOLOGY, Otto Rank. Fear of death, desire of immortality, nature of sexuality, social organization, creativity, according to Rankian system. 291pp. 5⅜ × 8½. 20485-5 Pa. $7.95

A THEOLOGICO-POLITICAL TREATISE, Benedict Spinoza. Also contains unfinished Political Treatise. Great classic on religious liberty, theory of government on common consent. R. Elwes translation. Total of 421pp. 5⅜ × 8½. 20249-6 Pa. $7.95

CATALOG OF DOVER BOOKS

PERSPECTIVE FOR ARTISTS, Rex Vicat Cole. Depth, perspective of sky and sea, shadows, much more, not usually covered. 391 diagrams, 81 reproductions of drawings and paintings. 279pp. 5⅜ × 8½. 22487-2 Pa. $6.95

DRAWING THE LIVING FIGURE, Joseph Sheppard. Innovative approach to artistic anatomy focuses on specifics of surface anatomy, rather than muscles and bones. Over 170 drawings of live models in front, back and side views, and in widely varying poses. Accompanying diagrams. 177 illustrations. Introduction. Index. 144pp. 8⅜ × 11¼. 26723-7 Pa. $7.95

GOTHIC AND OLD ENGLISH ALPHABETS: 100 Complete Fonts, Dan X. Solo. Add power, elegance to posters, signs, other graphics with 100 stunning copyright-free alphabets: Blackstone, Dolbey, Germania, 97 more—including many lower-case, numerals, punctuation marks. 104pp. 8⅛ × 11. 24695-7 Pa. $6.95

HOW TO DO BEADWORK, Mary White. Fundamental book on craft from simple projects to five-bead chains and woven works. 106 illustrations. 142pp. 5⅜ × 8. 20697-1 Pa. $4.95

THE BOOK OF WOOD CARVING, Charles Marshall Sayers. Finest book for beginners discusses fundamentals and offers 34 designs. "Absolutely first rate . . . well thought out and well executed."—E. J. Tangerman. 118pp. 7¾ × 10⅝. 23654-4 Pa. $5.95

ILLUSTRATED CATALOG OF CIVIL WAR MILITARY GOODS: Union Army Weapons, Insignia, Uniform Accessories, and Other Equipment, Schuyler, Hartley, and Graham. Rare, profusely illustrated 1846 catalog includes Union Army uniform and dress regulations, arms and ammunition, coats, insignia, flags, swords, rifles, etc. 226 illustrations. 160pp. 9 × 12. 24939-5 Pa. $10.95

WOMEN'S FASHIONS OF THE EARLY 1900s: An Unabridged Republication of "New York Fashions, 1909," National Cloak & Suit Co. Rare catalog of mail-order fashions documents women's and children's clothing styles shortly after the turn of the century. Captions offer full descriptions, prices. Invaluable resource for fashion, costume historians. Approximately 725 illustrations. 128pp. 8⅜ × 11¼. 27276-1 Pa. $10.95

THE 1912 AND 1915 GUSTAV STICKLEY FURNITURE CATALOGS, Gustav Stickley. With over 200 detailed illustrations and descriptions, these two catalogs are essential reading and reference materials and identification guides for Stickley furniture. Captions cite materials, dimensions and prices. 112pp. 6½ × 9¼. 26676-1 Pa. $9.95

EARLY AMERICAN LOCOMOTIVES, John H. White, Jr. Finest locomotive engravings from early 19th century: historical (1804–74), main-line (after 1870), special, foreign, etc. 147 plates. 142pp. 11⅜ × 8¼. 22772-3 Pa. $8.95

THE TALL SHIPS OF TODAY IN PHOTOGRAPHS, Frank O. Braynard. Lavishly illustrated tribute to nearly 100 majestic contemporary sailing vessels: Amerigo Vespucci, Clearwater, Constitution, Eagle, Mayflower, Sea Cloud, Victory, many more. Authoritative captions provide statistics, background on each ship. 190 black-and-white photographs and illustrations. Introduction. 128pp. 8⅞ × 11¾. 27163-3 Pa. $12.95

EARLY NINETEENTH-CENTURY CRAFTS AND TRADES, Peter Stockham (ed.). Extremely rare 1807 volume describes to youngsters the crafts and trades of the day: brickmaker, weaver, dressmaker, bookbinder, ropemaker, saddler, many more. Quaint prose, charming illustrations for each craft. 20 black-and-white line illustrations. 192pp. 4⅝ × 6. 27293-1 Pa. $4.95

VICTORIAN FASHIONS AND COSTUMES FROM HARPER'S BAZAR, 1867–1898, Stella Blum (ed.). Day costumes, evening wear, sports clothes, shoes, hats, other accessories in over 1,000 detailed engravings. 320pp. 9⅜ × 12¼. 22990-4 Pa. $12.95

GUSTAV STICKLEY, THE CRAFTSMAN, Mary Ann Smith. Superb study surveys broad scope of Stickley's achievement, especially in architecture. Design philosophy, rise and fall of the Craftsman empire, descriptions and floor plans for many Craftsman houses, more. 86 black-and-white halftones. 31 line illustrations. Introduction. 208pp. 6½ × 9¼. 27210-9 Pa. $9.95

THE LONG ISLAND RAIL ROAD IN EARLY PHOTOGRAPHS, Ron Ziel. Over 220 rare photos, informative text document origin (1844) and development of rail service on Long Island. Vintage views of early trains, locomotives, stations, passengers, crews, much more. Captions. 8⅞ × 11¾. 26301-0 Pa. $13.95

THE BOOK OF OLD SHIPS: From Egyptian Galleys to Clipper Ships, Henry B. Culver. Superb, authoritative history of sailing vessels, with 80 magnificent line illustrations. Galley, bark, caravel, longship, whaler, many more. Detailed, informative text on each vessel by noted naval historian. Introduction. 256pp. 5⅜ × 8½. 27332-6 Pa. $6.95

TEN BOOKS ON ARCHITECTURE, Vitruvius. The most important book ever written on architecture. Early Roman aesthetics, technology, classical orders, site selection, all other aspects. Morgan translation. 331pp. 5⅜ × 8½. 20645-9 Pa. $8.95

THE HUMAN FIGURE IN MOTION, Eadweard Muybridge. More than 4,500 stopped-action photos, in action series, showing undraped men, women, children jumping, lying down, throwing, sitting, wrestling, carrying, etc. 390pp. 7⅞ × 10⅝. 20204-6 Clothbd. $24.95

TREES OF THE EASTERN AND CENTRAL UNITED STATES AND CANADA, William M. Harlow. Best one-volume guide to 140 trees. Full descriptions, woodlore, range, etc. Over 600 illustrations. Handy size. 288pp. 4½ × 6⅜. 20395-6 Pa. $4.95

SONGS OF WESTERN BIRDS, Dr. Donald J. Borror. Complete song and call repertoire of 60 western species, including flycatchers, juncoes, cactus wrens, many more—includes fully illustrated booklet. Cassette and manual 99913-0 $8.95

GROWING AND USING HERBS AND SPICES, Milo Miloradovich. Versatile handbook provides all the information needed for cultivation and use of all the herbs and spices available in North America. 4 illustrations. Index. Glossary. 236pp. 5⅜ × 8½. 25058-X Pa. $5.95

BIG BOOK OF MAZES AND LABYRINTHS, Walter Shepherd. 50 mazes and labyrinths in all—classical, solid, ripple, and more—in one great volume. Perfect inexpensive puzzler for clever youngsters. Full solutions. 112pp. 8⅛ × 11. 22951-3 Pa. $3.95

PIANO TUNING, J. Cree Fischer. Clearest, best book for beginner, amateur. Simple repairs, raising dropped notes, tuning by easy method of flattened fifths. No previous skills needed. 4 illustrations. 201pp. 5⅜ × 8½. 23267-0 Pa. $4.95

A SOURCE BOOK IN THEATRICAL HISTORY, A. M. Nagler. Contemporary observers on acting, directing, make-up, costuming, stage props, machinery, scene design, from Ancient Greece to Chekhov. 611pp. 5⅜ × 8½. 20515-0 Pa. $10.95

THE COMPLETE NONSENSE OF EDWARD LEAR, Edward Lear. All nonsense limericks, zany alphabets, Owl and Pussycat, songs, nonsense botany, etc., illustrated by Lear. Total of 320pp. 5⅜ × 8½. (USO) 20167-8 Pa. $5.95

VICTORIAN PARLOUR POETRY: An Annotated Anthology, Michael R. Turner. 117 gems by Longfellow, Tennyson, Browning, many lesser-known poets. "The Village Blacksmith," "Curfew Must Not Ring Tonight," "Only a Baby Small," dozens more, often difficult to find elsewhere. Index of poets, titles, first lines. xxiii + 325pp. 5⅜ × 8¼. 27044-0 Pa. $7.95

DUBLINERS, James Joyce. Fifteen stories offer vivid, tightly focused observations of the lives of Dublin's poorer classes. At least one, "The Dead," is considered a masterpiece. Reprinted complete and unabridged from standard edition. 160pp. 5³⁄₁₆ × 8¼. 26870-5 Pa. $1.00

THE HAUNTED MONASTERY and THE CHINESE MAZE MURDERS, Robert van Gulik. Two full novels by van Gulik, set in 7th-century China, continue adventures of Judge Dee and his companions. An evil Taoist monastery, seemingly supernatural events; overgrown topiary maze hides strange crimes. 27 illustrations. 328pp. 5⅜ × 8½. 23502-5 Pa. $7.95

THE BOOK OF THE SACRED MAGIC OF ABRAMELIN THE MAGE, translated by S. MacGregor Mathers. Medieval manuscript of ceremonial magic. Basic document in Aleister Crowley, Golden Dawn groups. 268pp. 5⅜ × 8½. 23211-5 Pa. $7.95

NEW RUSSIAN-ENGLISH AND ENGLISH-RUSSIAN DICTIONARY, M. A. O'Brien. This is a remarkably handy Russian dictionary, containing a surprising amount of information, including over 70,000 entries. 366pp. 4½ × 6⅛. 20208-9 Pa. $8.95

HISTORIC HOMES OF THE AMERICAN PRESIDENTS, Second, Revised Edition, Irvin Haas. A traveler's guide to American Presidential homes, most open to the public, depicting and describing homes occupied by every American President from George Washington to George Bush. With visiting hours, admission charges, travel routes. 175 photographs. Index. 160pp. 8¼ × 11. 26751-2 Pa. $10.95

NEW YORK IN THE FORTIES, Andreas Feininger. 162 brilliant photographs by the well-known photographer, formerly with *Life* magazine. Commuters, shoppers, Times Square at night, much else from city at its peak. Captions by John von Hartz. 181pp. 9¼ × 10¾. 23585-8 Pa. $12.95

INDIAN SIGN LANGUAGE, William Tomkins. Over 525 signs developed by Sioux and other tribes. Written instructions and diagrams. Also 290 pictographs. 111pp. 6⅛ × 9¼. 22029-X Pa. $3.50

ANATOMY: A Complete Guide for Artists, Joseph Sheppard. A master of figure drawing shows artists how to render human anatomy convincingly. Over 460 illustrations. 224pp. 8⅜ × 11¼. 27279-6 Pa. $9.95

MEDIEVAL CALLIGRAPHY: Its History and Technique, Marc Drogin. Spirited history, comprehensive instruction manual covers 13 styles (ca. 4th century thru 15th). Excellent photographs; directions for duplicating medieval techniques with modern tools. 224pp. 8⅜ × 11¼. 26142-5 Pa. $11.95

DRIED FLOWERS: How to Prepare Them, Sarah Whitlock and Martha Rankin. Complete instructions on how to use silica gel, meal and borax, perlite aggregate, sand and borax, glycerine and water to create attractive permanent flower arrangements. 12 illustrations. 32pp. 5⅜ × 8½. 21802-3 Pa. $1.00

EASY-TO-MAKE BIRD FEEDERS FOR WOODWORKERS, Scott D. Campbell. Detailed, simple-to-use guide for designing, constructing, caring for and using feeders. Text, illustrations for 12 classic and contemporary designs. 96pp. 5⅜ × 8½. 25847-5 Pa. $2.95

OLD-TIME CRAFTS AND TRADES, Peter Stockham. An 1807 book created to teach children about crafts and trades open to them as future careers. It describes in detailed, nontechnical terms 24 different occupations, among them coachmaker, gardener, hairdresser, lacemaker, shoemaker, wheelwright, copper-plate printer, milliner, trunkmaker, merchant and brewer. Finely detailed engravings illustrate each occupation. 192pp. 4⅝ × 6. 27398-9 Pa. $4.95

THE HISTORY OF UNDERCLOTHES, C. Willett Cunnington and Phyllis Cunnington. Fascinating, well-documented survey covering six centuries of English undergarments, enhanced with over 100 illustrations: 12th-century laced-up bodice, footed long drawers (1795), 19th-century bustles, 19th-century corsets for men, Victorian "bust improvers," much more. 272pp. 5⅜ × 8¼. 27124-2 Pa. $9.95

ARTS AND CRAFTS FURNITURE: The Complete Brooks Catalog of 1912, Brooks Manufacturing Co. Photos and detailed descriptions of more than 150 now very collectible furniture designs from the Arts and Crafts movement depict davenports, settees, buffets, desks, tables, chairs, bedsteads, dressers and more, all built of solid, quarter-sawed oak. Invaluable for students and enthusiasts of antiques, Americana and the decorative arts. 80pp. 6½ × 9¼. 27471-3 Pa. $7.95

HOW WE INVENTED THE AIRPLANE: An Illustrated History, Orville Wright. Fascinating firsthand account covers early experiments, construction of planes and motors, first flights, much more. Introduction and commentary by Fred C. Kelly. 76 photographs. 96pp. 8¼ × 11. 25662-6 Pa. $7.95

THE ARTS OF THE SAILOR: Knotting, Splicing and Ropework, Hervey Garrett Smith. Indispensable shipboard reference covers tools, basic knots and useful hitches; handsewing and canvas work, more. Over 100 illustrations. Delightful reading for sea lovers. 256pp. 5⅜ × 8½. 26440-8 Pa. $6.95

FRANK LLOYD WRIGHT'S FALLINGWATER: The House and Its History, Second, Revised Edition, Donald Hoffmann. A total revision—both in text and illustrations—of the standard document on Fallingwater, the boldest, most personal architectural statement of Wright's mature years, updated with valuable new material from the recently opened Frank Lloyd Wright Archives. "Fascinating"—*The New York Times*. 116 illustrations. 128pp. 9¼ × 10¾. 27430-6 Pa. $10.95

PHOTOGRAPHIC SKETCHBOOK OF THE CIVIL WAR, Alexander Gardner. 100 photos taken on field during the Civil War. Famous shots of Manassas, Harper's Ferry, Lincoln, Richmond, slave pens, etc. 244pp. 10⅝ × 8¼.
22731-6 Pa. $9.95

FIVE ACRES AND INDEPENDENCE, Maurice G. Kains. Great back-to-the-land classic explains basics of self-sufficient farming. The one book to get. 95 illustrations. 397pp. 5⅜ × 8½. 20974-1 Pa. $6.95

SONGS OF EASTERN BIRDS, Dr. Donald J. Borror. Songs and calls of 60 species most common to eastern U.S.: warblers, woodpeckers, flycatchers, thrushes, larks, many more in high-quality recording. Cassette and manual 99912-2 $8.95

A MODERN HERBAL, Margaret Grieve. Much the fullest, most exact, most useful compilation of herbal material. Gigantic alphabetical encyclopedia, from aconite to zedoary, gives botanical information, medical properties, folklore, economic uses, much else. Indispensable to serious reader. 161 illustrations. 888pp. 6½ × 9¼. 2-vol. set. (USO) Vol. I: 22798-7 Pa. $9.95
Vol. II: 22799-5 Pa. $9.95

HIDDEN TREASURE MAZE BOOK, Dave Phillips. Solve 34 challenging mazes accompanied by heroic tales of adventure. Evil dragons, people-eating plants, bloodthirsty giants, many more dangerous adversaries lurk at every twist and turn. 34 mazes, stories, solutions. 48pp. 8¼ × 11. 24566-7 Pa. $2.95

LETTERS OF W. A. MOZART, Wolfgang A. Mozart. Remarkable letters show bawdy wit, humor, imagination, musical insights, contemporary musical world; includes some letters from Leopold Mozart. 276pp. 5⅜ × 8½. 22859-2 Pa. $6.95

BASIC PRINCIPLES OF CLASSICAL BALLET, Agrippina Vaganova. Great Russian theoretician, teacher explains methods for teaching classical ballet. 118 illustrations. 175pp. 5⅜ × 8½. 22036-2 Pa. $3.95

THE JUMPING FROG, Mark Twain. Revenge edition. The original story of The Celebrated Jumping Frog of Calaveras County, a hapless French translation, and Twain's hilarious "retranslation" from the French. 12 illustrations. 66pp. 5⅜ × 8½.
22686-7 Pa. $3.50

BEST REMEMBERED POEMS, Martin Gardner (ed.). The 126 poems in this superb collection of 19th- and 20th-century British and American verse range from Shelley's "To a Skylark" to the impassioned "Renascence" of Edna St. Vincent Millay and to Edward Lear's whimsical "The Owl and the Pussycat." 224pp. 5⅜ × 8½.
27165-X Pa. $3.95

COMPLETE SONNETS, William Shakespeare. Over 150 exquisite poems deal with love, friendship, the tyranny of time, beauty's evanescence, death and other themes in language of remarkable power, precision and beauty. Glossary of archaic terms. 80pp. 5³⁄₁₆ × 8¼. 26686-9 Pa. $1.00

BODIES IN A BOOKSHOP, R. T. Campbell. Challenging mystery of blackmail and murder with ingenious plot and superbly drawn characters. In the best tradition of British suspense fiction. 192pp. 5⅜ × 8½. 24720-1 Pa. $5.95

THE WIT AND HUMOR OF OSCAR WILDE, Alvin Redman (ed.). More than 1,000 ripostes, paradoxes, wisecracks: Work is the curse of the drinking classes; I can resist everything except temptation; etc. 258pp. 5⅜ × 8½. 20602-5 Pa. $4.95

SHAKESPEARE LEXICON AND QUOTATION DICTIONARY, Alexander Schmidt. Full definitions, locations, shades of meaning in every word in plays and poems. More than 50,000 exact quotations. 1,485pp. 6½ × 9¼. 2-vol. set.
Vol. 1: 22726-X Pa. $15.95
Vol. 2: 22727-8 Pa. $15.95

SELECTED POEMS, Emily Dickinson. Over 100 best-known, best-loved poems by one of America's foremost poets, reprinted from authoritative early editions. No comparable edition at this price. Index of first lines. 64pp. 5³⁄₁₆ × 8¼.
26466-1 Pa. $1.00

CELEBRATED CASES OF JUDGE DEE (DEE GOONG AN), translated by Robert van Gulik. Authentic 18th-century Chinese detective novel; Dee and associates solve three interlocked cases. Led to van Gulik's own stories with same characters. Extensive introduction. 9 illustrations. 237pp. 5⅜ × 8½.
23337-5 Pa. $5.95

THE MALLEUS MALEFICARUM OF KRAMER AND SPRENGER, translated by Montague Summers. Full text of most important witchhunter's "bible," used by both Catholics and Protestants. 278pp. 6⅝ × 10. 22802-9 Pa. $10.95

SPANISH STORIES/CUENTOS ESPAÑOLES: A Dual-Language Book, Angel Flores (ed.). Unique format offers 13 great stories in Spanish by Cervantes, Borges, others. Faithful English translations on facing pages. 352pp. 5⅜ × 8½.
25399-6 Pa. $7.95

THE CHICAGO WORLD'S FAIR OF 1893: A Photographic Record, Stanley Appelbaum (ed.). 128 rare photos show 200 buildings, Beaux-Arts architecture, Midway, original Ferris Wheel, Edison's kinetoscope, more. Architectural emphasis; full text. 116pp. 8¼ × 11. 23990-X Pa. $9.95

OLD QUEENS, N.Y., IN EARLY PHOTOGRAPHS, Vincent F. Seyfried and William Asadorian. Over 160 rare photographs of Maspeth, Jamaica, Jackson Heights, and other areas. Vintage views of DeWitt Clinton mansion, 1939 World's Fair and more. Captions. 192pp. 8⅞ × 11. 26358-4 Pa. $12.95

CAPTURED BY THE INDIANS: 15 Firsthand Accounts, 1750–1870, Frederick Drimmer. Astounding true historical accounts of grisly torture, bloody conflicts, relentless pursuits, miraculous escapes and more, by people who lived to tell the tale. 384pp. 5⅜ × 8½. 24901-8 Pa. $7.95

THE WORLD'S GREAT SPEECHES, Lewis Copeland and Lawrence W. Lamm (eds.). Vast collection of 278 speeches of Greeks to 1970. Powerful and effective models; unique look at history. 842pp. 5⅜ × 8½. 20468-5 Pa. $12.95

THE BOOK OF THE SWORD, Sir Richard F. Burton. Great Victorian scholar/adventurer's eloquent, erudite history of the "queen of weapons"—from prehistory to early Roman Empire. Evolution and development of early swords, variations (sabre, broadsword, cutlass, scimitar, etc.), much more. 336pp. 6⅛ × 9¼. 25434-8 Pa. $8.95

AUTOBIOGRAPHY: The Story of My Experiments with Truth, Mohandas K. Gandhi. Boyhood, legal studies, purification, the growth of the Satyagraha (nonviolent protest) movement. Critical, inspiring work of the man responsible for the freedom of India. 480pp. 5⅜ × 8½. (USO) 24593-4 Pa. $6.95

CELTIC MYTHS AND LEGENDS, T. W. Rolleston. Masterful retelling of Irish and Welsh stories and tales. Cuchulain, King Arthur, Deirdre, the Grail, many more. First paperback edition. 58 full-page illustrations. 512pp. 5⅜ × 8½. 26507-2 Pa. $9.95

THE PRINCIPLES OF PSYCHOLOGY, William James. Famous long course complete, unabridged. Stream of thought, time perception, memory, experimental methods; great work decades ahead of its time. 94 figures. 1,391pp. 5⅜ × 8½. 2-vol. set.
Vol. I: 20381-6 Pa. $12.95
Vol. II: 20382-4 Pa. $12.95

THE WORLD AS WILL AND REPRESENTATION, Arthur Schopenhauer. Definitive English translation of Schopenhauer's life work, correcting more than 1,000 errors, omissions in earlier translations. Translated by E. F. J. Payne. Total of 1,269pp. 5⅜ × 8½. 2-vol. set. Vol. 1: 21761-2 Pa. $10.95
Vol. 2: 21762-0 Pa. $11.95

MAGIC AND MYSTERY IN TIBET, Madame Alexandra David-Neel. Experiences among lamas, magicians, sages, sorcerers, Bonpa wizards. A true psychic discovery. 32 illustrations. 321pp. 5⅜ × 8½. (USO) 22682-4 Pa. $7.95

THE EGYPTIAN BOOK OF THE DEAD, E. A. Wallis Budge. Complete reproduction of Ani's papyrus, finest ever found. Full hieroglyphic text, interlinear transliteration, word-for-word translation, smooth translation. 533pp. 6½ × 9¼. 21866-X Pa. $9.95

MATHEMATICS FOR THE NONMATHEMATICIAN, Morris Kline. Detailed, college-level treatment of mathematics in cultural and historical context, with numerous exercises. Recommended Reading Lists. Tables. Numerous figures. 641pp. 5⅜ × 8½. 24823-2 Pa. $11.95

THEORY OF WING SECTIONS: Including a Summary of Airfoil Data, Ira H. Abbott and A. E. von Doenhoff. Concise compilation of subsonic aerodynamic characteristics of NACA wing sections, plus description of theory. 350pp. of tables. 693pp. 5⅜ × 8½. 60586-8 Pa. $13.95

THE RIME OF THE ANCIENT MARINER, Gustave Doré, S. T. Coleridge. Doré's finest work; 34 plates capture moods, subtleties of poem. Flawless full-size reproductions printed on facing pages with authoritative text of poem. "Beautiful. Simply beautiful."—*Publisher's Weekly*. 77pp. 9¼ × 12. 22305-1 Pa. $5.95

NORTH AMERICAN INDIAN DESIGNS FOR ARTISTS AND CRAFTSPEOPLE, Eva Wilson. Over 360 authentic copyright-free designs adapted from Navajo blankets, Hopi pottery, Sioux buffalo hides, more. Geometrics, symbolic figures, plant and animal motifs, etc. 128pp. 8⅜ × 11. (EUK) 25341-4 Pa. $6.95

SCULPTURE: Principles and Practice, Louis Slobodkin. Step-by-step approach to clay, plaster, metals, stone; classical and modern. 253 drawings, photos. 255pp. 8⅛ × 11. 22960-2 Pa. $9.95